ASTON MARTIN

POWER, BEAUTY AND SOUL

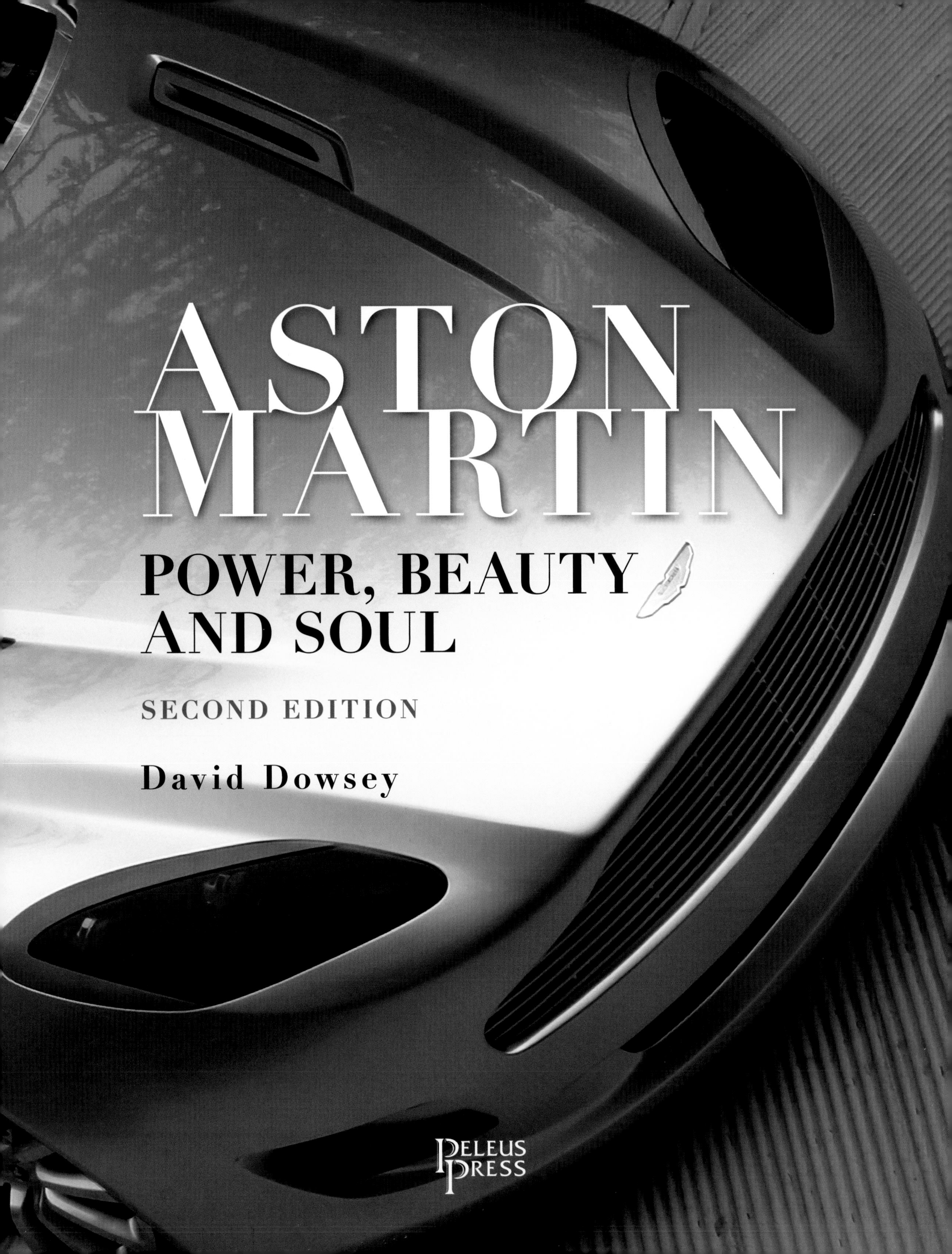

ASTON MARTIN

POWER, BEAUTY AND SOUL

SECOND EDITION

David Dowsey

PELEUS PRESS

Published in Australia in 2012 by
The Images Publishing Group Pty Ltd
ABN 89 059 734 431
6 Bastow Place, Mulgrave, Victoria 3170, Australia
Tel: +61 3 9561 5544 Fax: +61 3 9561 4860
books@imagespublishing.com
www.imagespublishing.com

Third reprint 2012
Copyright © The Images Publishing Group Pty Ltd 2012
The Images Publishing Group Reference Number: 1061

National Library of Australia Cataloguing-in-Publication entry:
Author: Dowsey, David.
Title: Aston Martin : power, beauty and soul / by David Dowsey;
               edited by Robyn Beaver.
Edition: 2nd ed.
ISBN: 978 1 86470 424 2 (hbk.)
Notes: Includes index.
Subjects: Aston Martin automobile.
               Aston Martin automobile - History.
Dewey Number: 629.2222

Designed by The Graphic Image Studio Pty Ltd, Mulgrave, Australia
www.tgis.com.au

Printed on 140gsm GoldEast Matt Art by Everbest Printing Co. Ltd.,
in Hong Kong/China

Contents

What's in a name?

The DB2's Gran Turismo concept set the scene for subsequent Aston Martins

The answer to the age-old question, 'What's in a name?' is *everything!* Especially when that name happens to be Aston Martin: a name revered around the world as representing the pinnacle in automotive sophistication, luxury and outright performance.

It is remarkable that Aston Martin has survived into the 21st century – a feat that at times looked improbable. The cars, and the accompanying mystique and charisma, are still produced simply because the good name of Aston Martin means so much to so many.

In 1912, when Lionel Martin and Robert Bamford set up their modest mechanical business in Henniker Place, Chelsea, it was possible for tiny concerns such as theirs to operate burgeoning motor car manufacturing businesses. The result was that roads, racetracks and showrooms were filled with a wonderful assortment of motoring exotica.

> 'Bruce Blythe took out his ink pen and on a napkin wrote, "The Ford Motor Company hereby agrees not to discuss or disclose any details relating to Aston Martin." How about that! That was our confidentiality agreement, written on a napkin.'
>
> *Peter Livanos*

Left to right: Aston Martin founders Lionel Martin and Robert Bamford; Carroll Shelby, right, approached David Brown, left, with the idea of combining a large-capacity engine in a DB3S chassis but his idea was rejected; Walter Hayes had deep connections within the Ford empire and was instrumental in Aston Martin's transition from private ownership to Ford ownership; Don Frey, pictured at Le Mans in 1966 during Ford's Total Performance era

Motor racing back then was extremely competitive and marques such as Bugatti, Hispano-Suiza, Auto Union, Maserati, MG, Salmson, Stutz, Vauxhall, Delage, Talbot-Lago, Darracq, Alfa Romeo, Mercedes, Lagonda, Lancia and Bentley actively campaigned on the world's great race tracks, road circuits and hill climbs. Scores of independent motor car manufacturers competed fiercely, not only on the racetrack, but also for the business of growing middle class populations who were taking to the newest form of transport with open arms.

When Lionel Martin's services were dispensed with and the company reorganised in 1925, all that was left to purchase, along with some basic tooling equipment, was the good name of Aston Martin. Similarly, when the Sutherland family bought the company in 1932, in effect what they purchased was 11 letters. David Brown, likewise in 1947, purchased little more than the Atom developmental car, some plans, some modest infrastructure and that all-important name: Aston Martin.

Ford's decision to purchase Aston Martin in 1987 couldn't have been based on large immediate fiscal returns. The only thing that could have possibly attracted Ford executives was the good name of Aston Martin: a name synonymous with quality and heritage. Aston Martin would surely bring a lot of prestige to the Blue Oval company. And it did.

In 1925, just months before the receivers were called in, Aston Martin displayed its wares at the Olympia Motor Show for the first time. Along with the fledgling marque were nearly 100 British motor car manufacturers, almost all of which have now vanished. Without Ford's takeover of Aston Martin, it too would be extinct.

Walter Hayes, then Ford's UK boss, and former Aston Martin Works Driver Carroll Shelby were instrumental in the early Ford–Aston Martin association. Shelby had the brilliant idea of combining a powerful, large-capacity American V8 engine with a stylish European body and chassis. Being very familiar with the cars, the first chassis on his shopping list was Aston Martin's DB3S. He approached David Brown and asked if he would be interested, but the idea was rejected. So Shelby and Hayes approached AC Cars and the Cobra was born.

The dual histories of Aston Martin and Ford are more intertwined than at first may be apparent. David Brown and Henry Ford II were long-time friends and during its 'Total Performance' years, Ford's bosses considered an acquisition of both Ferrari and Aston Martin. In 1963 Ford executive Don Frey approached John Wyer, then General Manager of Aston Martin Lagonda, with the idea of a Ford purchase of the company. Apparently, John Wyer was enthusiastic, but David Brown definitely was not. The sale didn't go ahead, but Wyer, who was a racing man through and through, left to join Ford Advanced Vehicles as General Manager.

Wyer's new role was to oversee the GT40 programme, which was an enormous success. The GT40 went on to dominate at Le Mans with four outright victories in 1966, 1967, 1968 and 1969. Ford gave up any ideas of an Aston Martin purchase and their paths did not cross again for a quarter of a century.

A further opportunity appeared when, in May 1987, Walter and Elizabeth Hayes were staying on the estate of Contessa Camilla Maggi in Italy with Victor Gauntlett and HRH Prince Michael of Kent, who were both piloting a DBR2 in the Mille Miglia. Inevitably, talk centred on Aston Martin, past and present. Later, Elizabeth was impressed with the V8 Volante Prince Michael used to drive her to the airport, and on her return home, urged her husband to consider buying the struggling company.

Meanwhile, Henry Ford II had retired and was spending a lot of time in England at his country house near Henley-on-Thames. Walter Hayes was a frequent visitor and over coffee one day Ford inquired, 'What shall we do today?' Hayes replied, 'We could always buy Aston Martin',[1] and continued to tell Ford of his experience at the Mille Miglia.

Henry Ford II set the purchase in motion in May 1987 by asking the President of Ford Europe, Alex Trotman, to investigate the acquisition of Aston Martin. Ford officially approached shareholders Peter Livanos and Victor Gauntlett on 1 July and from there things moved quickly.

Peter Livanos recalled: 'A friend of mine, Peter Sachs, asked me if I would be interested in selling Aston Martin to Ford. So

Left to right: John Wyer, pictured at Le Mans (at rear, third from left), moved to Ford when Aston Martin cancelled its racing programme at the end of 1963; Prince Michael of Kent, a well-known Aston Martin devotee; Victor Gauntlett was one of the giants in modern Aston Martin history, having led the company during some of its financially most difficult times; Henry Ford II was keen to ensure Aston Martin survived but he died shortly after the Ford Motor Company acquisition in September 1987

Left to right: Peter Livanos encouraged his family to support Aston Martin financially and was fundamental in the Ford acquisition of the company; Bruce Blythe; Sir Nick Scheele; Alex Trotman; and Ken Whipple were all in attendance at the dinner when Ford's official proposal was delivered to Gauntlett and Livanos

I spoke to my father and he said to me, "Well, sell it, keep it, why don't you go and hear what they have to say?"

'There were a number of people sniffing around Aston Martin during that 1986–1987 period. During that time Lamborghini was bought by Chrysler, and Ford was trying to buy Alfa Romeo. There was a whole bunch of little car companies being bought out by bigger companies.

'I said to Peter Sachs that we would be happy to talk to Ford, but since we are not on the market for sale, what we don't want to do is destroy the morale at the factory by people believing we are going to sell the company. He said that he would arrange a meeting with the senior people at Ford and it will either happen or not happen very quickly.' The deal was brokered in only ten days.

'Dinner was arranged at Grafton Street, Ford's London headquarters. Bruce Blythe, Walter Hayes, Alex Trotman, Nick Scheele, Ken Whipple, Victor Gauntlett and I attended and they simply said, "We would like to buy Aston Martin." The first question to us was, "What is your objective with Aston Martin?" My response was that I would love to see them do for Astons what people like Audi/Volkswagen do for Porsche in terms of support.

'The people at Ford said that they were interested because at Ford they can make 500,000 of anything, but it is nearly impossible for them to make five of anything. They thought there was a synergy because we had that expertise in building bespoke cars.

'Sometime after that dinner I spoke to my father and he said to go ahead and develop it. And Ford bought the company. I stayed on the Board for a few years and that was the end of that. The whole transaction was put together by Peter Sachs and Bruce Blythe. The negotiations were casual and friendly but the transaction was quite professional in its execution; it was put together by Goldman Sachs, representing Ford.

'There was a big question of confidentiality. We didn't want anything leaking out about these discussions and there was the inevitable, "The lawyers are going to get involved, so we had better write a confidentiality agreement." Bruce Blythe then took out his ink pen and on a Ford Motor Company napkin wrote, "The Ford Motor Company hereby agrees not to discuss or disclose any details relating to Aston Martin." How about that! That was our confidentiality agreement, written on a napkin.'

Ford purchased a majority shareholding in Aston Martin on 7 September 1987 for 'between 15 and 20 million pounds. Better than David Brown's one pound!'[2] said Victor Gauntlett. The resulting arrangement was that Ford owned 75 percent of Aston Martin and the Livanos family and Victor Gauntlett each retained 12.5 percent. As a condition of the sale Victor Gauntlett remained as Executive Chairman. Sadly, Henry Ford II died on 29 September, not seeing what was to become of the deal.

'The arrangement was really very simple,' explained Walter Hayes. 'We would own three quarters because I had argued quite strongly that Gauntlett should remain Chief Executive, the reason being that big companies do not understand small companies.'[3]

The purchase was given a tremendous amount of press, polarising the Aston Martin community in particular and the car-loving public in general. Howls about American 'imperialism' were heard loud and clear, as were fears that Aston Martin would lose its 'Britishness', simply becoming a high-priced badge-engineered Ford. With the benefit of hindsight, these fears have proven to be unfounded.

'There were a lot of people at the time who thought, "That's the end of it, it's going to be badge engineering," recalled Livanos. There was a very strong effort on behalf of Ford in the early days to counteract that and as a result, they left Victor Gauntlett running the company.

'Victor had an amazing personality, a very strong personality and he was able to convince the world that as long as he was Chairman, there was no question of the cars being badge engineered and that worked very well. Subsequent to Victor came Walter Hayes and he had an equally strong view. So, while there were people who were worried that was the end of Aston Martin as we knew it, the reality has turned out very different, as everyone can see.'

The fact is that in a world of globalisation, a tiny company in the middle of the English countryside, which hand-built ultra-expensive motor cars using methods sometimes dating back hundreds of years, could not compete with huge multinationals. It later became very apparent that the Ford takeover was not a whim. It was actually 25 years in the making and Henry Ford II's intention was to retain a great British automotive name.

Walter Hayes: 'Henry [Ford II] was a great Anglophile; his intention was simply to save a name that was going under. He believed that big companies could learn from small companies, for there are things big companies cannot do because they cannot afford them, like small volume limited editions.'[4]

Ford hoped to learn things from Aston Martin as well. The British company was to eventually become Ford's technological flagship and now acts as a pilot for limited runs of advanced technology and engineering. More importantly, Aston Martin put these cars into production, where Ford could not. Ford was able to use technology, researched and produced by Aston Martin, in much larger quantities in volume-produced Ford vehicles.

Ford took its adopted British marque very seriously. It funded and resourced Aston Martin as it built the last of the V-cars and was responsible for implementing the successful DB7 line and the Vanquish.

In 2003 Aston Martin took a quantum leap into the future with the opening of a new factory in Gaydon and the announcement of an all-new range of cars. This, if anything, was the news that finally allayed fears about Ford's commitment to Aston Martin.

'[Ford's purchase] was probably the key moment in turning that company from what was a privately held venture of wealthy industrial families from David Brown on, into a serious motor car company,' said Livanos. 'That was the moment in time that Aston Martin was made.'

Aston Martin went from strength to strength, rising to an enviable position of financial security; a position it had never before held in its long history. It was therefore a great surprise when Aston Martin and Ford parted company in 2007; after almost 20 years the Ford era came to an abrupt end with a formal announcement of the sale of Aston Martin delivered on 13 March 2007.

The Newport Pagnell cars still in production at the time of the Ford majority acquisition included the AMV8, V8 Volante, V8 Vantage Zagato, V8 Vantage, V8 Vantage Volante, Lagonda (Series 4), V8 Zagato Volante and the V8 Vantage Volante PoW Specification – an unprecedented eight-model line up. All used the Tadek Marek-derived V8 engine, in various states of tune, and all, except the Lagonda, shared the same basic chassis platform.[i]

The first eight chapters of this book feature cars that Aston Martin was constructing, or which were under development, when Ford Motor Company acquired the first 75 percent of AML shares. Some of the cars had been in production for many years and in developed form continued to be made.

Some of the featured cars are not strictly production models, such as the 6.3-litre Virage and Vantage V600, which were after-market conversions carried out at Works Service in Newport Pagnell; they have been included for completeness. Other cars such as the 20/20 Concept Car, Zagato Lagonda Rapide and Vantage Shooting Brake, are special cars designed or modified by outside styling houses or engineering companies and are included for interest's sake.

David Dowsey

It seems we already have quite a lot in common.

Ford built their first car in Britain in 1911. Lionel Martin built his first Aston Martin in 1914. So we're both among the oldest surviving marques.

We've both had illustrious careers in motor racing. Among our more famous victories, we've both won Le Mans.

The Shelby/Salvadori DBR1. Le Mans, 1959.

We've both made our share of unforgettable cars; from the Model T to the GT40 and 'Green Pea' to the Zagato.

And above all, in our different price ranges, we're both dedicated to quality.

The Amon/McLaren GT40 MKII Le Mans, 1966.

So imagine the cars that Aston Martin will build now that they've got Ford behind them. Aston with their craftsmanship and talent. And Ford with their technical and manufacturing resources.

Ford

Cars with a future.

Cars with a future: Ford was keen to allay fears that the Aston Martin brand would be diluted under its ownership

---

i   The Zagato cars used a shortened version of the AMV8 chassis

D B

The initials that created a legend

David Brown had been off the Aston Martin scene for 15 years when Ford Motor Company purchased the concern in 1987. Even so, the company's new owners appreciated the legacy the Yorkshireman had left behind. It wasn't long, then, before he was welcomed back into the fold.

Born in Huddersfield on 10 May 1904, Brown joined the family gear-making business, David Brown & Sons, as an engineering apprentice at 17. Established in 1860 by his grandfather, the firm had experience in car manufacture, among other things, from as early as 1908.

In 1932, 28-year-old Brown became Managing Director, and foundry and tractor arms were established prior to WWII. During the conflict the firm produced tank and aircraft gears. But immediately post-war, David Brown, it appears, was looking for a little fun to counter the seriousness of his duties.

Brown entered the British automotive manufacturing scene in a big way in 1947, saving not only Aston Martin but also Lagonda, another great British marque, when he purchased both companies. It was a fancy, but it made sense on a number of levels: he was wealthy, his factories were capable of building and assembling various components, and he had a passion for expensive cars.

Late in 1946 Brown saw an advertisement placed by Aston Martin owner Gordon Sutherland in *The Times* for the sale of a 'high class motor business'. It turned out to be Aston Martin, and Brown purchased the company in February 1947 for £20,500: with his own money.

The acquisition of Lagonda was more convoluted and expensive. Approached by a 'neighbour' with inside information that the struggling company was looking for a buyer, Brown approached Lagonda management to discuss terms. He also visited the Lagonda works in Staines and was given a prototype test drive by Walter Bentley.

But he was told that over £250,000 was being sought and that three offers had already been placed, by Armstrong Siddeley, Rootes and Jaguar. The price was out of Brown's league, but he wisely made a nominal offer of £50,000 to remain in the race. As it turned out, all three previous offers were later rescinded and Brown was the last man standing. His revised bid of £52,000 was accepted in September 1947, and so two of Britain's best-known marques were his for only £72,500.

Immediately post-war, David Brown, it appears, was looking for a little fun to counter the seriousness of his duties.

David Brown toasts the launch of the DB5 with actress Honor Blackman

The making of a car company

In 1913, businessman Lionel Martin and friend Robert Bamford formed Bamford & Martin Ltd, a motor garage business in London. When Martin later won on handicap at the Aston Clinton Hillclimb, in a specially tuned Singer Ten, his wife suggested the two names be linked. Aston Martin was born.

Martin wanted to design his own car and was having a special chassis built. In the meantime he mated a 1400 cc side-valve Coventry Simplex engine with an elderly Isotta Fraschini chassis, in which he competed in the Brighton Speed Trials. War intervened, however, and production was postponed.

Bamford left soon after war's end. Martin left in 1925, after production had begun in 1923 and around 50 road cars had been produced, along with some competition specials.

Between 1925 and the outbreak of WWII Aston Martin was kept alive by a string of individuals, including Gordon Sutherland, who sold the company to David Brown after the war.

The pre-war cars, while small in number, set the tone for Aston Martin. They were expensive, exclusively handmade, and competitive, having raced at Le Mans as early as 1928. Forebodingly, though, the company was a money-loser, a situation that has continued to shape the company's future.

The first car made under Brown's ownership was the Two-Litre Sports, now commonly called the DB1, which was announced at the 1948 London Motor Show. Styled by Lagonda's Frank Feeley, who went on to design several memorable Aston Martins, it featured open bodywork with a vestigial Aston Martin grille and Claude Hill's four-cylinder push-rod engine. With a £2331 price tag, only 16 were built before being deleted in 1950. In truth it was largely a carry-over from pre-war technology and not indicative of Brown's plans for the new company. The next car, however, was to be one of Aston Martin's best.

Brown purchased Lagonda to gain access to its Willie Watson/ WO Bentley-designed six-cylinder engine, having concluded that Claude Hill's four-cylinder engine was not powerful enough for the next generation of Aston Martins. It proved to be the first of many wise decisions.

Three examples of what became the DB2 (the first car to boast the famous initials) made their debut at the 1949 Le Mans 24-hour race: two with the extant Claude Hill push-rod four-cylinder engine and one with WO Bentley's twin-cam six-cylinder unit.

Embracing the new Italian Gran Turismo (GT) concept, the production DB2 made its first appearance at the 1950 New York Motor Show. The stylish two-seat coupe was penned, once again, by Frank Feeley and featured WO Bentley's 105 bhp six-cylinder engine. It was also available in 125 bhp Vantage form (the first car to use the higher specification designation still in use today).

Later available in drophead (convertible) form, the DB2 morphed into the DB2-4 in 1953. What the new model lost in sleekness was made up for in added practicality (the '4' denoting four seats). From 1957–59 the newly-styled but substantially similar DB MkIII was produced. It boasted a 162 bhp 3.0-litre engine, front Girling disc brakes, optional automatic transmission, and a new grille treatment that set the scene for almost every subsequent Aston Martin.

DB2
1950–1953

Chassis: Tubular steel frame

Body: Aluminium two-seat coupe styled by Frank Feeley

Suspension: Front – Independent with trailing arms and coil springs
Rear – Live axle with trailing arms and coil springs

Brakes: Girling hydraulic 12-inch drums (front and rear)

Steering: Worm and roller

Wheels: Dunlop 16-inch centre-lock wire

Tyres: Avon 6.00 X 16

Transmission: David Brown four-speed manual; final drive 3.77:1. Rear-wheel drive

Engine: 2580 cc cast iron in-line six-cylinder with twin chain-driven overhead camshafts and two valves per cylinder. Compression ratio 6.5:1. Twin 1.5-inch SU H4 carburettors

Power: 105 bhp/78 kW @ 5000 rpm
125 lb/ft/169 Nm of torque @ 3000 rpm

Top speed: 110 mph/177 km/h

Dimensions:
Length – 13 ft 6.5 in/4128 mm
Width – 5 ft 5 in/1651 mm
Height – 4 ft 5.5 in/1359 mm
Wheelbase – 8 ft 3 in/2515 mm
Weight – 2449 lb/1111 kg

Price when new: £2331[i]

Number built: 411[ii]

---

i   All prices quoted include UK Car Tax and VAT

ii Includes convertibles

David Brown was a racing enthusiast, having competed in car and motorcycle hill climbs in his youth. In fact, at one time he planned to race in his own Works Aston Martins, but John Wyer politely refused. Nevertheless, Brown wanted Aston Martin to compete in a well-planned series of events on the world stage. This he did, and with some success.

Employing John Wyer in 1950 to run the racing team proved to be among Brown's wisest decisions. Wyer went on to gather around him a team of high-calibre engineers, mechanics and racing drivers (including Stirling Moss, Jim Clark, Tony Brooks, Graham Hill, Peter Collins, Carroll Shelby, Jack Brabham, Bruce McLaren, Roy Salvadori and Reg Parnell) who were able to successfully compete with well-funded Works teams like Mercedes-Benz, Ferrari, Jaguar and Maserati.

The racing cars produced during Brown's reign included the successful DB3S and DBR1. Racing campaigns were also conducted with the DB2 (1949–53), DB3 (1951–53), Lagonda V12 (1954–55), DBR4 and DBR5 Grand Prix cars (1959–60), DB4 GT and DB4 GT Zagato (1959–63), and DP212, 214 and 215 Project Cars (1962–63).

Spanning 1949–63, the David Brown racing era included notable outright victories at Nurburgring (1957, 1958 and 1959), Spa (1957), Goodwood Tourist Trophy (1958 and 1959) and Le Mans (1959). Aston Martin eventually won the World Sports Car Championship with their DBR1 in 1959.

Top: The DB2 was a magnificent road car, and also a successful racing competitor **Above:** Finally bringing David Brown coveted Le Mans success was the Ted Cutting-designed DBR1, driven here by Carroll Shelby

DBR1
1956–1959

Chassis: Steel tubular spaceframe

Body: Aluminium two-seat roadster styled by Ted Cutting

Suspension: Front – Independent with trailing arms, torsion bars and Armstrong shock absorbers
Rear – de Dion axle with Watt's linkage, torsion bars and Armstrong shock absorbers

Brakes: Girling 12.0-inch discs (front); 11.5-inch discs (rear)

Steering: Rack and pinion

Wheels: Borrani 16-inch centre-lock wire

Tyres: Avon 6.00 X 16 (front); 7.00 X 16 (rear)

Transmission: David Brown five-speed manual; various final drives. Rear-wheel drive

Engine: 2992 cc alloy in-line six-cylinder with twin chain-driven overhead camshafts per bank and two valves per cylinder. Compression ratio 9.3:1. Triple Weber 50 DCO carburettors

Power: 250 bhp/186 kW @ 6000 rpm
195 lb/ft/264 Nm of torque @ 5500 rpm

Top speed: 158 mph/254 km/h

Dimensions:
Length – 13 ft 2.5 in/4026 mm
Width – 5 ft 4 in/1626 mm
Height – 3 ft 2.5 in/978 mm
Wheelbase – 7 ft 6 in/2286 mm
Weight – 1894 lb/859 kg

Price when new: N/A

Number built: 5

Taking Aston Martin firmly into a new era was the ground-breaking DB4, which was launched at the 1958 Paris Motor Show. It was a clean sheet design that in many ways set the mould for all future Aston Martins.

Ironically, what many consider to be the quintessential English car had an Italian-styled body. Despite Frank Feeley's excellent draughtsmanship on the DB2 and DB3S range of cars, his DB4 prototype (DP114/2) was disappointing, so newly-appointed General Manager John Wyer thought it best to have the coupe styled by Touring of Milan. The DB4's exquisite proportions are testament to the wisdom of his decision.

The new car did not have an easy birth: several technical problems were discovered after it was announced and a workers' strike at the Aston Martin factory delayed production. History shows this did not hurt the firm too much as the DB4 went on to become a popular model within the bounds of the company's limited production.

The two-plus-two-seat GT featured Tadek Marek's new 220 bhp 3.7-litre alloy six-cylinder engine (which had debuted in the DBR2 racing car), four-wheel Dunlop disc brakes and a luxurious leather-lined cabin. Over its production cycle, which yielded 1110 cars, several variants were produced including five distinct coupe series and, from 1961, a 250 bhp Vantage engine option and a convertible.

In addition, between 1959–63, a short wheelbase GT (which spurned special bodies by Zagato and Bertone, and the Project racing cars) was offered. The DB4 was also the basis for the long-wheelbase Lagonda Rapide, which was built from 1961.

Over its five-year lifecycle the DB4 was continually developed and improved into what essentially became the DB5. This new car was almost indistinguishable from the last DB4, which by

DB4
1958–1963

Chassis: Steel box-section chassis, steel superstructure

Body: Aluminium 2+2 coupe styled by Touring of Milan

Suspension: Front – Independent with wishbones and coil springs
Rear – Live axle with trailing links, coil springs and Watt's linkage

Brakes: Servo-assisted Dunlop 11.5-inch discs (front); 11.125-inch discs (rear)

Steering: Rack and pinion

Wheels: Dunlop 16-inch centre-lock wire

Tyres: Avon Turbospeed 6.00 X 16

Transmission: David Brown four-speed manual; final drive 3.54:1. Rear-wheel drive

Engine: 3670 cc alloy in-line six-cylinder with twin chain-driven overhead camshafts and two valves per cylinder. Compression ratio 8.25:1. Twin 2.0-inch SU HD8 carburettors

Power: 220 bhp/164 kW @ 5500 rpm
240 lb/ft/325 Nm of torque @ 4250 rpm

Top speed: 140 mph/225 km/h

Dimensions:
Length – 14 ft 9 in/4496 mm
Width – 5 ft 6 in/1676 mm
Height – 4 ft 3.5 in/1308 mm
Wheelbase – 8 ft 2 in/2489 mm
Weight – 2890 lb/1311 kg

Price when new: £3976

Number built: 1110[iii]

Aston Martin went to Italian stylists Touring of Milan for the DB4's superb lines

iii Includes convertibles

The DB5 brought enormous publicity to Aston Martin, but the company was not able to successfully capitalise on it

this time had incorporated the cowled headlights of the DB4 GT and had been lengthened to increase rear legroom. But many revisions, including the installation of the larger 4.0-litre engine (first used in the Lagonda Rapide), Girling disc brakes and a five-speed ZF gearbox, were enough, thought the company, to justify the new model designation.

By this time, Aston Martin was moving ever further from its sparse sporting origins and into the luxury arena. The DB5 offered, as standard, Sundym glass and electric windows, while options included air conditioning and a three-speed Borg Warner automatic transmission.

The high performance was still there, however, despite increased weight. The DB5 had a top speed of at least 143 mph and could sprint from 0–60 mph in 7.1 seconds. The Vantage engine, with its three Weber carburettors, was even faster, while retaining the comfort of the standard offering.

Along with a convertible (123 built), the DB5 was the subject of some 'specials', including a 272 bhp Vantage option, and a Shooting Brake conversion by Harold Radford Ltd of London (12 of which were made, including one for the personal use of David Brown).

Debuting in 1963, the DB5 is still probably Aston Martin's best-known car. Its use in the film *Goldfinger* created an enormous amount of publicity and plenty of orders to keep the factory busy. In its two-year production life, 1058 examples of all body styles were built.

Arriving in 1965, and a true model in its own right, the DB6 addressed some of the shortfalls of the DB5. But its longer wheelbase and Kamm tail, though providing superior rear passenger accommodation and improved stability, by necessity altered the superb lines of Touring's original DB4.

DB5
1963–1965

Chassis: Steel box-section chassis, steel superstructure

Body: Aluminium 2+2 coupe styled by Touring of Milan

Suspension: Front – Independent with wishbones and coil springs
Rear – Live axle with trailing links, coil springs and Watt's linkage

Brakes: Servo-assisted Girling 11.5-inch discs (front); 10.08-inch discs (rear)

Steering: Rack and pinion

Wheels: Dunlop 15-inch centre-lock wire

Tyres: Avon Turbospeed 6.70 X 15

Transmission: David Brown or ZF five-speed manual; final drive 3.31:1. Borg Warner automatic optional. Rear-wheel drive

Engine: 3995cc alloy in-line six-cylinder with twin chain-driven overhead camshafts and two valves per cylinder. Compression ratio 8.9:1. Triple 2.0-inch SU HD8 carburettors

Power: 242 bhp/180 kW @ 5500 rpm
280 lb/ft/380 Nm of torque @ 4500 rpm

Top speed: 143 mph/230 km/h

Dimensions:
Length – 15 ft/4572 mm
Width – 5 ft 6 in/1676 mm
Height – 4 ft 4 in/1321 mm
Wheelbase – 8 ft 2 in/2489 mm
Weight – 3233 lb/1466 kg

Price when new: £4175

Number built: 1058[iv]

iv Includes convertibles

David Brown had a DB5 coupe converted into a practical Shooting Brake: eleven other customers followed suit

The longer wheelbase, higher roofline and Kamm tail made the DB6 a more practical proposition

The larger DB6, which was only 17 lb heavier, carried over the DB5's 242-bhp engine, along with the 272 bhp Vantage option, while power steering and automatic transmission became regular options. Actually based on the shorter DB5 platform, a convertible was offered from 1965, launching the long-lived Volante name. The DB6-based Volante was unveiled the following year. Meanwhile, Harold Radford and FLM Panelcraft converted nine cars into DB6 Shooting Brakes.

In 1969, MkII versions of the coupe and Volante convertible were offered. Featuring wider wheels and tyres, along with flared wheelarches, at one point these cars could have worn DB7 badges. For the first time electronic fuel injection was offered, while power steering was by this time a standard feature.

Aston Martin's fortunes were running at an all-time high as the DB6 replaced the DB5. At one point an unprecedented 11 cars per week were being built, and in 1968 Brown was knighted for services to British export. Business was promising, but various factors conspired to bring Aston Martin down to earth; and although there were more 'DB' models in store, like the DBS and DBS V8, it was a downhill ride for Sir David Brown now that the racing team had been abandoned and the world was closing in around his other business interests.

Brown sold Aston Martin Lagonda in 1972 to Company Developments Ltd to help save his ailing primary manufacturing business. In the same year the David Brown Tractor division was also sold. Brown moved to Monaco in the late 1970s as a tax exile, but by 1990 the family interests in the 130-year-old company ceased to exist.

In 1993 Brown became Honorary Life President of Aston Martin Lagonda at the invitation of Walter Hayes, and his initials were reinstated on the DB7, a pre-production model which he saw and approved before his death at 89 in September 1993. His name now lives on in a new generation of Aston Martins.

DB6
1965–1969

Chassis: Steel box-section chassis, steel superstructure

Body: Aluminium 2+2 coupe styled by Touring of Milan

Suspension: Front – Independent with wishbones and coil springs
Rear – Live axle with trailing links, coil springs and Watt's linkage

Brakes: Servo-assisted Girling 11.5-inch discs (front); 10.08-inch discs (rear)

Steering: Rack and pinion

Wheels: Dunlop 15-inch centre-lock wire

Tyres: Avon Turbospeed 6.70 X 15

Transmission: ZF five-speed manual; final drive 3.73:1. Borg Warner three-speed automatic optional. Rear-wheel drive

Engine: 3995 cc alloy in-line six-cylinder with twin chain-driven overhead camshafts and two valves per cylinder. Compression ratio 8.9:1. Triple 2.0-inch SU HD8 carburettors

Power: 242 bhp/180 kW @ 5500 rpm
280 lb/ft/380 Nm of torque @ 4500 rpm

Top speed: 148 mph/238 km/h (Vantage)

Dimensions:
Length – 15 ft 2 in/4623 mm
Width – 5 ft 6 in/1676 mm
Height – 4 ft 5.5 in/1359 mm
Wheelbase – 8 ft 5.75 in/2584 mm
Weight – 3250 lb/1474 kg

Price when new: £4998

Number built: 1750ᵛ

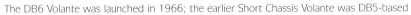

v   Includes MkI and MkII coupes and Volante convertibles

The DB6 Volante was launched in 1966; the earlier Short Chassis Volante was DB5-based

A M V 8
Last of the line

Aston Martin's DBS body and V8 engine formed a partnership that, in terms of longevity, had few rivals. The V8 engine was unveiled at the Racing Car Show in London in January 1967. The DBS was first shown at Blenheim Palace on 25 September the same year. Both were later brought together, as was always intended, in the DBS V8.

Its name changed to Aston Martin V8 in 1972, but for 20 years the car became the backbone of Aston Martin production in largely unchanged form. In fact, the engine was to survive, in modified form, until 20 October 2000, when the last 'Newport Pagnell' V8 left the Aston Martin factory in a Vantage Volante Special Edition.

Thoughts of replacing Aston Martin's extant six-cylinder unit with a V8 engine can be traced back to the late 1950s, after the 4.5-litre V12 Lagonda sports cars proved unreliable on the racetrack. But it was not until 1963 that Chief Designer Tadek Marek began work on the new power plant.

'It was buzzing along sweetly and we were all complimenting ourselves on how nice and smoothly the engine was running, when it stopped dead and the eerie silence was broken by steam starting to escape from all apertures.'

David Morgan

His brief was to produce a high-performance, low-stressed engine that would effortlessly power a Grand Touring car at speeds matching the best in the world well into the future. Who was to know at the time that the engine would be in production 37 years later?

Taking into account the increased frontal aspect of the yet-to-be-designed body and the inevitable weight increase, Marek calculated that the new engine would need to deliver 32 percent more power than the existing 3995 cc in-line six-cylinder engine, which produced a true 242 bhp in non-Vantage specification. This meant a power figure somewhere in the region of 300–350 bhp and a unit capacity of around 5.3 litres.

ASTON MARTIN: POWER, BEAUTY AND SOUL

One of the most important models in Aston Martin's history, the AMV8 was built for 20 years; this is a 1974 carburettor model

Clockwise from top: By the 1960s Aston Martins had grown enormously in size and engine capacity compared to this diminutive 1923 Bamford and Martin 1.5-litre side-valve four-cylinder Grand Prix car; The V8 engine was a tight fit in the DB4 engine bay; DB4 4YMC was fitted with an experimental V8 engine and used for extensive testing purposes; Until 2001 Newport Pagnell in Buckinghamshire was the headquarters of Aston Martin manufacturing; An Oscar India V8 being hand-built at Newport Pagnell in the 1980s

Left: The Lola–Aston T70 Mk III racing car was spectacularly unsuccessful but proved invaluable in the development of the production V8 engine Right: The first 5.0-litre Aston Martin V8 engine was fitted to the Lola–Aston racing car; pictured from left: David Morgan, Ted Fenwick, George Evans, Alan Crouch

'There were two technicians on the project; Ted Fenwick built the cylinder block assembly and I worked on the cylinder heads, inlet and exhaust systems,' said engineer David Morgan whose involvement in the V8 engine started with Marek's original blue prints. 'Along with George Evans I was also involved in the development and running the engines on the dynamometer.'

The first prototype engine, DP218, had a capacity of 4806 cc and was completed and bench tested for the first time on 29 July 1965. The engine block and heads were cast in alloy and several parts from the six-cylinder engine were retained.

'The first failure came soon after the first engine was running,' said Morgan. 'It was buzzing along sweetly and we were all complimenting ourselves on how nice and smoothly it was running, when it stopped dead and the eerie silence was broken by steam starting to escape from all apertures. With tails between our legs it was off the dyno and into the cradle to see what had happened. It was a big-end bolt failure.

'We soon put this thoroughly to right, replacing the handmade bolts with Unbrako X-type bolts and never had another failure. The initial 4.8-litre engine ran on downdraft 44 mm Weber carburettors with very short inlet manifolds. Performance was not good; well below the C-Type 4.0-litre six-cylinder output.'

After some initial running in and minor fettling the engine was tested at 275 bhp @ 5750 rpm running on Weber 46 IDA carburettors with a compression ratio of 8.36:1. After some further minor adjustments the engine produced 285 bhp @ 6000 rpm a few days later; only marginally better than the DBS Vantage engine, which produced a genuine 272 bhp.[i]

The next test had the V8 showing 297 bhp @ 6000 rpm. Work on the exhaust manifolds then pushed power up to 310 bhp @ 6000 rpm. Cam timing and carburettor tests brought the figure up to 319 bhp, then 325 bhp still at 6000 rpm.

In December 1965 AE Brico fuel injection was tried, which initially dropped horsepower down to 317 bhp, but a longer inlet tract greatly improved torque levels; before long power was back up to 320 bhp. Further improvements including induction alterations and a change in compression ratio to 9.0:1 produced a much better 329 bhp @ 6200 rpm. This particular engine was fitted to a DB5 (NPP 7D), chassis number MP222, and used for exhaustive testing on public roads.

Meanwhile, world-champion motorcyclist and Formula One driver, John Surtees, had won the 1966 Can-Am Championship in a Lola T70. He heard that a new Aston Martin engine was being developed and approached the company, which by this time had retired from competitive racing and proposed that Aston Martin supply V8 engines for the Lola T70 Mk III he was to campaign in the 1967 World Championship.

The company was interested, due in no small way to ex-racing Team Manager John Wyer, now working for Ford, who encouraged owner David Brown to supply Lola with the V8 engine. Tadek Marek however, was not amused. He had stipulated from the outset that the V8 engine was not to be used for competitive racing. Perhaps encouraged by the fact that a similar situation had arisen during the development of the 2.9-litre, used in the DB3S and DBR1, and 3.7-litre six-cylinder engines used with some success in the DBR2, he was persuaded otherwise.

A Chevrolet 5.9-litre V8 unit powered Lola and Surtees to the 1966 World Sports Car Championship and it was thought Aston Martin's V8 would deliver even greater results. A Chevrolet engine was borrowed from John Surtees and delivered to Newport Pagnell for further scrutiny. Following a thorough evaluation of the engine it was decided to increase the capacity of the Aston Martin V8 to 5.0 litres. This was done by enlarging the bore out to 97.75 mm, while retaining the 83 mm stroke, producing an engine of 4983 cc.

i Aston Martin claimed the exaggerated figure of 325 bhp

'The increased bore size allowed bigger diameter inlet valves, initially by shortening six-cylinder valves, and porting modification to improve the gas flow,' said Morgan. 'This head work alone gave us some 40 extra horsepower. But we needed to increase the inlet tract length so we fabricated cross-over manifolds, mated to 45 DCOE carburettors, as used on the six-cylinder.'

With a compression ratio of 9.1:1 and four 45 DCOE Weber carburettors, power was increased further to 332 bhp @ 5500 rpm with a very good improvement in torque. Later, a V8 engine with experimental Brico fuel injection was placed into a DB4 (4YMC), chassis number DP200/1, for further evaluation.

With the Lola–Aston partnership confirmed, progress continued with a view to producing greater power. Higher-lift camshafts and a reversion back to 48 IDA Weber carburettors produced a very promising 421 bhp @ 6500 rpm and 386 lb/ft of torque @ 5000 rpm. One of these engines was fitted to a Lola Mk III for a series of tests at Silverstone and Goodwood with drivers David Hobbs and John Surtees.

As always, racing, or in this case race testing, improved the breed and a series of breakages and shortcomings were detected in the engine. 'The initial engine for the Silverstone test was fitted with a modified wet sump system, which resulted in parts of a con-rod [coming off] on Hangar Straight,' said Morgan.

'Again Tadek Marek showed his real genius by working at home over the weekend and returning on Monday morning with detail drawings. Surtees later said that the dry sump system was the neatest system he had seen with everything contained within the sump, and oil pressure was rock-solid at all times.'

Cylinder head modifications and the addition of a higher-lift exhaust camshaft raised the power output once more to 450 bhp. By this time the 5.0-litre Aston Martin V8 engine had eclipsed the Chevrolet 5.9-litre unit in both power and torque. Things were looking very promising for a successful season with the Lola–Aston Martin T70 Mk III.

The public had its first view of Aston Martin's new V8 engine, in 5.0-litre guise, on John Surtees' stand at the Racing Car Show; while on Lola's stand, a new coupe was exhibited. No official announcement was made at the show regarding the impending collaboration, but it was plain to many that Aston Martin was about to return to the racetrack.

Being a new project, there were inevitable development problems. 'There were complaints that the engine wasn't developing enough power. I took the Lola–Aston Martin Le Mans car to the wind tunnel at MIRA and we did a lot of wind tunnel testing there which was all new and exciting for me,' said Development Engineer Mike Loasby.

'The drag was very high because the aerodynamic aids on the car were extreme. They made the car handle well but they made it slow. It was barely topping 190 mph but when we improved the aerodynamics it did over 200 mph easily. It had about 450-odd horsepower at the time.'

At the car's first race, the Nürburgring 1000 km, Lucas fuel injection was fitted. After Surtees recorded the second-fastest time in practice, behind Phil Hill's Chaparral, hopes were high. 'We went out to the Nürburgring and we frightened them all with it until the [rear] suspension broke,' recalled Surtees. The Lola was out of the race.

But if the Nürburgring 1000 km race was a disappointment, Le Mans proved even more so. One Lola–Aston retired at 59 minutes due to burnt pistons, the next at 2 hours 32 minutes with TV damper failure destroying the engine; but not before Hobbs had achieved 205 mph on the Mulsanne Straight. The failures ended any thought of continuing the partnership.

The V8 engine would have become a reliable and competitive race engine, but the initial development was extremely rushed. Had more time been allowed for thorough testing it would have been a success on the racetrack. 'Frankly, it could have been the first of the supercars. Lola–Aston Martin would have been a natural. It fell apart and it was a great shame,' said Surtees.

The DBS was always intended to take the V8 but had to make do with the existing 4.0-litre six-cylinder unit while prolonged development of the engine continued

David Brown's personal four-door DBS was equipped with a 5.0-litre V8 engine; a four-door V8 was never sold under his ownership but a revised version did enter production in 1974

The V8 engine was finally mated with the DBS body in 1969 with the DBS V8 the result

A post-race inspection of the dismantled engines back at Newport Pagnell revealed a degree of flexing, which resulted in chafing around the main bearing cap and some cracking around the main bearing housing. These failures however, did highlight the V8's weaknesses before it was put into production and proved once again that nothing tests an engine quite like endurance racing.

'When we had the problems with the V8 at Le Mans, the engines came back and were rebuilt and Tadek ran them on the test bed for 24 hours with a Le Mans-type exhaust system, which came out of the door in the workshop. It made a fearful noise. There were a few complaints from locals who phoned the police station, but couldn't get the police because they were out watching us,' remembered Loasby.

Oscar India

Oscar India was an internal reference used by Aston Martin employees for the 'new' V8 model, which was intended to be launched on 1 October 1978. Various theories exist as to what the code name meant: October 1 and October Introduction being the most common. Mike Loasby: 'Oscar India was so called so that we could refer to it amongst ourselves at Aston Martin without anybody knowing what it was called. The registration letters of the Cessna 152 aeroplane that Alan Curtis used to fly up from Blackbush to Cranfield in were Golf, Bravo, Foxtrot, Oscar, India (G-BFOI). We called the car "Oscar India" because people would think that we were referring to aircraft. It didn't stand for October Introduction; not in my book it didn't.'

After David Brown sold Aston Martin in 1972 a 'new' V8 model appeared with a reprofiled nose, while still retaining the fuel injected engine

Aston Martin returned to using carburettors in 1973, necessitating a larger bonnet scoop

'I well remember the Surtees race engine strip,' said Morgan. 'It had failed at Le Mans with a holed piston due to poor cooling on his car, which had experimental Ferrari-type bodywork, and a very late and unnecessary change of spark plug manufacturer.

'Once back at the factory we fitted another piston and ran the engine for 24 hours on the dynamometer, mimicking the Le Mans circuit. The engine completed the test in one piece, but on stripping the engine, once the front and rear mains were removed, we lifted the crankshaft, and what remained of the other bearing, out together.

'We had already known about the head gasket sealing problems, due to the cylinder head studs being too short and losing clamping loads quickly. We resolved this by extending the studs down to the main bearing bosses, waisting the studs so that they would stretch and dropping the clamping face in the cylinder head to just the other side in the combustion chamber, rather than clamp the whole head.

'We had found that the cylinder head distorted during tightening the head studs and distorted the valve seats and camshaft bearing housings. The 5.3-litre design limited the valve seat distortion, causing gas leakage and high hydrocarbons. We only really sorted the problem by using deformable valves on the later engines.'

Aston Martin's engineers were determined to fix the problem and the V8 underwent an extended series of tests and modifications, which delayed production of the engine. The V8's bottom end was modified and strengthened; ribbing was added for stiffness and, after extensive testing, cracking could not be detected. A testament to the bottom end's superb design was that it was used for the life of the engine and contributed to the V8's deserved reputation for rugged reliability and longevity.

Meanwhile, development of the rest of Aston Martin's new car continued. Harold Beach designed the chassis, which had independent front suspension and a de Dion rear end. The new body, the work of in-house designer, William Towns, was ready by 1967. The engine was not. As a result the DBS went into production with the familiar 4.0-litre six-cylinder unit.

Further tests in 1967 with AE Brico and Bosch fuel injection systems went ahead with the V8 engine, then delivering around 320 bhp. With the DBS by then in production Aston Martin was able to test the engine under 'real' conditions. In response to increasingly demanding emissions laws, Bosch fuel injection was chosen ahead of the AE Brico system or Weber carburettors.

Two years elapsed before Aston Martin's engineers were confident the V8 engine was ready for production. In the meantime, David Brown requested a four-door DBS with a 5.0-litre development V8 engine. 'David Brown's car had fuel injection and a cross-over exhaust. It was very quiet, but it developed about 280 bhp,' remembered Loasby.

Tadek Marek, an extremely important and influential figure in the post-war story of Aston Martin, retired in 1968, without seeing his masterpiece put into production. 'Working with Tadek was usually very good,' remembered Morgan. 'He was a very skilled designer but he had based the V8 design on the very successful 4.0-litre six-cylinder and saw the V8 as his final perfect engine. Unfortunately a V8 has very different stresses to a six-cylinder and Tadek wouldn't accept the need for changes, hence Alan Crouch's involvement.'

Alan Crouch, Senior Design Engineer working for Harold Beach, was given the task of completing Marek's work. Crouch had done a lot of work on the V8 since its inception in 1963 and carried out much of the redesign under the direction of Marek and Engineering Director, Dudley Gershon. The engine became considerably stronger as a result of his efforts.

Feeling now that the V8 was sufficiently robust, the bore and stroke were taken out to 100 mm and 85 mm respectively, creating a 5340 cc unit. In addition, new pistons, oil pump and Bosch, rather than the DB6 Mk II-sourced AE Brico mechanical fuel injection, were incorporated. In March 1969 the first 5.3-litre V8 engine was tested at 343 bhp @ 5000 rpm.

The DBS V8 was finally launched on 27 September 1969 at the Earl's Court Motor Show while the DBS and DB6 Mk II and Volante were still in production. The new car boasted a powerful and reliable production engine delivering 310–320 bhp @ 5000 rpm and 358 lb/ft of torque @ 4000 rpm.

The DBS V8 was equipped with Girling ventilated disc brakes and GKN 15-inch cast alloy wheels, shod in Pirelli Cinturato GR70 VR15 tyres; the only suitable tyres available at the time.

Road testers were impressed with the car and a top speed of 162 mph[ii] was recorded. A 0–60 mph sprint in 5.9 seconds did even more to enhance the DBS V8's reputation. Journalists commented that the balance of the car was upset a little in comparison to the DBS due to the slight increase in weight but perhaps the most telling criticism was that the car lacked low-down torque. This shortcoming was gradually improved as the car was developed. It was one of the fastest production cars in the world and was endowed with fine handling.

ii The road test car, however, produced 338 bhp @ 5500 rpm – *Aston Martin V8* by Michael Bowler

Top: Oscar India models contained several modifications including an enclosed bonnet scoop and Kamm tail **Above:** Fuel injection returned in 1986, this time by Weber-Marelli

Tadek Marek

Tadek Marek's engineering genius lay at the heart of Aston Martin's most famous cars. His six- and eight-cylinder engines graced the DB4 through to the V8, powering Aston Martin from 1958 to 1989 and his V8 engine lived on in modified form until late 2000.

Born in Krakow, Poland in 1908, Marek (pictured below right with Mike Loasby) studied engineering at Charlottenburg Technical Institute in Berlin, Germany. He became a keen racing driver, but his driving ambitions were curtailed by a serious accident in 1928. Marek began his working career at Fiat in Poland, and then moved to General Motors.

When WWII began he migrated to England and joined the Polish Army, spending most of his time designing tanks. At the end of the war he joined the United Nations and returned to Germany to help rebuild that country. In 1949 he joined the Austin Motor Company and finally moved to Aston Martin in 1954 as Chief Designer.

His first work included the update of the 2.6-litre six-cylinder that started life in the Lagonda saloons and DB2. He enlarged it to 2.9 litres and in this form it was used in the DB MkIII. Marek then produced the famed 3.7-litre six-cylinder DB4 unit, which was enlarged to 4.0 litres for the DB5, DB6 and DBS.

He was against having his engines raced, but they proved to be among the greats. Marek retired to Italy in 1968, just before the V8 was launched, but its longevity is a great testament to his immense talent. He died in 1982.

The DBS V8 came in for a name change and subtle restyling in 1972 after David Brown (by then Sir David) sold Aston Martin Lagonda Limited to Company Developments. The V8 cars then became known simply as Aston Martin V8s.

The biggest change from 1973 was the introduction of Weber carburettors. 'There were several reasons for the conversion to carburettors,' said Morgan, 'or rather away from the Bosch mechanical fuel injection system. Bosch was becoming more and more reluctant to produce the pumps, which had become very expensive. The work required to fit the fuel injection system took more hours than the build of the rest of the engine. The poor idle quality and the very complex setting-up problems didn't help either.

'We fitted a very efficient, four-into-one exhaust system and linked the twin exhausts under the centre of the car so pulses could split into two banks; this gave an extra 25 bhp alone. We were still short of torque at around 2000–3000 rpm; Aston Martin engines have always had impressive torque throughout the rpm range, so to fill the "hole" at 2500 rpm we had to develop the airbox to effectively give us a long inlet tract. This took some time and the very strong arms of John Holman, our experimental fabricator.

'The end result was very impressive and although slightly short of the massive torque provided by the long Bosch inlet tracts, the car was quicker to 60 mph and had excellent drivability.

'I will never forget taking the first carburettor car to the Weber factory in Bologna; they were extremely impressed with the drivability and the wide power band. Perhaps the biggest compliment came from John Wyer who visited the factory to see Harold Beach, our Head of Engineering. Wyer drove the car and was very impressed. If I hadn't driven that car I'd never have believed Webers could be that good.'

The cars underwent constant revision over the years but in reality changed only subtly. However, as is so often the case, the cars put on weight, became a little slower, a lot smoother and much more luxurious and refined.

Model	Production dates	Number built	Distinguishing features
DBS V8	Apr 1970 - Apr 1972	405 [iii]	Four 5.5-inch headlights, aluminium-fluted grille, GKN 15-inch alloy wheels, low bonnet scoop, Bosch mechanical fuel injection
AMV8 (Bosch fuel injection)	May 1972 - Jul 1973	288	Two 7-inch headlights, black mesh grille, GKN 15-inch alloy wheels, low bonnet scoop, Bosch mechanical fuel injection
AMV8 (Weber carburettor)	Aug 1973 - Sept 1978	967	Two 7-inch headlights, black mesh grille, GKN 15-inch wheels, large bonnet scoop, four Weber carburettors
AMV8 (Oscar India)	Oct 1978 - Jan 1986	291	Two 7-inch headlights, black mesh grille, GKN 15-inch alloy wheels, (BBS 15-inch alloy wheels from 1983), stainless steel exhaust system, revised suspension, integrated boot spoiler, enclosed bonnet scoop, walnut inserts and piped leather interior, four Weber carburettors
AMV8 (Weber-Marelli fuel injection)	Jan 1986 - Dec 1989	61	Two 7-inch headlights, black mesh grille, BBS 15-inch alloy wheels, walnut inserts and piped leather interior, flatter bonnet, Weber-Marelli fuel injection

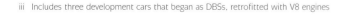

iii Includes three development cars that began as DBSs, retrofitted with V8 engines

Although at the factory they were only ever known as DBS V8s or AMV8s, the V8 cars can be grouped into five distinct categories, for ease of identification:

Model	Weight (lb)	0-60 mph (seconds)	Top speed (mph)	Power (bhp)
DBS V8	3800	5.9	162	310-320
AMV8[iv] (Bosch fuel injection)	3800	5.9	162	310-320
AMV8 (Weber carburettor)	3886	5.7	155	310
AMV8 (Oscar India)	3969	6.6	146	305
AMV8[v] (Weber-Marelli fuel injection)	4009	6.7	150	305

On 25 January 1986 at the New York Motor Show, a final development of the AMV8 was unveiled. Production of the new model began shortly afterwards with chassis number V8SGR12500.

This model was to prove the end of the line for the William Towns-styled V8. It was the last revision in a long series of updates for the aging model as Aston Martin bought time before the launch of its first new car in almost 20 years: the Virage.

The original DBS V8 delivered approximately 310–320 bhp[vi], but the V8 engine's power output was reduced in ensuing years to comply with increasingly rigorous emissions laws. In 1986 the company came full circle and returned to fuel injection.

Even with the benefit of this technology, the American-market cars were still down on power compared to European-specification models. Outputs were 305 bhp for the European cars and 262 bhp for the USA. It was not until the Virage was released with its new 32-valve engine that the American market was once again able to enjoy European-specification performance.

As with all the V8 cars since 1972, the appearance of the new AMV8 was very similar to its predecessors. The only immediately distinguishing feature was the almost flat bonnet. The BBS 15-inch cast alloy wheels were carried over from the later Oscar India cars, as was almost every other specification.

The Oscar India model introduced a level of luxury never before seen on an Aston Martin and the latest fuel-injected car continued that tradition. The V8s had evolved into sheer luxury by this time as the customer base changed and the cars moved into a new market.

The new AMV8 was no exception and every luxury item imaginable was available on the car, including electric aerial, mirrors and windows, stereo/cassette, heated rear window, air conditioning and cruise control. Chrysler's Torqueflite automatic transmission was the most popular option, although ZF five-speed manuals were also offered.

iv No published road test reports available; however this model shared the same mechanical specification as the DBS V8

v No road tests are available for this model

vi By the time of the release of the DBS V8, AML had stopped quoting bhp figures saying, like Rolls-Royce before them, that power was 'sufficient'. Figures for DBS V8/AMV8 from *Aston Martin V8* by Michael Bowler.

Top to bottom: DBS V8s can be identified by their four headlights; Fuel injected AMV8s featured a low bonnet bulge and dual headlights; Carburettor AMV8s had a higher bonnet scoop; Oscar India models introduced an enclosed bonnet scoop and revised interior; The shift to fuel injection meant the bonnet of the last series car was almost flat

Aston Martin Tickford

Tickford was originally a coachbuilding company based in Newport Pagnell, Buckinghamshire. Its roots can be traced back to 1820 when it was known as Salmons and Sons. It later branched out into making car bodies for clients including Alvis, MG and Rover and became known as Tickford in 1943. David Brown acquired the company name at the end of 1954 and eventually moved Aston Martin Lagonda to the site in Tickford Street, Newport Pagnell from 1955. Tickford later built the bodies for the Lagonda coupe and drop head coupe and the DB2/4 Mk II and DB Mk III.

Aston Martin Lagonda Ltd. established the subsidiary company, Aston Martin Tickford, in 1981 to utilise the talented engineering base at Newport Pagnell. Manufacturing Director, David Flint, was asked by the Board to head the new company, based in Blakelands, Milton Keynes, as Managing Director.

'Aston Martin was looking to widen its commercial base,' said Flint. 'Our engineering base was only being used to build a few cars per week, so it was decided to outsource our coachbuilding and engineering talent to other companies.'

Aston Martin Tickford conducted consultancy work for various companies, resulting in the Tickford Capri, Lancia Hi-Fi, Frazer Tickford Metro, Ford RS200 and RS500, Aston Martin Lagonda Tickford Limousine and Jaguar XJS Cabriolet, among others. It also conducted the engine development work for the Nimrod and EMKA racing car programmes, the Weber-Marelli fuel injection system, developed and supplied the 6.3-litre Virage V8 engine, provided performance development, calibration and Type Approval testing for the DB7 engine and conducted engine development work for Ford, Rover, Jaguar and General Motors.

During the restructure of Aston Martin in mid-1984, CH Industrials, headed by Tim Hearley, (pictured below) took full control of Aston Martin Tickford, which was converted into a separate company simply named Tickford. It conducted consultancy work for AML along with many other companies.

In 1991 Tickford teamed with Ford Australia to collaborate on Ford's high-performance vehicle division, Tickford Vehicle Engineering. In 2001, Prodrive bought a controlling interest in Tickford and the company became a part of David Richards' Prodrive group.

The biggest difference between the last AMV8 and its predecessors was the reversion to fuel injection; hence the almost-flat bonnet. Fuel injection had not been used since 1973, when the Bosch system was abandoned. This time, however, a Weber-Marelli electronically controlled sequential system delivered the fuel supply.

Aston Martin's V8 was the first production car outside Italy to use the new Weber-Marelli system. The main requirement for the new set-up was to match the power and torque characteristics of the carburettor car but with improved fuel economy. Aston Martin Tickford completed the application and homologation for the fuel injection and engine management system.

Powertrain and Engineering Manager Arthur Wilson recalls: 'The last AMV8 engine project was started by Aston Martin Tickford before the separation of the two companies. I was working for David Morgan who was Chief Engineer for Tickford, as Engine Development Engineer on that project. All hardware was finalised and a power map for the engine management completed. The emission and drivability map and emission certification was still to be done.

Top: Original Bosch mechanical fuel-injected engine from the DBS V8
Above: Weber-Marelli fuel injection was a feature of the last AMV8 variant

Top to bottom: The Tickford-enhanced Ford Capri; Oscar India interiors took Aston Martin into Rolls-Royce territory with hitherto unheard of luxury; Late fuel-injected cars show how little the interior changed over time

'Early in 1984 I was offered the position in charge of engines in a new Engineering Department at AML, set up by Michael Bowler as Head of Engineering. This had been necessary due to the separation. Chris Bale took over from me at Tickford and completed the project for AML, with me being the AML end of this project.'

Only 61 Weber fuel injected AMV8s were built between 1986 and 1989, which made it the scarcest of the DBS V8/AMV8 series. The AMV8 overlapped the Virage for a short time until the new model was in full production. The AMV8 gracefully disappeared from the catalogue in December 1989 with chassis number V8VKR12701/R after providing sterling service for 20 years.

AMV8 [vii]
1986–1989 [viii]

Chassis: Steel box-section chassis, steel superstructure

Body: Aluminium 2+2 coupe styled by William Towns

Suspension: Front – Independent with unequal length double wishbones, coil springs and anti-roll bar
Rear – de Dion axle with coil springs and Watt's linkage

Brakes: Servo-assisted Girling 273 mm ventilated discs (front); 263 mm inboard-mounted ventilated discs (rear)

Steering: Power-assisted rack and pinion

Wheels: 15-inch BBS alloy

Tyres: Avon Turbospeed 235/70 VR15

Transmission: Torqueflite three-speed automatic; final drive 3.058:1. ZF five-speed manual; final drive 3.33:1. Limited-slip differential. Rear-wheel drive

Engine: 5340 cc alloy V8 with twin chain-driven overhead camshafts per bank and two valves per cylinder. Compression ratio 9.25:1. Weber-Marelli fuel injection. Fully catalysed exhaust system

Power: 305 bhp/227 kW @ 6000 rpm
320 lb/ft/434 Nm of torque @ 3000 rpm

Top speed: 150 mph/241 km/h

Dimensions:

Length	15 ft 4 in/4674 mm
Width	6 ft /1829 mm
Height	4 ft 4.25 in/1327 mm
Wheelbase	8 ft 6.75 in/2610 mm
Weight	4009 lb/1818 kg

Price when new: £55,000 [ix]

Number built: 61

AMV8 – Last of the line

---

vii Specifications quoted throughout are typical for each model, but owing to the hand made nature of Aston Martins, specifications could vary according to individual customer's requirements

viii Dates quoted encompass the public launch to the last example built

ix All prices quoted include UK Car Tax and VAT

V 8   V o l a n t e

V8 wings

Since the inception of the automobile, motorists had enjoyed years of open-top touring. But during the 1970s American politician Ralph Nader and government legislation almost eliminated convertibles, especially in the United States. The convertibles produced during that era were often ugly hybrids with ungainly Targa roofs and rollover bars.

Virtually every Aston Martin model had been available in an open version, but a convertible had not been created after the demise of the DB6 Mk II Volante in November 1970. A lack of finances meant there was no DBS convertible and with Aston Martin's American market on the wane in the early- to mid-1970s, there was no pressing need to develop a V8 version either.

The situation had thawed by mid-decade and at the behest of his customers, AML's representative in the US, Rex Woodgate, along with Los Angeles dealer Chuck Vandergriff, petitioned Aston Martin to construct a V8 convertible. They even engaged automotive artist Dale W. King to fashion a design sketch of what a V8 convertible would look like to hasten the decision.

It worked, but because of the prevailing safety legislation, the V8 Volante was a long time coming. Harold Beach had designed a convertible platform by the end of 1976 and in mid-1977 consultants Woodall Nicholson constructed a prototype. After inevitable development problems had been solved, production was confirmed. The V8 Volante was launched on 21 June 1978, almost nine years after the first V8 had been announced. Production began in mid-1978, but the Volante was only sold in the US for the first twelve months.

The name Volante, 'flying' in Italian, was coined by Aston Martin's Sales Administrator, Kent Monk, and was first used to describe what is now known as a Short Chassis Volante. Previously, all roofless Aston Martins were either known as drop head coupes or convertibles.

The first V8 Volante was launched while the original carburettor V8 Saloon was in production. The arrival of the Volante provided Aston Martin with the perfect opportunity to revise the V8 Saloon to create a more luxurious touring car. The changes involved a neater, redesigned bonnet and burr walnut cappings and piped leather interior.

The V8 Volante proved to be one of Aston Martin's best sellers during its life span of more than 10 years

The name Volante, 'flying' in Italian, was coined by Aston Martin's
Sales Administrator, Kent Monk, and was first used to describe
what is now known as a Short Chassis Volante.

Top: DB6 convertibles were known as Volantes, a name Aston Martin has continued to use **Above:** Two men who played vital roles in the Volante story: Rex Woodgate (left) petitioned Aston Martin to build a convertible V8 for his US customers and Kent Monk, the man responsible for the Volante name

The V8 engine had also entered its so-called Stage 1 tune by this time, which involved fitting new camshafts and larger diameter inlet valves, raising the compression ratio and recalibrating the carburettors. New damping and the Vantage's stainless steel exhaust system had been installed, too. The changes to the new Volante pre-empted those of the upcoming Oscar India V8 Saloon, which was launched in October of the same year.

The Volante was based on the AMV8, sharing most of the same mechanical components, fittings and setups. However, the platform chassis was revised by Harold Beach with added strengthening to increase rigidity. Welding extra box-section members in the sills and reinforcing the base and sides of the windscreen pillars created the strengthening required. As a result the Volante was very strong, but the extra bracing and powered hood pushed the car's weight up to 3950 lb.

The beautifully constructed hood was the work of George Moseley, designer of the Rolls-Royce Corniche hood. It was fully lined and incorporated a plastic rear window. With handbrake engaged, and with the touch of a button, the Smiths electronic and hydraulic lifting rams raised and lowered the roof in a matter of seconds. It was an exceptional system, but the stowed hood and leather tonneau cover spoiled the neat lines of the car somewhat.

The hood mechanism and restyled flat rear deck conspired to rob the already-small boot. To make the best use of the space, exquisite fitted leather luggage by Tanner Krolle was available as an optional extra.

Top: Rex Woodgate commissioned this sketch from artist Dale W. King to show to the Aston Martin board **Above:** Carburettor-equipped V8 Volantes were fitted with plastic rear windows; heated glass became available in May 1987

Journalists praised the excellent suspension, brakes, Adwest rack and pinion power-steering, outstanding handling and elegant looks of the convertible. Performance was still brisk, but predictably, top speed was down to around 140 mph; but *Motor* still recorded a commendable 7.7-second 0–60 mph sprint for an automatic car.

A revised Volante was unveiled at the New York Motor Show on 25 January 1986. The new model shared similar enhancements seen on the last AMV8, unveiled at the same show; namely the reversion to fuel injection and the accompanying flat bonnet. Avon GR70 VR15 tyres and BBS 15-inch cross-spoke wheels were

standard equipment, while almost all other specifications and dimensions matched the AMV8 Saloon. Chrysler Torqueflite three-speed automatic transmission was the preferred choice for most customers; by now, the very expensive ZF manual gearbox was £1281 extra. From May 1987 a heated glass rear window became available.

Power was quoted as 305 bhp @ 6000 rpm and 320 lb/ft of torque @ 3000 rpm, which resulted in a claimed top speed of more than 140 mph, with the 0–60 mph sprint coming up in 6.7 seconds. Production started during 1986 at chassis number V8CGL15440.

Harold Beach

Harold Beach began his career as an apprentice at the famed coachbuilding firm, Barkers, in 1928. He went on to work for a number of automotive companies before joining Aston Martin in September 1950 as a Design Draughtsman, rising to become Chief Engineer in 1956. During his early years with the company he worked on the DB2 range of cars and abortive designs for new Lagondas. He was responsible for the chassis platforms for the DB4/5, Lagonda Rapide, DB6, DBS, AMV8-based Lagonda and V8 Volante. He retired at the beginning of 1978 after production of the V8 Volante was secured.

Model	Weight (lb)	0-60 mph (seconds)	Top speed (mph)	Power (bhp)
V8 Volante (1978-1986)	3950	7.7	140	305
V8 Volante (1986-1989)	4009	6.7	145	305

Like the AMV8, the Volante overlapped Virage manufacture by several months. When the new coupe model was in full production the Volante was phased out to allow the Newport Pagnell factory to dedicate itself fully to the Virage. The fuel-injected V8 Volante was finally withdrawn late in 1989 after 216 examples had been constructed. A convertible Aston Martin would not be available for another three years.

Above: Like the coupe, the fuel-injected V8 Volante included an almost flat bonnet **Opposite top:** Connolly leather, Wilton carpet and walnut cappings were standard V8 Volante specification **Opposite bottom:** Fitted luggage by Tanner Krolle was optionally available to capitalise on the car's small boot

The changes to the new Volante pre-empted those
of the upcoming Oscar India V8 Saloon, which was
launched in October of the same year.

Model	Production dates	Number built	Distinguishing features
V8 Volante (Weber carburettor)	Jun 1978 - Jan 1986	439	Oscar India-style AMV8 convertible body, walnut inserts and piped leather interior, GKN 15-inch alloy wheels, (BBS 15-inch wheels from 1983), four Weber carburettors
V8 Volante (Weber-Marelli fuel injection)	Jan 1986 - Oct 1989	216	Weber fuel injection-style AMV8 convertible body, walnut inserts and piped leather interior, BBS 15-inch alloy wheels, Weber-Marelli fuel injection

V8 Volante
1986–1989

Chassis: Steel box-section chassis, steel superstructure

Body: Aluminium 2+2 convertible styled by William Towns

Suspension: Front – Independent with unequal length double
   wishbones, coil springs and anti-roll bar
   Rear – de Dion axle with coil springs and Watt's linkage

Brakes: Servo-assisted Girling 273 mm ventilated discs (front);
   263 mm inboard-mounted discs (rear)

Steering: Power-assisted rack and pinion

Wheels: 15-inch BBS alloy

Tyres: Avon Turbospeed 235/70 VR15

Transmission: Torqueflite three-speed automatic; final drive
   3.058:1. ZF five-speed manual; final drive 3.33:1. Limited-
   slip differential. Rear-wheel drive

Engine: 5340 cc alloy V8 with twin chain-driven overhead
   camshafts per bank and two valves per cylinder. Compression
   ratio 9.25:1. Weber-Marelli fuel injection. Fully catalysed
   exhaust system

Power: 305 bhp/227 kW @ 6000 rpm
   320 lb/ft/434 Nm of torque @ 3000 rpm

Top speed: 145 mph/233 km/h (approx)

Dimensions:
Length	15 ft 4 in/4674 mm
Width	6 ft /1829 mm
Height	4 ft 6 in/1371 mm
Wheelbase	8 ft 6.75 in /2610 mm
Weight	4009 lb/1818 kg

Price when new: £68,500

Number built: 216

V 8 V a n t a g e Z a g a t o

Two great names reunited

The Aston Martin–Zagato association is legendary. Their collaboration on the DB4 GT during the early 1960s was a high point for the two companies. The DB4 GT was the only DB Aston Martin fitted with Zagato coachwork and since the mid-1970s the press had speculated as to whether a Zagato-bodied Aston Martin V8 would ever be constructed.

For various reasons, past administrations did not or could not build a Zagato-bodied V8 car. Chairman Victor Gauntlett, however, was a well-known enthusiast of Zagato Aston Martins, being the owner of one of the original 19 DB4 GT Zagatos, and was keen to revive this glorious past association.

When, by happy coincidence, the Aston Martin show stand was placed near that of Carrozzeria Zagato at the Geneva Motor Show in March 1984, an idea occurred to the AML Chairman. The thought was further promoted by co-owner Peter Livanos' visit to the Ferrari stand at the same show, where potential customers were clamouring to be first in line for one of its 200 limited-edition, £75,000 cars.

'It was the unveiling of the Ferrari 288 GTO at the Geneva Motor Show; the first of those low-volume supercars produced by sports manufacturers,' recalled Peter Livanos. 'Everyone wanted a GTO, myself included, but you just couldn't get one; they were like hen's teeth.'

'Victor Gauntlett used to tell people that Zagato modelled the bulge on his belly.'

Richard Williams

At the same show Porsche also displayed one of its own limited-edition 959 models, which sold for £110,000. If other manufacturers could produce limited-edition runs of a particular model, and customers were prepared to pay incredible prices for them, why not Aston Martin?

The motoring world was in the middle of the classic car boom in 1984 and customers were prepared to pay almost anything for a quality car with a pedigree. 'With all this furore about low-volume sports car production, Guido Cantele, the CFO of

Carrozzeria Zagato's styling of the short-chassis V8 Vantage polarised opinion

Zagato at that time, met with Victor Gauntlett and me and handed us the Zagato brochure and said, "Why don't you let us make you a prototype?" Victor and I thought it was a great idea and that was the initial introduction to the subsequent meeting with the Zagato brothers, where we decided to make the first Zagato V8,' recalled Livanos.

Wanting to take advantage of the situation, Gauntlett, Livanos and Elio and Gianni Zagato met to discuss the possibility of rekindling the famous association. The idea gathered momentum and by the end of the show the plan was already becoming a reality.

Carrozzeria Zagato

Founder of Carrozzeria Zagato, Ugo Zagato, was born on 25 June 1890. As a teenager, he worked in Germany before moving to Carrozzeria Varesina in Milan, then the Costruzioni Aeronautiche Pomilio aeroplane factory in Milan, making biplanes.

This experience, and the recognition of how aeronautical construction techniques could be used in motor car manufacture, led him to establish Carrozzeria Ugo Zagato and C. in 1919. Zagato's early designs became known for their lightweight, stylish, wind-cheating bodies.

Zagato's early efforts included bodies for the Fiat 501 and Alfa Romeo 1500 cc and 1750 cc sports cars and his cars became famous in the 1930s for their success in the gruelling Mille Miglia. Ugo's commissions came not only from major manufacturers, but also from private buyers wanting a competitive edge.

During WWII Zagato constructed commercial vehicles but the factory was destroyed in bombing raids. Work continued and in 1947 the famous 'panoramica' was introduced on the Fiat 1100, using Plexiglas for low weight and elegant curves. Zagato also prepared Fangio's Formula One World Championship-winning Alfa 159, but it was in GT racing that the carrozzeria earned its fame, with Ugo's son Elio winning many Italian titles. Some of the company's outstanding designs during that period included the Fiat 8V, Alfa Romeo 1900 SS2 and the Abath Zagato.

Ugo died in 1968 and sons Elio and Gianni succeeded him as joint heads of the company. Several factory moves were made and over the years Zagato constructed bodies for marques including Fiat, Lancia, Rolls-Royce, Bugatti, Isotta-Fraschini, MG, Ferrari, Maserati, Alfa Romeo, Lamborghini and Toyota.

In July 1986, shortly after the launch of the V8 Vantage Zagato, Victor Gauntlett learnt that Zagato was very close to receivership. To ensure the project was completed Aston Martin Lagonda Ltd. purchased a 50 percent share in the financially fragile carrozzeria.

The Ford acquisition of AML in 1987 did not include Zagato, so around the time the last V8 Zagato Volante was built, Aston Martin Lagonda Ltd. disposed of its share in Carrozzeria Zagato to a Japanese company.

The factory in Terrazzano di Rho, to which Zagato moved in 1962, was later closed but the Zagato styling business continued under Ugo's grandson, Dr Andrea Zagato. Zagato and Aston Martin reunited with the release of the DB7 Zagato in 2002.

In April 1984, Peter Livanos and Director of Engineering, Michael Bowler, visited Carrozzeria Zagato in Milan to discuss the brief, confirm performance targets and assess associated engineering factors. A stripped and lightened V8 Vantage 'mule' (VNK 360S), V8/11967/RCAV, an ex-demonstrator factory car, had already been timed at 175 mph with a 437 bhp version of the Vantage engine, but this was obviously not enough. AML and Zagato wanted to produce a supercar capable of taking on the fastest cars in the world. A top speed of 186 mph and a 0–60 mph sprint in less than five seconds was thought to be sufficient.

At the time it was felt that the V8 engine had reached its developmental limit. Therefore a lighter body with low drag coefficient and lower frontal area was needed. This was where Zagato came in.

In July 1984, Gianni Zagato and Chief Stylist Giuseppe Mittino visited Newport Pagnell to present a styling sketch and to study the V8 chassis. While Zagato and the Aston Martin Board discussed projected costs and related matters, Mittino collected drawings and ideas regarding what existing componentry could be used. 'Mittino was Chief Stylist, but the Zagato brothers also had a hand in the design, too,' recalled Bowler.

It was decided that a production run of 50 cars would provide the right balance between exclusivity and design and tooling costs, and would ensure advance orders. At the beginning of 1985 Aston Martin agreed in principle to proceed with the project and on 1 March 1985, exactly one year after conceiving the idea, a design sketch of the V8 Vantage Zagato prototype was unveiled.

Simply co-joining these two famous names was enough to sell the car sight unseen. There was no full-sized mock-up, scale model or even photographs – the only image prospective customers had was a styling sketch. All 50 cars were sold by August of the same year.

During the car's development several potential clients were taken to the Zagato factory to see the prototype taking shape. Deposits of £15,000 were needed from prospective customers in order to secure a car, but the initial price, quoted as £87,000, quickly rose to £95,000.

Aston Martin still used manual drawing techniques at that time and, while Zagato was capable of using computer aided design (CAD), it was quicker for them to continue using the same design techniques as AML. The complete body design was drawn up in full size with all contour lines and section shapes. The necessary supporting structure was then constructed and its attachment to the main platform was designed. Concurrently, a full-size body buck was fashioned in wood.

The construction of the cars was complicated – the chassis were constructed at Newport Pagnell, then shipped to Milan where the bodies were built and interiors fitted. The wooden buck was sized to allow the aluminium panels to be laid on top and beaten into final shape by Zagato's skilled panel beaters. Moulds for the glass areas and composite reinforced polyester front and rear panels were then taken directly from the body buck. The preparation took a great deal of time; the master body buck was completed in Zagato's workshops by September 1985.

'Arguably there should have been a completely hand-built prototype but the time scale and the near-production work that is still involved in a one-off made it both impossible and uneconomical for this particular exercise' said Bowler at the time. 'However, to go from sketches to complete pilot production cars in 12 months is very rapid progress, which can only be achieved when two companies can work together as well as Aston Martin and Zagato have done.'[5]

Giuseppe Mittino's design was dictated largely by function. Aluminium and other weight-saving materials were used to achieve lightness. Both the nose and rear sections were constructed from glass/aramid-hybrid composite, stiffened with metal-reinforced polyurethane foam, and then bolted to shock-absorbing bumpers.

Flush-fitting glass with an all-encompassing, 'girdle' design was used for aerodynamic efficiency. Crafted by Saint Gobain in France the glass was complex and expensive to design and make. The driver and passenger windows were fixed, containing small, drop-section glass. Vision was excellent, being almost totally unimpeded. The rest of the body was constructed from hand-formed aluminium panels beaten into shape on bucks and fitted to the frame attached to the shortened Vantage chassis.

While Carrozzeria Zagato planned to trim the Vantage's weight by 10 percent and projected a drag factor of 0.29, Aston Martin had its own challenges. One of the dilemmas was balancing the difficult task of making detail changes without upsetting Type Certification laws.

Nevertheless, the platform and running gear required many modifications if the car was to achieve its ambitious targets. The V8 Vantage was 15 ft, 4 in long and 6 ft, 2 in wide; the V8 Vantage Zagato was shortened to 14 ft, 4.75 in and narrowed to 6 ft, 1.75 in, but retained the Vantage's wheelbase. The suspension was also revised in deference to the car's lighter weight. Re-certification laws prevented any further changes to the chassis.

The Mittino design was stout and aggressive with the lack of rear overhang giving the car powerful rear haunches, enhanced by the aerodynamically necessary inbuilt spoiler. 'The wind tunnel testing was undertaken by Ray Mallock,' recalled Richard Williams. 'The little tail spoiler was his idea.' The rear treatment created 120 lb of downforce at 150 mph.

In the interests of aerodynamic performance the bonnet was lowered as far as possible and the underside contained an aerodynamic venturi. The calculated coefficient of 0.29 was never attained but a still-respectable 0.32 was achieved in the wind tunnel at Southampton University.

Top to bottom: Giuseppe Mittino's adaptation of the famous grille was similar to an elongated version used by Frank Feeley on the DB2; Aston Martin's lifelike V8 Vantage Zagato model; Weight was saved by paring down the interior but it was still nicely trimmed in leather

Left to right: Badges contained both the Aston Martin wings and Zagato's 'double Z'; A V8 Zagato outside Aston Martin's old Newport Pagnell headquarters; Features included Zagato-designed wheels, flush-fitting glass and an unsightly bonnet bulge; Zagato's first collaboration with Aston Martin produced the DB4GT Zagato – it proved to be a hard act to follow

The car featured both Zagato and Aston Martin design signatures. The roof contained a hint of the famous 'double-bubble', a long-established Zagato trademark, allowing for a low aerodynamic shape while providing adequate headroom for both occupants.

A salute to Aston Martin was the stylised grille. The angular shape, however, lacked the flare of the Touring design, looking more like an elongated version of the 'bowler hat' grille of Frank Feeley's DB2. Other special Zagato touches included unique circular badges on the nose and boot, 'Zagato Milano' badging behind the front wheel arches and 'Z'-embossed flush-fitting door handles.

'For the badge design with the Aston Martin and Zagato symbols on it, I went to Outline Creative and worked with Howard Potter,' said Director, Customer Relations Kingsley Riding-Felce. 'We worked together on a number of briefs to show Victor Gauntlett.'

The twin-seat interior, trimmed in alcantara and leather was functional, if not luxurious, although air conditioning and a stereo were standard equipment. It was quite a departure from the usual Aston Martin fare, being more in line with exotic Italian sports cars. The interior was designed and fitted-out in-house by Zagato with a view to weight saving. The seats were the same as used in the Zagato-designed Lancia Delta S4. The dashboard, with Smith's dials, hinted at the Aston Martin grille.

Aston Martin had recently introduced the Weber-Marelli fuel injection system on its AMV8s and at one stage consideration was given to its use in the V8 Zagato. However, it was finally decided to continue with Weber carburettors, thus creating a problem with the styling. A hump on the bonnet was needed to clear the four carburettors and, unlike the earlier AMV8's power bulge, the Zagato prototype's hump drew harsh criticism.

'The hump on the prototype was fabricated by the Engineering Department,' recalled Bowler. 'This was the car that most press people drove. Production cars had a nicely designed Zagato hump, which was never unsightly.'

'I was developing an engine upgrade for the then-current Vantage model, which would eventually become known as the 580X,' recalled Arthur Wilson. 'Certifying to the emissions standards of the time using carburettors was becoming increasingly difficult, so initially a version of this engine specification was released to our Service Department to offer to customers with a Vantage.

'Eventually we succeeded in gaining full certification for the 580X engine using 48 IDF carburettors; it was never certified using 50 IDFs so they were only available as an aftermarket fitment. The fully emissions and drive-by noise test compliant production engine produced 410 bhp @ 6000 rpm and 395 lb/ft @ 5000 rpm. This could be increased to 437 bhp @ 6250 rpm and 400 lb/ft @ 5000 rpm by fitting the 50 IDF carburettors and a sports exhaust system from the manifolds back.'

The engine chosen for the V8 Vantage Zagato was the 410 bhp 580X version. 'When we certified it, we certified it for the Zagato. But it was the same engine as the 580X Vantage off the line, which wasn't publicised very much. This was a shame, as I don't think there was ever a magazine road test on a 580X Vantage. Most of the books that mention the Vantage quote the earlier car's performance figures. Bearing in mind the hefty power increase in the 580X, it would have made interesting reading.'

The production 580X engine utilised four 48 IDF Weber carburettors, higher-lift camshafts, larger porting to the cylinder heads and a 10.2:1 compression ratio. Only a few cars were converted to 50 IDF carburettors; because they were hand-drilled, costly and time consuming to make, they were eventually discontinued.

To help achieve the car's high-speed performance targets, the prototype's final drive was changed from 3.31:1 to 3.06:1. All other production Zagatos were supplied with the 3.31:1 final drive as used on the V8 Vantage, although owners could retrofit the 3.06:1 to match the sprinting capacity of the prototype. Unique Zagato-designed Speedline 16-inch wheels,

which aided ventilation of the large Girling disc brakes, were used in place of the standard Vantage wheels.

The V8 Vantage Zagato was launched at the Geneva Motor Show in March 1986. A single car graced the Aston Martin stand; another posed on Zagato's stand and a third was perched atop the Beau Rivage Hotel overlooking Lake Geneva. All three were painted in the same evocative racing red to emphasise the car's sporting heritage. It was all calculated to create maximum exposure, and it worked. The first production Vantage Zagato, was delivered on 14 July 1986.

Aston Martin prepared a special car, 370 lb lighter than standard, to publicly demonstrate the model's projected maximum speed of 186 mph. So confident was Aston Martin that Le Mans was chosen as a public proving ground. Ex-works driver, Roy Salvadori was engaged to drive the car on the famous Mulsanne Straight at a pre-race demonstration event in June 1986. Embarrassingly, fuel starvation problems – caused by a blocked roll-over breather valve in the fuel tank, and only discovered back at Newport Pagnell – robbed the car of its ultimate performance. 'I didn't record the actual speed, it was too embarrassing,' remembered Bowler. 'It spluttered down the straight at around 150 mph.'

Aston Martin was redeemed, however, when on 8 July Jose Rosinski of French motoring magazine, *Sport-Auto*, officially timed the factory prototype at 185.52 mph, only marginally short of the projected target. The 0–60 mph sprint was achieved in 4.7 seconds 'on the high axle, which just allowed 60 mph in first at 6800 rpm,' said Bowler.

The model proved to have fine handling and enormous capability. But, although it provided close to the ultimate in outright performance, the reaction to the body design was mixed. That it had its followers, however, is certain: Victor Gauntlett and Peter Livanos each bought one.

V8 Vantage Zagato
1986–1988

Chassis: Steel box-section chassis, steel superstructure

Body: Aluminium 2+2 coupe styled by Giuseppe Mittino of Carrozzeria Zagato

Suspension: Front – Independent with unequal length double wishbones, coil springs and anti-roll bar
Rear – de Dion axle with coil springs and Watt's linkage

Brakes: Servo-assisted Girling 273 mm ventilated discs (front); 263 mm inboard-mounted discs (rear)

Steering: Power-assisted rack and pinion

Wheels: 16-inch Speedline alloy

Tyres: Goodyear Eagle 255/50 ZR16

Transmission: ZF five-speed manual; final drive 3.31:1.[i] Limited-slip differential. Rear-wheel drive

Engine: 5340 cc alloy V8 with twin chain-driven overhead camshafts per bank and two valves per cylinder. Compression ratio 10.2:1. Twin SU fuel pumps and four Weber 48 IDF/3 carburettors[ii]

Power: 410 bhp/306 kW @ 6000 rpm
395 lb/ft/536 Nm of torque @ 5000 rpm
437 bhp/326 kW @ 6250 rpm
400 lb/ft/542 Nm of torque @ 5000 rpm
(optional engine with 50 IDF carburettors)

Top speed: 186 mph/299 km/h

Dimensions:
Length	14 ft 4.75 in/4388 mm
Width	6 ft 1.25 in/1860 mm
Height	4 ft 3 in/1295 mm
Wheelbase	8 ft 6.75 in/2610 mm
Weight	3637 lb/1650 kg

Price when new: £95,000

Number built: 52

---

i   A 3.06:1 differential could be fitted to match the prototype, but only as an aftermarket option

ii Some of the first cars were produced with 50 mm Weber carburettors

V8 Vantage

Up the ante

The Vantage name has been used to denote higher performance engine options available on Aston Martin road cars since 1951, beginning with the DB2. When the DBS V8 was launched in 1969 it was thought it would only be a matter of time before Aston Martin's engineers developed a Vantage version.

A prototype DBS V8 Vantage, (222 HOH) DBS/5002/R, fitted with a 5.0-litre engine with race-derived camshafts, 48 IDA 'race' carburettors and producing 384 bhp was first tested in 1969. With Chief Engineer Mike Loasby at the wheel, the car achieved 172 mph. However, due to changes of ownership and the difficult financial climate at the time, the V8 Vantage did not materialise for several years.

'When we got the company going again after being in receivership in 1974 and 1975 we needed to get it making some money quickly,' recalled Mike Loasby. 'At the start we had so little money we emptied the old 'experimental' stores and sold lots of bits, which were of no use at all. We did lots of detail changes to the standard (V8) car, then we thought, 'Well we could probably make a bit more money if we made a Vantage version,' which we did.

'The idea was to turn the wick up a bit and, dare I say it, put some inexpensive aerodynamic aids on it and sell it for a lot more money so we could get the company into profit.'

Mike Loasby

'We up-rated and modernised the suspension as far as we could on the standard production car, which was producing about 320 horsepower then. Then we did a Vantage version of it. We also introduced a new [larger diameter] exhaust system [with both banks converging within the centre cruciform], which was partly responsible for the 25 bhp power improvement, but was also a much nicer noise. It gave you something between a V8 and a V12, a much happier noise that we continued with all the way till the end of production.

The V8 Vantage was Britain's answer to the supercar war being fought out mainly among Italian and German manufacturers

David Morgan

David Morgan joined Aston Martin in 1963 as a technician in the experimental department. 'Initially I was based at Newport Pagnell but I drove to Feltham every day,' said Morgan. 'It wasn't long before they found us space and we set up a workshop at Newport. The Feltham operation closed down and the expensive land sold for housing. Very few people transferred; George Evans being the only Development Engineer.

'I specialised in the engine work, after working with George on the C-Type Vantage six-cylinder; mainly cylinder head gas flowing, then assisting with the dynamometer development and finally the carburettor calibration on the road.'

Morgan became a specialist on Weber carburettors, conducting all the development work on the various Weber carburettor V8s. He was also closely involved in the fuel injection development on the DB6, DBS and DBS V8, working in cooperation with AE Engineering and later Bosch.

Morgan was heavily involved with the V8 engine development for the Lola-Aston sports racing car, attending races and participating in the strip and analysis of the engines post-Le Mans. He was later promoted to Development Engineer and was involved in gaining the US Federal Emissions certification for the carburettor V8.

Morgan worked for Weber as Resident Engineer in Vauxhall during the factory closure in 1974, rejoining Aston Martin in January 1975 as Chief Development Engineer at the request of Mike Loasby. He participated in the development of the Lagonda, working on both the engine and handling of the car. 'There were a lot of headaches with the Lagonda,' he said, 'but its novel shape and advanced electronics did create a lot of interest.'

Morgan was also heavily involved with the development of the V8 Vantage, contributing to the engine, handling and aerodynamics. He transferred to Aston Martin Tickford in the early 1980s as Chief Development Engineer, becoming a director in 1985 and a shareholder in 1986.

'Tickford began following a 10 percent redundancy of engineering staff at AML and we were about to have a much higher round,' remembered Morgan. 'After the resurrection of AML we had built up a really good engineering department, so rather than break it up, it was decided to keep it together and sell their services to the motor industry.'

It was at Aston Martin Tickford that Morgan was involved in the development of the V8 racing engines used by EMKA, Cheetah and Nimrod sports cars. Later he developed the 6.3-litre V8 engine conversion for Works Service. As well as his work for Aston Martin, Morgan was director of a large engine engineering team that successfully completed many major Tickford projects for Ford engineers in the UK, USA, Germany, India, Brazil and Australia and General Motors engineers in USA, Germany and Belgium.

Morgan retired from the automotive industry in July 2002.

'The idea was to turn the wick up a bit and, dare I say it, put some inexpensive aerodynamic aids on it and sell it for a lot more money so we could get the company into profit. It was a little matter between two or three of us and we decided that it would be a great idea to do a Vantage; it wasn't handed on as a company project. We discussed it amongst ourselves and we thought we could do it without too much trouble. It was good fun. It wasn't like running a company; you did what you really wanted to do. We made the kind of cars that suited us because we were enthusiastic motorists and, luckily, lots of other people wanted the same things too. We had the Vantage up and running within a year.'

Loasby initially engineered a Vantage option for existing V8 models, to be offered by the Service Department as an after-market conversion. But as development proceeded, a stand-alone model became a reality. A pre-production 'Vantage' version of the AMV8 Saloon, (OKX 136P), V8/11429/LCA, was first demonstrated in June 1976 at an Aston Martin Owners' Club race meeting when the standard AMV8 was using Weber carburettors.

'The car that I raced at the [AMOC] St John Horsfall meeting really was a standard production car. Everybody called it the Vantage, but it wasn't,' said Loasby. 'It didn't have Vantage performance; it didn't have the Vantage aerodynamics. It might have had a few more horsepower than the standard production car; it may have been the forerunner of it, but it wasn't the Vantage. I am pretty categorical about that.'

The 'real' Vantage was first announced on 18 February 1977. Starting with chassis number 11640, and built especially for Director George Minden, the Vantage sold for a £4000 premium over the AMV8. The new car was both mechanically revised and had a stylistic identity all its own.

'We blanked the front end of the bonnet off on the Vantage, we flared the headlights in and blanked the radiator grille, all of which improved the drag and lift dramatically. We needed four headlights to my mind because that was the only way you could see where you were going when you were going that fast,' said Loasby.

There has been some conjecture as to the origins of the Vantage body accoutrements. Ex-Aston Martin dealer and racing driver Robin Hamilton claims his DBS V8-based Le Mans racing car was the inspiration; Loasby disagrees. 'Robin Hamilton came to the company and wanted company support for his racing, but we couldn't do it because, for a start, we didn't have any money. But we said we would give him what help we could in terms of engine development information although we didn't do any work as far as I can remember, apart from running his engine on our test-bed, perhaps. I don't know if he took any hints from us from the point of view of aerodynamics. We certainly didn't take any from him.

'The things we did by way of aerodynamics on the Vantage were the current fashion. We put a spoiler on the front because that car had terrible front-end lift, a big, deep spoiler which we knocked up in aluminium and the tail flip-up we put on because that was actually reminiscent of the Lola-Aston Martin T70 we did in 1967.'

'Mike Loasby was responsible for the Vantage development,' recalled David Morgan. 'He agreed to finance a session in MIRA's wind tunnel with Robin Hamilton. To make it look a bit worthwhile he asked if I would prepare a revised version of the V8 to test at the same session. I agreed and got a panel beater to fabricate new spoilers as per our ideas, including blanking plates for the grille and headlight covers.

'During the session Robin tried lots of ideas to improve drag and reduce lift – not downforce in those days. We had the last hour and started by testing the standard car, then fitted all the spoilers and retested the car. It was amazing; drag went down by over 10 percent and all the lift was lost.

'The result was exactly what Robin had been trying to get. [Emissions Engineer] David Orchard was driving the V8 and had driven up in standard spec and back with all the new spoilers. He was very excited by the difference in handling and the extra 10 mph top speed.'

Top to bottom: The first V8 'Vantage' driven by Mike Loasby at the AMOC St John Horsfall race meeting; Robin Hamilton's DBS V8-based RHAM Le Mans race car in 1979 guise shows some of the aerodynamic aids also incorporated on the production Vantage; A first series V8 Vantage showing the add-on bonnet bulge enclosure and rear spoiler

Jaguar purchase

During 1989 Ford executives approached Jaguar with an offer to purchase the famed British company, heading off General Motors which also considered buying into the concern. On 1 December 1989 the Jaguar Board approved Ford's £1.6 billion offer and during 1990 the final arrangements for the sale were completed.

'To start with, the [body enhancements] were simply bolted on, then they very rapidly became a production thing,' added Loasby. '[Hamilton's] car and ours both bore a resemblance to the fashion of the time. His front end was much lower than ours and it had a large splitter that ours didn't because ours was a road car.' Although the alterations were a little gauche, the new aerodynamic aids were effective. 'Front-end lift, which had been dramatic at some 400 lb at 140 mph, was reduced to practically nothing.'

Changes to the Vantage's Stage 2 engine included bigger inlet valves, revised camshafts and larger diameter exhaust system and new 48 IDF Weber carburettors. The alterations produced 375 bhp @ 6000 rpm and 380 lb/ft of torque @ 4000 rpm, which propelled the car from 0–60 mph in 5.4 seconds with a top speed approaching 170 mph. It was the fastest accelerating car in the world at the time. In addition, the suspension was stiffened and Koni shock absorbers fitted. The AMV8 alloy wheels remained the same, but tyres were changed to Pirelli CN12 255/60 VR15.

'The ever-important ingredient in the original Vantage specification was the Pirelli CN12 tyres; again Mike was responsible,' said Morgan. 'We had met the Pirelli engineers during tyre testing a few years before and they suggested trying the CN12s. These were developed for Maserati, which was also front-engined, and didn't need to suppress oversteer like Porsches. But the CN12s were really race-spec rather than road tyres. They were superb and really put the final touch to the Vantage.'

At this stage an automatic transmission was not officially available but a small number were made. 'Our original plan was not to do any automatic Vantages because we had not done

any serious testing with the automatic gearbox,' said Loasby. 'We were not sure it would take the power, but we made some and they worked alright.'

With the introduction of the Oscar India V8 in 1978, the V8 Vantage adopted similar styling changes, including the integral rear spoiler and closed bonnet bulge. When BBS 15-inch wheels were adopted on the V8 Saloon, the Vantage followed suit. Inside the cabin, the leather dashboard and headlining and optional walnut trim gave the car a more luxurious air. Power was also boosted to 390 bhp.

'What we decided to do from a styling point of view was establish the rear spoiler into the general styling to make it look really stylish, instead of adding on bits and pieces. It looked quite nice, I thought. That's when we decided to change the bonnet line: instead of putting the scoop at the front we put it at the back,' said Loasby.

The last variant of the V8 Vantage was unveiled at the Birmingham Motor Show in October 1986 and sold for £5000 more than the AMV8. Styling remained much the same as the previous Vantage, including the power bulge on the bonnet – demanded by the use of carburettors – while the standard AMV8 changed to fuel injection.

The V8 Vantage now produced 410 bhp @ 6000 rpm and 395 lb/ft of torque @ 5000 rpm with the four 48 IDF/3 Weber carburettor engine. The improvements to the engine output were achieved through higher-lift camshafts, modified porting

Vantage engines remained at 5.3 litres but power increased to as much as 437 bhp by the end of production in December 1989

to the cylinder heads and a higher compression ratio, which was changed to 10.2:1. There was also a more powerful option with four 50 IDF Weber carburettors delivering 437 bhp @ 6250 rpm and 400 lb/ft of torque @ 5000 rpm.

'The 580X was very much a mix of the Nimrod (Le Mans racing car) and a project we had done for a South African customer (DP2000),' remembered Arthur Wilson. 'He had an altitude problem with his Vantage and was tired of being passed by turbo Porsches so he wanted an upgrade. So we did a South African-spec Vantage. We could have called the 580X the South African-spec Vantage, except that South Africa was politically out of favour at that time. So we thought of another name and called it the 580X.

'The X-Pack name was something that our Service Department came up with to describe a conversion package that we had engineered for them while developing the production 580X. So X-Pack should only really apply to converted cars. I didn't like it at the time because Ford had an X-Pack for its Ford Capri and Cortinas and it didn't sound appropriate for Aston Martin. But 580X was just a way of coming up with a name and avoiding 'South African-Spec'. It was pretty much a Nimrod cylinder head, to be honest, with different cams. Although quite a lot of what went into the South African-Spec was in there as well.

'We provided an option of modified 48 IDF carburettors bored out to 50 mm for the 580X. But it was very much a special job. The carburettors had to be bored by Weber concessionaires at Sunbury-on-Thames; it was a tricky operation. Whether you wrecked the carburettor or not depended on how good the casting was. Gradually the later carburettors became more susceptible to failure, so it came to an end. When they had been bored out and returned to AML, I would rebuild them on the bench by hand. They did give out a bit more power. There weren't that many of them made; we did 35 with standard 48 mm carburettors. We did an automatic and a manual version of the 580X Vantage.'

Model	Weight (lb)	0-60 mph (seconds)	Top speed (mph)	Power (bhp)
V8 Vantage (1977-1978)	3886	5.4	168	375
V8 Vantage (1978-1986)	3969	5.2	168	390
V8 Vantage (1986-1989) (437 bhp optional)	4009	5.2	175[i]	410

Apart from the engine up-rating and other minor changes, the last V8 Vantages were little changed from the preceding model; differential ratios, suspension, steering and exterior dimensions remained much the same. ZF five-speed manual gearboxes were standard equipment but, for the first time, Chrysler's Torqueflite automatic transmission became an official option.

i   Using optional 437 bhp engine

While early Vantages had optional walnut cappings, later cars were as luxurious as the standard saloons and Volantes

Mike Loasby

Mike Loasby started his automotive career as an apprentice at Alvis Cars. 'I was a draughtsman then, designing anything that came up on the cars except the bodies, which were made by Park Ward,' he said. When Alvis was taken over by Rover in 1965 he moved to Coventry Climax as Senior Designer, Engines.

'That didn't last very long because they had more or less stopped racing. I got bored, [then] a friend of mine sent me an advertisement out of the *Coventry Evening Telegraph* that said Aston Martin was looking for a Development Engineer and I got that job. I had finished racing at that point, having raced both Lotus Climax and Brabham Cosworth F3 racing cars. So I went to work at Aston Martin in 1967 as a Development Engineer, the only one, working for Tadek Marek.

'When Tadek retired I became head of our little experimental department, working alongside Harold Beach who was in charge of the design department. Towards the end of 1969, I was invited to join Triumph Motor Company in Coventry as Executive Engineer on engine design. I stayed there for quite a few years and left them at the end of 1974, having been invited to become Chief Engineer at Aston Martin, which was a dream job, a fantastic opportunity. I went back to the company to work, effectively, for Fred Hartley. There were only a small number of us there to keep the company open. But we got the company going and then people like Alan Curtis came along, and the company changed.

'[From] 1976 I was Chief Engineer until the 'night of the long knives' in 1977. Fred Hartley was pushed out and David Flint and I were elevated to directors. Fred was promoted sideways, and so was I in due course; I was effectively pushed out. I was made Managing Director of Aston Martin Engineering Limited, but we never did anything.

'I became Director of Engineering in 1977 but at the end of 1978 I was invited to join DeLorean Motor Company as Product Engineering Director in Northern Ireland. I worked there for about three years and when the company closed down, my wife and I decided that we didn't want to work for anybody else ever again and we set up our own company, Midland Design Partnership, covering many aspects of engineering design.

'I have at various times been engine, transmission, suspension, chassis and body designer. The one thing that I have never done, because I am not capable of it, is actually style a body. I can take a styling exercise and convert it into the real three-dimensional thing, but I can't draw pictures.'

Loasby was recalled by AML in 1989 to work as a consultant on the Virage, Vantage, Lagonda Saloons and Shooting Brakes and Special Series Vantages. During that time he ran the Engineering Department for nine months before Rod Mansfield arrived. He left Aston Martin for the last time in 1998.

Top: While the V8 Vantage had supercar performance, it could seat two rear passengers in reasonable comfort **Above:** The V8 Vantage looked menacing yet retained a certain elegance; the mesh grille on this particular car is original

Model	Production dates	Number built	Distinguishing features
V8 Vantage	Feb 1977 - Sept 1978	38[ii]	Carburettor AMV8 body with add-on rear spoiler, blanked-off bonnet scoop and front air dam, GKN 15-inch alloy wheels, 375 bhp engine
V8 Vantage	Oct 1978 - Sept 1986	181	Oscar India AMV8 body with integral rear spoiler, front air dam, optional walnut inserts and piped leather interior, GKN 15-inch alloy wheels, (BBS 15-inch alloy wheels from 1983), 390 bhp engine
V8 Vantage	Oct 1986 - Dec 1989	137	Oscar India AMV8 body, walnut inserts and piped leather interior, Ronal 16-inch alloy wheels, (Compomotive, OZ, MSW and Ronal alloy wheels also used), 410 bhp or optional 437 bhp engine

ii   Includes 13 'cosmetic' Vantages for the US market

V8 Vantage
1986–1989

Chassis: Steel box-section chassis, steel superstructure

Body: Aluminium 2+2 coupe styled by William Towns

Suspension: Front – Independent with unequal length double wishbones, coil springs and anti-roll bar
Rear – de Dion axle with coil springs and Watt's linkage

Brakes: Servo-assisted Girling 273 mm ventilated discs (front); 263 mm inboard-mounted discs (rear)

Steering: Power-assisted rack and pinion

Wheels: 16-inch Ronal alloy

Tyres: Goodyear Eagle 255/50 VR16

Transmission: ZF five-speed manual; final drive 3.33:1
Torqueflite three-speed automatic; final drive 3.058:1.
Limited-slip differential. Rear-wheel drive

Engine: 5340 cc alloy V8 with twin chain-driven overhead camshafts per bank and two valves per cylinder. Compression ratio 10.2:1. Twin SU fuel pumps and four Weber 48 IDF/3 or 50 IDF carburettors

Power: 410 bhp/306 kW @ 6000 rpm
395 lb/ft/536 Nm of torque @ 5000 rpm
437 bhp/326 kW @ 6250 rpm
400 lb/ft/542 Nm of torque @ 5000 rpm
(optional engine with 50 IDF carburettors)

Top speed: 175 mph/282 km/h

Dimensions:
Length	15 ft 4 in/4674 mm
Width	6 ft 2 in/1880 mm
Height	4 ft 4.25 in/1327 mm
Wheelbase	8 ft 6.75 in/2610 mm
Weight	4009 lb/1818 kg

Price when new: £59,500

Number built: 137

V 8 V a n t a g e V o l a n t e

Open air power

As soon as the V8 Volante was unveiled, customers requested a higher performance Vantage option. Initially the company would not comply due to fears that the roofless car would not cope with the engine's power. But behind the scenes, a handful of unofficial Vantage-specification Volantes were delivered quietly to some special customers.

It took Aston Martin eight years to officially comply with customers' requests for a higher performance Volante. But finally, at the Birmingham Motor Show on 8 October 1986, news of a V8 Vantage Volante was released. Production began at chassis number V8CHR15538.

While the high-performance engine pushed the car back towards the supercar league, the handsome lines of William Towns' original DBS shape were altered almost beyond recognition. The impetus for the car's aggressive styling came from a customer who visited Works Service to have his Volante personalised.

'Many owners had requested a slightly different body styling on their cars,' said Kingsley Riding-Felce, then Director of Works Service. 'One particular owner of a Volante wanted his car to have side sills. Mind you, this was back in the eighties and what might make you cringe today was very popular then. So we put side sills on the car to extend it out to make it look different. This was some of the inspiration for the Vantage Volante with the side skirts and wide wheel arches.'

> Behind the scenes a handful of unofficial Vantage-specification Volantes were delivered quietly to some special customers.

The new body incorporated the Vantage-style blanked-off radiator grille with twin Cibie driving lights and deep chin spoiler, while a prominent spoiler was fashioned at the rear. The 16-inch wheels and 255/50 VR16 Goodyear Eagle tyres required additional flaring of the wheel arches and accompanying glass fibre sill skirts were added.

'The flared wheel arches were done at William Towns' house in Oxfordshire,' said Riding-Felce. 'William clayed one side of the car according to Victor Gauntlett's wishes with the new wheels and tyres and this was approved.'

Inspiration for the Vantage Volante's styling came from a customer request at Aston Martin's Works Service

Top: William Towns was responsible for the Vantage Volante's restyle **Above:** The Vantage Volante's rear spoiler detracted from the original convertible's graceful lines

The V8 Vantage Volante adopted the suspension setup of the V8 Zagato, which consisted of up-rated front springs, new progressive rate dampers, altered geometry of the double wishbone front suspension and a lowering of the ride height.

In line with the last V8 Vantages, the car retained Weber carburettors. Power output was quoted at 410 bhp @ 6000 rpm and 395 ft/lb of torque @ 5000 rpm with the standard engine. The 437 bhp optional X-Pack engine was available at extra cost.

With a top speed of 164 mph and a 0–60 mph dash in just 5.3 seconds, the V8 Vantage Volante was hailed as the world's fastest four-seat convertible, and at £93,500, it came close to being the most expensive.

V8 Vantage Volante
1986–1989

Chassis: Steel box-section chassis, steel superstructure

Body: Aluminium 2+2 convertible styled by William Towns

Suspension: Front – Independent with unequal length double wishbones, coil springs and anti-roll bar
Rear – de Dion axle with coil springs and Watt's linkage

Brakes: Servo-assisted Girling 273 mm ventilated discs (front); 263 mm inboard-mounted discs (rear)

Steering: Power-assisted rack and pinion

Wheels: 16-inch Ronal alloy

Tyres: Goodyear Eagle 255/50 VR16

Transmission: ZF five-speed manual; final drive 3.33:1
Torqueflite three-speed automatic;[i] final drive 3.058:1.
Limited-slip differential. Rear-wheel drive

Engine: 5340 cc alloy V8 with twin chain-driven overhead camshafts per bank and two valves per cylinder. Compression ratio 10.2:1. Twin SU fuel pumps and four Weber 48 IDF/3 carburettors

Power: 410 bhp/306 kW @ 6000 rpm
395 lb/ft/536 Nm of torque @ 5000 rpm
437 bhp/326 kW @ 6250 rpm
400 lb/ft/542 Nm of torque @ 5000 rpm
(optional engine with 50 IDF carburettors)

Top speed: 164 mph/264 km/h

Dimensions:
Length	15 ft 4 in/4674 mm
Width	6 ft 2 in/1880 mm
Height	4 ft 6 in/1371 mm
Wheelbase	8 ft 6.75 in/2610 mm
Weight	4009 lb/1818 kg

Price when new: £93,500

Number built: 167[ii]

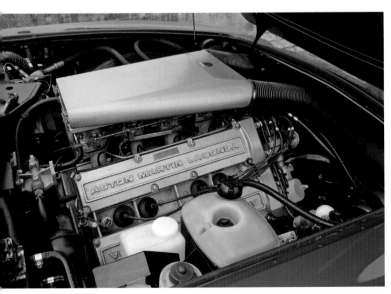

Top to bottom: The 16-inch wheels and Goodyear Eagle tyres required additional flaring of the wheel arches and sill skirts; Connolly leather, Wilton carpet and walnut cappings added to the car's considerable weight; Carried over from the V8 Vantage, the 5.3-litre V8 engine was available in 410 bhp and 437 bhp forms

i   Automatic transmission was officially unavailable but a small number were built.

ii Includes 58 fuel injected 'cosmetic' Vantage Volantes for the US market, and 27 PoW Specification Vantage Volantes.

Lagonda

Living on the wedge

Since David Brown merged Aston Martin and Lagonda in 1947, the once-famous Lagonda marque has been outshadowed by its younger stablemate. For several years the 2.6-litre and 3.0-litre Lagonda saloons were constructed alongside the DB2, but the Lagonda badge quietly disappeared early in 1958. The Lagonda name has since mainly been used for stretched four-door models, and has become a brand name of Aston Martin rather than a genuine marque in its own right.

Brown was a well-known devotee of Lagonda and was sincere in his efforts to revive the marque. He sent Lagonda back to Le Mans in 1954 and 1955 with the 4.5-litre V12 sports cars and put the DB4-based Lagonda Rapide into production in 1961. Later, he had a Lagonda-badged four-door V8 DBS specially constructed, but the car never entered production under his ownership. Brown had done his best to lift the profile and image of Lagonda, but in truth the marque stalled under his leadership and never recovered.

Following Company Developments' takeover of Aston Martin, its new £14,040 four-door V8 saloon was announced at the London Motor Show in October 1974. Named Aston Martin Lagonda V8, the car entered production the same year, but struggled to find a market. Only seven were built before being deleted in June 1976.[i]

When Victor Gauntlett arrived at AML he was told consideration was being given to closing down the manufacturing of Aston Martins altogether and production would concentrate solely on Lagondas.

When the new management of Aston Martin Lagonda (1975) Ltd. created its blueprint for the future, once again the Lagonda name was broached. It was originally intended that the V8 Lagonda of 1974 be reintroduced. 'After I returned to the company in 1975, we built a further [AMV8-based] Lagonda in 1976,' remembered Mike Loasby.

The directors were determined to breathe new life into Lagonda and to produce a unique line of cars with the hope of attracting a new customer base. In February 1976 plans were

i   Seven cars were made, but eight chassis were built. Chassis number eight has been made into a four-door Lagonda by Roger Bennington at Stratton Motor Company. It used a number of original parts and panels Aston Martin was holding in stock.

The last of the line Series 4 Lagonda had William Towns' original sharp edges rounded off

Top to bottom: Lagonda was acquired by David Brown, who was keen to develop the marque; The DB4-based Lagonda Rapide was another attempt by David Brown to breathe life into the Lagonda marque; David Brown commissioned this four-door V8-engined DBS for his personal transport, but it never entered production under his stewardship; Four-door AMV8-based Lagondas entered production when Company Developments took over Aston Martin, but only seven were built

put in place with the ambitious target of producing a totally new Lagonda in only eight months.

'Everybody on the board was equally keen, but George Minden was the artistic inspiration,' said Loasby. 'He was a very good chap to have around, as long as he didn't get too involved with the engineering side of things. George was the aesthete, I think you could say.'

Aston Martin was not in a position to create a new engine, so it was decided to power the new four-door car with the extant V8. William Towns was once again asked to design the car and his wedge-shaped vision created a sensation when first shown to the press at The Bell Inn at Aston Clinton in Buckinghamshire on 12 October 1976.

At the London Motor Show later that month an incomplete Lagonda was the star of the event. Around 200 orders were taken on what was then thought to be a £20,000 motor car. Buoyed by the unprecedented exposure, Aston Martin quoted bold production and delivery dates, which were to cause some concern in the months ahead.

Alan Curtis later said, 'The company promised delivery dates for the Lagonda at the 1976 Motor Show that we didn't have a cat in hell's chance of keeping. During 1977 we went through a crucial development phase with the car, and I must confess that at times I thought we made an appalling mess of the whole thing. We'd underestimated the time it would take to develop the car, which, after all, contained many innovations for the automotive world, and some of the costings were sheer guesswork. We made the necessary moves to bring the programme into some semblance of shape, but in my view, we only cleared the hurdle of development in March 1978.'[6]

Most journalists predicted the Lagonda would remain no more than a dramatic concept car. But they were wrong. After some delays the first car was delivered to its owner, Lady Tavistock, a new director of the company, in an embarrassing publicity stunt on 24 April 1978. With the press in waiting, the car was *pushed* to the gathered assembly because the electrical system had not yet been perfected.

Manufacturing Director, David Flint: 'We worked for two days and two nights solid trying to fit this harness from Cranfield Institute of Technology into the car. We had nearly finished when we were told we had better send the car out "right now". I'd had enough by this time and I said, "If you want to push this car out, you can do it yourself, I'm going home," so I went home.'

Only three cars were carefully hand-built during 1977. Full production didn't begin until later in 1978 and by late 1979 the original list price of £24,570 had more than doubled to £49,933. The Series 2[ii] Aston Martin Lagonda was something of an enigma; it was thoroughly futuristic in design and concept inside and out, yet it was traditionally coachbuilt and contained an engine and other components that could be traced back to the 1960s.

ii Unlike the AMV8s, the Factory actually used a series designation for the Lagonda

Mike Loasby had the task of designing the substantial platform chassis. Working with him were Production Engineering Manager, Laddie Bunker and Chief Draughtsman, Jess Line. 'We designed a new chassis because the chassis on the V8 was very expensive; we actually designed a two-door version first,' said Loasby. 'The original idea had been to put a new skin on the old chassis because we wanted to give it new life, but the old chassis was so expensive it really was not worth doing.

'We realised we would never be able to introduce it without altering the production line. We couldn't afford that and we couldn't afford our own new front suspension, so we decided that we would have to do a new car, building the Lagonda alongside the existing production line. All the chassis jigs at that time were for different wheelbases; Aston and Lagonda, the two-door and the four-door, so we could easily make the short chassis and the long chassis. We never made the short chassis.'

Loasby concluded that the rear seat and luggage load could be substantial, so self-levelling rear dampers were incorporated. 'We wanted self-levelling dampers to make the car level with all of the various load situations, with passengers and luggage.

'The only carry over bits from the AMV8 to "my" Lagonda were the differential, gearbox and the middle part of the engine; it wasn't the bottom end or top end of the engine. The heads were modified, the inlet manifolds were new, the sump was new and so on. They weren't carry-over parts. Not one little bit. The front suspension was Jaguar, in the main; it had a "Jaguar" front upright and top link. We did our own new bottom link and incorporated new geometry. The wheels were Jaguar, the steering was Adwest, which was not carried over and the chassis was totally new,' explained Loasby.

'We started on the car at the beginning of 1976. William [Towns] and I spent about two weeks working through every interface detail between the chassis superstructure and the body.'

The servo-assisted brake package contained 11.1-inch front discs and 10.4-inch inboard ventilated discs at the rear. The 15-inch disc wheels were shod in Avon 235/70 HR15 tyres. 'On the first cars we made our own wheel trims, which were terribly attractive,' continued Loasby. 'They were the ones William wanted and I don't think any subsequent ones really looked as nice. Such was the hurry we only had time to make two wheel trims, and for the first TV pictures they were only on one side of the car; if pictures of the other side were required we had to swap them around. The moving pictures were taken with the car rolling down a slope as the engine was not complete either.'

The V8 engine was mounted far back in the engine bay and due to the car's lower bonnet line a smaller air box was required. The engine was de-tuned to 280 horsepower so it could fit under the bonnet.

'The Lagonda had a lower air box to clear the very low bonnet line, which affected maximum power on the carburettor version,' said Arthur Wilson. 'The later fuel injection cars were more on par with the Astons. The Lagonda engine was the first V8 engine to have the 2.1-inch inlet valves in an attempt to alleviate the breathing problem associated with the low air box. After that they were used in the first Vantage engines and then became standard for all engines.'

'The Lagonda's shape meant further restriction on intake tracts and exhaust systems, plus the US was introducing automatic transmissions with lock-up torque converters,' said David Morgan. 'The initial engine in the Lagonda was hopeless when the torque converter locked up and [was] pretty poor at other times. So a revised power curve was required. We fitted the largest inlet valves possible and redesigned the cam profiles and effectively pulled the power curve down by 500 rpm. Typically the lock-up transmission was never released for production but it was a better engine.'

In line with the Lagonda's limousine-like status, the only transmission considered was the Chrysler Torqueflite three-speed automatic with a final drive ratio of 3.31:1. For such a large car it performed amazingly well; it could travel at up to 145 mph quietly and in complete comfort.

Best remembered for this design, William Towns made extensive use of the then-current trend in sharp, straight edges. The striking finished product provoked wildly fluctuating opinion.

William Towns later explained: 'Aston Martin is a rather strange company to work for. I get hired usually to do scale models in clay, but because making full-size clay bucks is such a costly procedure, they move straight on to drawings. A great deal therefore depends on the skill and accuracy of the draughtsman.

'They had a man called Bert Thickpenny, who was a draughtsman at Tickfords. He'd done the drawings for the Austin Healey 100, and he was the man who made the DBS into such a well-surfaced car. When it came to the original Lagonda, they had a different draughtsman, who was not in the same class, and none of the surfaces were translated very well from the scale model onto the drawings.'

But Mike Loasby contended: 'I can't say I remember any problems on the body surfaces because what we did was go from the scale model, which he produced, to a full-size wooden structure with him being involved at every stage. Maybe he wasn't too keen on some of the lines he had been specified, but, if he was, he certainly didn't say so at the time. We didn't have any problems with our draughtsmen.

'William liked low, wide cars [but] we had to rein him in a bit on the Lagonda. The design of the body was very different to everything else. It was classic William Towns. We altered very little of the design after William's first presentation. We altered the plan shape at the front by narrowing it a little, and we altered the grille because we thought it wasn't quite wide enough, but that's about all. It stayed very much as he wanted it, which is

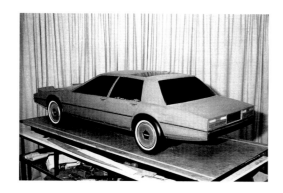

Top to bottom: William Towns' original scale model; Constructing the chassis platform; The wooden body buck; An early prototype nearing completion; Lagondas used a revised Aston Martin V8 engine

Mike Loasby (far right) and Alan Curtis (right) discuss progress of the Lagonda's futuristic interior

unusual. I think he was happy with the finished production model. He bought one; or his bank manager did.

'We carried on with the new car and were intending to introduce it at the Motor Show as planned. That went wrong because the publicity was such that we had to finish it before the show. We had television from everywhere in the world at Astons. It was unbelievable. We actually took something like seven-and-a-half months to build the car from scratch.'

While the Lagonda's body was striking, the space-age interior was even more so. Making use of state-of-the-art electronics, the interior featured a digital dashboard, the first ever produced. It caused consternation for both Aston Martin and Cranfield Institute and delayed production of the car for two years.

'We only made the first prototype, which didn't drive, in 1976 and it was put into production in 1978/79. That's pretty good,' contended Loasby. 'The electronics delayed production a bit. Most of the problems were sorted out after I left.'

The car was an electronic tour de force. Approximately 40 touch-sensitive buttons controlled almost every aspect of the car's performance, including the pop-up headlights, window lifts, air conditioning, cruise control, door locks and electrically adjustable seats. The digital LED display on the dashboard contained information on all of the car's systems, such as distance travelled, vehicle speed and fuel economy.

'One of the novel items on display and one of major interest was the seat position memory system,' recalled Loasby. 'I think we were the first to have three-position memory buttons fitted in the driver's door so that the seat position could be adjusted before the driver got in. This came about because my wife is about a foot shorter than me and if she jumped into "my" seat she couldn't reach anything and if I jumped into "hers" I took my knee cap off on the steering column on the way in.'

David Morgan wasn't impressed with some of the Lagonda's electrical shortcomings though. 'During the first test drive [the

William Towns' uncompromising styling created a sensation when the Lagonda was unveiled in 1976

seat] decided to move as close to the steering wheel as possible of its own accord,' he said. '[The car] would raise and lower a single headlight as it felt like it too!'

'For the show we had the first car built up to look as though it had the electronics in it, but it didn't. We had an electronic buck on the stand, which was just the passenger compartment of the car without a roof and it had all of the electronic displays working on it, or looking as though they were. That was built by a company called Fotherby Willis. They were very keen on doing it. But when Fotherby Willis said they had financial problems and couldn't complete the contract and started putting the screws on Curtis, Curtis dropped them,' explained Loasby.

'He made a bit of a mistake in going to Cranfield for the electronics. The mistake to my mind was that you should never get any academic on anything because they will never finish the job and they will never get it to work. The boot wasn't big enough to contain [the electrics] for a start, so that started us manoeuvring things around until we could get an electronic system that would work. Aston Martin's decision to go to the US for the electronics was right. Cranfield made a fearful mess of the electronics because, even though they were at the forefront of technology, they had no idea of the realities of what you could and couldn't do in a car.'

When Cranfield Institute was unable to satisfactorily develop the complicated electronics, Steve Coughlin approached Brian Refoy at Javelina Corporation in Texas. He specialised in making and developing aircraft instruments and was entrusted to successfully develop the Lagonda's electronic instrumentation and switchgear to production stage.

William Towns

Born in 1936, William Towns joined the Rootes Group in 1954 as a designer of small componentry. He joined Rover in 1963 and while there worked on the 2000 model and Le Mans Rover-BRM Gas Turbine car.

Towns joined Aston Martin in 1966 as a seat and interior designer and, although Cyril Honey was then Chief Body Engineer, Towns' design talent came to the notice of David Brown. His DBS body styling was the forerunner of a long line of designs for Aston Martin including the Aston Martin Lagonda V8 (four-door), AMV8, Lagonda and Bulldog concept car.

Towns also designed the Aston Martin MGB update and submitted an unsuccessful Virage design and scale model to Victor Gauntlett in 1986. As a freelance stylist he worked on the Jensen Healey and Reliant's SS2 and SST. Towns died in June 1993 at the age of 56.

Top to bottom: Styling was futuristic but all Lagondas were traditionally coachbuilt; The last Lagonda was produced in January 1990; Aston Martin Tickford produced three Lagonda limousines at £110,000 each; Lagondas had various dashboards over their 14-year production; this is a late series version

The interior was luxuriously appointed with leather seats and full Wilton carpeting, but the rear accommodation fell some way short of limousine comfort. The non-traditional dashboard and console and single-spoke steering wheel were a radical departure for Aston Martin; but that was precisely the point. The company's new directors, Alan Curtis, Peter Sprague, George Minden, Denis Flather and Fred Hartley were keen to showcase the company's engineering talent and to announce to the world that Aston Martin was back in business in a big way.

'We had to show that Aston Martin was back in business with a different car,' said Loasby. 'Many articles written at the time said that there were a lot of carry-over parts and this didn't reflect the fact that it was totally new. There was no carry over of the chassis and no carry over of the suspension, and certainly none on the instrumentation.'

The Lagonda initially sold very well, particularly in the Middle East, and helped to finance the company while providing Aston Martin with a lot of positive publicity. In fact, when Victor Gauntlett arrived at AML late in 1980, he was told that consideration was being given to closing down the manufacturing of Aston Martins altogether and that production would concentrate solely on Lagondas. Gauntlett fought strongly to block this move and was eventually successful.

A twin turbocharged V8 was developed in 1980, but the project was abandoned because of the high cost. 'It was a quick car,' said Arthur Wilson, 'but the really amazing thing about the turbo Lagonda was how well the car handled it. We put Vantage wheels and tyres on it and it handled like a dream.'

In 1983 Tickford developed an £85,000 'enhanced' Lagonda, which included a body kit, BBS wheels and altered interior. Only five were sold. A Tickford stretched limousine was also available for £110,000, but only three found customers.

The updated Series 3 Lagonda was released on 25 January 1986 at the New York Motor Show and featured Weber-Marelli fuel injection, increased power to 305 bhp and a revised rear axle ratio of 3.058:1. Seventy-six were built.

The new Series 4 Lagonda, starting with chassis number LOHR13540, was launched at the Geneva Motor Show in March 1987. The justification for the new series designation was the extensively updated body design. By 1987, sales were flagging; the car was coming to the end of its useful life. The once-fashionable wedge shape was by now a little passé, so AML commissioned William Towns to give the Lagonda a final facelift.

Towns transformed the car, but in doing so lost its original spirit. The razor-sharp lines of the Series 2 and 3 models were gently rounded off and the sills were deepened, which created a more contemporary look. Every panel was different from the preceding model. The pop-up headlights were replaced with fixed units, while the fog lamps were moved to the thicker-set

The Aston Martin Lagonda came in for numerous running changes during its 14-year life span and four distinct series can be followed:

Model	Production dates	Number built	Distinguishing features
Aston Martin Lagonda (MP/230/1)	1969	1	Stretched four-door DBS body, wire-spoked wheels, development 5.0-litre V8 engine
Aston Martin Lagonda V8 (Series 1)	Aug 1974 – May 1976	7 [iii]	Four-door AMV8 body, horseshoe-shaped grille, headlight wipers, Cosmic fire paint, central locking, GKN 15-inch alloy wheels
Aston Martin Lagonda[iv] (Series 2)	Oct 1976 – Jan 1986	462	Wedge-shaped body, steel 15-inch wheels with aluminium wheel covers, (BBS 15-inch wheels from 1983), LED dashboard display with touch sensitive buttons, single-spoke steering wheel, pop-up headlights
Lagonda (Series 3)	Jan 1986 – Mar 1987	76	Wedge-shaped body, BBS 15-inch wheels LED dashboard display, three-spoke steering wheel, pop-up headlights, Weber-Marelli fuel injection
Lagonda (Series 4)	Mar 1987 – Jan 1990	98	Revised wedge-shaped body with rounded edges and deeper sills, Ronal 16-inch alloy wheels, two-spoke steering wheel, revised interior and dashboard with push-button switches, six fixed headlights, Weber-Marelli fuel injection

chin spoiler. Other detail changes included new 16-inch, 18-spoke alloy wheels fitted with 255/60 VR 16 Avon Turbospeed CR27 tyres.

Inside, the once cutting-edge digital instrumentation and the traditional luxurious leather interior were now balanced; the new pleated leather seats were more akin to their Aston Martin stablemates and the steering wheel was a two-spoke version shared with the AMV8.

The infamous dashboard was given a facelift, too. The fascia still featured digital readouts on fuel consumption, average speed, air conditioning, temperature and distance travelled, but the touch-button controls were replaced by more traditional items. The Series 4 Lagonda also featured 'voice commands', first offered in 1984 on the Series 3 model, reminding the driver to switch off headlights, fasten seatbelts and other information. The voice commands could be programmed in German, French, Arabic and English.

The Series 4 was a more highly developed car. Many of the Lagonda's early problems had been resolved by this time, but it was too late. The new model, built at the rate of one per week, found only 98 buyers. The Lagonda, once Aston Martin's best-selling model and saviour, disappeared quietly with chassis number LOTR13645 in January 1990 after 636 (Series 2–4) cars had been made.

Model	Weight (lb)	0–60 mph (seconds)	Top speed (mph)	Power (bhp)
Aston Martin Lagonda V8	4400	N/A [v]	N/A	N/A
Aston Martin Lagonda (Series 2)	4551	7.9	148	280
Lagonda (Series 3)	4622	Not tested	Not tested	300
Lagonda (Series 4)	4622	8.4	145	305

Lagonda Series 4
1987–1990

Chassis: Steel box-section chassis, steel superstructure

Body: Aluminium four-seat sedan styled by William Towns

Suspension: Front – Independent with unequal length double wishbones, coil springs and anti-roll bar
Rear – de Dion axle with coil springs and Watt's linkage

Brakes: Servo-assisted Girling 273 mm ventilated discs (front); 263 mm inboard-mounted discs (rear)

Steering: Power-assisted rack and pinion

Wheels: 16-inch Ronal alloy

Tyres: Goodyear Eagle 255/50 VR16

Transmission: Torqueflite three-speed automatic. Final drive 3.058:1. Limited-slip differential. Rear-wheel drive

Engine: 5340 cc alloy V8 with twin chain-driven overhead camshafts per bank and two valves per cylinder. Compression ratio 9.3:1. Weber-Marelli fuel injection. Fully catalysed exhaust system

Power: 305 bhp/227 kW @ 5500 rpm
340 lb/ft/461 Nm of torque @ 4000 rpm

Top speed: 145 mph/233 km/h

Dimensions:

Length	17 ft 4 in/5283 mm	
Width	5 ft 11.5 in/1816 mm	
Height	4 ft 3 in/1302 mm	
Wheelbase	9 ft 6.5 in/2916 mm	
Weight	4622 lb/2097 kg	

Price when new: £95,000

Number built: 98

iii Seven cars were made, but eight chassis built

iv In 1983 the 'Aston Martin' prefix was dropped and the car thereafter became known simply as Lagonda

v No road tests conducted on this model

V8 Zagato Volante

Zagato drops its top

The announcement of the V8 Vantage Zagato in 1985 aroused immense interest. Plentiful firm deposits were received and all 50 examples were spoken for within five months, leaving some collectors disappointed. Hopeful prospective customers demanded an increase over the limited production run of 50 cars, even at the high price of £95,000.

But honourably, Victor Gauntlett kept his word, almost: 52 cars were made. Original buyers breathed a collective sigh of relief. They were promised exclusivity and they got it.

The solution that would please everyone was to produce an open version of the V8 Zagato with a different engine specification, which was approved in November 1986. It was a fairly predictable decision, given that open Aston Martins have always been exceedingly popular. Carrozzeria Zagato's Giuseppe Mittino was once again entrusted with the design, which he began at the end of 1986.

The Volante Zagato followed the same build process as the Vantage Zagato coupe. Aston Martin constructed a rolling chassis, complete with engine, transmission, suspension and wiring and sent it to Zagato. In Milan a new superstructure was added to mount the aluminium body panels. This time, however, the frame required additional stiffening below the waistline to compensate for the convertible's lack of roof.

'Chassis rigidity is actually stiffer than that of the Vantage Zagato in both torsion and bending modes, albeit with a small weight penalty of approximately [77 lb],' wrote Michael Bowler. 'The basic platform is the same as that for the Vantage Zagato and therefore has the advantage of incorporating that car's excellent suspension package.

'While it may sound easy just to cut the roof off a coupe and change the front, considerable work has gone into the new car both in engineering, tooling and homologation requirements. The small production run of new cars means higher amortisation costs per car; to keep these within reasonable bounds the Volante Zagato will only be offered in UK specification.'[7]

Officially, the Zagato Volante was not produced in Vantage form; its fuel injected engine therefore allowed a flatter bonnet line

'Victor said he just couldn't help himself, he had to make more.'

Richard Williams

Top: Zagato's interior design was not as luxurious as most Aston Martin models but it did help save weight **Above:** The hood, with a plastic rear window, was a very neat fit with the rear body work **Opposite:** The Volante's frontal treatment was closer to Giuseppe Mittino's original coupe sketch

Once completed, the Zagato cars were returned to Newport Pagnell and brought into Works Service where the tanks and fuel lines were flushed and the cars given a thorough check and valet before being handed to the customer or dealer.

The first Zagato Volante was unveiled at the Geneva Motor Show in March 1987. The car on the company's stand actually started life as one of the 52 coupes; Victor Gauntlett's own car no less, chassis number V8XGR20042. The first production Zagato Volante was chassis number V8ZJR30010.

The purpose of the car was somewhat different to the Vantage version and alternate performance targets were set. The V8 Vantage Volante had already been announced in October 1986 and it was felt that there was no need to produce a Vantage Volante Zagato.

The engine came from the V8 Saloon using the Weber-Marelli sequential fuel injection system and for this reason the Volante had a flat bonnet. Power was cut severely in comparison to the berlinetta model, but buyers of these cars were not seeking outright performance.

Like many other V8 cars, some V8 Vantage Zagatos and Zagato Volantes were later modified to take 437 bhp 5.3-litre Vantage engines, 6.3-litre and 7.0-litre engines. So unofficially, some V8 Vantage Zagato Volantes exist.

Model	Weight (lb)	0-60 mph (seconds)	Top speed (mph)	Power (bhp)
V8 Vantage Zagato	3637	4.7	186	437
V8 Zagato Volante	3929	5.5 (approx)	155	305

Outwardly, the Volante Zagato differed from the coupe model in several ways. It had a power-operated soft top with a plastic rear window for lightness and a traditional tonneau cover. In addition the flat bonnet flowed down to a distinctive new 'grille' that was more faithful to Mittino's original coupe sketch. The Volante also incorporated three tiers of lighting, including a set of flip-up headlights and full door glasses and retractable rear quarter glasses. The interior, individual specifications aside, replicated the coupe.

It was decided that a production run of only 25 cars would provide the correct balance of exclusivity and profits. Production didn't stop at that though. 'Victor said he just couldn't help himself, he had to make more,' recalled Richard Williams. Thirty-seven open Zagatos were constructed, including two prototypes. The larger production run raised some eyebrows among buyers who, having already spent £125,000, were looking at the Zagato Volante in purely speculative terms.

V8 Zagato Volante
1987–1988

Chassis: Steel box-section chassis, steel superstructure

Body: Aluminium 2+2 convertible styled by Giuseppe Mittino of Carrozzeria Zagato

Suspension: Front – Independent with unequal length double wishbones, coil springs and anti-roll bar
Rear – de Dion axle with coil springs and Watt's linkage

Brakes: Servo-assisted Girling 273 mm ventilated discs (front); 263 mm inboard-mounted discs (rear)

Steering: Power-assisted rack and pinion

Wheels: 16-inch Speedline alloy

Tyres: Goodyear Eagle 255/50 ZR16

Transmission: ZF five-speed manual; final drive 3.33:1
Torqueflite three-speed automatic; final drive 3.058:1
Limited-slip differential. Rear-wheel drive

Engine: 5340 cc alloy V8 with twin chain-driven overhead camshafts per bank and two valves per cylinder. Compression ratio 9.25:1. Weber-Marelli fuel injection. Fully catalysed exhaust system

Power: 305 bhp/227 kW @ 6000 rpm
320 lb/ft/434 Nm of torque @ 3000 rpm

Top speed: 155 mph/249 km/h (approx)

Dimensions:
Length	14 ft 8.5 in/4480 mm
Width	6 ft 1.25 in/1860 mm
Height	4 ft 3.5 in/1305 mm
Wheelbase	8 ft 6.75 in/2610 mm
Weight	3929 lb/1782 kg

Price when new: £125,000

Number built: 37

V8 Vantage Volante PoW Specification

A prince's car for a king's ransom

While no one could argue with the performance of the Vantage Volante, not everyone was enamoured with its overtly masculine looks. One such customer was HRH Prince Charles. Offered a car as a gift from The Amir of Bahrain, His Highness Sheikh Isa bin Salman Al-Khalifa, the long-time Aston Martin enthusiast wanted a Vantage-engined V8 Volante, but preferred the clean lines of William Towns' original design. The Factory obliged the Prince and produced a car to his individual specifications. The Prince of Wales' Specification Vantage Volante is now one of the most collectable Aston Martins of all.

When the order for the new car was received, Kingsley Riding-Felce visited the Prince's office to discuss the proposal. It was agreed that the Prince would want the most powerful convertible model and a manual gearbox. The only open-top car fitting that description was the Vantage Volante, but the Prince of Wales wanted a subtler look.

It was suggested that a car looking like a standard Volante, but with the Vantage performance running gear intact, would be a worthy compromise. Aston Martin manufacturing took a standard Volante, slightly flared the wheel arches to accommodate the larger tyres and wheels of the Vantage, deleted the side skirts and incorporated a redesigned new front valance.

'The only problem was that we got a call from the Prince's office one day. They believed someone was trying to offer the Prince's car for sale.'

Kingsley Riding-Felce

Modifications were made to the interior including a redesigned centre box with a glass jar for sugar cubes, for the Prince's polo horses, and the addition of a Nardi steering wheel and special gear knob in matching wood. The interior was finished in a special mushroom-coloured trim, without contrast stitching, and the car was painted a particular shade of British Racing Green. The PoW Volante was delivered to Prince Charles at Highgrove on 17 July 1987.

Replicas of HRH Prince Charles' car subsequently became known as PoW Specification Vantage Volantes; a total of 27 were built

'Victor Gauntlett saw this car and said, "Gosh, I'll have one of those as well",' said Riding-Felce. 'I remember writing, 'Build to PoW Specification,' and that's how we got the name that is still used today. Another customer saw the car and he wanted one and so on and it got to be known as the PoW Specification Volante.'

Top to bottom: Two PoW models were produced with the flip tail of the 'regular' Vantage Volante; A wood-rimmed Nardi steering wheel and matching wooden gear knob were standard equipment; HRH Prince Charles V8 Vantage Volante undergoing preparations for auction at Works Service

The PoW package proved irresistible. Twenty-two were built, all in right-hand-drive and all but one with manual transmission. In addition, five 'cosmetic' PoW Vantage Volantes were built for the US market, but the rubber-bumper, fuel-injected cars missed out on the X-Pack Vantage engine.

To confuse the situation somewhat, two PoW Specification Volantes, chassis numbers V8COR15690 and V8COR15835, were built with the tail spoiler of the standard Vantage Volante. Often referred to as 'flip-tail' PoW Specification Vantage Volantes, they are yet another splendid example of the hand-built nature of Aston Martins.

The PoW Specification cars retained the Vantage mechanicals but were devoid of the boot spoiler, extensively flared wheel arches, prominent sills and large front air dam. The pure lines of the original V8 Volante were retained, including the traditional open mesh grille and power bulge on the bonnet. The result was the best of both worlds: a car with outstanding performance in a refined package.

The interior followed the existing lines of the V8 Volante and typically featured a walnut-faced oddments box in place of the ashtray, centre arm-rest with a cubby box, recessed switches and matching wood-rimmed Nardi steering wheel and gear knob.

The PoW Specification cars proved a minor sales success for Aston Martin, but their unexpected popularity created a concern for the Prince's office. 'The only problem was that we got a call from the Prince's office one day. They believed someone was trying to offer the Prince's car for sale,' said Riding-Felce. 'I explained that several cars were built to the same specification and although one of them had been offered for sale as the PoW Specification, it was not the Prince of Wales' own car.'

Late in March 1994 Prince Charles acquired a Virage Volante with PoW paint and trim, converted to 6.3-litre specification to match the performance of his V8 Vantage Volante. This car too, lacked the flared wheel arches of the Works Service conversion.

In September 1995, after consultation with the Amir of Bahrain, Prince Charles sold his V8 Volante, chassis number V8CHR15581, for £111,500 at a Sotheby's auction, with all proceeds going to the Prince of Wales' Charities Trust. Prince Charles still owns his Seychelles metallic blue DB6 Mk II Volante, affectionately known as 'The Old Lady', which was presented to him by Queen Elizabeth II and The Duke of Edinburgh for his 21st birthday on 14 November 1969.

In a speech to mark the opening of Aston Martin's new Gaydon factory in Warwickshire in March 2004, Prince Charles told the collected workers: 'One of the reasons that I have been a huge fan of Aston Martin for 34 years is because I have always recognised that it is a real work of art, what all of you manage to put together. I am devoted to my 34-year-old car, which I do love. It rattles a bit, like I do, but otherwise it has done nothing but give real pleasure and enjoyment all these years.'

Kingsley Riding-Felce

Kingsley Riding-Felce joined Aston Martin on 17 May 1976 after running his own automotive business. Within six months he had moved into the service department to work as a chassis technician; he then spent a short time as a service technician, before taking up a role in service reception, which was to become a fundamental part of the business.

In 1980 Victor Gauntlett offered Riding-Felce the opportunity to broaden his experience within Aston Martin by developing the dealer network. Riding-Felce assumed a new role at Aston Martin's then offices at 33 Sloane Street, London. At the same time he also took responsibility for the company's marketing and presence at international motor shows.

In 1986, Riding-Felce was asked to manage Service, Parts Operations, Technical Operations and Warranty. This was later to become Works Service, which under his control grew to become a valuable and integral part of Aston Martin Lagonda. It is internationally recognised as the place to have Aston Martin or Lagonda motor cars maintained and restored.

Riding-Felce is a board director of Aston Martin with overall responsibility for Works Service and Customer Relations. He has an international reputation with clients and Aston Martin enthusiasts alike, is well-known for his extensive knowledge and enthusiasm for both Aston Martin and Lagonda marques and is regarded as the custodian of the company's heritage. He is also a Trustee of the British Motor Industry Heritage Trust and the Aston Martin Heritage Trust.

BUCKINGHAM PALACE

From: The Private Secretary to T.R.H. The Prince and Princess of Wales
17th February 1987

Dear Mr Riding Felce

Thank you for your letter of 5th February. His Royal Highness is happy with the colour proposed for the car, the leather, and for the hood. His Royal Highness prefers the green carpet and suggests a slightly lighter green to edge it. His Royal Highness prefers manual transmission. I look forward to hearing from you.

Riddell

Sir John Riddell

K. J. Riding Felce, Esq.

HRH Prince Charles' specifications led to the creation of a unique model

V8 Vantage Volante PoW Specification
1987–1989

Chassis: Steel box-section chassis, steel superstructure

Body: Aluminium 2+2 convertible styled by William Towns. Modified by Works Service

Suspension: Front – Independent with unequal length wishbones, coil springs and anti-roll bar
Rear – de Dion axle with coil springs and Watt's linkage

Brakes: Servo-assisted Girling 273 mm ventilated discs (front); 263 mm inboard-mounted discs (rear)

Steering: Power-assisted rack and pinion

Wheels: 16-inch Ronal alloy

Tyres: Goodyear Eagle 255/50 VR16

Transmission: ZF five-speed manual; final drive 3.33:1
Torqueflite three-speed automatic; final drive 3.058:1. Limited-slip differential. Rear-wheel drive

Engine: 5340 cc alloy V8 with twin chain-driven overhead camshafts per bank and two valves per cylinder. Compression ratio 10.2:1. Twin SU fuel pumps and four Weber 48 IDF/3 or 50 IDF carburettors

Power: 410 bhp/306 kW @ 6000 rpm
395 lb/ft/536 Nm of torque @ 5000 rpm
437 bhp/326 kW @ 6250 rpm
400 lb/ft/542 Nm of torque @ 5000 rpm
(optional engine with 50 IDF carburettors)
305 bhp/227 kW @ 6000 rpm
320 lb/ft/434 Nm of torque @ 3000 rpm
('Cosmetic' USA engine)

Top speed: 168 mph/270 km/h (est)

Dimensions:

Length	15 ft 4 in/4674 mm
Width	6 ft/1829 mm
Height	4 ft 6 in/1371 mm
Wheelbase	8 ft 6.75 in/2610 mm
Weight	4009 lb/1818 kg

Price when new: N/A

Number built: 27[i]

---

i Includes five 'cosmetic' PoW Vantage Volantes built for the US market

Zagato Lagonda Rapide
Another curiosity

Over the years, the Aston Martin–Zagato relationship has borne much fruit, even though production numbers remained predictably low. The DB4 GT Zagato, V8 Vantage Zagato, Zagato Volante, DB4 GT Zagato Sanction II and III, DB7 Zagato and Zagato Vanquish Roadster are all desirable classics.

However, there is another Aston Martin Zagato, or more properly, Lagonda Zagato model that never achieved the esteemed status of its stablemates. The awkward-looking Lagonda Rapide styling exercise by Zagato is another painful reminder that the best days of Lagonda are very distant indeed; the Zagato Lagonda Rapide remained a speculative one-off show car.

The company described the concept as a production possibility for the 1990s: 'The Lagonda Rapide Zagato is designed as a comfortable two-door, four-seater within the elegant lines of a three volume shape. The original angular lines of the Lagonda have given way to a more rounded shape, which Zagato has evolved to suit the classic traditions of this long-standing marque.'

'In truth it was largely to give Zagato something to display at the Geneva Motor Show. Even if it had been brilliant the production space wasn't really available, rather like the [Lagonda] Vignale.'

Michael Bowler

Rapide is a revered name in Lagonda history. It graced the M45R, which won the Le Mans 24-hour race in 1935, and was thought fitting for the Zagato styling exercise. The full-scale mock-up, described as a coupe by Zagato, was designed by Marco Pedraccini, with assistance from Gianni Zagato, and was built on an Aston Martin-supplied shortened Lagonda chassis at Zagato's workshops in Milan. Being a styling exercise only, the mock-up did not feature any running gear, electrics, moving suspension parts or interior.

'The problem with the style was that we tried to recapture Frank Feeley's wing sweeps,' recalled Michael Bowler, who was seconded to Zagato at that time. 'But someone decided to leave a kink in the waistline to allow an easy sightline for the external mirrors. If this had been straightened, the car would have lost its broken-backed look.

'In truth it was largely to give Zagato something to display at the Geneva Motor Show. Even if it had been brilliant the production space wasn't really available, rather like the [Lagonda] Vignale.'

The Zagato Lagonda Rapide, DP2051, broke from more recent Lagonda tradition by having only two doors. The standard Lagonda wheelbase was shortened by 7.9 inches and was 4.3 inches taller, providing ample headroom. '[This is] a car you don't have to climb down into but rather, step into,' said Gianni Zagato. The front featured rectangular headlights and a three-section grille crafted from a single piece of polished stainless steel, that Zagato suggested created a 'new corporate identity' for Lagonda.

The most controversial point of the design was the unusual front quarter window shape and kinked waistline. 'The flowing curves of earlier days are recaptured in the side view, where the sweeps over the front and rear wings converge at the top of the door panel, a feature that also improves lateral visibility,' explained Zagato.

Its bonnet and headlights were vaguely reminiscent of the William Towns-styled Lagonda and the Virage. The wheels were large silver-painted Lagonda-badged units with vents echoing those of the V8 Vantage Zagato; they were actually constructed from wood. The styling exercise also featured large dark 'glass' areas to disguise the fact that the car contained no interior.

The Lagonda's only public appearance was fleeting. The dark metallic green saloon was unveiled at the Geneva Motor Show in 1988 on the Carrozzeria Zagato stand, tellingly not on Aston Martin's, as it was a Zagato styling exercise, not an Aston Martin Lagonda product.

Any thoughts of placing the Zagato Lagonda Rapide into production were dismissed when Victor Gauntlett and Walter Hayes saw the car. Unimpressed, they rejected the idea immediately.

After the Zagato Lagonda Rapide, Aston Martin did not work with Zagato for some time. Former head of Ford Motor Company, Jac Nasser, recalled, 'I don't think that there was a policy on *not* using Zagato, but in the past small companies needed to outsource some of their design and development work. With Aston Martin able to source a much bigger resource pool [at Ford], there was less need for it to outsource work.'

In the company's brochure, Zagato ambitiously stated its intentions to create a convertible version of the Rapide: 'An open version of this coupe was envisaged from the start, a classic cabriolet with an electrically powered hood already under development within Zagato Industrial Design, the Styling and Prototype department of Zagato.'

This statement appears to be totally unfounded and after the cool reception received by the Rapide coupe, all signs pointed to a cessation of Aston Martin–Zagato projects in the future, but both companies had some more surprises in store.

Top: Described in Zagato's literature as a coupe, the Rapide was an unusual Lagonda in having only two doors **Above:** The Zagato Rapide project never entered production; the unique show car was neglected and on-sold by Zagato

Zagato Lagonda Rapide
1988

Chassis: Steel box-section chassis, steel superstructure

Body: Wood, plastic and foam four-seat coupe styled by Marco Pedraccini of Carrozzeria Zagato

Suspension: Front – Independent with unequal length double wishbones, no springs or shock absorbers fitted
Rear – de Dion axle, no springs or shock absorbers fitted

Brakes: Not fitted

Steering: Not fitted

Wheels: 15-inch wood

Tyres: Goodyear Eagle 255/50 VR15

Transmission: Not fitted

Engine: Not fitted

Power: N/A

Top speed: N/A

Dimensions:

Length	16 ft 8.8 in/5100 mm
Width	6 ft 2.5 in/1890 mm
Height	4 ft 7.5 in/1410 mm
Wheelbase	8 ft 10.5 in/2700 mm
Weight	N/A

Price when new: Not available for sale

Number built: 1

Virage

Last of the few

The beginning of the end? Or the end of the beginning? Neither, really. The Virage was the last production car conceived by Aston Martin before the Ford takeover and was a watershed in the company's history. All the models produced at the time of the Ford acquisition in late 1987 belong to a different era. The Ford story really starts with the Virage because, although its origins pre-date the American company, and Aston Martin was given a free hand in its design, the Virage was produced with the backing of Ford Motor Company.

Some considered Ford's ownership of Aston Martin the end of *real* Aston Martins and the Virage the last of the genuine article. But that has been said about the last side-valve Lionel Martin car, the 1.5-litre Sports of 1925, the DB6 Mk II and the DBS V8. In reality the Virage was no more or less an Aston Martin than any other car produced in the company's long history.

Alan Curtis, one of Aston Martin's saviours after Company Developments sold out, had mentioned back in 1976 that the V8 was outdated, being already seven years old. Ever since, a replacement had been sought, but unstable financial conditions made the development of a new car impossible.

It became very clear during the mid 1980s that the aging V8 Saloon could not survive yet another makeover. Something new was needed to secure business, but what, when, and more importantly, how much?

As DP2034 was nearing completion, Aston Martin found a novel way of naming its new car: it conducted a competition.

Huge multinationals like General Motors and Ford spend billions of dollars developing new cars – amounts that Aston Martin simply couldn't afford. The prohibitive development costs could cripple a small company like Aston Martin, especially if the car was unsuccessful. It was not possible, therefore, to develop the new model on a totally clean sheet of paper.

Aston Martin had to build on the extant Mike Loasby-designed Lagonda chassis, albeit in largely modified form. The engine, too, had some carry over parts, but was totally reworked and modernised to produce an up-to-date, emissions-clean unit.

The basic Virage design spanned several new models and many variants

Above: The 5.3-litre V8 engine design of Tadek Marek (left) still lay at the heart of the Virage engine but by this time it was considerably altered; Mike Loasby (right) returned to Aston Martin to help with Virage improvements

Victor Gauntlett had a number of bold ambitions as Executive Chairman: he wanted to develop a new V8 model, return to racing, and create a new, smaller car, more in line with the earlier DB models.

All three ambitions were eventually realised, but not in the way Gauntlett had first envisaged. The first priority was to create the new V8 model. Gauntlett gave approval for the project in late 1985 with Engineering Director Bill Bannard responsible for the project's development.

Designated Development Project 2034, work commenced with the following brief:

- Front-engined unleaded V8 able to meet all known and projected world emissions regulations
- Engine to be of equal or greater power to the preceding model
- Rear-wheel drive
- 2+2 coupe with reasonable luggage accommodation
- Utilise as many existing components as possible
- Evolutionary body design with reduced drag
- Traditional coachbuilt aluminium body of simpler construction
- Completion within two years

Tadek Marek's V8 was to be used in DP2034, but updated and fitted with a new four-valves-per-cylinder head to meet the car's modern emissions-clean objectives. Although Aston Martin possessed the engineering expertise to develop the head, the project was outsourced. The tender for the new cylinder head development was given to Callaway Engineering in Connecticut, USA, well-known for its work on four-valve racing engines and its 200-mph 'hot' Corvettes.

Arthur Wilson: 'What prompted the 32-valve engine was the changing European emissions regulations that were heading towards similar levels as America. The US Federal version of our engine was pretty low on power, due in part to the necessary low compression ratio to operate on lower-grade unleaded fuel and to comply with the NOx limit regulations. Simply put, NOx is a pollutant influenced by combustion temperature, hence the need for a low 8.1:1 compression ratio. The US cars of the time were producing around 260 bhp and it was unlikely that we could have sold many cars in European markets at that power output.

'We needed a better cylinder head, one that could run a higher compression ratio without getting into detonation on low-grade fuel. Detonation causes localised hot spots that result in NOx. We weren't alone and the modern trend was for a very compact combustion chamber with a low surface-to-volume ratio: a pent-roof type with three, four or five valves. We chose the four-valve route. The hemispherical head used with a domed piston, if you look at it in profile, has a crescent-shaped combustion chamber, which has the potential for long flame travel and residual pollutants at its extremities.

'It was going to be a major step to come up with a new cylinder head and pretty expensive for us but we had to keep up with developments if we wanted to stay in business. We talked to the top runners of the time, like Cosworth and Tickford, but the price tag was pretty horrendous.

'Peter Livanos had what they call a "neighbour" in America, Reeves Callaway, who was doing some pretty clever things with engines. He had an innovative way of containing project costs, essentially by using an off-the-shelf valve pack from another manufacturer. He would design the combustion chamber and the rest of the cylinder head around that and provide a cam profile to suit, which was a pretty attractive proposition from where we were sitting, so we went that route.'

Engine development started in April 1986 with Chief Engineer Tim Good heading the Callaway team in the US and Arthur Wilson working on the rest of the engine at Newport Pagnell. The first development engine was tested at Aston Martin in May 1987. It produced 338 bhp @ 5000 rpm and 370 lb/ft of torque @ 4000 rpm, but this was run without the hindrance of a catalytic converter and leaded fuel, so was a little deceptive.

Wilson continues: 'The idea was that Callaway would come up with a cylinder head including cam covers and a chain-drive mechanism for us to develop an engine based on that cylinder head at Newport Pagnell. So that went ahead and I went over there for the first run. There was a problem with the timing chain tension, which allowed a camshaft oscillation that upset the engine management timing trigger mechanism. We sorted that and the engine ran fine, although the compression ratio was a bit high and we had to use aviation fuel to run it. Apart from that it seemed to run okay. I came back to the UK and we waited for our first pair of cylinder heads to start engine development proper.'

Although the original design proposal by Heffernan and Greenley called for side air vents, the Virage was made without them; this car had them retro-fitted

The new cylinder head was the mastermind of freelance engineer Hans Hermann, who was invited on to the team by Reeves Callaway. Hermann designed the racing head for the AMR-1 Group C racing car first, then the Virage head. Catalytic converters and a Weber-Marelli fuel injection system, first seen on the last AMV8s in 1986, were used but with a new calibration.

Arthur Wilson designed the new cylinder block at Newport Pagnell. 'The original intention was to have a bolt-on, four-valve cylinder head for the existing V8 engine,' he said. 'However, I managed to convince Bill Bannard, who was Engineering Director at the time, that this would restrict future development. So I was allowed to design a new cylinder block as long as I could retain the capability to produce the old block from the same casting pattern work.

'I was responsible for the design and development of all the 32-valve engines that followed. Callaway was commissioned to design the first four-valve cylinder head. All engine development was done by Aston Martin at Newport Pagnell, as were the rest of the engine and engine system's design and development. Callaway went on to develop the successful racing version of the engine, but that was very different. During this period we had a good working relationship with Callaway and information flowed freely between both projects.

'There were setbacks during development, as there always are, but we achieved our performance targets, which were to match the European version of the 16-valve engine, but running catalysts and three-star 95 RON Octane fuel.

'Roy Goldsmith, who was in charge of the Certification Department, did a survey of world markets and he decided 95 octane fuel would be okay, except in Australia. For the European market we didn't need catalysts at that time, but we wanted a single world market model.

'Everything worked out, but there were limitations with that head design. I re-designed the combustion chamber fairly early on because of the production problems. The original combustion chamber was very contoured, which is fine unless you got a slight shift in the casting process and then the seats would be recessed on one side and stand proud on the other. It was something we did a lot of work on, trying to resolve it. But in the end we decided that we were asking too much from our casting supplier, so I redid the combustion chambers, which gave us better consistency with valve seat-relative-to-chamber surface. It also gave us a small reduction in NOx.

'We were doing emission test work with the Weber people in Italy at that time and up until that point we had been selecting

75

Arthur Wilson

Arthur Wilson began working for Aston Martin in the engine build shop early in 1959 when the DB Mk III and DB4 were both in production. 'I spent some time in production engine building and gradually I took on the rectification of engines with the road test department,' recalled Wilson. 'Eventually, I was pretty well on permanent loan to that department doing engine work and carburettor tuning; I became the man on carburettors, essentially.

'In the early 1970s Aston Martin was just about to put carburettors on the V8 engine and David Morgan approached me and suggested that I might like to apply for a job in what was then the Experimental Department. I worked directly for David Morgan, who was Chief Engineer on engines at that time. Eventually the engineering side of Astons became Aston Martin Tickford, which did work for Aston Martin and other manufacturers, as well as the endurance race engines for the Nimrod and EMKA teams.

'Early in 1984 AMT and AML separated, leaving AML without an engineering department. Michael Bowler was given the task of setting up a new department at Newport Pagnell for AML and he offered me the position in charge of engine development. It was a bit of a wrench to leave Tickford. I had learnt a lot during that time, particularly from Alistair Lyle who was Chief Engine Designer. But the opportunity to be in charge of engine development for Aston Martin was too much to turn down.'

Arthur Wilson retired from his position as V8 Powertrain Engineering Manager/Chief Engineer at Aston Martin in September 2000 after 41 years' service.

the best cylinder heads for them to work on, hoping to sort out the combustion chamber in the meantime. In the end I had to change the combustion chamber shape. We didn't tell the Weber people but they spotted it straight away, NOx went down which was good in one way, but it did upset the balance of their calibration.

'Bill Bannard originally wanted the new cylinder head to be retrofitted to existing 16-valve engines. Callaway was quite prepared to do that. But when we started to look at it in more detail, it became obvious that the stud spacing on the original block would restrict the inlet ports to the end cylinders. So I had a talk to Bill Bannard about it and convinced him that we should alter the stud position. You had to have a good argument with Bill because he was a pretty astute old boy, but he could see my reasoning.

'From that point on, it was a new block. That was pretty complicated because being low volume, any tooling costs had to be kept to a minimum. So we had to be pretty clever about it and came up with pattern work changes that would allow us to make 32-valve blocks or 16-valve blocks with much the same tooling and pattern work. We ended up having to machine some bits off that we didn't want in each case.'

The completed production engine developed 306 bhp @ 6000 rpm with 340 lb/ft of torque @ 3700 rpm. The engine was mated to a ZF five-speed gearbox or three-speed[i] Chrysler Torqueflite automatic transmission. The engine was not much more powerful than the one it replaced, however the new car ran on unleaded fuel, met all known emissions requirements and could be sold in all world markets without modification.

Concurrent with the engine development, Victor Gauntlett put out a tender in April 1986 for the all-important body design; a deadline was set for 13 August that year. Five competing concerns produced designs within the four-month period, including Richard Oakes, John Evans, Mike Gibbs, the partnership of John Heffernan and Ken Greenley and William Towns.

The designer of the DBS, Lagonda and futuristic Bulldog concept car, Towns was invited to join the tendering process but was late with his submission and did not keep within the brief. Gauntlett wanted to give Towns a decent chance and instructed him to try again. He came back again with disappointing design drawings and a quarter-scale clay model.

While Towns would have been a sentimental choice, the tender was awarded on 8 October to John Heffernan and Ken Greenley, although the design was largely Heffernan's work. The two designers, who worked out of Olympia, in West London, first formed their partnership in 1983. Formerly of the General Motors Design School, Heffernan and Greenley were lecturers at the Royal College of Art and their design credits included the Panther Solo and Bentley 90.

While the Virage's new cylinder head was being designed in the USA by Callaway Engineering, the rest of the engine development was conducted at Newport Pagnell under the direction of Arthur Wilson

i   Four-speed Chrysler Torqueflite automatic transmission became standard from 1993

The Virage's aluminium bonnet flowed all the way to the front headlights, but still hinged forward like many Aston Martin models before it

By this time Aston Martin had invested in CAD technology at Newport Pagnell and it was used for the first time on the Virage. Initially, Ford's involvement with the project was limited to providing financial resources and development technology like CAD, leaving Aston Martin to develop and launch the new car.

The updated engine and new body sat atop a chassis with origins dating back to the Lagonda of 1976. The Virage's chassis sections, including the front bulkhead, front chassis rails, cross members, rear seat pan, rear wheel arches and boot were from the Lagonda, but the sub-frame was new from the front bulkhead back. It was shortened and adjusted and included a new 'A' frame rear suspension. The use of existing, albeit revised, sections was one reason Design Engineer Malcolm Pearson and his team were able to complete their brief in such a short time.

A modified short-chassis two-door Lagonda 'mule' underwent 36,000 development miles to fine tune the chassis, suspension and newly modified 32-valve engine. Incidentally, William Towns, hoping it would become a production reality, always envisaged a two-door Lagonda and had designed one back in

the 1970s. The Virage chassis, too, was always seen as a platform for a new long-wheelbase Lagonda, slated for introduction in around 1992. In production form, at least, it never arrived.

Chassis and Handling Engineer, Scott Ellis, was responsible for the suspension. Ellis conducted thousands of development miles in the Virage prototype. But it was the rear suspension layout that later came in for the most criticism. The car was underpinned by a lightweight aluminium de Dion axle, radius arms, Watt's linkage, coil springs and telescopic dampers at the rear and unequal length wishbones, coil springs, coaxial spring dampers and anti-roll bar at the front. The rear suspension was the car's Achilles' heel and the later Vantage and V8 Coupe reverted to a more traditional rear end similar to the earlier V8 models.

Later, Loasby, working as a consultant, revised the front and rear suspensions to improve the geometry and mechanical integrity. The revisions were principally for the later Vantage, but were introduced across the board as soon as possible in the later V8 Coupe.

Top: The interior was very luxurious, but was gradually developed due to customer criticism **Above:** After aerodynamic testing, the car's substantial rear deck was raised higher than the initial design dictated

The brake package included large PBR ventilated discs; the rear set moved outboard to aid cooling. At this stage, ABS was not offered. The wheels were five-spoke 16-inch cast alloy, shod in specially developed Avon Turbospeed 255/60 VR16 tyres.

The interior was designed by John Heffernan and produced with the assistance of Anglo-Swedish Consultants, who constructed the clay model. Aston Martin's Engineering Development Department brought the interior to production under the direction of Alan Stevens. The car was trimmed in Connolly hide with contrasting piping and Wilton carpet and walnut veneer cappings were featured on the dashboard and doors.

As DP2034 was nearing completion, Aston Martin found a novel way of naming the car: it conducted a competition. Held within the factory and AMOC, Gauntlett stipulated the new car was to have a name, not simply a number designation or acronym. The name was to start with V to continue the series of V names: V8, Vantage and Volante. AMOC member Jeff Bines coined the Virage name, it being French for corner.

Befitting the announcement of the first new Aston Martin in more than two decades, the Virage was unveiled at the International Motor Show in Birmingham on 18 October 1988 to the sound of fanfare trumpets. Vying for interest at the same show were Jaguar's XJ220 and Ferrari's F40, but the Virage attracted considerable interest and positive press. More importantly, 54 firm orders and deposits were taken at the show.

Its reception from the motoring press was mixed. Most writers praised the handsome body but some expected more performance. The 0–60 mph dash in 6.8 seconds was disappointing, since after all, the DB6 could out-sprint it way back in 1966. But the DB6 was neither as comprehensively equipped, nor crippled by power-sapping emissions equipment.

Virage production began promisingly with the first customer car, chassis number AMSLR50000, delivered in December 1989. In 1990 and 1991, production figures of 178 and 168 respectively boded well for the future. But with the introduction of the Virage Volante and the more powerful Vantage in 1992, production of the coupe almost came to a halt. After what initially looked like a successful production run, only 411 Virage coupes were constructed before the V8 Coupe replaced it in 1996.

It was early days, but this was the dawning of a new era.

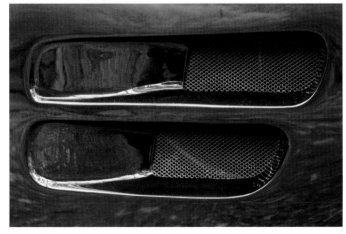

Top: Detailing on later 'V' cars included recessed badges **Above:** Twin air vents were also featured on the Limited Edition model

Reeves Callaway

The son of Callaway Golf Company founder Ely, Reeves Callaway was a successful Formula Vee competitor during the early 1970s. He later became a race car instructor and during this time completed his first turbo-charger installation on an ex-race school BMW 320i at his home in Connecticut. Its subsequent success led to the foundation of Callaway Engineering in 1985.

Callaway Engineering and associated business Callaway Cars are best known for their 'tuned Corvettes', one of which, 'Sledgehammer', held the record for the 'World's Fastest Street Car' with a top speed of 254.7 mph set in 1988. From 1986 Callaway Engineering developed the new cylinder head for the Virage and the engines for the AMR-1 racing cars.

Virage
1988–1994

Chassis: Steel box-section chassis, steel superstructure

Body: Aluminium 2+2 coupe styled by John Heffernan

Suspension: Front – Independent with unequal length double wishbones, coil springs, coaxial spring dampers and anti-roll bar Rear – de Dion axle, radius arms, Watt's linkage, coil springs and telescopic dampers

Brakes: Servo-assisted PBR 330 mm ventilated discs (front); 289 mm ventilated discs (rear)

Steering: Power-assisted rack and pinion

Wheels: 16-inch alloy

Tyres: Avon Turbospeed 255/60 VR16

Transmission: ZF five-speed manual; final drive 3.33:1. Torqueflite three-speed automatic[ii]; final drive 3.058:1. Limited-slip differential. Rear-wheel drive

Engine: 5340 cc alloy V8 with twin chain-driven overhead camshafts per bank and four valves per cylinder. Compression ratio 9.5:1. Weber-Marelli fuel injection. Fully catalysed exhaust system

Power: 306 bhp/228 kW @ 6000 rpm 340 lb/ft/461 Nm of torque @ 3700 rpm

Top speed: 155 mph/249 km/h

Dimensions:

Length	15 ft 7 in/4745 mm
Width	6 ft 1.5 in/1856 mm
Height	4 ft 5.5 in/1359 mm
Wheelbase	8 ft 6.75 in/2610 mm
Weight	4233 lb/1920 kg

Price when new: £125,000

Number built: 411

ii Four-speed automatic from 1993

A M R - 1
Aston Martin goes racing

Over the years, Aston Martin's sporting reputation has been greatly enhanced by competing on the world's racetracks. From Lionel Martin's early record-breaking light cars of the 1920s to Bertelli's Le Mans attempts in the 1930s, to the successful David Brown racing era spanning 1948 to 1963, Aston Martin took on the best in the world and won.

When David Brown announced at the end of the 1959 season that Aston Martin, having won the World Sports Car Championship, would withdraw from sports car racing, the accountants gave a collective sigh of relief, but customers and Aston Martin's distributors did not.

French distributor Marcel Blondeau was instrumental in convincing Aston Martin to briefly return to Le Mans in 1962 and 1963. The project cars were a half-hearted effort, however, and Aston Martin finally retired from factory racing in 1963. With the long-term prospect of racing again with Aston Martin all but lost, John Wyer joined the Ford GT40 project in 1963, creating an early Ford–Aston Martin association.

> 'It came as a genuine surprise that Ford Motor Company agreed to proceed with the AMR-1 project only one month after acquiring the company.'
>
> *Ted Cutting*

The brief return to sports car racing did prove one thing: Aston Martin's rightful place was on the racetrack. But racing had cost every owner, from Lionel Martin to David Brown, a great deal of money. Through the financially troubled 1970s and 1980s, the owners simply did not have the capital to return to racing as a Works Team.

Privateers such as Robin Hamilton flew the flag at Le Mans in 1977 and again in 1979 with his modified DBS V8, while the Aston Martin Tickford V8-engined racers, Nimrod, EMKA and Cheetah, competed in the early 1980s.

Robin Hamilton created Nimrod Racing Automobiles Limited in 1981 with a two-car team, while another car was run by Viscount Downe, all with the support of Pace Petroleum

Ford allowed the AMR-1 programme to continue after its acquisition of Aston Martin, but it was not to last beyond 1989

The Livanos family underwrote the project to the tune of £26 million, which was to be used over a projected six-year period for the development of the first cars and the day-to-day running of the racing programme.

Limited. The chairman of Pace at the time was Victor Gauntlett, who had joined the Aston Martin board, and had acquired a 50 percent shareholding in the company in December 1980.

'Victor Gauntlett introduced me to Robin Hamilton, the father of the Nimrod programme and my family agreed to buy some funding in Nimrod,' said Peter Livanos. 'It was largely an amateur exercise that was clearly under-funded, so inevitably did not go anywhere. But it was an interesting first visit to Le Mans and it gave me the bug for the Le Mans 24-Hour race, which is one of the most important motor racing events in the world.'

After taking full-time control of AML, Gauntlett and Livanos turned their minds to Factory racing. The decision to proceed with development was made in 1986. 'As my family became more involved in the factory and were beginning to feel more confident, I suggested to Victor Gauntlett that we might go back to Le Mans and do the project in-house – we should make our own car,' said Livanos. 'We got Richard Williams and Ray Mallock involved and they created the AMR car.'

It was believed the current V8 engine was the place to start; after all, privateers had developed it out to 820 bhp and the Nimrod cars had performed admirably in the 1982–84 World Sports Car Championship. The RS Williams/Lord Downe team finished third overall in 1982, despite being massively under-funded compared to teams like the all-conquering Porsche concern.

In August 1987 Aston Martin announced that it was developing a Group C sports car. An agreement had been struck between Gauntlett and Livanos in the middle of the previous year to establish a team and compete in endurance racing events with a wholly Aston Martin car, not just an Aston Martin engine in another manufacturer's chassis.

When on 7 September 1987, only one month after the announcement, Ford acquired a controlling interest in AML, it came as a genuine surprise that approval was given to proceed with the project. Livanos made sure the continuation of the AMR programme was written into the contract when his family relinquished its 75 percent stake in Aston Martin. Approval to continue was only given provided Ford didn't have to fund the programme and that production cars would not be compromised. To ensure this happened, Ford deemed the racing programme and day-to-day running of the company to be two separate entities.

A subsidiary company was set up in Milton Keynes to oversee the racing programme and to separate the racing and production cars. Proteus Technology Ltd. (Protech) was a separately funded part of the Proton Group, a holding company for the joint interests of the Livanos family and Gauntlett. Protech was 75 percent owned by Proton while Williams and Mallock, whose shares were in the name of Ecurie Ecosse, owned the remainder.

There has been some confusion over the Ecurie Ecosse involvement in the AMR project. Ray Mallock explained, 'Ecurie Ecosse was not announced in conjunction with the car. It was, in fact Ray Mallock Limited (RML) that was originally contracted to manage the design and build of the first car. What brought Ecurie Ecosse into the picture was that I elected to have my shares in Proteus Technology in the name of Ecurie Ecosse in recognition of the contribution that the Ecurie Ecosse team made in creating a platform from which the Aston AMR-1 programme could develop.'

The Livanos family underwrote the project to the tune of £26 million, which was to be used over a projected six-year period for the development of the first cars and the day-to-day running of the racing programme. A 36,500-square-foot headquarters in Milton Keynes was established and opened by HRH Prince Michael of Kent on 2 June 1989. Previously the AMR cars had been prepared at Ray Mallock Limited's premises in Northamptonshire. All work now was transferred to Milton Keynes and a farmhouse and grounds at Tertre Rouge was purchased to use as a base at Le Mans.

The Federation Internationale du Sport Automobile (FISA) proposed that stock block engines would be allowed, so long as the car was homologated in Group B, which required 200 units to be built. Callaway Engineering was commissioned to produce the AMR's engines under the direction of Richard Williams.

Top: Carroll Shelby piloting the Le Mans and World Sports Car Championship-winning DBR1/2 in 1959 **Above:** The Aston Martin-powered Nimrod race car at Le Mans

Aston Martin returned to Le Mans in 1962 with Project 212 but the British team's racing days were soon to come to an end

News of the racing engine first broke in May 1988 when *Automobile* magazine reported under the headline 'Callaway Aston Martin': '... spotted on a dynamometer in Reeves Callaway's shops was an Aston Martin DOHC V8 ... Aston Martin's Chairman, Victor Gauntlett allows that the 6.4-litre engine's development is being underwritten by enthusiast-patron Peter Livanos with an eye to World Prototype endurance racing.'

Hans Hermann, of Callaway Engineering, was responsible for the four-valve head and development of the racing version of the V8. Four different Virage-based engines were planned in the hope that all possible formulas would be covered. Designated RDP87-1 (Race Development Project 1987), 5.0-litre, 5.3-litre, 6.0-litre, 6.3-litre and 6.4-litre engines were all considered, in order to cover IMSA and Group C regulations. The 5.0-litre and 6.4-litre development was cancelled, while the standard 5.3-litre was used only for testing purposes.

The standard 5.3-litre engine was tested at 570 bhp @ 7500 rpm in April 1988, so it looked promising for the larger capacity engines. A 687 bhp 6.0-litre version, ready in August, was finally chosen for the AMR-1 programme. Coupled to the engine was a new purpose-designed transaxle five-speed gearbox built in-house with Hewland internals.

While work was conducted on the engine in the US, Max Boxstrom was engaged to develop the chassis and body design. The first quarter-scale model was completed in September 1987 and wind-tunnel tested at MIRA and Southampton

Richard Williams

Born in 1945 Richard Williams joined Aston Martin at Feltham as an apprentice in 1963. He left in 1966 to join actor and motor sport enthusiast, Peter Sellers' 'Sellers' Racing', preparing his race and road cars. In 1968 he set up his own business, RS Williams Ltd, restoring, servicing and selling Aston Martins.

He became involved in racing Aston Martins in the early 1970s when Lord Downe invited him to prepare and run his DBR1 and Project 212 sports cars and later, he managed Downe's Nimrod sports car between 1982 and 1984, finishing third in the World Sportscar Championship in 1982. During 1984 RS Williams constructed the famous Lightweight DB4s and from 1985 Williams was Team Manager for Ecurie Ecosse, running its Group C2 cars, which won the C2 Championship in 1986 and finished second in 1987.

During 1988 he became Managing Director of Proteus Technology, which developed the AMR cars and in 1989 acted as Team Manager of the AMR team. But when the project was wound down, Williams returned to his previous business working with Aston Martins in Cobham. Aston Martin appointed RS Williams Ltd. as a Heritage Specialist in 2002.

Williams' company has been instrumental in developing a number of special Aston Martins, including the Sanction II and III DB4 GT Zagatos and the 6.3-litre and 7.0-litre V8 engines. Williams also helped develop the AMR-1 cars and DB7 V8 Le Mans engine. With his vast experience, Richard Williams is one of the most respected names in the modern Aston Martin story.

Ray Mallock

Ray Mallock came from a family deeply involved in motor racing; his father, Arthur, was a racing car designer and constructor.

Like Richard Williams, Mallock was an Aston Martin apprentice. He began his racing career in 1969 and left Aston Martin in 1971 to go into business with his father. He successfully drove Formula 2, Formula 3, Formula 5000 and sports cars and developed a very good reputation as a test driver and development engineer. He played a leading role in the Aston Martin Nimrod project along with Richard Williams.

In 1985 Ecurie Ecosse commissioned Ray Mallock Ltd. to design, develop and construct its C2 car. He continued to race during this time: he was runner-up in the C2 Driver's Championship in 1985, 1986 and 1987 and was a member of the 1986 Ecurie Ecosse Championship winning team. In 1987 Mallock was appointed Engineering Director of Proteus Technology and designed the AMR-1 team cars.

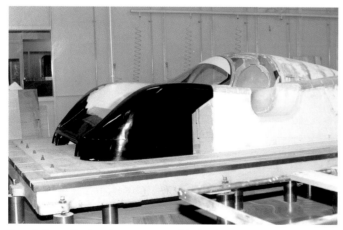

Top: Callaway Engineering was responsible for the development of the AMR-1 engine Above: A buck used to design the AMR-1 body

University. Ex-Williams Formula One employee, Paul McBride, built the carbon and Kevlar tub. The body was manufactured using carbon-fibre panels.

Ray Mallock was employed as Engineering Director, while Richard Williams was appointed Team Manager responsible for overseeing the project. Sixty people, some of whom had experience running the Nimrod and Ecurie Ecosse C2 cars eventually became involved in the project. Protech's Operations Director, Michael Bowler, dealt with team movement, homologation issues, press and sponsorship; former Aston Martin Chief Racing Designer, Ted Cutting, the man responsible for the design of the Le Mans-winning DBR1, was appointed by Victor Gauntlett to liaise between Richard Williams and himself and to provide technical support.

'Victor sent me down to assess the project while the building of the car was taking place,' said Cutting. 'I reported back to him favourably. I had minimal involvement with the team, which was probably a wise idea. Max Boxstrom said that after he had spent an hour with me he had to "spend an hour in a dark room." I was probably out of date by then. If you don't live with motor racing every day, you soon get out of date. I went with the team to Brands Hatch, but I didn't go to Le Mans.'

Ray Mallock Limited was given the contract to manage the design and prototype build of the first car. While development work was conducted, inevitable delays occurred and the proposed debut at Spa in September 1988 came and went. The first complete car, AMR-1/01 was unveiled privately to Ford and Aston Martin senior management at Newport Pagnell on 23 October 1988. Its first test run, at the hands of Ray Mallock, was on 28 November, at Silverstone.

It was always intended that the new car would not be raced unless considered competitive. After promising, exhaustive testing, the go-ahead was given at the start of January and the official announcement was made on 25 January 1989 that the AMR team would compete in the World Sports Car Prototype Championship. Drivers engaged for the 1989 season were Brian Redman, David Leslie, David Sears, Ray Mallock, Michael Roe, while Stanley Dickens and Costas Los were recruited later in the season when required.

The AMR-1 programme suffered a setback when, during testing at Donington Park, David Leslie, who had been responsible for much of the development and testing of the new car, crashed AMR-1/01 badly. Axle failure was deemed the cause, but the crash meant the team was not ready for the Championship's first race at Suzuka in Japan; Proteus Technology was fined £250,000 for missing the race.

The second round of the season at Dijon saw AMR-1/01 finish its first race in 17th position; a creditable performance considering its lack of development and practice time. At Le Mans two cars were entered, both wearing black bands in respect for the great John Wyer who passed away on

8 April. 'The two cars ran well although both experienced severe porpoising on the Mulsanne straight as a result of high downforce created by the bodywork,' recalled Ray Mallock. While AMR-1/03 expired in the early hours of the morning, AMR-1/01 crossed the finish line in a respectable 11th position.

'The team came away from Le Mans with many lessons learnt and the time was put to good use in the period leading up to the next race, Brands Hatch, with many detail changes to the suspension, steering and general set up,' said Mallock.

At Brands Hatch AMR-1/04 was very competitive, finishing in a fine fourth place; its best performance of the season. At Germany's Nürburgring, the scene of some of Aston Martin's most famous victories, AMR-1/04 could not replicate the domination of the earlier DBR1s and finished in eighth place. Donington was the scene of a sixth and seventh placing for AMR-1/05 and AMR-1/04 and at Spa in Belgium, another favourite circuit during Aston Martin's racing glory days in the 1950s, there was a further solid seventh position for AMR-1/04.

Michael Bowler

Michael Bowler is a trained engineer, but he chose a motor journalism career when he graduated from university. He worked for *Motor* magazine for seven years before becoming Sports Editor. In 1973 he was the Founding Editor of *Thoroughbred and Classic Cars* magazine before leaving in 1981 to join Pace Petroleum.

Through Pace Petroleum, Bowler was responsible for all of Aston Martin's motorsport sponsorship and became Director of the Nimrod team in 1982. In 1984 he set up the new Engineering Department at Aston Martin following the foundation of Aston Martin Tickford. In February 1985 he was appointed Special Projects Director, then spent 18 months at Carrozzeria Zagato overseeing the new Aston Martin-Zagato cars. In 1989 he became Operations Director of Proteus Technology, but left in February 1990 when the AMR programme was wound down.

Wearing black bands to mark the death of John Wyer, the red, white and blue livery reflected a sponsorship deal with Mobil; one of these five cars, AMR-1/02, was never completed

AMR-1/05, the lightest and most potent car, used a 6.3-litre, 721 bhp Version II V8 engine and was 132 lb lighter than the first cars. But another eighth place was all that it could achieve at the final race of the season in Mexico. These sound results put the AMR-1 into sixth place overall at the end of the season, with Sauber-Mercedes winning the Championship.

Work had begun on AMR-2, and had progressed as far as using a 6.3-litre engine, installed in an AMR-1 body for testing purposes. A new AMR-2 body was being developed for the 1990 season that was to have a more efficient aerodynamic shape, allowing a projected top speed of 230 mph. 'This was specifically aimed at reducing drag with Le Mans in mind, but maintaining the high levels of downforce of the AMR-1,' remembered Mallock.

Top: AMR-1 was the first official Aston Martin team entry in sports car racing for a quarter of a century **Above:** The AMR-1 team finished sixth in the 1989 World Sports Car Prototype Championship with a best result of fourth at Donnington

Max Boxstrom

Max Boxstrom was born in Sweden before moving to Canada where he developed an interest in racing cars. Upon arriving in the UK in 1966 he worked on Formula 2, Formula 3 and Formula 5000 cars. He then formed Race Cars International to run Formula 3 Brabhams and Chevrons, winning the 1969 Shell Motor Sport Championship. He joined Frank Williams in 1974 before forming the well-known Dymag wheel manufacturing business. In 1985 he worked with Ray Mallock on the Ecurie Ecosse C2 cars that won the 1986 championship, then became involved in the AMR-1 programme. It was originally envisaged that Boxstrom would design the 1991 3.5-litre Group C Aston Martin, but he left the team in mid-1989 to concentrate on his business interests.

Top: V8 engine development spanned from 5.0 to 6.4 litres but AMR-1 only used the 6.0- and 6.3-litre units while racing **Above:** Top speed for the AMR-1 was 217 mph; the 6.3-litre version was thought to be capable of 235 mph, but it never reached that speed in its only race in Mexico

But there were serious doubts as to whether Le Mans would proceed for that season as the Automobile Club de l'Ouest (ACO) and FISA couldn't agree on certain terms. Le Mans was Aston Martin's raison d'être for participating in sports car racing and the doubts over its running caused indecision over Aston Martin's entire racing future.

Meanwhile, Ray Mallock had replaced Max Boxstrom as Designer and testing continued on the AMR-2 project in the hope that all would be resolved. AMR-2 was to retain the AMR-1 tub but had a radically different body shape and a Version III V8 engine. The new chassis was to differ from the existing one in several key areas: engine installation, suspension pick-up points and torsional rigidity.

But almost as quickly as the dream had materialised, it vanished. The promising AMR cars met their demise in December 1989 when, as Aston Martin was preparing for another season in the World Sports Car Championship, FISA changed the engine capacity for Sports Cars to 3.5 litres for the 1991 season. It wasn't worth continuing with the V8 engine for a single year, so the AMR project was disbanded in February 1990.

'The funding levels at that time were beginning to grow astronomically and it became quite clear to all at the factory that the family either had to decide to support the factory and its operations or racing; it couldn't do both. So again the AMR project was not taken to its conclusion and it died an early death,' said Peter Livanos.

'It was a much more serious effort than Nimrod and was much more successful; with a fourth place at Brands Hatch, it did quite creditably. But the funding required to keep it going and to make it into a winning car would have been astronomical.'

Aston Martin was left with a very capable car, an extensively developed AMR-2 prototype and plans for a new Tony Southgate-designed chassis for the 1991 AMR-3. However, its 6.3-litre engine was nearly twice that of the 1991 allowable capacity limit and Protech had no way of developing a brand new engine in time.

Ford had a proven 3.5-litre Cosworth Formula One engine. Protech had been in negotiations with Ford management to obtain the engine, but the request was refused. Jaguar got it and went on to a high-profile, if unsuccessful, Formula One career and Aston Martin did not participate in Factory racing for 16 years.

Above: Ted Cutting, designer of the World Championship-winning DBR1, was employed as an advisor to Victor Gauntlett on the AMR-1 project
Right: AMR-1's dashboard contained a computer relaying vital information back to the pits
Below: AMR-1's large wing and rear venturi made the most of 1980s aerodynamics

Peter Livanos

Peter Livanos is one of several individuals to come to the rescue of Aston Martin during its long history. Born on 18 August 1958 Livanos' family made their fortune in the shipping business, but he soon became interested in motor cars. While studying at Columbia Engineering School, the 21 year old was seeking to purchase a sports car. His eventual choice was to have far-reaching consequences.

'In 1979 I saw an advertisement for a Ferrari Daytona, which was being sold by a company called Aston Martin North America,' recalled Livanos. 'So I went down to see the car. I couldn't afford it, but while I was there I was introduced to an AMV8. The President of Aston Martin North America, Maurice Hallowell, said, "Well, why don't you try this?" I responded that I had never driven an Aston Martin, but would love to try it. He said to take the car and bring it back tomorrow.

'I thought that was very generous and off I went in this car. I spent the evening with it and the next day. I really, really enjoyed the whole atmosphere of what it was and I was very touched by the gesture. So I ended up buying the car. But in each of the first three weeks that I had it, it had a major breakdown. The half-shaft broke, the clutch broke and the differential broke and on every occasion, I brought the car back and they said how unusual it was for that to happen to an Aston Martin.

'By the third time I felt that they may have been pulling the wool over my eyes. But they were very pleasant, I enjoyed the experience; they were nice people. But when I went to pick up the car for the third time I was expecting an enormous bill because it was a used car and there was no question of there being any warranty in my mind. I said that I wanted to discuss the bill, but I was told that there was no bill – the car shouldn't have broken down and even though there was no warranty, it shouldn't have happened to me. There was no charge made for the repairs. I asked if I could at least buy them dinner, and that is how my involvement started.

'I got a chance to meet the top people who were running the North American Aston Martin operations and later, I met Victor Gauntlett, who had taken over the factory with Tim Hearley. I had a Greek friend, Nick Papanicolaou, who loved the cars as well and together we got involved in the US operations. Very shortly after that, Pace Petroleum had its problems and Nick did the negotiations to buy the whole factory; we bought out the Pace and CH Industrials shares in Aston Martin. Nick absolutely adored the cars and he adored the factory that produced the cars. He really put a lot of effort into it.'

Livanos encouraged his family to invest in the company, which they did, and once again, Aston Martin was saved. A fan of motorsport, Livanos was financially involved in the Nimrod programme and later became the major financial backer of the AMR project.

'It was an incredible learning experience at Aston Martin. Incredible! It was a business venture that would have, in any circumstances, been difficult to make a success of and as the regulations were tightening up it became clearer and clearer that small-volume car manufacturers were a dying breed,' recalled Livanos.

After the Ford Motor Company purchased 75 percent of Aston Martin in 1987, Livanos retained a 12.5 percent stake in the company before finally selling the remainder of his holding in July 1994 when Ford became the 100 percent stakeholder. Livanos resigned from his position as Director of the company on 22 July 1994.

> 'As the regulations were tightening up it became clearer and clearer that small-volume car manufactures were a dying breed.'
>
> *Peter Livanos*

AMR-1
1988–1989

Chassis: Carbon fibre monocoque

Body: Kevlar, carbon and honeycomb Group C sports racing car designed by Max Boxstrom

Suspension: Front – Independent with double wishbones, coil springs over dampers and anti-roll bar
Rear – Independent with double wishbones, inboard-mounted coil springs over dampers and anti-roll bar

Brakes: Servo-assisted 14-inch ventilated discs with AP Racing four-piston callipers

Steering: Power-assisted rack and pinion

Wheels: 14-inch (front); 15-inch (rear) Dymag alloy

Tyres: Goodyear Eagle 25.5 x 12.0 17 (front). 27.5 x 14.5 17 (rear)

Transmission: AMR five-speed manual transaxle. Rear-wheel drive

Engine: Mid-longitudinally mounted 5998 cc[ii] alloy V8 with twin chain-driven overhead camshafts per bank and four valves per cylinder. Zytec engine management system

Power: 5998 cc engine – 687 bhp/512 kW @ 7750 rpm
501 lb/ft/679 Nm of torque @ 5500 rpm

6299 cc Version II engine – 721 bhp/538 kW @ 7750 rpm
530 lb/ft/719 Nm of torque @ 6750 rpm

Top speed: 217 mph/349 km/h

Dimensions:

Length	15 ft 8 in/4775 mm
Width	6 ft 6.25 in/1987 mm
Height	3 ft 4 in/1016 mm
Wheelbase	9 ft 6 in/2896 mm
Weight	1988–2178 lb/904–990 kg

Price when new: N/A

Number built: 4[iii]

---

ii One 6299 cc engine built and fitted to AMR1/05 in September/October 1989

iii AMR-1/02 not completed. The tub was used for in-house development and to mock up seating and pedals. A sixth car, AMR-2/01, was in development at the time Proteus Technology was wound up, but was never raced by the team. The AMR-2 chassis, incorporating many detail changes, was constructed and was to be tested with an AMR-1 body; the AMR-2 body was still in development and was never fitted. After the closure of Protech AMR-2/01 was completed at Richard William's workshops and subsequently sold.

DB4 GT Zagato
Sanction II

Rebirth of a legend

The DB4 GT Zagato Sanction IIs are essentially 1960s vehicles, built *new* in 1991 to, as Victor Gauntlett put it, 'tidy up a bit of Aston Martin history.' The highly desirable DB4 GT Zagatos have spawned several copies over the years, but the Sanction II cars are not among them. These are Aston Martin Lagonda products, though they weren't built at the Newport Pagnell factory.

It is ironic that the most collectable road-going Aston Martin was a dismal sales disappointment in its day. Aston Martin simply couldn't sell the expensive coupes when new and while 23 were slated for construction, only 19 were built, the last few of which were offloaded to HWM to sell as a 'job lot,' as Gauntlett recalled.

The short-chassis DB4 GT, styled by Touring of Milan debuted at the London Motor Show in October 1959. It was designed as a production road-racing car and an intended production run of 100 cars ensured homologation for racing. They were highly sought after, even at £4534.

> Very conscious that DB4 GT Zagatos were fetching up to £1.7 million at auction, a thought occurred to Gauntlett: what if AML and Zagato were reunited and built the four 'un-built' cars?

The following October, at the London Motor Show at Earls Court, a special edition DB4 GT was shown with lightweight coachwork styled by Ercole Spada of the Milanese coachbuilding firm, Carrozzeria Zagato.

Starting with chassis number DB4GT/0176/R, the intention was to build 23 Zagato-bodied cars finishing with chassis number DB4GT/0200/R. (The first one built was chassis number DB4GT/0200/R to satisfy homologation requirements). An astronomical price tag of £5470 and the much cheaper Jaguar E-Type scuttled that idea and only 19 Zagato DB4 GTs were constructed. Chassis numbers 0192, 0196, 0197 and 0198[i] were not built and when the DB4 was superseded in 1963, it looked as though the remaining four cars would never be completed.

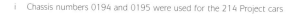

i   Chassis numbers 0194 and 0195 were used for the 214 Project cars

Sanction II Zagatos married the styling of the originals with sympathetic upgrades to improve the driving experience

The resolution of the Zagato DB4 GT story had to wait until 1991. Very conscious that DB4 GT Zagatos were fetching up to £1.7 million at auction in the late 1980s, a thought occurred to Gauntlett: what if AML and Zagato reunited and built the four 'unbuilt' cars? 'Victor contacted four prospective clients with the proposal that they could buy a Zagato at "half the price",' recalled Richard Williams. Plenty of money could be made from the project, reasoned Gauntlett, and there was. It was a brilliant marketing strategy.

The unused DB4 GT chassis numbers occurred in the midst of the Zagato production run so it was decided to construct the cars using Zagato coachwork according to Ercole Spada's original design. AML had already renewed acquaintances with Zagato during the V8 Zagato project and the carrozzeria was looking for work outside Italy because the bulk of the Italian motor industry was under Fiat control, which engaged its own designers.

'Just prior to the [AMR] team being formed we [RS Williams Ltd.] were commissioned by AML Ltd. to build the four remaining DB4 GT Zagatos. These were to be known as the Sanction II cars,'[ii] said Williams.

Approval for the project was given in 1987, 'when Peter Livanos and I owned Aston Martin and Aston owned half of Zagato so no one was in a position to say no,' said Gauntlett. 'Gianni [Zagato] was a willing accomplice of course.'

Williams was commissioned to oversee the Sanction IIs, but he was already committed to the AMR programme. The Zagato project was put on hold. The winding down of the AMR World Sports Car Team in 1990 enabled Williams to complete the project.

RS Williams produced four rolling chassis to DB4 GT specification from three DB4s and one DB5 platform, with extra strengthening to improve torsional rigidity, at its workshops in Cobham. The first chassis was finished and shipped to Carrozzeria Zagato in Milan in January 1989. The last of the four chassis was completed and shipped in April.

Williams' own DB4 GT Zagato (DB4GT/0181/L) was sent on ahead to Zagato's workshops, as Zagato still owned the copyright to the design. It was stripped, studied and new patterns were taken so that the bodies for the Sanction IIs could be replicated as closely as possible. Only two employees from 1960 were still working at the famous coachbuilder and because the tooling and bucks had been disposed of years ago the four cars were actually completed in the workshops of ex-

Top: The beautifully styled DB4 GT by Touring was unveiled at the 1959 London Motor Show **Above:** The DB4 GT Zagato was one of Ercole Spada's first designs **Opposite:** 2VEV is among the most famous genuine DB4 GT Zagatos; it competed at Le Mans in 1961 for the Essex Racing Stable

ii 'Sanction' was a term used by some carmakers in the past. It eventually fell out of favour and was replaced by 'Mark'.

Zagato employee, Mario Galbiatti. Michael Bowler, who worked closely with Zagato on the V8 Zagatos, acted as liaison between the British and Italian companies.

Once each of the four rolling chassis had been bodied to original specification, they were painted in Richard Williams' RSW Green. 'This colour was specially formulated by us and has been used on our DB4 lightweights, my own DB4 GT Zagato and the Sanction II cars,' said Williams. The nearly completed cars were shipped back to England to be finished and road tested at RS Williams under the watchful eye of Project Manager and Director of RS Williams Ltd., Neil Thompson. The end result was a complete success: the Sanction II cars were almost indistinguishable from the originals. 'Very few people would be able to see the difference,' said Williams.

Outwardly, the only discernible differences were the Borrani 15-inch wheels and larger 205/70 VR15 Goodyear Eagle tyres in place of the original 16-inch wheels and 6.00 x 16 Avon Turbospeed Mk IIs. Small adjustments were also made to the front suspension geometry, including a different, stronger anti-roll bar with altered pick-up points and revised spring rates and dampers and the live rear axle, which featured different damper settings. The differential ratio was also changed from 3.31:1 to 3.07:1. Three of the bonnets incorporated a trio of Zagato-style bubbles, while a single example incorporated a DB4-style single bonnet bulge. Inside, the interior faithfully replicated the originals.

The original six-cylinder engine's capacity was increased from 3670 cc to 4212 cc, like Williams' DB4 Lightweight racers. The engines retained a twin plug head while the compression ratio was changed from the original 9.7:1 to 9.82:1. The triple Weber 50 DCO1/SP carburettors were also fitted with extended inlet manifolds and alternators took the place of the original dynamos.

The original DB4 GT Zagato engines produced a true 272 bhp @ 6000 rpm and 250 lb/ft of torque @ 3700 rpm. The new 4.2-litre engine in the Sanction II cars boasted a genuine 352 bhp @ 6000 rpm and 330 lb/ft of torque @ 4600 rpm. The new cars were the best of both worlds; almost identical to the prized originals, they were more powerful and better to drive due to unseen and sympathetic changes.

Model	Weight (lb)	0-60 mph (seconds)	Top speed (mph)	Power (bhp)
DB4 GT Zagato	2550	6.1	153.5	272
DB4 GT Zagato Sanction II	2798	5.5	160	352

All four cars were completed by July 1991 and with Gianni Zagato, Victor Gauntlett and Mario Galbiatti in attendance, were unveiled to their new owners at RS Williams Ltd. in Cobham on 22 July 1991, 31 years after the original made its debut. The cars sold for a rumoured £750,000 and have since commanded very high resale prices, but have not attracted the fanatical following of the originals, which sell for a good deal more.

Debate still continues regarding the Sanction cars. Perhaps the last word should be left to Gauntlett, who said at the launch in 1991, 'It is nonsense to regard [the Zagato Sanction IIs] as part of the original line ... as far as I'm concerned a production line is like a car because it has a continuous history and our production line for the Zagato does not have a continuous history ... they are approved replicas blessed by Aston and Zagato. So these are true Works-approved replicas. To me "Works replica" is an honourable expression.'[8]

Victor Gauntlett

Victor Gauntlett was born in 1942 and, after leaving school, joined the RAF before entering the oil industry in 1963. After working for BP and CFP he set up his own business, Pace Petroleum, in 1972. Through Pace, Gauntlett funded many motoring events and was Nigel Mansell's personal sponsor during his early Formula One career.

Gauntlett bought his first Aston Martin because he had 'had a pretty good time of it in the 1970s with Pace Petroleum.' On 5 May 1980, Gauntlett was driving around Brands Hatch with friend Alan Curtis in his Speed Six Bentley. Curtis told Gauntlett that Aston Martin was facing financial difficulty and capital was needed, to which Gauntlett replied, 'Well, you haven't asked me.'

Gauntlett considered his support of Aston Martin as 'industrial sponsorship'. 'We were sponsoring left, right and centre, why not sponsor a decent bit of British traditional engineering?' he thought. On 28 May 1980 he invested £250,000 and became a 10 percent stakeholder in AML through Pace Petroleum. Shortly afterwards Gauntlett was appointed a director of the company and upon the departure of Alan Curtis and Peter Sprague he took joint ownership of AML in partnership with CH Industrials in December 1980. In January 1981 he became Executive Chairman of the company.

Gauntlett launched Aston Martin Tickford in 1981 and took a shareholding in the Nimrod racing programme. He persuaded the Livanos family in late 1984 to purchase 75 percent of the company, while retaining 25 percent. In 1987 Gauntlett, along with Peter Livanos and Walter Hayes, was instrumental in Ford Motor Company buying 75 percent of Aston Martin. Part of the deal was that Gauntlett was to stay in charge of the company for three years. He stayed longer, leaving in September 1991.

Under Gauntlett's direction, Aston Martin produced the AMV8, Lagonda, V8 Vantage, V8 Volante, V8 Vantage Volante, V8 Vantage Zagato, Zagato Volante, Virage, DB4 GT Zagato Sanction II and AMR-1. He also initiated the 'DB4 for the nineties' project, which became the DB7. Walter Hayes succeeded him as Executive Chairman.

In preparation for his life beyond Aston Martin, Gauntlett set up Proteus Petroleum in 1988. After leaving AML he continued with the business until selling it in 1998. In 2002 he became Chairman of Automotive Technik Holdings, a manufacturer of military vehicles.

Throughout that time Gauntlett remained active, serving as a council member of The Air League, a trustee of the National Motor Museum, the RAF Museum and the Museum of Army Flying. He was also a Freeman of the City of London and a Master of the Worshipful Company of Coachmakers and Coach Harness Makers. He was a great enthusiast of British automotive and aviation history and owned a number of important cars and aeroplanes including a Blower Bentley and a DB4 GT Zagato along with a De Havilland Rapide and Mk I Spitfire. Gauntlett died suddenly on 31 March 2003 at age 60.

Top to bottom: Engines were expanded to 4.2 litres; Running gear included David Brown four-speed manual gearboxes; Rolling chassis taking shape; Superleggera lattice framework to which the lightweight aluminium panels were attached

From left: Victor Gauntlett, Mario Galbiatti and Gianni Zagato all played a part in the creation of the Sanction II cars

ZAGATO CAR S.R.L.
stabilimento e uffici Amministrativi
20017 Terrazzano di Rho (Milano) Italia
Tel. (02) 9301635 Telex. 332526 ZAGATO I
Telefax (02) 9310285 ZAGATO I

Cod. Fiscale IVA 01257260184
Sede Soc. in Bergamo - Cap. Soc. L. 1.380.000.000
Tribunale di Bergamo - Reg. Soc. 16937 Vol. 15986
C.C.I.A.A. Bg. 187636 - C.C.I.A.A. Mi. 1058551

June 1990.

Victor Gauntlett Esq.,
49-51, Cheval Place,
London, SW7 1EW.

Dear Victor

I am delighted to confirm that work is progressing well on the four DB4 GT Zagato works replicas and we hope that Galbiati will have them all pannelled before the Summer holidays. Whilst I know that you felt it appropriate to pay Zagato a fee regarding these cars Elio and I feel that it is unnecessary and inappropriate in the light of our relationship over the past few years. We are plesed to help in this project that will see four more great motorcars on the road. Indeed with our two companies involved in the project the word replica is almost unnecessary!

Should you need any further help on the project please let me know and it will be my pleasure to assist.

Best regards

Gianni Zagato.

Top: Gianni Zagato politely declines a licensing fee offer by Victor Gauntlett Middle: Bodies undergoing construction at Mario Galbiatti's workshops in Italy Above: Richard Williams performing the final inspection before handing over to new owners

DB4 GT Zagato Sanction II
1991

Chassis: Steel box section chassis, steel superstructure

Body: Aluminium two-seat coupe styled by Ercole Spada of Carrozzeria Zagato

Suspension: Front – Independent with transverse unequal wishbones, coaxial spring damper units and anti-roll bar Rear – Live axle with coil springs, parallel trailing links, telescopic dampers and Watt's linkage

Brakes: Girling discs (front and rear)

Steering: Power-assisted rack and pinion

Wheels: 15-inch Borrani alloy

Tyres: Goodyear Eagle NCT 205/70 VR15

Transmission: David Brown four-speed manual; final drive 3.07:1. Limited-slip differential. Rear-wheel drive

Engine: 4212 cc alloy in-line six-cylinder with a chain-driven twin overhead camshaft with two valves and two plugs per cylinder. Compression ratio 9.82:1. Twin SU fuel pumps and three 50 DCO1/SP Weber carburettors

Power: 352 bhp/262 kW @ 6000 rpm
330 lb/ft/447 Nm of torque @ 4600 rpm

Top speed: 160 mph/257 km/h

Dimensions:

Length	13 ft 10.5 in/4229 mm
Width	5 ft 6 in/1676 mm
Height	4 ft 2 in/1271 mm
Wheelbase	7 ft 9 in/2362 mm
Weight	2798 lb/1269 kg

Price when new: £750,000

Number built: 4

6.3-Litre Virage

When enough is not enough

Initially, Aston Martin was selling every Virage it could build. But it soon became evident that the new model was falling short of customer satisfaction. The Virage had gained a reputation for being a huge step sideways for Aston Martin. The revised 32-valve V8 engine was able to meet worldwide emissions requirements, but it was thought by some that the Virage was no better than the V8 model it replaced – and in some respects worse.

Journalists complained about the unsatisfactory suspension layout, overly large turning circle, dashboard instrumentation and underwhelming performance. It became apparent that some changes had to be made to the existing car.

As part of the Customer Satisfaction Programme, cars were brought into Works Service and, under the direction of Andy Warner, 32 customer service items were dealt with in an effort to improve the Virage. The modifications were designed by Mike Loasby and incorporated onto the Factory experimental car by Richard Williams prior to the inclusion on production cars.

> The more powerful engine necessitated further modifications and a lot of development work to the rest of the car to make it the complete package.

Newly appointed Executive Chairman, Walter Hayes, had already initiated development work on the Virage Vantage in 1990. However, it became apparent the new Vantage would require much more than just engine modifications and Aston Martin's stretched development engineers would not be able to complete the car for some time.

To bridge the gap while the Vantage was in development, AML gave approval for an 'enhanced' Virage. Victor Gauntlett had already approved the project before he resigned and Hayes enthusiastically received it, announcing the new 6.3-litre Virage on 28 January 1992.

'In 1983 one of our technicians who came off the shop floor, like myself, was David Eales. He was a very good technician and had gone overseas many times as Product Support Engineer,'

The 6.3-litre Virage was comprehensively redesigned to produce what many thought the Virage should have been in the first place

recalled Kingsley Riding-Felce. 'He was travelling the world fixing all of the problems on customer cars and was asked by Bill Bannard if he would join as Service Manager.

'We worked very well together and we became aware that customers were coming to us saying that they needed more power and wanting to know how performance could be improved. Prior to that, the company had provided some development on the two-valve V8 engine, developing bigger air box induction and larger exhaust diameters for the manifolds. Breathing had been improved, but we really wanted more power to meet our customers' expectations.

'In the meantime, while we were thinking about this, Richard Williams, one of the leading Aston Martin specialists, was working on a programme to make the 5.3-litre engine 1000 cc bigger. There are a lot of good reasons why 6.3 litres was thought to be a very good configuration. There was one red car, 7 EXY, which Richard used as a demonstration car to promote the 6.3 engine. An article in *Classic Car* caused a great deal of interest – so much interest that David and I said we would really like an opportunity to sell the 6.3 engine.

'At this time Richard was contemplating closing his business and concentrating fully on running Aston Martin's Group C Racing Team up in Milton Keynes. So we asked Victor Gauntlett whether it was possible to purchase the car and the intellectual rights to the 6.3 engine from Richard Williams. That in fact was what we did and we received an invoice dated 6 April 1989 for the purchase.

'So we had this car with a tremendous engine, but further development was needed as we realised the power far exceeded the capabilities of the car and its handling. Our engineers were extremely busy at the time developing our new car for the future so there was not an opportunity for them to pick up our requirements. So we went to an outside handling specialist called Rhoddy Harvey-Bailey.

'Rhoddy is well-known in the motoring world; he is an extremely clever handling and ride specialist; his background was with Alfas in Italy. Rhoddy came down, talked to us, went away and did a development programme on the car for us, then came back and really transformed the car. Not only did he improve the ride and handling, but also the balance of the car, which made such a big difference in the way it braked and the way it felt on the road.

'It was a much better balance for the performance that the 6.3 engine was now giving out, so we decided we were now in a position to sell this package. We told customers that if they were going to have the engine done, they had to have the suspension done as well. This involved new front and rear anti-roll bars that had not been previously fitted, new springs, new dampers and so on. It was a whole new package. We had tremendous success with it and we went on to do a lot of conversions.'

Having succeeded with the two-valve 6.3-litre engine, Works Service turned its attention to the Virage. 'We wanted to have a new car for Virage conversions, a new demonstrator with a

Works Service created the 6.3-litre Virage due to customer demand for more performance and greater handling

four-valve engine. We had managed to get a Vantage body-in-white from our engineering team, which was being considered for the Vantage. We really wanted to make this car very special, with a real macho look that our customers wanted. A lot of time was spent trying to get it right and to get it sorted, because we wanted to offer a Virage upgrade that we had offered with the two-valve 6.3-litre Vantage.'

Principal Engineer for Special Vehicle Operations, Steve Bolton, was given the task of transforming the car. 'At that time we also had help from somebody, very quietly, who was going to play a leading part in the future: Steve Bolton,' said Riding-Felce. 'Steve is an incredible engineer; he has been involved in all the Works Service jobs since the 6.3.

'He really is a *whole car* engineer, which is very rare. He specialises in things like suspension, ride and handling, but he also has a very good understanding of everything else. He is very quiet with an easy way of going about things; he really is a genius and has some wonderful ideas. He has a full understanding of what customers want and what we want. That was our first time working with Steve, and he gave up a lot of his extra time above and beyond, which is so typical of him, in developing the 6.3-litre package.

'What was required from me was to work on something that would differentiate the car dynamically and visually,' Bolton recalled. 'I already realised that one of the key features we could use was already evident in the Vantage.

'We decided to introduce the 18-inch Goodyear tyres on 10-inch-wide rims, which were on the V8 Vantage, onto the 6.3 Virage. The car looked significantly different because the wheel arches had to be pulled out. The styling cues for the rest of the body meant that it had a more aggressive front spoiler splitter and some changes to the rear.

'The adoption of the 18-inch wheels also meant we could use larger brakes, rather than the Virage's standard brakes. We went to AP Racing, a respected industry leader in brakes, and we had some bespoke brakes made that were able to sit inside the wheels.'

To accommodate the large wheel and tyre combination, both the front and rear fenders were cut and flared out by the skilful body builders at Newport Pagnell. A unique boot-mounted spoiler, deeper sills, an extended rear valance and a bigger front air dam were fashioned from glass fibre and neatly incorporated into the design.

Another important body modification was the reinstatement of the horizontal air vents behind the front wheel arches. First incorporated into the prototype DB4 of 1958, the air vents have become one of Aston Martin's most enduring trademarks. This feature was removed from the first Virages, even though the original design featured them.

No design drawings exist for this car; the body modifications were all carried out by hand and eye. David Eales recalled, 'The flared arches and wheels, side vents and sill features were sculptured out of clay in the Service Department prior [to the work commencing].'

Riding-Felce: 'We started with the wheels and we really started to work on the rear wing shapes, which took a lot of time, a lot of evening cups of coffee with a lot of thought, but we knew instinctively what we wanted. We wanted the car to have haunches, we wanted it to look beefy, but we wanted it to look sexy. We wanted it to look like it had put on a little bit of weight in the right places and have an elegant shape to it. We eventually got that shape, which was fantastic.'

The 6.3-litre Virage was designed as an after-market conversion to existing customers' Virages; it was not a new car. There were to be no 'official', made-to-order, 6.3-litre Virages as the Vantage was on the way. A few, however, were made for a well-known collector.

'The 6.3-litre Virage wasn't offered as a production model because it did not conform to Type Approval. Of course, in the UK you could get away with that, as many cars were modified after being registered, but in countries like Germany, this was a problem. We did discuss obtaining some limited Type Approval but as the Vantage was already in development, this was not considered effective,' said Eales.

The enhanced car was never called Virage Vantage. 'At one point, it was seriously considered as the Virage Vantage,' said Eales, 'but the one flaw with the car was the rear suspension. The Virage used a triangular rear sub-frame, which, in hindsight, was of poor design, as you would get a lot of "squat" when accelerating. To overcome this on the 6.3-litre version we took away the rubber mounting and fitted rose joint suspension. This was also done on the front and the changes improved the car's handling considerably. But as a recognised weakness, on the Vantage a different rear chassis was later developed which made the car even better. Of course, we couldn't just change the Virage chassis without re-Type Approval.'

'In the meantime,' continued Riding-Felce, 'we were developing the engine and obviously didn't have the support that we needed, because everybody was very busy trying to develop the Vantage. So we worked with Tickford Engineering and we put a plan together with David Morgan, who had left Aston Martin to go and join Tickford many years earlier. He knew the Aston Martin V8 very, very well. David was super. We worked with him and his team and eventually we got to a point where we had 465 bhp with a very high level of torque for the four-valve engine that we could put into the car.'

'During the early days the V8 engine stood up pretty well but from around 1980 onwards it wasn't good enough,' said David Morgan. 'It was a mistake that Aston Martin didn't go for a stretch to around 6.0 litres; this would have given the car a much-needed lift in performance and, I am sure, better sales.'

'The 32-valve engine was initially poor, but the 6.3-litre 32-valve engine that I up-rated as a project for Aston Martin Service produced a performance level that should have been in production during the mid 1980s. We supplied some 70 sets of update kits to Service, for the after-market. They had about the same performance as the Tickford 5.3-litre race engine used in EMKA and Nimrod.'

Modifications to the 6347 cc engine included bore and stroke modifications, new crankshaft with special Cosworth racing

Wide Body Volante

When the Virage Volante was announced in March 1992, it too became available with the optional 6.3-litre upgrade, provided the car was first road-registered. All the coupe's enhancements and body modifications could also be incorporated into the Volante. Several standard Volantes were converted to resemble the 6.3-litre cars while retaining the original running gear. These 5.3-litre cars are referred to as Wide Body Volantes.

Body modifications, including the flared wheel arches, were carried out by hand and eye

Top: Large AP Racing disc brakes, with ABS, hid behind 17-inch OZ alloy wheels **Above:** Like the 5.3-litre Virage engine before it, all 6.3-litre units were 'signed' by the engine builder

pistons and a compression ratio of 9.5:1. 'The heart of the kit were highly-modified cylinder heads with the valve centre moved, ports bored out and carefully controlled fettling, periodic bench flow testing as quality control, larger diameter solid tappet cups, larger valves all-round and specially redesigned high-lift camshafts, which vastly improved breathing. The all-important larger diameter exhaust system achieved better flow-through by the incorporation of tuned-length manifolds,' said Morgan.

The 6.3-litre Virage also incorporated modified Weber/Alpha sequential fuel injection and a re-mapped engine management system. Sports mufflers and special exhaust catalysts were added. The changes produced a 40 percent increase in available power. Transmission options included a five- or six-speed ZF manual or a three- or four-speed Torqueflite automatic gearbox.

The engine, which boasted a plaque on its black cam covers proudly announcing 'Built to 6.3-litre specification', was tested at 465 bhp @ 5750 rpm and 460 lb/ft of torque @ 4400 rpm. (Aston Martin's literature claimed 500 bhp @ 6000 rpm and 480 lb/ft of torque @ 5800 rpm).

The more powerful engine necessitated further modifications and much development work to the rest of the car to make it the complete package. 'So we eventually had these huge AP brakes which were wonderful, we had these huge wheels and tyres, we had the 465 bhp engine and we had a hell of a package to take to the market [at the end of] 1991. That's really when we launched the Virage 6.3-litre conversion,' said Riding-Felce.

'After the first car had been made,' said Bolton, 'one of the main problems that we encountered was that the car had excessive rear squat, whereby the increase in torque available meant that under acceleration the rear of the car would squat down, which would mean that the front would rise.

'This is a peculiarity of the Virage's suspension, because the thrust lines between the wheel centre and where it drives into the body were at an inclined angle, which means that when you drive the car quickly the rear of the car bobs down. Over the course of a few days we devised a way of making a linkage that decoupled the forward thrust axis for the lateral thrust axis to eliminate the squat.

'This was done with a linkage consisting of two rose joints and two spherical bearings, which raised the thrust axis by 1.7 inches, which was sufficient to eliminate the squat and turn the car into something more dynamic. That was the beginning of the 6.3-litre Virage and of creating special vehicles for special customers.'

The front and rear suspension was reworked to include different spring and shock absorber ratings, revised roll bars and wishbone mountings to cope with the additional power. A first for Aston Martin was the incorporation of a Bosch-designed ABS system into the braking package. In addition

Vantage-bodied 6.3-litre Virage

Another 6.3-litre Virage variant exists; the Vantage-bodied 6.3-litre Virage. 'We have completed a number of Vantage-bodied 6.3 conversions,' explained Kingsley Riding-Felce. 'In other words, when the Vantage came out, a number of customers bought their 6.3 Virages back and we put a Vantage front and rear on them. That makes these cars very unique in that they look like Vantages, but they have 6.3-litre engines.'

the AMR-1-derived 14.0-inch discs were, at the time, the largest to be fitted to a road car. The Virage's Avon tyres were also updated to 285/45 ZR18 Goodyear Eagles, fitted to 18-inch OZ alloy wheels.

The interior was little altered from the Virage. However a CD player, telephone and TV system could be installed as options. To complete the conversion the car was re-sprayed and detailed. The first 6.3-litre Virage was delivered in early 1992.

'I will never forget David and I taking our first drive into Milton Keynes in that car,' said Riding-Felce. 'The customer had a car that was an absolute pleasure to drive, a lot of fun, a lot of the right kind of noises and what a lot of our customers wanted. We did a great many conversions; it was a very, very successful programme.'

Autocar achieved 0–60 mph in 6.1 seconds and 0–100 in 13.8 seconds in wet conditions and admitted that better times were probably achievable in different circumstances. But it couldn't match the 0–60 mph in 5.5 seconds, 0–100 mph in 11.5 seconds and the 174 mph top speed claimed by Aston Martin.

Model	Weight (lb)	0-60 mph (seconds)	Top speed (mph)	Power (bhp)
Virage	4233	6.8	155	306
6.3-litre Virage	4340 (approx)	6.1	174 (claimed)	465

Works Service's 6.3-litre conversion worked extremely well as it kept client interest in the marque and improved the reputation of Aston Martin, if not the Virage. But it was much more than that. In a difficult economic climate, the success of the 6.3-litre Virage provided Aston Martin with much-needed work and capital while the world waited for the upcoming Vantage.

David Eales makes a point to Kingsley Riding-Felce at Works Service during 6.3-litre development

6.3-Litre Virage
1992–

Chassis: Steel box-section chassis, steel superstructure

Body: Aluminium 2+2 coupe or convertible styled by John Heffernan; modified by Works Service

Suspension: Front – Independent with unequal length wishbones, coil springs, coaxial spring damper units and anti-roll bar
Rear – de Dion axle, radius arms, Watt's linkage, coil springs, telescopic dampers and anti-roll bar

Brakes: Servo-assisted 355 mm ventilated discs with AP Racing four-piston callipers (front); 280 mm ventilated discs with AP Racing four-piston callipers (rear). ABS

Steering: Power-assisted rack and pinion

Wheels: 18-inch OZ alloy

Tyres: Goodyear Eagle GS-D 285/45 ZR18

Transmission: ZF five- or six-speed manual; final drive 3.54:1 or 3.33:1. Torqueflite three- or four-speed automatic; final drive 3.058:1. Limited-slip differential. Rear-wheel drive

Engine: 6347 cc alloy V8 with twin chain-driven overhead camshafts per bank and four valves per cylinder. Compression ratio 9.5:1. Weber-Alpha sequential fuel injection

Power: 465 bhp/347 kW @ 5750 rpm
460 lb/ft/624 Nm of torque @ 4400 rpm

Top speed: 174 mph/280 km/h (claimed)

Dimensions:
Length	15 ft 7 in/4737 mm
Width	6 ft 3 in/1944 mm
Height	4 ft 3.5 in/1321 mm
Wheelbase	8 ft 6.75 in/2610 mm
Weight	4340 lb/1969 kg (approx)

Price of conversion: Approximately £50,000 depending upon exact specification

Number converted: 65 (approx)[i]

i   Includes 2- and 4-valve conversions

Virage Volante

Soft top tradition continues

With the Virage coupe launched and successfully in production, thoughts turned to producing a convertible. A speculative two-seater prototype was unveiled at the British International Motor Show in October 1990. Some customers, however, rued the fact that the show car lacked rear seats. Aston Martin added them and the two-seater idea was abandoned.

The 2+2 model was later unveiled at the Geneva Motor Show in March 1992, with production starting at chassis number AM1CNR60001. The Volante proved so popular that the coupe was quickly overshadowed. Coupe production never recovered and only around 165 further examples were constructed.

A convertible was part of Heffernan's original styling exercise and in anticipation the coupe chassis was designed with ample torsional strengthening. 'As we didn't want to have to change it too drastically when we came to do the Volante we designed [the coupe] from the start without a roof,'[9] said Design Engineer Malcolm Pearson. AML's Research and Development Department and engineering consultant, Hawtal Whiting, undertook development to production stage.

> Production by this time had dropped to about one car per week with Volantes accounting for almost all of that output.

With some notable differences, the Volante closely resembled the coupe in specification which, by this time, had come in for some running development changes. In March 1993, the Volante received a new four-speed automatic transmission; manual gearboxes were a no-cost extra. Final drive ratios were also lowered to achieve better response at the sake of top end speed. New 17-inch alloy wheels and 255/60 ZR17 Avon tyres and ABS were included, as were the trademark air vents.

In response to customer criticism, the Virage's all-in-one dashboard was revised. The new fascia reverted to traditional dials housed in walnut, which improved the interior markedly. Revised switchgear, an updated entertainment system and a new steering wheel with airbag were also incorporated.

When the popular Volante arrived, production of the Virage coupe almost ceased; the dual air vents are absent from this car

'With these changes the Virage has become an even better car from both the driving and aesthetic points of view,' said Walter Hayes. 'Our customer research has shown that the original concept, although a very good one, could be improved upon and that we have done.'

The Volante included a fully lined, power-operated hood, complete with heated glass window and drop-down rear-quarter windows. With the hood raised the car possessed a sleek profile. When lowered, however, the tonneau cover was cumbersome, though it was better than the two-seat Volante

prototype. The hood also encroached into the boot space and already small rear seats and hampered rearward vision. If constructed, the two-seater, with its luggage platform and lockable stowage compartment, would have been a welcome production option.

Aston Martin had always been vulnerable to recession and by 1992 found itself in a very difficult trading market. Production by this time had dropped to about one car per week with Volantes accounting for almost all of that output. Virage coupes were only being built to order.

Aston Martin Juniors

Launched alongside the Virage Volante at the Geneva Motor Show in 1992 was the 4:7 scale Virage Volante Junior (pictured right, below); an £18,000 fully working 'toy' for 'the younger Aston Martin owner who will not yet have had the opportunity or age qualification to obtain a driving licence.'

Developed by Kingsley Riding-Felce with the assistance of outside suppliers, the cars featured accurate glass-fibre Volante bodies, Connolly leather seats and Wilton carpet, a radio/cassette, Honda GXV 160 5.5-horsepower unleaded four-stroke engines, five-speed automatic transmission and suspension by shock absorbers and coil springs. Five were built, three right-hand-drive and two left-hand-drive, comprising chassis numbers 90001–90005.

Between July 1986 and January 1991 Aston Martin built 25 V8 Volante Juniors. Featuring chassis numbers J001–J0025, the authentic scale replicas featured Honda GXV 160 vertical-shaft engines and fully trimmed interiors.

At the height of the original James Bond phenomenon Aston Martin apprentices built two one-third scale DB5 Volantes (pictured right, above) with 'secret agent' extras including operational water jets. One was presented to HRH Queen Elizabeth II on a Royal visit to Newport Pagnell in April 1966, the other was built for HRH Prince Reza of Persia.

Convertible versions of the Virage were very elegant, but as the 'V' cars evolved they grew further from their sporting origins

Diamond Jubilee Virage Volante

To celebrate the Aston Martin Owners' Club (AMOC) Diamond Jubilee in 1995, AML, in association with Cartier of London, created a one-off Virage Volante Cartier Special Edition. The silver automatic convertible, chassis number AMCCR60200 – with wide-body coachwork, a standard 5.3-litre engine and adorned with Cartier diamond, emerald and ruby jewellery – was unveiled at the Silver Jubilee Ball at the Dorchester Hotel in March 1995. The whole package was reputed to be worth £750,000.

Virage Volante dashboard instrumentation returned to a more traditional layout after criticism of the Virage's all-in-one instrument cluster

Virage Volante
1992–1995

Chassis: Steel box-section chassis, steel superstructure

Body: Aluminium 2+2 convertible styled by John Heffernan

Suspension: Front – Independent with transverse unequal length wishbones, coaxial spring damper units and anti-roll bar
Rear – de Dion axle, radius arms, Watt's linkage, coil springs and telescopic dampers

Brakes: Servo-assisted PBR 330 mm ventilated discs (front); 289 mm solid discs (rear). ABS

Steering: Power-assisted rack and pinion

Wheels: 17-inch OZ alloy

Tyres: Avon Turbospeed 255/60 ZR17

Transmission: Torqueflite three- or four-speed automatic with Sport and Comfort modes; final drive 3.54:1. ZF five-speed manual; final drive 3.54:1. Limited-slip differential. Rear-wheel drive

Engine: 5340 cc alloy V8 with twin chain-driven overhead camshafts per bank and four valves per cylinder. Compression ratio 9.5:1. Weber-Marelli sequential fuel injection

Power: 306 bhp/228 kW @ 6000 rpm
340 lb/ft/ 461 Nm of torque @ 3700 rpm

Top speed: 155 mph/249 km/h

Dimensions:
Length	15 ft 7 in/4745 mm
Width	6 ft 0.5 in/1856 mm
Height	4 ft 7 in/1397 mm
Wheelbase	8 ft 6.75 in/2610 mm
Weight	4321 lb/1960 kg

Price when new: £149,000

Number built: 223

Middle: Following tradition, the folded hood was stored under a leather tonneau cover **Above:** The Volante's hood contained a heated glass window which allowed for adequate rearward vision

i   A two-seat Virage Volante prototype, DP2054, was unveiled in October 1990 at the British International Motor Show but did not enter production. Two were constructed but DP2054/1 was used for crash testing. The left-hand-drive DP2054/2 survives but has since been modified to a 2+2 with a blue-printed high-performance engine modified by Works Service.

Virage Shooting Brake
Aston Martin's own estate wagon

Aston Martin Shooting Brakes have been constructed on DB5, DB6 and DBS chassis over the years by body builders Harold Radford and FLM Panelcraft, but never by Aston Martin itself. The John Heffernan-based Virage Shooting Brake was a first for Aston Martin, being either hand-built from scratch or converted entirely at Newport Pagnell, not contracted to an outside body builder.

Code-named DP2099, the first Virage Shooting Brake was unveiled at the Geneva Motor Show on 3 March 1992 and the first production model, chassis number AMSLL50435, was delivered in the same year.

'It is a splendid long-distance touring car as well as being extraordinarily versatile, and great attention has been paid to comfort as well as function,' said Walter Hayes upon its launch. 'It is expensive because it is unique and it will provide a lifetime of dependable service for sportsmen and dog owners, Embassies and golf clubs, expensive hotels and classic car enthusiasts.'

Even though the first two examples came straight off the factory floor, subsequent owners had to have a road-registered Virage to hand over to the factory for conversion if they wanted a Shooting Brake. It was aimed at hunting or golf enthusiasts, but in truth it was simply a more practical and useable high-performance motor car.

The inspiration for the Shooting Brake arose from a difficult trading period for Aston Martin. 'In 1989 Astons wanted some work done on the Virage,' said Mike Loasby, 'because the Virage that had been introduced into production wasn't doing what it should have done and we made a lot of detail changes to make the car acceptable. That effort came to an end for me and there was a bit of a lull, and it was decided we should make some two-door Estate cars.

'The idea was, to cut down the amount of work, to use an Escort rear door and modify it to fit, which we did on the first couple, not entirely satisfactorily because they were very heavy. We did it in the production department with me overseeing the project. We chopped the back end of the car and the whole roof off and started on the shop floor, literally.' The compact and well-designed rear end also made use of Renault 21 Savannah Estate taillights and incorporated thoughtful design touches like a rear window wiper with drainage recess and re-routed exhaust pipes.

Shooting Brake versions of the Virage produced almost the same performance as the donor coupe with the added benefit of more storage space

It was a first for Aston Martin as the Shooting Brakes were either hand-built from scratch or converted entirely at Newport Pagnell, not contracted to an outside body builder.

Top: The Ford Escort rear door blended very well with the existing Virage body work **Above:** Front passenger accommodation remained much the same as for the Virage coupe

The Shooting Brake was almost identical in specification to the Virage. Just about any option could be accommodated, but the basic design featured a two-door, four-seater body with upward-lifting rear door supported by gas struts. The design included individual fold-down rear seats with a 50/50 split, a large parcel shelf for luggage, luggage blind, electrically operated rear ventilation windows, fold-down dog guard grille, rear storage pockets, luggage tie-down points, carpeted rear floor and fold-out flap to protect the rear bumper when loading.

'We did two-door Shooting Brake Virages for various European customers with bespoke fitted luggage. I designed these various luggage boxes of differing sizes that fitted in the back for clothes, shoes and make up and things like that. The last one that I did cost £10,000 for a set of luggage! Another one had a special briefcase mounting; things like that. I am a master of constructing things out of cardboard. What I used to do was envisage the thing and make it up in cardboard and have the wood workers and trimmers make it up in the proper materials. It would look beautiful,' said Loasby.

Due to the revised roofline, the Virage Shooting Brake provided greater rear headroom and, with slightly improved accommodation and a possible 28 cubic feet of luggage space, about four times that of the coupe, the car became an honest carriage for four adults and their luggage. It was a big vehicle, but only half an inch longer than the coupe, which says rather a lot. The rest of the dimensions were almost identical, including the wheelbase. The Shooting Brake was 132 lb heavier than the coupe and had a claimed 152 mph and 0–60 mph in 7.6 seconds performance; not far short of the coupe. It was touted as 'The fastest estate car in the world.'

All Virage Shooting Brakes were originally configured in right-hand drive, but two were subsequently returned to the factory for conversion to left-hand drive. Several examples were finished in green and a single example, the second prototype DP2099/2, was painted in 'Martini Rosso' burgundy. 'We did a green one and a red one. I only did two or three at the time. We certainly did some in Service, too and we did some 6.3-litre conversions,' said Loasby.

Kingsley Riding-Felce: 'We had carried out some two-door Shooting Brake conversions on Virages for customers, because the engineering work had been done. We did this specialist coachwork in Works Service, but it was becoming clear that the world was a changing place – legislation did not allow us to do this kind of work in all markets. There were different rules and regulations in Germany, in Europe and in the US, so it became more than evident that we had to redirect our thinking.'

Between 1992 and 2000, Aston Martin produced eight two-door Shooting Brakes. The first two examples were built in production from the beginning; subsequently three conversions were carried out at Works Service on Virage coupes and three from the later V8 Coupe.

Aston Martin Shooting Brakes

David Brown commissioned a DB5-based Shooting Brake (HPP 3C) for his personal use in 1965. So as not to interrupt production at Newport Pagnell, which was at an all-time high, a complete DB5 was sent to coachbuilder, Harold Radford Ltd. in London, which converted the car into a very handsome Shooting Brake (pictured below). Brown was at the height of his fame at this time and photos of him and his Shooting Brake in the social pages led to a further eleven being converted by Radford.

When the DB6 (pictured bottom) arrived, six customers ordered a practical Shooting Brake version, including David Brown. This time, the longer wheelbase and Kamm tail of the new model meant the finished design by Radford was not quite as elegant as the DB5 version. An additional three DB6 Shooting Brakes were constructed by FLM Panelcraft, which also converted a single DBS example.

Above: A V8 Coupe Shooting Brake captured in Paris; three were thus converted **Top right:** The Virage Shooting Brake still wore the Aston Martin badge

Virage Shooting Brake
1992–1999

Chassis: Steel box-section chassis, steel superstructure

Body: Aluminium four-seat Shooting Brake styled by John Heffernan

Suspension: Front – Independent with transverse unequal length wishbones, coil springs, coaxial spring damper units and anti-roll bar
Rear – de Dion axle, radius arms, Watt's linkage, coil springs and telescopic dampers

Brakes: Servo-assisted Girling 330 mm ventilated discs (front); 289 mm solid discs (rear) ABS

Steering: Power-assisted rack and pinion

Wheels: 16-inch OZ alloy

Tyres: Avon Turbospeed 255/60 ZR16

Transmission: Torqueflite four-speed automatic; final drive 3.54:1. ZF five-speed manual; final drive 3.54:1. Limited-slip differential. Rear-wheel drive

Engine: 5340 cc[i] alloy V8 with twin chain-driven overhead camshafts per bank and four valves per cylinder. Compression ratio 9.5:1. Weber-Marelli fuel injection

Power: 306 bhp/228 kW @ 6000 rpm
340 lb/ft/461 Nm of torque @ 3700 rpm

Top speed: 152 mph/245 km/h

Dimensions:
Length	15 ft 7.5 in/4757 mm
Width	6 ft 0.5 in/1856 mm
Height	4 ft 3.5 in/1320 mm
Wheelbase	8 ft 6.75 in/2610 mm
Weight	4365 lb/1980 kg

Price when new: £165,000

Number built: 8[ii]

i   6346 cc engine also offered

ii Includes three V8 Coupe conversions

Vantage
2 + 2 = 550

The naming of Aston Martin's new high-performance model made a subtle, yet telling point. Eager to distance itself from the Virage designation after its underwhelming reception, Aston Martin discarded the Virage prefix, opting instead simply for Vantage. The Virage name later disappeared altogether, replaced by the V8 Coupe in 1996. Although it appeared heavily based on the Virage, the Vantage was a new car with 60 percent new components; Aston Martin wanted people to know that.

There was always going to be a Vantage version of the Virage and historical precedents suggested the Virage be built with that in mind. The original 306-bhp engine was capable of producing more power, but its potential was not exploited – that was the Vantage's role.

'It was a transitional time for Aston Martin,' said engineer Steve Bolton. 'We had new cars coming along, which we had been working on but the company was going through some real changes. Rod Mansfield, our Engineering Director, who had been seconded from Ford Motor Company, left us, so for a short period of time we were without an Engineering Director. At that time Tom Walkinshaw was responsible for overseeing the work that we were doing for the Vantage.

'Seven customers had pre-ordered and paid deposits for Vantages so it was decided to begin by building just seven cars. Consequently, the design had to be changed because for seven vehicles you would not put down tooling to do a production run for a number of complex parts. Instead of having large forged wishbones, we sought fabricated parts that didn't require any tooling so we could still make the job, but it didn't commit the company to a large amount of expenditure.'

Development work on the Vantage started in 1989, as the first production Virages were nearing completion. Programme Manager Mike Booth arrived at Newport Pagnell at the end of 1990 when the Vantage plans were in their infancy and oversaw its overall development. Arthur Wilson was responsible for all engine development, which had already been established by the time Booth arrived.

'A computer analysis of the power requirement for the performance targets had been conducted by Andrew Marsh, who was Vantage Project Manager before Mike Booth arrived,

Although resembling the Virage, almost every body panel on the Vantage was different save for the roof and door skins

'There was some concern over the social acceptability of such power at that time, so the quoted 550 bhp was conservative.'
Arthur Wilson

Left and right: The full-size Vantage clay model under review with different wheel options

and who had previously worked for me on engine development,' said Wilson. 'This analysis had initially identified a need for 480 bhp. Later, this was to rise to 500 bhp. By this time the first development engines were running. We were still using Weber-Marelli fuel injection, which was later changed to the Ford EEC IV.'

The aim was to produce a 186-mph supercar but as power increased, other modifications were required and when the suspension and brakes were strengthened, weight crept up too. It became evident that this Vantage was going to be a more comprehensive package than past Vantages, which consisted mainly of engine upgrades.

While having a unique body and its own identity, the 1992 Vantage's engine was also more highly developed than its previous namesakes, with a horsepower differential of 79.7 percent over the Virage engine. With nearly 80 percent more power than the standard Virage, Booth was concerned the chassis, suspension and brakes were being overworked. He decided early on to have a fundamental evaluation of the car and many components were redesigned to meet the same performance potential of the engine. A total transformation incorporating body, chassis and component modifications for DP2055 was needed, hence the delay in development. The 6.3-litre Virage filled the resulting gap.

Model	Weight (lb)	0–60 mph (seconds)	Top speed (mph)	Power (bhp)
6.3-litre Virage	4340	6.1	174 (claimed)	465
Vantage	4368	4.6	186	550

It was thought at one stage the 6.3-litre Virage might detract in some way from the Vantage's presence. Fears were allayed, however, upon the 550-bhp Vantage's debut, when solid orders were received, while Works Service successfully carried on with its 6.3-litre conversions.

The V8 engine had been extensively redesigned for the Virage and then Works Service created the 465 bhp 6.3-litre version. But this was not certified, and even if it was, a lot more power

was needed if the car was to reach 186 mph. It was calculated that to propel the Vantage at this speed, no less than 500 bhp would be needed.

'As we got into the 32-valve engine things changed more and more,' recalled Wilson. The Vantage required a new-design four-valve cylinder head and extensive engine redesign to achieve 550 bhp. As an emissions-clean engine, I couldn't see the Virage engine going much further in power, certainly not a 50 percent increase. During development we had experienced this detonation problem at maximum torque that was a real problem.

'I was asked initially to produce a 460-horsepower motor, which went up to 480 fairly quickly, and then they put it up to 500. The detonation limitation of the Virage head meant that we could never get that sort of power out of it.'

Instead of basing the Vantage's 550-bhp engine on the successful 6.3-litre version, Wilson decided that the 32-valve 5.3-litre unit would be the basis. Extra power would have to be found by other means.

'About the time that I was thinking about the Vantage, the Eaton company had done the Ford Thunderbird using its M90 supercharger, which looked about the right size and had a lot of product validation testing behind it for Ford. My recommendation was that we go with the supercharger route and that we should do it in-house. Victor Gauntlett and Engineering Director Andrew Woolner accepted my recommendation and we went ahead.

'To me [supercharging] was the only way to go for that horsepower. With turbocharging, the low-speed torque was not that great until things got going and also the turbo would have to [go] before the catalyst, which would take some heat out of the exhaust, which we would need to light off the catalyst. The catalyst would also be a problem at the time because the technology was not where it is today.

'But with the supercharger, you have steam engine-like torque right from the word go. It, perhaps, doesn't make the maximum power that a turbo could, but it would have great torque all the

Model	Year	Standard engine (bhp)	Vantage engine (bhp)	% Differential
DB2	1951	105[i]	125	19.0
DB4	1963	220	250	13.6
DB5	1965	242	272	12.4
DB6	1967	242	272	12.4
DBS	1967	242	272	12.4
AMV8 (Weber carburettor)	1977	310	375	21.0
AMV8 (Oscar India)	1977	305	375	23.0
AMV8 (Weber-Marelli fuel injection)	1986	305	437 (optional)	43.3
Virage	1992	306	550	79.7

way through the range. It wouldn't interfere with the catalyst; we could run a low compression ratio so it wouldn't produce a lot of NOx. We could run short cam timing so it wouldn't produce a lot of HC or CO. It would give good fuel consumption due to the high torque at low rpm, enabling high gearing to be used during cruise. Eventually everyone was convinced and we went that way.

'We needed to have a fairly wide operating range so we didn't have to gear everything up, which would have had a bad effect on the available torque. The 6.3 580X didn't make as much power in terms of bhp as the standard 580X 5.3, purely because it didn't rev. It had a lot more torque but not the horsepower, nor did it make it at the right rpm for a 186-plus-mph car.'

As Wilson developed the engine he was able to produce more and more power until he was told by Booth to 'take it back a bit'. 'The torque figure was in the 600-plus range. We were on target for power at 500-plus horsepower, but the torque was raising concerns over transmission reliability. I changed the cam timing to push the power up-range, which gave a very flat torque curve and reduced the peak torque to a more tolerable 550 lb/ft. Power went up to 550-plus, which is why we came to overshoot the horsepower target for the project. There was some concern over the social acceptability of such power at that time, so the quoted 550 bhp was conservative.

'[Each] Vantage engine cost around £12,000 to make, taking one man about one-and-a-half weeks to build. It wasn't thrown together, let's put it that way. Having said that, our engines were [always] expensive, due to the low volumes.'

A Ford engine management system, coupled with a new crankshaft, Cosworth pistons and other modifications, helped produce 550 bhp and 550 lb/ft. The engine was mated to a ZF six-speed manual gearbox, the same as used on the 6.3-litre Virage. The Vantage also boasted suspension changes to cope with the extra power and to overcome the shortcomings of the Virage design.

The development programme was protracted and inevitable problems arose. 'We were getting a phenomenon called axle tramp,' recalled Bolton, 'whereby if you do a fast start, rather than the car just spinning its wheels, the back axle would start leaping up and down. There were a number of different ways of addressing the problem to control the rear wheels while this huge amount of power was trying to be deployed. We needed stronger springs and shock absorbers, which was fine on a race car or dragster, but it totally ruined the ride of the car when you wanted to be civilised on the road.

'We made seven cars at that point but we still had to find the fix for this power to be deployed without the rear axle tearing itself out. The big breakthrough was made when we converted the car to a torque tube. A prototype tube was made by folding up steel plate, which was used in the chassis. We cut the mounting off the existing axle and welded them to it. It was a totally standard prop shaft complete with universal joints.'

The experimental turbo-charged 728 bhp V8 Bulldog; Aston Martin's engineers preferred the supercharging route for the new Vantage

---

i   Exaggerated and fluctuating power figures have been quoted by the Factory and motoring journalists in the past. To keep up with the horsepower war initiated by American manufacturers, who wildly inflated their horsepower figures, Aston Martin in turn inflated its quoted figures. To complicate matters further, Aston Martin decided to back out of the battle in the 1970s and stopped quoting bhp figures, merely stating that power was 'adequate'. This led to some journalists conjuring up unlikely bhp figures.

Formula One legend Jackie Stewart was appointed to the Aston Martin board by Walter Hayes and assisted with development of the Vantage

Bolton recounted, 'It was at this stage that Walter Hayes brought in Jackie Stewart and Adrian Reynard from Reynard Racing. They were friends of Walter and he brought them in for their acknowledged expertise in rapid problem solving. Jackie Stewart drove it and said that it was now acceptable. He had also driven the car previously when it was pre-torque tube. Over the course of a weekend he took one of our early prototypes to Scotland and while it was up there, *Autocar* reviewed it. A favourable report appeared in *Autocar* and Jeremy Clarkson also reviewed the car, featuring it on *Top Gear*, extolling its virtues as a bit of a beast.

'After we built the initial seven cars it was so successful it became a mainstream programme. It was only going to be built in the hundreds, then it was 200 and eventually it went into respectable figures. Even in the very last version of the car, the Le Mans, built years later, the torque tube was exactly the same design as the original. It wasn't bettered and there was no need for a re-design. If it works, why change it?'

Virage designer John Heffernan, who considers the Vantage his masterpiece, designed the updated body. Although closely resembling the original Virage design, Heffernan subtly changed the car's shape, creating a more aggressive body. Almost every part of the car was changed. The only exterior panels carried over from the Virage were the roof and door skins.

The front featured new rectangular headlights and re-profiled grille. The spoiler was also enlarged and reshaped and the bonnet more smoothly integrated. Twin side vents were added and the front and rear wheel arches flared to accommodate the larger wheels and tyres. The rear featured four round taillights and a built-in rear spoiler that helped to promote 150–170 lb of down force. The new body had a Cd of 0.34 compared to the Virage's 0.356.

The interior was also updated. The cabin was lined with Connolly leather, Wilton carpet, walnut trim and featured electrically heated Recaro seats and a new four-spoke steering wheel. The rear seats, at one stage in danger of being omitted, were also improved and new map pockets and a larger glovebox incorporated.

The new Vantage was one of the most powerful production cars in the world and the most powerful production Aston Martin ever. It had a measured top speed of 186 mph and could sprint from 0–60 mph in 4.6 seconds and 0–100 mph in 10.1 seconds.

'After the Vantage project, the engineering department was pretty much wound down,' said Bolton. 'So there was an engineering workshop going spare and because we were only going to make seven cars it was decided that they would be made in that workshop by a small team led by Mike Booth, going to make seven cars it was decided that they would be made in that workshop by a small team led by Mike Booth, away from the main production area. Engines were built by the production engine builders in the main engine build area under the control of Arthur Wilson.'

Five prototypes were constructed and used for exhaustive testing purposes; Aston Martin was determined to thoroughly develop the car before beginning production. The Vantage was unveiled at the British International Motor Show on 20 October 1992, with production starting at chassis number AM1RR70001.

There was nothing like the Vantage being produced by any other manufacturer and it soon became the mainstay of production. From an envisaged original production run of only seven cars, the Vantage became quite a good seller for Aston Martin with 511 constructed.

Jackie Stewart

Formula One World Champion Jackie Stewart was appointed an Executive Director of Aston Martin by Walter Hayes. While his Stewart/ Ford Formula One team took up much of his time, Stewart acted as an advisor during the development of the Vantage and DB7 and ambassador for the marque that his brother, Jimmie, briefly raced for in the 1950s. Stewart vacated his position during 1996.

Top: With two Eaton superchargers, the Vantage's engine was capable of more than 550 bhp **Above:** The Vantage was fitted out like no other supercar with luxurious Connolly leather, Wilton carpet and walnut fascia panels

Vantage
1992–1999

Chassis: Steel box-section chassis, steel superstructure

Body: Aluminium 2+2 coupe styled by John Heffernan

Suspension: Front – Independent with unequal length double wishbones, coaxial spring damper units and anti-roll bar
Rear – de Dion axle, longitudinal radius arms, transverse Watt's linkage, coaxial spring damper units and anti-roll bar

Brakes: Servo-assisted PBR 362 mm ventilated steel discs with AP Racing four-piston callipers (front); 286 mm solid steel discs with sliding aluminium callipers (rear). ABS

Steering: Power-assisted rack and pinion

Wheels: 18-inch alloy

Tyres: Goodyear Eagle 285/45 ZR18

Transmission: ZF six-speed manual; final drive 3.77:1. Limited-slip differential. Rear-wheel drive

Engine: 5340 cc alloy V8 with twin chain-driven overhead camshafts per bank and four valves per cylinder. Compression ratio 8.2:1. EEC IV engine management system. Two Eaton Roots type M90 superchargers with air to liquid intercoolers. Fully catalysed exhaust system

Power: 550 bhp/410 kW @ 6500 rpm
550 lb/ft/746 Nm of torque @ 4000 rpm

Top speed: 186 mph/299 km/h

Dimensions:
Length	15 ft 7 in/4745 mm	
Width	6 ft 4.5 in/1944 mm (excluding wing mirrors)	
Height	4 ft 4.5 in/1330 mm	
Wheelbase	8 ft 6.75 in/2610 mm	
Weight	4368 lb/1981 kg	

Price when new: £189,950[ii]

Number built: 511

ii 1997

Vantage – 2 + 2 = 550

Lagonda Vignale
Concept Car

Flame rekindled

When Walter Hayes learnt Ford's Chief Designer, Jack Telnack, was working on an updated Lincoln Town Car, the thought of rekindling the dormant Lagonda marque appeared. Ian Callum was in the early stages of designing the DB7 at this stage and his brother, Moray, working at Ford's Ghia Design Studio in Turin, was asked to style what was to be called the Aston Martin Lagonda Vignale. Callum's brief was to develop a design study for a Lagonda concept car with production possibilities, one that was to test the waters for an Aston Martin-based saloon/limousine.

'At Ghia I did a large Aston Martin show car design, that maybe could have become a Lagonda,' said Moray Callum. 'It was a two-door coupe but it was very much in the Vignale (Lagonda) vein. It was very large and ostentatious but it was not a sports car; it was more like an old Bentley. We did a full-size proportional model. This was around the time that Victor Gauntlett moved on and nothing became of that design. That was my first dealing with Aston Martin.

'John Oldfield was driving it on this extremely windy road and he was flying towards a corner and everyone in the car was thinking "Oh, my god!" Let's just say we nearly didn't have that car for very long!'

Moray Callum

'Then the Vignale project came around. Tom Scott, who was the Director of Advanced Design at Ford at that time, had been in discussions about what Aston Martin could do to stretch its brand – what it could do to expand its market. I knew at the time that Ian was working on the DB7 and Aston Martin was going through a resurgence stage and they approached me. One of the advantages of Ghia was that we weren't seen as a Ford studio, we were seen as an international studio based in Italy, which gave us a sort of neutrality, which is why we got a lot of these exciting projects.

'There was an internal competition within Ghia and everybody was given the opportunity of submitting a scale model. My model was chosen and then I did a full-size model. I was in charge of the whole programme. It was a great car to do because

ASTON MARTIN: POWER, BEAUTY AND SOUL

This special replica of the original Lagonda Vignale, codenamed XM02, was created and built at Newport Pagnell for evaluation purposes for a possible production run that never eventuated

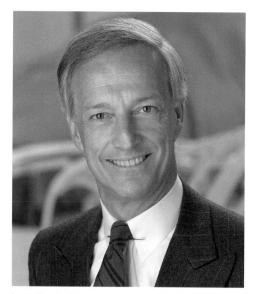

Left: Ford's Chief Designer Jack Telnack did the update design for the Lincoln Town Car that inspired the Lagonda Vignale **Right:** The original Ghia-built prototype had many subtle differences from the later 'production' car

money was no object in what I could try and portray. There were some great discussions about how we could spend money. We wanted to make an emotional car with great extravagance and the flamboyance of cars like Duesenbergs and Delahayes.'

Fortunately, Aston Martin was now in the situation of being able to call on the wider resources of Ford worldwide. As Hayes put it, 'It is nice to be able to phone up your big brother and ask him to do the airbags.' Known for its expertise in the design and finish of concept cars, Ghia was a natural partner in the project.

Hayes stated at the time that, 'although we have no firm programme for production of a car of this type, we believe it is appropriate to continue to investigate and research its appeal with potential customers. We believe there is a right and natural place for a handmade luxury car in the future, but it has to be fuel efficient and innovative and capable of being a car for life.'

Filippo Sapino, Managing Director of Ghia added, 'As a result of our discussions with Aston Martin Lagonda, we decided that our primary objective was to create a design concept for the Lagonda Vignale that would be regarded as timeless. We believe that a car in this class should be capable of meeting the needs of at least two decades.'

Launched at the Geneva Motor Show on 2 March 1993, coincidentally the debut of the DB7, the Lagonda Vignale was featured in numerous publications and, with an eye cocked in the direction of the lucrative North American market, two cars were shown to potential clients at a number of events in the US.

It was a stunning design. The organic shape disguised the car's enormous size, which was 5 inches longer in the wheelbase than the Lincoln Town Car and wider than a Rolls-Royce Silver Shadow.

'We started working on the Vignale in 1992,' recalled Callum. 'We pretty much did what we wanted to do. We wanted to do something striking and individual. Aston Martin had done the original (1960s) Lagonda Rapide, which were very good looking cars, and then it did the four-door DBS which it called a Lagonda, then it did the Bill Towns Lagonda. There was no continuity of what a four-door Lagonda should be so it gave us a bit of freedom.

'There wasn't a lot of effort to design a recognisable front end because Lagonda wasn't really that well known then. It had such a chequered history that there wasn't that much DNA to hold on to. We just tried to reproduce a flamboyance about the car. There was nothing like it at the time. We wanted to show that luxury cars could be sexy and emotional.'

The bulbous styling was aerodynamically efficient; a straight line was barely discernible. It was tall, rounded and high-waisted with short windows and short front and rear overhangs. It was big, but incredibly well proportioned. Ornamentation was kept to a minimum with only a nickel strip running end-to-end along the waistline and a nickel surround for the grille.

The body was constructed from aluminium panels placed over an extruded-aluminium frame. Based on a Lincoln Town Car floor pan, it incorporated the Lincoln independent front suspension and a de Dion rear end. The underpinnings of what may have become the production car were thought to be based on a version of the aluminium modular frame developed for the Ford Contour concept car with all-round independent suspension. The Vignale used unique AZE 18-inch cast alloy wheels with specially made Lagonda-embossed 255/55 ZR18 Goodyear tyres.

Powered by Ford's Lincoln alloy 4.6-litre DOHC four-valves-per-cylinder V8 coupled to a Lincoln four-speed automatic transmission the Vignale produced around 190 bhp and 260 lb/ft of torque. The Lincoln V8 engine was not intended for any future production Lagonda; something far more potent was envisaged: a 5.9-litre V12 producing in the region of 400 bhp and 400 lb/ft of torque.

A distinctive feature of the intended V12 engine, it was said, was that six of the 12 cylinders could be shut down when not needed; in heavy traffic or under light load, ensuring low emissions and excellent fuel economy. The remaining six cylinders were more than sufficient for town driving. Surprisingly for such a large motor car, the powerful engine had a projected performance of 150 mph.

The 5.9-litre V12 engine, later fitted to Project Vantage, had its origins back with the Lagonda Vignale. Ford's press release stated that, 'Aston Martin engineers, drawing on the worldwide resources of the Ford Motor Company, have identified an advanced concept for a 5.9-litre V12 engine that could be developed for the Lagonda Vignale.'

The interior was the work of designer David Wilkie, working alongside Sally Wilson, who chose the luxurious materials. Like the later Project Vantage, it looked modern and was a departure from previous Lagondas. The Art Deco-inspired interior featured nickel sill plates, an almost flat load floor with Lagonda-embossed woollen Wilton over-carpets, woollen headlining and four electronically adjustable, aniline-dyed parchment leather seats. With the rear centre armrest retracted, up to five passengers could be accommodated.

The dashboard, pedals and steering wheel made extensive use of nickel plating, while the dash itself was constructed from a single piece of laminated beech wood featuring five round analogue dials, with central rev counter, and an AM/FM radio/cassette player. The three-spoke beech wood, leather and aluminium steering wheel swung away for access when the driver's door was opened and returned to its original position when closed.

'The trunk was lined with wood, with stainless steel inserts like those found on boats,' recalled Callum. 'There were a lot of touches that were real quality on that car. The interior was

Ford's Lincoln Town Car was the basis for the original Vignale Concept Car

Carrozzeria Vignale

Born in 1913, Alfredo Vignale founded Carrozzeria Vignale in Turin in 1946 and produced the first body there in 1948. Vignale's designs have graced many of the great Italian marques, including Ferrari, Maserati and Lancia.

In 1961 Vignale began producing cars under its own name, but the venture was unsuccessful and Vignale became part of Ghia in 1969. Alfredo Vignale died in a motoring accident three days after selling the company.

The Lagonda Vignale was not the only Aston Martin to be bodied by the famous Turin-based carrozzeria. A left-hand drive DB2/4, chassis number LML/802, was specially built for King Baudouin of Belgium in 1954. Chassis LML/608 and DB3/3 were also clothed in Michelotti-designed coachwork by Vignale, the latter being destroyed in an accident.

designed to be very much like a gentlemen's club. The front seats were like armchairs and the rear seat was like a couch.'

The car featured advanced electronics and touch controls for door operation, seat adjustment and satellite navigation. The rear featured power-operated workstations; one desk featured a built-in laptop computer, the second a vanity set. To cope with the complicated electronic systems, most of which were fully functioning, a built-in battery charger with European and US voltage systems was fitted.

AML was serious about building the Lagonda Vignale. John Oldfield stated in 1994 that the car could be hand-made at Aston Martin. 'I don't see us giving up Newport Pagnell,' said Oldfield, 'the only question is what to produce here. Like the Lagonda Vignale, for example, a lot depends on the platform. But if the car uses aluminium and less steel it could be built here at Newport Pagnell.

'Inside there's a lot of work to be done. It's not passenger-friendly and needs a load of redevelopment. But the car … is probably close to what we have in mind. And it's right for Aston Martin to get us into the four-seat, four-door sporty sedan market; a lot of people would like an Aston Martin Lagonda that seats four people in comfort.

'We'll have the work done before the year's end, and without having to go back to the parent company for approval; as long as we put forward a plan that makes sense, getting approval in the US is usually a formality.'[10]

Oldfield was very fond of the car, having test driven it in Italy. 'John Oldfield came to Turin and we picked him up for dinner in the hills of Turin,' said Callum. 'While we were having dinner we organised for the Lagonda to be parked outside for him to drive. He got in it and he just drove it thinking it was a

Above: A full-size model of the Lagonda Vignale nears completion at Newport Pagnell Below: The Aston Martin-built Lagonda Vignale was sold to a special client in the Far East Opposite: The 'Newport Pagnell' Lagonda was built on a smaller platform to the original and was powered by a V12 engine drawn from the PAG group; unlike the Ford original it was traditionally coachbuilt in aluminium

Carrozzeria Ghia

Ghia and Garaglio was founded by Giacinto Ghia (1887–1944) and became known as Carrozzeria Ghia in 1926. Famous for its designs for Lancia, Alfa Romeo, Chrysler, VW and De Tomaso, it became part of De Tomaso Automobili in 1967.

Ford owns the Italian carrozzeria and through that company, Vignale. Ford purchased 84 percent of the Turin-based carrozzeria in 1970; the remaining 16 percent was acquired in 1973 whereupon the Ghia badge began appearing on premium Ford products. Ghia was later downgraded by Ford to a small studio for the design of prototypes.

Carrozzeria Ghia bodied a Giovanni Savonuzzi-designed Aston Martin DB2/4 Mk II, chassis number AM/300/1/1132, for the famous racing driver Harry Schell. Before he took delivery of the car known as 'Super Sonic', it appeared at the Turin Motor Show in 1956.

'It was a good studio,' said Moray Callum who worked at Ghia during the mid 1980s and early 1990s. 'It was owned by Ford but we got to work on six or seven brands from Aston Martin to Jaguar, Ford to Lincoln and Mercury to Volkswagen and AC; it was great from that point of view.'

While with Ghia, Callum completed a design study and clay model for a large Aston Martin coupe in 1990. The luxurious long wheelbase two-door car never reached production.

real car, but this was a show car that you would normally drive at only 30 mph. He was driving it on this extremely windy road and he was flying towards a corner and everyone in the car was thinking "Oh, my god!" It started raining and it had a Plexiglas windshield and the windscreen wipers stopped. He was flooring the car; he was doing probably 70 or 80 km/h and by the time he put the brakes on, which weren't very good … let's just say we nearly didn't have that car for very long!'

While Oldfield admired the car the business case did not meet approval and the Lagonda went no further than concept stage. 'Amazingly, for a brand that has been really alone for a long time it still has very good recollection among the enthusiasts,' said Ford CEO, Jac Nasser. 'There are so many luxury brands out there that I doubt whether it could be a stand-alone brand.'

'I think the Vignale Lagonda was a blind alley,' said CEO Bob Dover later. 'My concern was to get Aston Martin revitalised and the business turned around. Aston Martin was well known, but Lagonda, the further you got away from England the less it was known. It seemed a huge and unnecessary task for us to try and do it and in terms of big four-door cars, which the Lagonda tended to be post-war, the top end of the market was tiny. Even Jaguar struggled with Daimler to get limousines going.

'But for stylish sporting cars with a big traditional English-style front-engine, rear-wheel drive layout there was a gap in the market and Aston Martin already had that heritage

with the DB cars. That seemed to me more sensible; the company had a much better chance doing that than the Lagonda. Frankly, with the Vignale, the badge could have gone any place, there weren't that many Lagonda cues, except the extreme luxury and that it was very stylishly done. The concept itself was brilliant but there was just no way we had the market or the dealers ready to run with it.'

The Vignale concept car was unique among post-war Lagondas because it had a body, chassis *and* engine that did not belong to any other Aston Martin. Even though the initial two cars were constructed from Ford components and it was never put into production, it still had the distinction of being a unique, purpose-designed Lagonda.

Ford Motor Company owned the original Sorrento Blue publicity car until June 2002 when Christie's sold it at auction, along with numerous Ford concept cars. The reserve was set at a modest US$60,000–120,000, which proved a remarkable underestimation; it sold for US$403,500 (£274,490).

The second car, used by Ford at various public relations events, while a running vehicle, was not a fully engineered vehicle. It was destroyed after the publicity events finished and the car was no longer needed.

A third and very special Lagonda Vignale, codenamed XM02, which had some notable differences from the Ford-produced vehicles, was hand-built at Newport Pagnell during 1995 as part of an evaluation process with a view to production.

'We were asked to do a productionised Lagonda at Ghia and we did a full-sized prototype with Aston Martin engineers. There was a serious look at putting it into production,' said Callum.

'We designed the clay model and the car was made at Newport Pagnell. We partly designed the interior at Ghia and the sheet metal was done at Aston Martin. This was about the time when I left Ghia in 1995. I never saw the finished car in the flesh; only photos. It was narrower and I don't think it had the same presence and drama as the original car.'

Built on a different platform, sourced from within PAG, and slightly smaller, the metallic burgundy car was subtly altered to include a different front with larger headlights, a larger grille with Lagonda badge, separate front indicators, rectangular fog lights and reshaped air intake. It also had different door mirrors, side indicator lights and similar, but different, alloy wheels.

The interior remained quite faithful to the original prototype. Remaining left-hand-drive, the Art Deco theme was continued but many detail changes were made. The wood-accented steering wheel, with airbag, contrasted strongly with the radical

original. A centre console was introduced, complete with automatic transmission lever and metal handbrake lever to the right of the driver's seat. An instrument cluster, similar to the original, was employed, as was the large timber dashboard. The doors used larger wooden veneers and heavier-set armrests that incorporated switches for the powered windows. The suede-lined interior roof featured aircraft-style lighting controls.

In the rear, ample leg and head room, along with plush seating, ensured passenger comfort. The seats, door and dashboard sections were covered in mushroom-coloured leather with contrasting piping and buttons. A retractable centre armrest and control panel was also featured. The Lagonda featured a V12 engine and utilised parts sourced from within the Ford empire.

'This car was based on the car made by Ford, but it was slightly smaller than the Lincoln-based cars,' said Kingsley Riding-Felce. 'It was a lot prettier, too. [Chief Body Engineer] Shaun Rush was responsible for the body-in-white.'

'The Lagonda Vignale was probably the most enjoyable project I worked on at Astons,' said Shaun Rush. 'I really thought that this could be our next production vehicle. I visited Ghia in January 1995 to look at the full-size epowood model together with other associated tooling and parts that Ghia were supplying to us.'

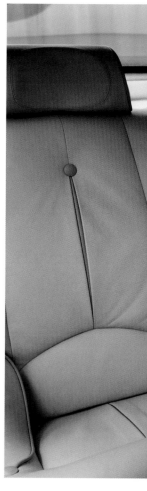

Left: The 'production' interior followed the basic design of the concept car with several changes
Right: The seating in the original Ghia-built car could accomodate five passengers, while the 'Newport Pagnell' Lagonda Vignale had rear bucket seats for two only

'We took plaster casts and GRP reversals from this master model at Newport and then made tooling from those. The whole of the aluminium outer skin was made from flat sheet at Newport. We were able to showcase all our skills and it was a fine example of using both advanced design technology such as CAD together with Newport's traditional coachbuilding skills to produce a fully finished running vehicle in a short space of time.

'It was shown to senior management at Bloxham in October 1995 and it was apparently well received,' said Rush. 'The whole vehicle was stunning and you could see the potential for a low-volume luxury limousine. I was disappointed that it never made it into production; it was the best thing we ever made.'

'Everyone was aware of this car's importance in trying to secure the programme for us,' continued Riding-Felce. 'This was the plan to put it into production. It was a very serious thought, but DB7 was the future at the time. To introduce yet another car was a step too far.'

When the programme was cancelled, Riding-Felce sold the Vignale, DP2138, to a collector in the Far East for £1,300,000. After making some spare panels, the tooling was destroyed.

Moray Callum

Moray Callum was born in Dumphries, Scotland. He studied industrial design at University in Edinburgh and did a postgraduate degree, sponsored by Chrysler, at London's Royal College of Art.

'I started working for Chrysler in the UK in the Whitley studios in the late 1970s,' said Callum. 'Then I moved to Paris and worked for Peugeot. I was there for about four-and-a-half years and then I was offered a job at Ghia in Italy where I worked for seven years.

'It was then suggested I move to the US and a few years later Ghia closed down. I worked as Design Manager (for Ford) on advanced car programmes and trucks up until 2001.' Callum then moved to Mazda, where he designed the award-winning MX-5 before returning to Ford in the US in 2006.

Lagonda Vignale Concept Car[i]
1993–1997

Chassis: Lincoln steel-perimeter floor pan, extruded aluminium frame

Body: Composite 4/5-seat saloon styled by Moray Callum

Suspension: Front – Independent with coil springs and stabiliser bar
Rear – de Dion axle with self-levelling shock absorbers

Brakes: Servo-assisted Girling ventilated discs

Steering: Power-assisted rack and pinion

Wheels: 18-inch AZE alloy

Tyres: Goodyear 255/55 ZR18

Transmission: Lincoln four-speed automatic with touch-button control; final drive 3.08:1. Rear-wheel drive

Engine: Lincoln 4605 cc alloy V8 with twin chain-driven overhead camshafts per bank and four valves per cylinder. EEC IV engine management system

Power: 190 bhp/142 kW @ 4200 rpm
260 lb/ft/353 Nm of torque @ 3200 rpm

Top speed: 140 mph/225 km/h (est)

Dimensions:

Length	17 ft 5.5 in/5236 mm
Width	6 ft 5 in/1955 mm
Height	4 ft 9 in/1449 mm
Wheelbase	10 ft 2.75 in/3118 mm
Weight	N/A

Price when new: Prototypes not available new. First prototype sold at auction for £274,490. Second prototype destroyed. Production car sold for £1,300,000

Number built: 3[ii]

---

i   Specifications for 1993 prototype

ii One destroyed

D B 7
DB legend revived

Victor Gauntlett's dream of ushering in his 'DB4 for the 1990s' ended when he resigned in September 1991 to pursue other business interests. Gauntlett had originally agreed to preside as Chairman of Aston Martin for three years from September 1987, but stayed four – until the DB7 project had started. 'My use-by date had come,' he said of his departure.

Meanwhile, Walter Hayes had retired early in 1989, having been with Ford since 1961. But with the resignation of Gauntlett, Hayes was asked by Ford Chairman Harold 'Red' Poling if he would accept the position of Executive Chairman of AML. 'As I felt a responsibility for it,' said Hayes, 'I said I would do it until the age of 70, but not beyond.'[11]

The Virage was in production by this time and the classic car boom at its zenith. Financially, the company was stable; it was not making much money, but importantly, it was not losing any money. High on the AML board's agenda was how to capitalise on the positive market. Virage production was running at five cars per week and steps were taken to boost this to six – a drop in the ocean in terms of the worldwide automotive industry, but a significant shift in operations for Aston Martin.

'We drove it into the Aston dealership in Kensington. The Ford executives couldn't believe it. I have never seen a reaction like that before or since in my life.'

Ian Callum

But things changed overnight when the world was stung by the sudden downturn in the financial market in the late 1980s. The demand for high-priced performance cars dried up almost immediately. Aston Martin went into survival mode. Thoughts of expansion ceased and plans were executed to keep the company viable. If Aston Martin was to stay in business, a new car was needed and it was needed soon.

Over a lifetime, Hayes had built up important business contacts in the automotive world and was well placed to usher in a new era at Aston Martin. He had been a board member of

Opposite: The DB7 cemented Ford's commitment to the British marque

AML since 1990 and in preparation for his stewardship had put together a strategy for the future, presenting it to Ford executives in March 1991. He concluded that if Aston Martin was to survive, it would have to expand its range to include a cheaper sports car. He also stated there was no way the antiquated Newport Pagnell factory could cope with building a higher-volume car – a suitable facility had to be found.

Many legends surround the pricing of Aston Martin's cars. One states that a friend of David Brown sidled up to him at a party and asked if he could buy a car at cost price. The man was rather surprised when DB said he would be delighted to oblige and that it would be '£1000 over list'. Another states that if everybody who intended to buy an Aston Martin were given £50 by AML not to buy a car, Aston Martin would have been a lot better off.

Like all good fables, they may have contained an element of truth but the fact was that Aston Martin rarely made any money, simply because the company never charged enough for its cars. Things started to change dramatically during the 1970s when the price of the AMV8 rose from £19,657 in 1970 to £55,786 in 1987. This had little impact on profits however, and Aston Martin's perilous financial position remained.

By the time the Virage arrived it cost £125,000 and rose to £134,604 just over three years later, placing Aston Martin near the top of high-priced production car values, Rolls-Royce and Bentley included. Cars by famous marques such as Ferrari, Mercedes-Benz, Jaguar and Lamborghini could be bought for a good deal less.

'Really, with the benefit of hindsight, things had got a little bit out of hand,' said Managing Director, Nick Fry. 'When the Virage was priced everyone was a little shocked that it was to be nearer £130,000 compared with about £80,000 for its predecessor. Of course, it remained a very expensive car to build, but even at the extremely high prices we charged it was not profitable to make. When Walter Hayes came along and started to run the company full time, I think it was on day two, he told me he had decided we must have a lower-priced car. It was fairly obvious to Walter the way things were going we knew we had to have this small car.'

It was simple economics and the sums were not adding up. Skilled labour in England was expensive and this is why other companies like General Motors, Ford and Volkswagen were outsourcing construction of their cars to countries like Mexico and Spain where the wages were significantly lower.

The Virage engine alone took 56 hours to hand-build and cost £12,000; a single aluminium front fender took 25 hours to hand form and it took 40 hours to paint a car. It was painfully obvious, even to the casual observer that an £80,000 car couldn't be built in that way. Hand-building cars had a place in the company but certainly didn't fit into plans for a lower-priced, higher-volume model.

Top: TWR-designed 'flying saucer' wheel trims were a feature of early cars but were later deleted **Above:** The DB7 was the DB6 MkII's spiritual successor

Scottish-born Tom Walkinshaw started his motorsport career in 1968, racing Formula Ford. He was hired by Ford to drive touring cars in 1974 and won his class in the British Touring Car Championship driving a Ford Capri.

Tom Walkinshaw Racing (TWR) was established in 1976, winning the British Touring Car Championship in 1980 and 1981 in a Mazda RX-7. In 1982 TWR began to race Jaguars in the European Touring Car Championship. The following year Walkinshaw won the title with a Jaguar XJS.

During the 1980s TWR began building cars for the IMSA series in the United States and for Holden Special Vehicles in Australia. But it was with Jaguar that Walkinshaw was to have his greatest success. In 1987 and 1988 Jaguar won the World Sportscar Championship and the Le Mans and Daytona endurance classics. A further World Championship was won in 1991. In 1994 TWR teamed with Volvo, winning the British Touring Car Championship in 1998.

Meanwhile, TWR began producing Jaguar XJ220s and in late 1991, Walkinshaw was appointed Managing Director of Aston Martin Oxford. TWR subsequently designed and built DB7s at Bloxham. TWR at that time employed 1400 people, almost three times that of Aston Martin.

In 1992 Walkinshaw began his involvement with Formula One, becoming Benetton's Engineering Director and later becoming Team Manager at Ligier. He went on to purchase a majority stake in the Arrows Formula One team. The team fell into grave financial difficulties and in 2002 went into liquidation. Soon afterwards, Walkinshaw's TWR empire also closed down.

A new facility would be needed for Aston Martin's new car. Hayes considered his options, which included old Rolls-Royce and Lotus facilities or even a factory in continental Europe. The answer ultimately lay with stablemate, Jaguar.

The Jaguar XJ220 was being constructed at a custom-built facility in the grounds of Wykham Mill, near Bloxham, Oxfordshire and was coming to the end of its production life. The soon-to-be-vacated factory was seen as the perfect choice for the construction of the new Aston Martin. Bill Hayden, Chairman of Jaguar said to long-time friend Walter Hayes, 'I've got no use for that factory after the 220 finishes so if Aston Martin want it, being all part of the family, then have it.'[12]

In late 1991, Hayes contacted Tom Walkinshaw, who was a partner in JaguarSport, and formed Aston Martin Oxford Ltd. in partnership with Walkinshaw's TWR Group; the share split being 75 percent Aston Martin and 25 percent TWR. Walkinshaw was appointed Managing Director.

'TWR was responsible for the engineering development [of the DB7],' said Bob Dover. 'TWR and JaguarSport set up a factory to produce XJRs and things and it had made the Jaguar

XJ220 at one point. Aston Martin took that factory over to do the DB7 and it was a very troubled time because the DB7 was quite different from the XJ220. We didn't have the craftsmanship background [there] that we had at Newport Pagnell and the volume was much higher than Aston Martin had done [previously].'

Meanwhile, Jaguar had been working on an XJS replacement since the early 1980s with what would have become the new F-type, the XJ41. When Ford purchased the company, the newly appointed head, Bill Hayden, quickly set about re-establishing Jaguar's financial status. He decided Jaguar should concentrate its efforts on building and developing its current range of cars. When it was realised Jaguar was in a very precarious financial position, Ford needed much more than an expensive sports car if Jaguar was to fulfil its potential as part of the Ford stable. The project was scrapped in March 1990.

Walkinshaw was peering into the future, beyond the XJ220 project, and had recruited stylist Ian Callum in 1990 to design some future Jaguar models. Callum had been Design Manager at the Ford-owned Carrozzeria Ghia when he came to the attention of Walkinshaw.

Top to bottom: A cut-away drawing illustrates the DB7's neat packaging; The DB7 was well trimmed but the 'tombstone' seats were not popular with all customers; A six-cylinder engine was chosen to align the DB7 with the earlier 'DB' models

Shortly afterwards, Walkinshaw was asked to quickly develop an F-type concept car, code-named Project XX for the motor show circuit. The project went as far as having an XJ41-based, Ian Callum-designed body, fitted atop the XJS floorpan. An alloy AJ16 4.0-litre in-line twin-turbo six-cylinder engine, replacing the elderly AJ6 unit, was also in the pipeline. It was seen as being too expensive to develop and build and once again Ford's bosses shelved Project XX.

Jaguar's and TWR's attempt to create a new sportscar did not make financial sense for the numbers that Jaguar needed to sell. But the proposal did suit Aston Martin.

Once the go-ahead for Ford's version of DP1999 (what would become the DB7) was received, Hayes decided to use as much of the stillborn TWR Project XX as possible. Hayes asked to see Callum's body design, but this was quickly dismissed; it was not an Aston Martin shape and couldn't be adapted. But the engine, some other mechanicals and the floorplan were all seen as being suitable for the new car.

It was unrealistic for Aston Martin to start completely from scratch, so the DB7 was underpinned by Jaguar's XJS platform. Walkinshaw knew the XJS intimately, having turned the car into a race-winner during the 1980s. It was felt this was a very good platform on which to build DP1999, but Aston Martin was very coy about the fact.

'There is no question that the new car had to share a platform and as many unseen panels and running gear components as possible if it was to have any chance of viability,' said past Director of Engineering Michael Bowler. 'Project XX was XJ41 married to an XJS. The DB7 took over and used Jaguar components but Walkinshaw made the car behave and feel completely different.

'Ford's coyness at the time is just as likely to have been due to the use of the XK8's prototype tooling very early in the DB7 run and well before the XK8 had been launched. It doesn't actually matter. The car gave Aston Martin a new lease on life and it never felt like a Jaguar or looked like one. It can be regarded as the start of the Aston Martin role as Jaguar's hi-tech research department.'

Aston Martin's use of proprietary parts was nothing new. As Hayes bluntly put it, 'The acquisition by Ford of Aston Martin and Jaguar has enabled it to use the resources of these specialist companies. I know exactly where to go in Ford for anything we might want. And if you have the opportunity to use these facilities you'd be damn silly not to.'[13]

The 'Jag in drag' debate raged on in the press and the matter was exacerbated in 1996 when Jaguar released its XK8 Coupe. The body design, also by Ian Callum, resembled the DB7 and the proportions and layout were similar. The DB7, however, was 5.2 inches shorter, 1.2 inches lower and 7.8 inches narrower.

Model	Engine	Weight (lb)	0-60 mph (seconds)	Top speed (mph)	Power (bhp)
Jaguar XK8	4.0-litre V8	3800	6.1	155	290
DB7	3.2-litre supercharged six-cylinder	3802	5.7	165	335

Nick Fry

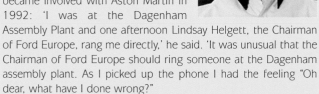

Born in 1956, Nick Fry graduated with a Degree in Economics from the University of Wales in 1978 and began working for Ford Motor Company soon after, spending the next 20 years within the Ford group.

Fry remembered very well how he became involved with Aston Martin in 1992: 'I was at the Dagenham Assembly Plant and one afternoon Lindsay Helgett, the Chairman of Ford Europe, rang me directly,' he said. 'It was unusual that the Chairman of Ford Europe should ring someone at the Dagenham assembly plant. As I picked up the phone I had the feeling "Oh dear, what have I done wrong?"

'Lindsay asked me to come up and see him that afternoon at Ford Europe headquarters and he handed over a photo of a clay model of what was to become the DB7. A strong recommendation came from Bruce Blythe, the Chief Strategist from Ford Europe; he knew me quite well. There were a lot of business and product issues that needed sorting out for the DB7. That's why they chose me.

'To start with, I was Operations Director but I was promoted to Managing Director three months later. The principal project I was involved with was the DB7; that was the reason I was sent there. At that time Aston Martin was part-owned by Ford and part-owned by the Livanos family. It was agreed that Ford would fund the DB7 in its entirety and obviously Ford wanted its own man to go in and ensure that its investment was spent wisely. That was my principal reason for going.

Fry is adamant that Ford's involvement with Aston Martin was responsible. 'Ford's involvement with Aston Martin has been completely positive. Without an association with a big manufacturer, a company like Aston Martin was unlikely to survive.

'Ford brought access to things like test facilities, intellectual property in technology and its legal team. On occasion we would use the Ford Lommel test facility to drive the cars around. Those types of facilities you really can't buy; you can only get by association with a big manufacturer.

'Ford looked after Aston Martin very well', said Fry. 'It basically allowed the operating management to principally to do their own thing. I think Ford were very good in that respect, where other motor manufacturers would have gone in with lead boots. I've only good things to say about Ford in terms of the way they treated the situation.'

Fry became Managing Director of Prodrive in 2001, later becoming Group Managing Director. The following year he was appointed Managing Director of the BAR Formula One team, becoming CEO in November 2004. In 2006 he became CEO of the new Honda Grand Prix team.

Things were starting to fall into place. Red Poling had granted Hayes £1 million to develop a prototype and Ford offered assistance with the development of the car. Outline proposals were completed in late 1991 and the decision to proceed was made in March 1992. Walkinshaw was responsible for overseeing production of the new cars while Ford's Mike Moreton oversaw the assembly at Bloxham.

Codenamed DP1999, the basic brief for the DB7 was:

- Front mounted six-cylinder engine
- Rear-wheel drive
- 2+2 coupe body
- Pressed steel and composite construction
- Price below £80,000
- Production of around 1500 units per annum

In line with previous DB models, and to help position the car below the V8 line up, it was decided to produce an in-line six-cylinder motor. Development of a totally new engine was prohibitively expensive, even with Ford's backing, so it was decided to outsource the engine development or to acquire a completely developed one.

Hayes approached both Mercedes-Benz and BMW to see if one of their six-cylinder engines could be used. But Jaguar once again came to the fore and offered the AJ6 six-cylinder engine block that was used in its XJ saloons.

The DB7 engine was developed and assembled at TWR's Kidlington factory under Aston Martin's supervision. Geraint Castleton-White, the man responsible for Jaguar's XJ220 turbo-powered V6, was in charge of engine development. The twin chain-driven, double overhead cam, in-line six-cylinder engine consisted of a unique TWR-designed alloy four-valves-per-cylinder head mated to the existing Jaguar block.

An important addition was the single Eaton supercharger. The water-intercooled supercharger was fitted with a bypass valve and had maximum boost pressure of 14 psi. The engine boasted 335 bhp @ 5500 rpm and 360 lb/ft of torque @ 3000 rpm, which was more powerful than the Virage's V8 powerplant.

Hayes was well aware of Ian Callum's talents and allowed him a certain amount of artistic freedom in the car's design. But Callum's brief was plain and to the point. He was to create a modern car that looked like a direct descendant of the DB6; in short, the kind of car David Brown would have made in the 1990s. Hayes had Callum study a DB4 GT Zagato Sanction II and a DB5 in the flesh, as well as copious amounts of photographs of other Aston Martins. Famously, Hayes is said to have pointed to the photographs on the wall and exclaimed, 'Like that!'

Callum had been aware of DB Aston Martins since childhood and was thrilled when asked to design the new model. 'They put an Aston DB5 in the design studio,' said Callum, 'which I respected but I could have drawn an Aston from memory; it was so ingrained in me from my childhood. The design of the DB Astons was very pure and I think there is a lot of that in the DB7.

'At one stage the DB7 may have been a V12 and also, I believe could have been a four-wheel drive platform, but Walter Hayes thought that a six cylinder would suit the car better, being more in line with the earlier DB engines, so we went with the six-cylinder. That was a very good engine, a very strong engine.

'But the problem was that when we were developing the car it didn't fit under the bonnet line. I showed Tom and he said the car would have to come up a bit in the front. I didn't like that but I did it on the clay model and I showed Tom, who said that he didn't like it either, and suggested that we drop the engine.

'So we had to rebuild the front subframe to fit the engine. I can tell you the engineers were not impressed when Tom said that we were going to drop the engine to fit it under the bonnet. They suggested lifting the bonnet, but we didn't want to do that.

'That car had to sit well so we developed it. We also redesigned the back end to make it sit right and I think one of the best things about the car is that it sits absolutely perfectly because I insisted on it. It started off as a Jaguar but everything was redesigned and changed.'

When the shape had been approved by Hayes and Ford's US Chief Designer, Jack Telnack, Callum made two-dimensional design sketches of the yet-unnamed Project NPX, (Newport Pagnell eXperimental), and started working with TWR's chief modeller, Andrew Miles, very early on. 'I [designed] the car on

my own,' said Callum. 'It meant so much to me. I knew that it had to be nothing-but-perfect. That was absolutely paramount in my mind.'

Sir David Brown was shown Callum's sketches and, impressed, asked Hayes and Managing Director Nick Fry to show him the clay model. Upon studying the design he was so obviously delighted he insisted it be called DB7.

In a later letter to Hayes, Sir David Brown wrote: 'I am of course delighted and very honoured that the new Aston Martin should be designated a "DB". From what I have seen of it I am sure it will be a world-beater and more than worthily uphold the "DB" tradition.'

Nick Fry recalled, 'We were wondering what to call this thing. It didn't have a name at all but both Walter Hayes and I felt that we really wanted to get back to the kind of cars designed in the DB era. When we were looking at the styling of the vehicle we had a DB5 in the styling studio in Kidlington and at one stage we also had a DB4 GT Zagato. They were always the kind of role model that we were following.

'Walter and I went to see Sir David Brown in his office in London. We went down to lunch and had a nice conversation. Then we went back to his apartment and showed him pictures of the car, which was a bit beyond the clay model at that stage and we literally asked his permission which he gave immediately. Clearly, from his body language and from what he said, he was absolutely thrilled that we wanted to continue the line. In fact Sir David and Lady Brown subsequently came to a number of events including tours of the factory. They both were very eager to participate and I think he was very much an Aston Martin man right up to his death.

'I think the DB initials contributed to the DB7's success because, certainly at that stage, Aston Martin was still very much unknown. It was well known among real enthusiasts, but if you go out into the wider public, especially in places like North America, it was virtually unknown. In many cases it was called "Austin Martin"; people thought it had something to do with the old Austin car company. Aston Martin was clearly well known for James Bond and Prince Charles, but you had to hark back into history to jog people's memories. The car was good enough that it would have been a success anyway, but calling it a DB was very, very helpful. Heritage is something you can't buy.'

At this stage however, there were no guarantees that the project would reach production. 'I had done a 1:1 clay model,' said Callum, 'and Tom Walkinshaw had said that we were going to get the Ford people together to show them the car. Tom had raised their expectations so we had to have something pretty special to show them.

'All we generally used to do was develop a business plan and a clay model. But Tom was talking to me in the design studio and I remember him walking away and when he reached the doorway he turned around – I knew it was coming – and asked what would be better than a clay model. I replied that a fibreglass model would be better, but a proper car would be even better than that. He agreed that was what we should do.'

On 26 March 1992 a running prototype was presented to four Ford Executives in London. 'It was a metal car and it was hand built,' explained Callum. 'We built that car in three months and we drove it into the Aston dealership in Kensington. The Ford executives couldn't believe it. I have never seen a reaction like that before or since in my life. They were astounded that the car had been built, and finished. We explained that it wasn't quite finished, but it certainly proved a point.

'We put on a presentation and had video footage, taken from a helicopter, of the car driving around Tom's estate. It was very impressive. It was a great piece of showmanship. We got the funds to finish the car and bring it to production but in Ford terms the DB7 was very, very cheap. It was very good value, I can assure you. I think it may have cost them something like US$40 million. It just goes to show you what you can do with some autocratic decision making.

'The politics of the car were troublesome; some people wanted to protect the brand and didn't want to do [the DB7]. But Walter Hayes, in his wisdom, was cunning. He managed to manoeuvre through the politics and get the project done.'

The DB7 was launched at the Geneva Motor Show on 2 March 1993. The metallic grey left-hand-drive car caused a sensation and was crowned "Car of the Show".

'I call this my "happy car",' said Callum. 'It changed my life and has allowed me to do what I really want to do. The reaction to the car was tremendous. It gave me a lot of satisfaction to know that I had created something so nice, so successful. I became known as a successful designer and that was great for me. I got a lot of work from that and I was able to make a very good living out of designing.'

Walter Hayes (pictured left with King Hussein of Jordan) was the driving force behind the DB7

The DB7 name

DB7 was first mooted back in 1967 for William Towns' new Aston Martin coupe design, which was to replace the DB6. However, two prototypes, MP 226, designed by Touring of Milan had previously been shown at the 1966 London, Paris and Turin Motor Shows and, evoking the DB3S racing car's mystique, were subsequently named DBS.

It was later decided not to put these two-seat coupes into production and the William Towns-styled car was produced instead. The DBS name remained in people's minds however, so DBS was chosen for the Towns design and, in a not-entirely-logical move, the DB7 name was overlooked.

The DB7 was given a further opportunity to appear in July 1969, when the updated DB6 appeared. Although several changes had been made to the car and the flared wheel arches and bigger tyres gave it a slightly different look, it was not a totally new model, so DB6 Mk II was chosen instead.

When the V8 engine was placed in the DBS in 1969 the new model was simply called DBS V8; DB7 was never considered for the V8 variant. The DBS and the DBS V8 were the last models to bear the famous DB initials; in February 1972 David Brown sold Aston Martin to Company Developments and the DB prefix was dropped. It was not until 1993, 21 years after the close of the David Brown era that the DB initials again graced an Aston Martin.

The re-introduction of the DB initials didn't come about by accident. Walter Hayes, a man renowned for his sense of tradition, was keen to recreate the glory days of the marque so went straight to the source: Sir David Brown. Brown was invited by Hayes to become Honorary Life President of AML in 1993 and his portrait was hung in the Newport Pagnell boardroom.

Sir David was delighted to be reacquainted with the company. When Hayes asked Brown for his permission to call the new car DB7, Brown was more than happy to oblige, quipping that if people looked hard enough, someone was sure to uncover a batch of DB7 badges at Newport Pagnell, for he recalled having some made in the late 1960s.

Bloxham

Once home to Jaguar's XJ220 production and situated on the 11.5-acre grounds of Wykham Mill in Oxfordshire, the Bloxham plant was the home of the DB7.

With DB7 production set for 1500 cars per annum, the Newport Pagnell facility was clearly unsuitable; a new, bigger, more modern factory was required. Unlike Newport Pagnell however, Bloxham was more of an assembly plant; the production line assembled DB7s from components constructed elsewhere. The engines came from TWR in Kidlington, while the bodies were initially painted at Rolls-Royce in Crewe.

Always intended as a stop-gap measure, Bloxham was used by Aston Martin for 10 years and all DB7 models were produced there. But it became obvious that if Aston Martin was going to expand a new larger, purpose-built facility was needed.

'As far as Bloxham was concerned, we had already developed the site,' said Bob Dover. 'We couldn't get any more vehicles on because we had taken the volume up and up; we had built a paint and small trim shop at Bloxham. All that got put on hold as we bought Gaydon.'

After the final DB AR1 model was completed in early 2004 the site was broken up into industrial units and sold off. Aston Martin's future now lay elsewhere.

Cheapest Aston Martin

Although a lot cheaper than the V cars, the DB7 was not the cheapest Aston Martin built. Another model took that mantle when a 24-speed Aston Martin mountain bike was launched at the 1994 Geneva Motor Show. The state-of-the-art bicycle was made by custom bike maker, Charles Roberts, but received 12 coats of paint, in any choice of colour to match an owner's car, and was finished by Aston Martin at Newport Pagnell.

It was fitted with high-quality accessories and came complete with an Aston Martin badge. 'This we are doing for a bit of fun,' said Managing Director Nick Fry. 'We hope people will come to the factory in the same way as they do for the cars and specify the bike for themselves and have it tailored like a suit.'[14] With a starting price of £3495.60 for the basic model, only a handful were made.

Having established the DB7 programme Walter Hayes retired in January 1994 and was succeeded by John Oldfield. Production started in the middle of that year and the first car, chassis number SCFAA111VK100001, was delivered in September. Only 30 cars were produced during the latter half of that year. It was a different story in 1995, when an unprecedented 645 cars were manufactured at the Oxford plant.

The DB7 featured a host of firsts for Aston Martin, including the first production steel body, the use of composite materials, fully independent rear suspension, driver and passenger airbags as standard and side impact bars in the doors.

Callum's design was masterful. The links to Frank Feeley's DB2 could be seen from the rear, the powerful haunches recalled the DB4 GT Zagato and the grille was reminiscent of the DB3S. It was a slippery body with a drag coefficient of 0.31 and had all the hallmarks of past classic Aston Martins, yet looked entirely up-to-date and was certainly no pastiche.

Chrome was kept to a minimum with plating only on the door handles, rear number plate shroud and air intake flash. The design was pure, totally devoid of spoilers, side skirts, air dams or pop-up lights.

One feature of Callum's design that didn't make production was the Targa-style roof. The sunroof-sized detachable panel fitted into its own leather carry case and stowed in the boot.

The body was constructed from composite and zinc-coated, electro-treated steel. Closed sections were wax-injected and the front wings, bonnet, bumpers, sills and boot lid were moulded in composite materials by TWR's Advanced Structural Technology division. Upon completion they were sent to the Rolls-Royce factory in Crewe to be painted then transported to Bloxham where they were hand-assembled and completed.

The interior was the work of TWR's Neil Simpson. He and Callum were both Royal College of Arts students and had worked on the Escort Cosworth together while with Ford. 'We didn't have a brief for the DB7, because we did a lot of it before AML saw it, or even knew about it,' said Simpson. 'Tom Walkinshaw had strong ideas, especially about the rear seats and brought in his Porsche 911 Turbo as an example. When AML became involved Walter Hayes wanted some wood; I didn't. Once the basic shape was resolved we became very involved with the AML sales and marketing team and we really sorted out all the niceties of the colour and the trim with them. They really knew their customer base, but at that time we were looking at a whole new group of potential buyers. It was all new territory for us.'

While in the Aston Martin tradition, Simpson said, 'we didn't see why the interior had to be olde worlde. The interiors should be beautiful to look at and touch, they should be exotic and cosseting; sportier than a Bentley and more sumptuous than a Ferrari. The trick was to get the highest quality and the handmade look to work well together.

'Though [Ian Callum] left me alone, he'd had 12 years with Ford, mainly in interiors and was very experienced and had a particularly good eye. Tom and Walter were very close to the project. It was a very big deal for Aston and us.'

The car was trimmed in Connolly leather and Wilton carpet with walnut veneer on the dash, console and doors. The dashboard contained analogue dials and a new four-spoke steering wheel.

The DB7 featured air conditioning, cruise control, electronically controlled windows and front seats, heated front and rear windscreens and mirrors, central locking and an alarm/immobiliser. The car was fully optioned; the only things to choose were paint and trim colours, transmissions and stereo systems.

Fine tuning was undertaken by Tom Walkinshaw, TWR test driver, David Hudson, race car builder, Adrian Reynard, Eric Broadley of Lola and ex-Grand Prix drivers Jackie Stewart and Peter Gethin. During its two-year development, more than 30 DB7 prototypes, including pilot production cars, were built for testing and evaluation, far more than any Aston Martin before it. The prototypes were extensively road tested in the UK, US, Australia and at Ford's Lommel test track in Belgium.

In the past, only one or two prototypes were typically built, and after demanding testing and evaluation were serviced, valeted and sold as used cars; Aston Martin simply couldn't afford not to. But in the age of litigation, Ford demanded all prototypes be destroyed. 'Victor would have found a way to sell the prototypes, but Ford could not,' remarked Michael Bowler.

If Aston Martin was to realise its potential for volume sales, the North American market was crucial and it was in January 1996 at the Detroit Motor Show that the DB7 was finally launched there. 'At the press launch we had a stage, on to which Stirling Moss was going to drive a DB4, with me as passenger,' recalled CEO David Price, who replaced John Oldfield in October 1995.

'I was to get out and do my speech. Unfortunately, at the dress rehearsal the previous evening, when the doors at the back of the stage slid open, the DB4 wouldn't start! We discovered a severe electrics problem that was not instantly fixable, so the only answer was to put the battery on charge until the very last minute and hope the car would start at the critical moment. Fortunately it did, but I was far more nervous about the possibility of pushing the car on stage (shades of the Lagonda V8 launch in the UK) than I was about speaking to a large US press audience about the DB7.' The DB7 was very well received in the US market and sales there were strong.

The DB7 saved Aston Martin. Without it, the company would almost certainly be no more. It was the first totally new car conceived from beginning to end while Aston Martin was under Ford control and as such, will be remembered as a seminal work in the company's history.

The DB7 became the most successful selling Aston Martin up to that point; Ford thus continued its promotion and development. The DB7 could well be the most important Aston Martin of all.

Ford Motor Company purchased the remaining 25 percent of shares in Aston Martin Lagonda Ltd on 1 July 1994. Obviously buoyed by the early positive reaction to the DB7, Ford committed itself 100 percent to the future of the company.

Bob Dover: 'The DB7 clearly saved the business, thanks to a lot of people. Aston Martin wouldn't be around if it wasn't for Peter Livanos and Victor Gauntlett; it certainly wouldn't be around without the enthusiasm and commitment of Ford.'

DB7
1993–1999

Chassis: Steel semi-monocoque body shell

Body: Composite and pressed steel 2+2 coupe styled by Ian Callum

Suspension: Front – Independent with double wishbones incorporating anti-dive geometry, coil springs, monotube dampers and anti-roll bar
Rear – Independent with double wishbones, longitudinal control arms, coil springs, monotube dampers and anti-roll bar

Brakes: Servo-assisted 284 mm ventilated discs with alloy four-piston callipers (front); 305 mm solid discs with sliding aluminium callipers (rear). Drum handbrake. ABS

Steering: Power-assisted rack and pinion

Wheels: 18-inch Speedline alloy

Tyres: Bridgestone Expedia 245/40 ZR18

Transmission: GM (or ZF) four-speed automatic with Sport Mode; final drive 3.058:1
Getrag five-speed manual; final drive 3.54:1. Limited-slip differential. Rear-wheel drive

Engine: 3228 cc alloy in-line six-cylinder with a chain-driven double overhead camshaft and four valves per cylinder. Compression ratio 8.3:1. M90 Eaton supercharger with bypass valve and liquid intercooler. Zytec engine management system with sequential fuel injection system. Fully catalysed exhaust system

Power: 335 bhp/250 kW @ 6000 rpm
361 lb/ft/489 Nm of torque @ 3000 rpm

Top speed: 165 mph/266 km/h

Dimensions:

Length	15 ft 1.5 in/4646 mm[i]	
Width	5 ft 9.5 in/1830 mm	
Height	4 ft 1.5 in/1238 mm	
Wheelbase	8 ft 5 in/2591 mm	
Weight	3802 lb/1725 kg	

Price when new: £78,500

Number built: 1605

i   The American-delivered cars were 3 inches (76 mm) longer owing to the more bulbous bumpers needed to meet safety legislation

DB7 – DB legend revived

Lagonda Saloon
Four-door reprieve

Various administrations, including Ford, have tried to revive the once-famous Lagonda name. The wedge-shaped Lagonda of the late 1970s came the closest, having a body design and chassis unique to that car, but a Lagonda with direct links to its roots had not been seen since 1958. After the demise of the Lagonda in 1990, the great name laid dormant until the arrival in 1993 of the Virage-derived four-door Lagonda Saloon and Shooting Brakes.

'We were operating in a difficult trading period,' recounted Kingsley Riding-Felce, 'and we thought, "What can we do? We can't continue to suffer. We can't have recessional thinking because with recessional thinking you go inwards instead of outwards. Let's try and sell ourselves out of trouble, let's try and do something!"

'We came up with this idea for an ex-engineering Virage. We spoke to a very good customer and said that if he were to buy this ex-engineering Virage, we would be happy to coachbuild the car to four-door specification as part of the package.

'We spoke to a very good customer and said that if he were to buy this ex-engineering Virage, we would be happy to coachbuild the car to four-door specification as part of the package.'

Kingsley Riding-Felce

'We would be able to use for the coachwork services the original Engineering Director, [Mike Loasby], who was involved in manufacturing and designing the original four-door Lagondas that were built back in the early 1970s. The company built seven of those: eight chassis, seven cars. Effectively, those seven cars were about a foot longer and had four doors.

'Mike Loasby said that he would be happy to come back and help us make a four-door version of the Virage, but to make it really the car that it should be, we decided to fit the 6.3-litre engine, the bigger brakes, the suspension upgrade and everything for the 6.3 conversion, but we won't put the big wheels and tyres on it. Naturally Steve Bolton would engineer

The stretch to four doors did not detract from the Virage's elegant lines

While not featuring the coupe's extensively flared wheel arches, the Lagonda Saloon was built to full 6.3-litre specification

something that would be more in keeping with the car, which he did. The customer agreed to it and we built that first four-door car, which was fantastic.'

'First we did the two-door (Virage) Shooting Brakes,' recalled Loasby. 'Then we did a four-door saloon, which went to a well-known Aston Martin customer, and a four-door Shooting Brake conversion of the Virage that went to a German gentleman.'

Painted Hunter Green, these two cars were used for publicity purposes and photographs. The impetus for further cars came when an order for a number of four-door Virages arrived from the Far East when the company was approached directly by the representative of a very special customer on 24 March 1993.

'The decision to make these (four-door) Estates and Saloons had been taken and they weren't finished but they were well on their way when the gentleman's representative came around and said, "Ha, I'll have those!"' remembered Loasby. 'Kingsley said he was sorry, but the cars were for somebody else. He repeated, "I want those", and it all went on from there. So we made some more.'

'When we let the world know about these cars it gave an "overseas collector" the interest to come and see us,' said Riding-Felce who dealt directly with the customer. 'Once we had orders from them to build these cars we didn't build them for anybody else and we didn't want to. They asked for exclusivity and they got it.'

Aston Martin built the modified chassis in production and the engineering and body work was carried out by the Special Projects Group that included Mike Loasby, Shaun Rush, Ray Brown, Trevor Stone, Joe Camozzi, George Burns, Arnold Heaton, Allen Pooley, Neil Morris, Ian Hartley, Peter Killick, Steve Bolton, Dave Townsend and the Manager for Special Projects, Kingsley Riding-Felce.

Apart from the added weight and the 12-inch extension in length, the Lagonda saloon was equipped much the same as the 6.3-litre Virage. The conversion, however, was more involved than first impressions may indicate. The Saloon had a completely new structure and panels behind the A-pillar. The front Virage-sourced doors were shortened, new, strengthened B-pillars were incorporated into the chassis design and new rear doors, a notch-back rear and relocated fuel filler caps were added. 'The rear windows of the saloon car were a matter of interest,' said Loasby. 'They were actually off a Rover Metro. They just happened to fit and it was possible to have them heated.'

The altered wheelbase was more easily facilitated by the fact that an altered Lagonda chassis was chosen for the Virage. Originally it was intended to give Aston Martin a common platform to incorporate future different wheelbases and therefore, models.

The Lagonda Saloon offered the customer the best in bespoke motoring, as almost any option was possible, including body and trim colour, seating configuration, airbags, CD player, TV and video or security devices. Even though 5.3- and 6.3-litre V8

Left: Rear windows were sourced from the Rover Metro **Right:** Kingsley Riding-Felce (second from left) inspecting the progress of a Lagonda Saloon

engines and manual and automatic gearbox options were available, all nine cars were chosen with the larger engines and automatic transmissions. Special polished split-rim 18-inch alloy wheels were chosen and fitted with Goodyear Eagle 285/45 ZR18 tyres to give the cars a distinctive look.

The price tag for one of these cars was not for the faint-hearted. Walter Hayes recounted that when a prospective customer enquired about the four-door Lagonda Saloon, he was told the price would be quite high. The customer rebuffed, 'Did I ask how much it would cost?'[15] The price of the Lagonda Saloon was 'quite high' at approximately £250,000.

'John Heffernan never designed the four-door [Virage-based] Lagondas,' said Loasby. 'He did the two-doors, certainly, but aft of the windscreen, we did it on those particular cars. John Heffernan wasn't terribly complimentary when we showed him the four-door cars. But then stylists aren't usually when they see that somebody else has messed with their design.

'I have to say, they didn't come out as well as I would have liked them to either, because when you talk to panel beaters, in the main, they are very good at making things off production jigs, but they are not very good at constructive work, so they didn't quite carry them off as well as they might have done. But the customers liked them.'

Development took 12 months, but the Lagonda Saloon was not a production car. A converted ex-engineering mule was used to avoid costly Type Approval on the first example. Those going to the Far East were built new, but registration laws were not a problem for that customer.

The first Lagonda Saloon, used in the publicity photos, was chassis number DP2034/5, while the collection of six saloons bound for the Far East, bore the chassis numbers 50279 (Cannock Black), 50401 (Cobalt Blue), 50402 (Emerald Green), 50405 (Titanium Grey), 50406 (Litchfield Black) and 50407 (Titanium Silver). In addition to the six 'standard' Lagonda Saloons, two long-wheelbase versions, chassis numbers 50427 (Special Red) and 50428 (Special Black) were also constructed; they both contained an 18-inch stretch to create rear leg room more in keeping with a limousine.

Lagonda Saloon
1993–1996

Chassis: Steel box-section chassis, steel superstructure

Body: Aluminium four-door saloon modified by Special Projects Group

Suspension: Front – Independent with transverse unequal length wishbones, coaxial spring damper units and anti-roll bar
Rear – de Dion axle, radius arms, Watt's linkage, damper units, single rate springs and anti-roll bar

Brakes: Servo-assisted Girling 355 mm ventilated discs with AP Racing four-piston callipers (front); 280 mm ventilated discs with AP Racing four-piston callipers (rear). Bosch four-channel ABS

Steering: Power-assisted rack and pinion

Wheels: 18-inch OZ alloy

Tyres: Goodyear Eagle 285/45 ZR18

Transmission: Four-speed Torqueflite automatic; final drive 3.058:1. Limited-slip differential. Rear-wheel drive

Engine: 6347 cc alloy V8 with twin chain-driven overhead camshafts per bank and four valves per cylinder. Compression ratio 9.5:1. Weber-Alpha sequential fuel injection. Fully catalysed exhaust system

Power: 495 bhp/369 kW @ 5750 rpm
480 lb/ft/651 Nm of torque @ 4400 rpm

Top speed: 170 mph/274 km/h (claimed)

Dimensions:
Length	16 ft 7 in/5050 mm[i]
Width	6 ft 1 in/1854 mm
Height	4 ft 5.5 in/1365 mm
Wheelbase	9 ft 6.2 in/2900 mm
Weight	4497 lb/2040 kg

Price when new: £248,000 (approx. depending on exact specification). Conversion price £115,000

Number built: 9

i   Two constructed 18 inches (457 mm) longer than the Virage coupe

Lagonda Shooting Brake

Les Vacances

'Inspiration for these new Lagondas,' said Walter Hayes in November 1993 upon the launch of the Lagonda Saloon and Shooting Brake, '… is entirely due to the owners … The renewal of individual demand for a more capacious four-door has been met through the expansion of our coachwork facilities and they are very special examples of British bespoke craftsmanship and the heritage of Aston Martin Lagonda.'

Aston Martin's Works Service Special Projects Group constructed the first Lagonda Shooting Brake: a stretched version of the Virage-based three-door Shooting Brake in 1993. As tradition decreed, it was named Lagonda by virtue of the number of doors. 'The green cars used in the publicity photos were called Lagonda. I won that argument. I argued that all four-doors should be called Lagondas. You can call "two-doors" Aston Martins, but it didn't seem right to me to call "four-doors" Aston Martins,' remarked Mike Loasby.

Like the Virage and Virage Volante, the car could be ordered with, or converted to, 6.3-litre specification. The fitment of a 6.3-litre engine alone cost an extra £28,116 in an already expensive package. Manual and automatic transmission could also be specified, along with almost any option the customer demanded. The German owner of the first car, chassis number DP2099/1, and the subsequent collection of six cars ordered by 'an overseas client' from the Far East, chassis numbers 50246 (Emerald Green), 50251 (Black), 50403 (Cobalt Blue), 50404 (Titanium Grey), 50408 (Titanium Grey), 50409 (Titanium Silver), all specified 6.3-litre engines and four-speed automatic transmissions.

> Having satisfied the demands of a special collector, many, more radical, specials were to follow in subsequent years.

The mechanical package remained almost the same as the Lagonda Saloon, including the large AP Racing brakes, polished split-rim 18-inch alloy wheels and Goodyear tyres. The Far East cars had some special interior features including bespoke fittings for carrying supplies, fitted luggage and dark tinted windows.

The five-door Lagonda Shooting Brake was the most capacious car ever constructed by Aston Martin

Clockwise from top left: The coachbuilt body taking shape; Window mechanisms were drawn out in cardboard; Lagonda grilles were attempted on both the Saloon and Shooting Brake but were abandoned for traditional Aston Martin frontal treatments; All seven Lagonda Shooting Brakes featured 6.3-litre V8 engines and four-speed automatic transmissions; The interior being mocked up

The luxurious interior followed that of the Virage Shooting Brake with an important and unique feature: it could be fitted with an optional rear-facing children's seat in the luggage compartment. This seating configuration could accommodate six passengers.

Regarding the creation of the Lagonda Shooting Brake, Kingsley Riding-Felce remembered, 'At the time we were doing a lot of coachbuilding and we talked about doing a Shooting Brake. We had a very good customer from Europe who said that he would buy an ex-engineering Virage, but specified that it should be a left-hand drive, four-door Shooting Brake, and it should be called 'Les Vacances' (The Vacation). So we built him a four-door Shooting Brake. We did a press release on these cars to try and create some interest around the world, to see if anyone would like some coachbuilding to take place.' They did.

'For the four-door Estates what we did was take the Virage chassis, which wasn't strictly all as I designed it; the whole front end, the bulkhead was the same, all the floor and the back end was the same basically, but it had some under-frame members added. We chopped them behind the front seats and [made them] a foot longer,' said Loasby.

The first Shooting Brake differed from the 'Far East' cars, however. 'When we did the [Far East] cars, we didn't make them a foot longer, they were a bit more than that, we made them 9 feet 10.2 inches in the wheelbase, instead of 9 feet 6.2 inches as earlier on. Those cars were a different kettle of fish from my point of view. They weren't done as before,' said Loasby.

The Lagonda Saloons and Shooting Brakes proved to be the beginning of a very exciting time for the Special Projects Group. Having satisfied the demands of a special collector many, more radical, specials were to follow in subsequent years.

Other Lagonda Shooting Brakes

In the early 1950s the Aston Martin Racing Department used a Tickford-converted 2.6-litre Lagonda, chassis number LAG/50/530 (pictured below at far left along with an AEC Regal transporter), with a wooden Shooting Brake body, to transport personnel and spares to sports car races. The Service Department also used a similar car, chassis number LAG/50/542, at the Feltham Factory during the 1960s.

The original Lagonda Shooting Brake was badged 'Vacances' at the request of the German customer

Lagonda Shooting Brake
1993–1996

Chassis: Steel box-section chassis, steel superstructure

Body: Aluminium four-door Shooting Brake modified by Special Projects Group

Suspension: Front – Independent with transverse unequal length wishbones, coaxial spring damper units and anti-roll bar
Rear – de Dion axle, radius arms, Watt's linkage, damper units, single rate springs and anti-roll bar

Brakes: Servo-assisted Girling 355 mm ventilated discs with AP Racing four-piston callipers (front); 280 mm ventilated discs with AP Racing four-piston callipers (rear). Bosch four-channel ABS

Steering: Power-assisted rack and pinion

Wheels: 18-inch OZ alloy

Tyres: Goodyear Eagle 285/45 ZR18

Transmission: Four-speed Torqueflite automatic; final drive 3.058:1. Limited-slip differential. Rear-wheel drive

Engine: 6347 cc alloy V8 with twin chain-driven overhead camshafts per bank and four valves per cylinder. Compression ratio 9.5:1. Weber-Alpha sequential fuel injection. Fully catalysed exhaust system

Power: 495 bhp/369 kW @ 5750 rpm
480 lb/ft/651 Nm of torque @ 4400 rpm

Top speed: 170 mph/274 km/h (claimed)

Dimensions:
Length	16 ft 7 in/5050 mm
Width	6 ft 1 in/1854 mm
Height	4 ft 5.5 in/1365 mm
Wheelbase	9 ft 6.2 in/2900 mm or 9 ft 10.2 in/3000 mm
Weight	4497 lb/2040 kg

Price when new: £254,000 (approx. depending on exact specification). Conversion price £121,000

Number built: 7

Limited Edition Coupe

Limited edition of a limited run

The Virage was a popular seller when first launched, but as time marched on it began to lose its appeal, especially when the Volante and Vantage were unveiled. To compound the problem, a recession and news of the impending release of the DB7 discouraged buyers to the point that, during 1992 and 1993, Virages were literally trickling out of Newport Pagnell at one or two cars per week.

To promote business, Aston Martin produced a small number of Virage-based specials, including Shooting Brakes and four-door saloons. But by 1994 Virage orders had virtually stopped and Aston Martin was left with nine unsold chassis. To sell the cars a Limited Edition Coupe was conceived and unveiled at the British International Motor Show in October 1994.

Aston Martin had never previously used the Limited Edition badge, but in this case it was justified. Costing around £3000 more than the standard model, only nine examples were made, encompassing chassis numbers AMSRR50411 to AMSRR50419; a very limited edition run by anybody's standards.

It was important for Aston Martin to increase the power output of the V8 because it would, in part at least, justify the price premium over the DB7.

All nine cars were painted in the same dark, metallic British Racing Green and the interiors trimmed in saddle brown Connolly leather upholstery with beige and green trim. Burr elm was featured on the instrument panel and doors and a brass plaque, noting the car's chassis number and original owner's name, was fitted to the fascia panel. A driver airbag came as standard.

Outwardly, two aspects set the Limited Edition Coupe apart from the standard Virage: the unique 'continuous V' grille and five-spoke, 18-inch alloy wheels. The engine was more powerful, too.

Outwardly the main difference between the Limited Edition Coupe and the donor Virage was the continuous V-shaped grille

143

Limited Edition Coupes featured saddle-brown leather trim, burr elm inserts and a plaque stating the name of the original owner on the dashboard

John Oldfield

John Oldfield was born on 13 January 1937 and studied at the Cranfield Institute of Technology, obtaining a Masters Degree in Science. He joined Ford in 1958 as an engineer responsible for suspension, steering, transmission and chassis design. In 1973 he was appointed Manager of Light and Large Car Development for Ford of Europe. In 1974 he was promoted to Chief Engineer of Ford in Brazil and in 1976 became Chief Engineer for Ford Chassis Engineering in Europe, moving on to Chief Vehicle Engineer for the Escort programme.

Between 1980 and 1983 he acted as Vice President responsible for Ford Product Development, then Director of Vehicle Engineering in Europe. He then moved to Ford in North America for one year as Executive Director of Engineering and Manufacturing, becoming engineer in charge of planning, design and development of the Ford Mondeo.

He was appointed Ford European Vice President for Product Development in 1989 and became Vice President of Ford Motor Company in January 1991.

Oldfield succeeded the retiring Walter Hayes as Executive Chairman of AML on 1 February 1994. Being an enthusiastic engineer, Oldfield became involved in the development of the DB7, driving the prototype cars. He vacated his position in October 1995 due to ill health and died in 2002.

Virage Lynx Turbo
1995/2002

Limited Edition Coupe chassis number AMSRR50413 was possibly the ultimate Virage in terms of performance and perhaps the most outrageous Aston Martin road car ever made. Having already had a 7.0-litre engine conversion carried out by RS Williams, the owner took the car to Lynx Motors International for a major mechanical overhaul. The conversion work included a 720 bhp, turbo-charged engine producing 1140 lb/ft of torque. Alterations were also made to the transmission and suspension, while at the owner's request the body remained standard, save for the necessary air intakes in the front valance and larger wheels and tyres.

Car for life

Aston Martin's 'Car for Life' programme is a commitment to owners of classic post-1950s Aston Martins that the factory will supply parts and restoration services 'for life'.

'We feel we have a special responsibility to every member of this family,' said Walter Hayes. 'We see no reason why cars we are making today should not be in perfect condition 75 years from now, or longer. The philosophy behind the idea is that someone does not buy one of our cars then disappears. There is a bond between us and them.'

The Car for Life programme was the brainchild of Walter Hayes and Kingsley Riding-Felce. 'We had this impasse at Works Service,' remembered Riding-Felce. 'We had not been able to move forward. Walter Hayes was desperately trying to get the DB7 programme approved and part of that was he saw revenue coming in from Works Service to keep the company going. We had discussions; he saw opportunities here and made me a Director. He felt that if I were given the right levels of confidence and assurance, we could really take the business forward.

'We planned a lot of things and the more we talked about it, the more it became obvious that an Aston Martin really is a Car for Life. It never dies, it doesn't matter what you do, you can't really kill it because if you've got the chassis plate we can make the car again.

'Mr Hayes thought the cars never die because they can be returned, serviced, painted and repaired. Certainly in those days, when we were building cars that were more traditionally coachbuilt, it was a lot easier to make them right-hand drive, left-hand drive, automatic, manual, whatever. So all these discussions came back to a Car for Life and a new emphasis was placed on the business.

'Mr Hayes contacted one of his old pals in the video business and he came up with his cameras. He called in a lot of favours from his old colleagues like Innes Ireland and we did a video called *A Car for Life*. We then started to do some literature and tried to reinvent the after-sales business.

'We did a lot of work with parts, trying to push that forward saying, "What parts haven't we got? What parts do we need?" I put a team together and set about getting them, because if we can support the business with the right level of parts, it really is a Car for Life.'

'The engine followed Virage specifications,' recalled Arthur Wilson, 'but a small yet significant upgrade in performance was achieved simply by fitting the new cylinder heads created for the Vantage; no other changes were made. This resulted in a power increase from the 306 bhp and 340 lb/ft of torque from the Virage to 335 bhp and 350 lb/ft of torque for the Limited Edition Coupe, which was a good demonstration of the effectiveness of the new-design cylinder heads.'

It was important for Aston Martin to increase the power output of the V8 because it would, in part at least, justify the price premium over the DB7, which had surpassed the Virage's 306 bhp by about ten percent.

Limited Edition Coupe
1994

Chassis: Steel box-section chassis, steel superstructure

Body: Aluminium 2+2 coupe styled by John Heffernan

Suspension: Front – Independent with double wishbones, coil springs, coaxial spring dampers and anti-roll bar
Rear – de Dion axle, radius arms, Watt's linkage, coil springs and telescopic dampers

Brakes: Servo-assisted Girling 330 mm ventilated discs (front); 289 mm ventilated discs (rear). ABS

Steering: Power-assisted rack and pinion

Wheels: 18-inch alloy

Tyres: Avon Turbospeed 255/60 ZR18

Transmission: Torqueflite four-speed automatic; final drive 3.058:1
ZF five-speed manual; final drive 3.33:1. Limited-slip differential. Rear-wheel drive

Engine: 5340 cc alloy V8 with twin chain-driven overhead camshafts per bank and four valves per cylinder. Compression ratio 9.75:1. EEC IV engine management system. Fully catalysed exhaust system

Power: 335 bhp/250 kW @ 6000 rpm
350 lb/ft/475 Nm of torque @ 4300 rpm

Top speed: 155-plus mph/249-plus km/h

Dimensions:

Length	15 ft 7 in/4745 mm
Width	6 ft 4 in/1940 mm
Height	4 ft 4.5 in/1330 mm
Wheelbase	8 ft 6.75 in/2610 mm
Weight	4233 lb/1920 kg

Price when new: £137,500

Number built: 9

DB7 V8 Le Mans
Target 24 Hours

In the absence of a full Works team, several Aston Martin-powered privateer outfits raced at Le Mans during the 1970s and 1980s. In the mid-1990s French motor sport enthusiast and publisher Michel Hommell also tried to return Aston Martin to the famed endurance race.

'Fond of Bugatti, Michel Hommell made a deal with the new Italian management and the French importer (of Bugatti) to enter an EB 110 SS in the GT class at Le Mans in 1994,' said ex-racing driver and journalist Jose Rosinski, leader of Hommell's team. 'This was to be the very first race of this new car. It ran like a train during the first two-thirds of the race, up to eighth in the general classification and second in GT when the turbos started to fail one after the other … and there were four!

'The promising experience encouraged Michel Hommell to start again in 1995, but the new Bugatti operation turned sour. However, the French importer, British Motors, was also the Aston Martin concessionaire in Paris. So they made contact with Aston Martin, which was then in the process of launching the DB7 and found their idea appropriate.

'[The car] was purchased on a special order without an engine, transmission and different other items at a special price. During the fall of 1994 Aston Martin organised a meeting with TWR representatives, RS Williams and ourselves. TWR agreed to supply contracts with different English contractors for tanks, brakes etc. and Williams to build two of its V8 racing engines to Le Mans 1995 technical regulations and sell them to us, as well as service them during tests and the race.

'Putting the V8 into the DB7 was unanimously decided during this meeting as the best chance to be ready in time and competitive, considering the short period of time available. The engine derived from the 1989 V8 AMR. It was 6299 cc [105.5 x 90 mm] and had 2+2 overhead camshafts, 32 valves, Zytec electronic injection, 60 mm diameter air restrictor, 11.2:1 compression ratio and a dry sump. It produced 619 bhp @ 6600 rpm and 500 lb/ft of torque @ 5800 rpm.'

John Watson at RS Williams built the AMR-1-derived engine and Neil Thompson dyno tested it at Williams' Cobham premises. The transmission was a ZF six-speed synchronised gearbox with special gears and an 85 percent limited-slip differential by the French firm, SADEC.

ASTON MARTIN: POWER, BEAUTY AND SOUL

A protracted build period precluded thorough development, meaning the DB7 V8 narrowly missed out on a Le Mans berth

The GT1 class allowed entrants to use *any* engine produced by the engine supplier; not necessarily the unit fitted to the *production* model on which the racing car was based.

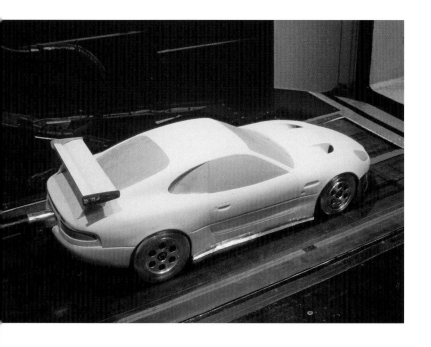

Michel Hommell

Michel Hommell started motor racing in the 1960s in the Coupe Renault 8 Gordini formula. He then successfully launched two motor sport magazines, *Echappement* and *Auto Hebdo* and owns and runs one of the most prosperous groups of specialist magazines in France.

'Michel Hommell has managed to rebirth a small town in Brittany called Lohéac and dedicate the whole place to motorsport,' said Jose Rosinski. 'There he built a circuit, a factory to make a small production of sports racing cars, the Hommell Berlinettes and Roadsters, with Peugeot 2.0-litre engines amidships and a tubular space frame, and a huge Museum named Manoir de l'Automobile, which has become one of the most important in France. This is the place where the Aston Martin DB7 V8 can be seen, sometimes even on the track, which surrounds the museum.'

Top: A model of the DB7 V8 Le Mans undergoing wind tunnel testing **Above:** Compared to the production car, the race version retained the spirit of Ian Callum's original

Top: All exterior panels were remodelled in lightweight composite carbon fibre and aluminium but the profile of the car remained distinctly DB7
Above: The interior was pure race car but the DB7's interior door handles and some wood veneer still remained

Above: The V8 engine was a tight fit in the DB7's engine bay Below: The DB7 V8 Le Mans undergoing testing in France

'The chassis was built at Changé, near Le Mans,' added Rosinski, 'in the Synergie company premises, by a team consisting of ex-Rondeau personnel who were very experienced in Le Mans peculiarities. Chief designer Philippe Beloou modified the standard chassis by relocating the engine, roll cage and suspension. The weight distribution was modified to 45 percent front and 55 percent rear, the battery was moved into the cabin and the alternator over the rear axle. The car used Alcon four piston brakes with carbon discs, 375 mm front and 325 mm rear.

'The body had doors, wings and front bonnet made in carbon, which kept the weight down to 2932 lb; it was [3802 lb] in standard form. The body modifications were made by ex-Venturi designer, Gerard Godfroy. The car was tested and tuned in a wind tunnel by Max Sardou, one of the best renowned French aerodynamicists.'

Recalling his part in the making of the DB7 V8, Richard Williams stated, 'We were involved with only the engine of this car. We prepared a 6.3-litre engine based on the AMR-1 engine that we had successfully used in the World Sports Car Championship in 1989.'

Model	Weight (lb)	0–60 mph (seconds)	Top speed (mph)	Power (bhp)
DB7	3802	5.7	165	335
DB7 V8	2932	4.0 (est)	200	619

The DB7 V8 was entered in the 1995 Le Mans 24-hour race in the GT1 category by the French Manoir de l'Automobile team. The GT1 class allowed entrants to use *any* engine produced by the engine supplier; not necessarily the unit fitted to the *production* model on which the racing car was based. The DB7 V8's 6.3-litre powerplant qualified because it was an option for the Virage.

Not being among the 20 invited entries, Hommell and his team needed to qualify for the race in the pre-qualifying weekend at the end of April. The car was only completed a few days before the practice sessions and furious development work continued day and night leading up to the all-important pre-qualifying sessions.

'The Le Mans operation was properly funded and carefully planned,' said Rosinski 'but Aston Martin was unexpectedly slow to deliver the car and Synergie started to build it much too late. It was completed just in time, but at the expense of the development programme, which was reduced to one session of two hours only. So the DB7 V8, which took to the track at the Le Mans pre-qualifying session, came practically straight from the workshop, far from being fully developed.'

Drivers for the qualifying sessions were ex-Le Mans winner Eric Helary and Alain Cudini. The best recorded lap time, 4.09.97 with Helary at the wheel, was narrowly beaten by the Lister Storm GTS, which set a best time of 4.08.74. There would be no Aston Martin at Le Mans.

'Considering the fact that it missed the target only narrowly – it was bumped off for approximately one second – its performance in these conditions was far from disgraceful, especially if you take into account the fact that it was substantially a modified production car and not one purpose-made for racing, like the Lister for instance, or even the McLaren. But its full potential must have been impressive, as demonstrated by the fact that it ran nearly 8 seconds faster than the Bugatti EB 110 SS, which put in such a good show the year before!'

For Hommell and his supporters, the dream of another Aston Martin assault on Le Mans did not materialise. How it would have performed in the gruelling 24-hour race can only be left to speculation; racing successfully against spectacular GT1 opposition from Jaguar XJ220Cs, Ferrari F40s, McLaren F1 GTRs and Porsche 911 RSRs would have been an extremely difficult task.

DB7 V8 Le Mans
1995

Chassis: Steel semi-monocoque body shell. Modified by Synergie

Body: Composite, carbon fibre and pressed aluminium 2+2 coupe styled by Ian Callum. Modified by Gerard Godfroy

Suspension: Front – Independent with double wishbones, coil springs, monotube dampers and anti-roll bar
Rear – Independent with double wishbones, longitudinal control arms, coil springs, monotube dampers and anti-roll bar

Brakes: Servo-assisted 375 mm ventilated discs with Alcon four-piston callipers (front); 325 mm carbon discs with Alcon four-piston callipers (rear)

Steering: Power-assisted rack and pinion

Wheels: 18-inch BBS alloy

Tyres: Dunlop Racing 280/650 R18 AV (front). 300/710 R18 AR (rear)

Transmission: ZF six-speed manual; final drive 3.33:1. Limited-slip differential. Rear-wheel drive

Engine: 6299 cc alloy V8 with twin chain-driven overhead camshafts per bank and four valves per cylinder. Compression ratio 11.2:1. Zytec electronic fuel injection

Power: 619 bhp/462 kW @ 6600 rpm
500 lb/ft/678 Nm of torque @ 5800 rpm

Top speed: 200 mph/322 km/h (approx)

Dimensions:

Length	15 ft 7 in/4646 mm
Width	5 ft 9.5 in/1830 mm
Height	4 ft 1.5 in/1238 mm
Wheelbase	8 ft 5 in/2591 mm
Weight	2932 lb/1330 kg

Price when new: N/A

Number built: 1

DB7 GT

Gentleman's racer

Aston Martin had been keen to return to racing since the untimely demise of the AMR project, but it couldn't afford to. All company efforts were concentrated on the production cars and on gaining financial stability. After the successful launch of the DB7, however, thoughts once again turned to racing the new car. Ferrari and Porsche had their own one-make racing series so a similar application for the DB7 seemed obvious.

Early in 1995, after a number of requests from customers, the AML Board of Directors met and agreed in principle to support the construction of a DB7 racing car with a possibility of developing a single-make racing programme. Aston Martin sought out companies and suppliers to assist in the development of the car and on 15 May 1995 an agreement was signed between Managing Director of Prodrive Holding Ltd., David Richards and Managing Director of AML, Nick Fry.

Richards recalled, 'The DB7 GT was intended for a race series. It was meant to be a race car but we only built one. We did all the design work and we built the car; it was actually commissioned by Aston Martin. We ran the car just in testing, but it all came to naught in the end.'

> ## Luxuries like electric windows, stereo system and air conditioning were dispensed with but the cabin was still nicely fitted out for a race car.

'Two cars were built for the purpose of evaluation for the [DB7] single-make series,' remembered Kingsley Riding-Felce. 'The first testing of one of those cars was out in Pembery in Wales with Andy Wallace driving. Works Service then took one of those cars and made it into a real gentleman's racer.'

The precedent for a racing derivative of the road-going DB7 was created in 1960 when the DB4 was shortened and lightened to become the DB4 GT. That model went on to some competition success in the hands of drivers Stirling Moss, Jim Clark and Lex Davison.

Two DB7 GTs were constructed and evaluated for a possible one-make racing series, which did not eventuate

David Price

David Price came to Aston Martin with more than 30 years experience with Ford Motor Company. 'I joined Ford in 1964,' said Price, 'and worked principally in finance and product planning. I then came back in the 1980s into program management, which was a new development at the time for Ford. I was the Program Manager for all engine and transmission programmes in the 1980s. In the late-1980s through to the 1993 launch I was Program Manager for Mondeo [Europe] and Contour [US].

'I [was] in South America working on the break up of the joint venture involving Volkswagen and Ford in Argentina and I got a phone call from Jac Nasser at five o'clock on a Thursday morning in October 1995. He asked if I would like to be Chairman of Aston Martin and said to come as soon as I could. I was on a plane that night and in the office for a board meeting on the Monday morning. Things happen fast at Ford!

'I had a reasonable knowledge of the company, in that I understood its product, starting in the days when, as a young teenager, I drooled over the DB4 at the London Motor Show. Brilliant though the product was, I wondered if it was right for the modern world. It was a company I held great respect for, but it was difficult to comprehend in the 1990s.'

Price presided over the US launch of the DB7 and DB7 Volante, the V8 Coupe and development of the V8 Volante. He left Aston Martin in early 1997 to take up a senior position with a major UK engineering firm.

Driving Dynamics

The development experience gleaned from the DB7 GT proved invaluable. The components and set-ups used on the racers led to the after-market Driving Dynamics package, which was launched in 1998 by Works Service. The package provided owners of standard DB7s with up-rated AP Racing brakes with ABS, adjustable suspension, traction control and a catalysed competition sports exhaust.

The DB7's body could also be modified with a Visual Dynamics package, which included sill extensions, deeper front spoiler, modified rear bumper with extended valance, modest boot spoiler and Works-prepared badge. Five-spoke magnesium wheels could also be fitted. Customers could choose individual items starting from £797 to the full package at £34,000.

The Prodrive car differed from the DB4 GT in that the wheelbase was not shortened. The DB7 GT was, however, stripped to the bare essentials and the side glass replaced by Perspex, which lightened it considerably. A roll cage was built in and the brakes and suspension up-rated to cope with racing conditions. The green Prodrive car, chassis number 100001, was notable for its painted red nose.

The AML board investigated the possibility of developing its own racing DB7s and put forward the idea of developing two versions of the racing car. One was to be exclusively for track work, the other for combined track and road use. But early on the idea of a road and track car was abandoned. All efforts were concentrated on developing a gentleman's racer. The Customer Service Division (now Works Service) acquired a press car, chassis number 100006, and totally dismantled it in readiness for the detailed rebuild in the mould of Prodrive's prototype.

The body shell was taken to Safety Devices where a roll cage was fitted. The car was then placed in the hands of the Competitions Department. The cabin was fitted with adjustable black leather Recaro competition seats and the interior was trimmed in all-black leather, Alcantara, carpet and quilted vinyl. A driver's-side cut-off switch and fire extinguisher were also supplied. An oval plaque on the dashboard stated: 'DB7 GT prototype 001 Aston Martin Lagonda Ltd. Competitions Department Newport Pagnell Buckinghamshire'.

Special lightweight aluminium bonnet, boot and front wing panels were produced and aluminium door frames fabricated to accommodate Perspex side windows. Standard front and rear windows were fitted, as were different mirrors. Luxuries like electric windows, stereo system and air conditioning were dispensed with but the cabin was still nicely fitted out for a race car.

Above: Stirling Moss at the wheel of the DB7 GT which, although a stripped-out race car, was still neatly trimmed. **Opposite top:** Stirling Moss testing the Works-prepared DB7 GT at Goodwood

The Works-prepared DB7 GT was painted metallic Almond Green with a yellow snout and large white roundels, much like the Aston Martin DB3S and DBR1 racing cars of the 1950s. The car certainly looked the part, but it was strictly for the track; it was not road-legal.

A TWR-developed supercharged 3.2-litre engine with aluminium radiator and oil cooler was installed, as was a competition clutch, five-speed manual transmission and specially tuned exhaust with centre catalyst. The Prodrive-developed competition brakes included a new master cylinder and driver's balance valve, while the rear suspension featured a new oil-cooled rear axle and Penske gas shock absorbers, which could be adjusted by the driver from inside the cabin. The front suspension was modified and included a newly designed upright, with uprated adjustable dampers, modified springs and roll bar.

CEO John Oldfield was very enthusiastic about Aston Martin returning to racing. 'There's lots of ambition,' said Oldfield. 'What we'd like to do is go back to Le Mans, and probably Daytona as well, with the DB7. The Aston Martin name is still strong enough and a lot of people will support us.'

The completed DB7 GT was tested at MIRA and once final specification had been decided, Le Mans-winner and ex-Formula One driver Andy Wallace thoroughly tested the car at Millbrook and Pembrey with the Prodrive team. During October 1995 a customer clinic was held at Goodwood to assess possible interest and Stirling Moss was called in to demonstrate the car. A dozen wealthy potential clients were each allowed six laps of Goodwood at racing speeds. Riding-Felce said at the time Aston Martin would need to find 25 buyers and a sponsor if the series was to get underway.

'At last, an Aston with a nice gearbox,' said Stirling Moss in reaction to the car. 'The steering is much lighter than I'm used to but the turn-in is good, the adhesion is good and there's plenty of torque from the engine. A grid full of these would make quite a sight. Certainly an expensive sight.'[16]

Oldfield was replaced at the helm by David Price in October 1995 and the Aston Martin board discussed the possibility of continuing on with development, but the proposal was eventually abandoned. At a time when Aston Martin desperately needed to focus its resources for the V12 DB7 development, a decision not to pursue the project was made by Price early in 1996 because he 'could not get support from senior Ford management.' No longer needed, the Works sold its DB7 GT, (A7 AML), on 28 March 1996.

Riding-Felce recalled, 'I was lucky enough to be involved in the original development programme for a single-series make DB7. We had some days down at Goodwood testing the first AA1 sports racing car. Unfortunately the series didn't go ahead, but we built some wonderful motor cars and, in fact, two of those cars are now in private ownership. It really epitomised the gentleman's racer and could have been a very exciting programme.'

DB7 GT
1995

Chassis: Steel semi-monocoque body shell

Body: Composite, aluminium and pressed aluminium 2+2 coupe styled by Ian Callum. Modified by Aston Martin Competitions Department

Suspension: Front – Independent with double wishbones, coil springs, monotube dampers and anti-roll bar
Rear – Independent with double wishbones, longitudinal control arms, coil springs, monotube dampers and anti-roll bar

Brakes: Servo-assisted 14.5-inch ventilated discs with AP Racing six-piston callipers (front); 12-inch ventilated discs with AP Racing four-piston callipers with fully adjustable balance valve (rear)

Steering: Power-assisted rack and pinion

Wheels: 18-inch Speedline alloy

Tyres: Bridgestone Expedia 245/40 ZR18

Transmission: Getrag five-speed manual; final drive 3.77:1. Limited-slip differential. Rear-wheel drive

Engine: 3228 cc alloy in-line six-cylinder with a chain-driven double overhead camshaft and four valves per cylinder. Eaton M90 supercharger. Competition exhaust system

Power: 385 bhp/287 kW @ 6500 rpm
400 lb/ft/542 Nm of torque @ 4500 rpm

Top speed: 180 mph/290 km/h (approx)

Dimensions:
Length	15 ft 1.5 in/4646 mm
Width	5 ft 9.5 in/1830 mm
Height	4 ft 1.5 in/1238 mm
Wheelbase	8 ft 5/2591 mm
Weight	3086 lb/1400 kg (approx)

Price when new: N/A

Number built: 2

DB7 GT – Gentleman's racer

DB7 Volante

La Volare Sei

The DB7 Volante was unveiled at both the Los Angeles and Detroit Motor Shows in January 1996. At the Detroit launch, Stirling Moss and Alex Trotman, President of Ford Europe, drove the much-anticipated convertible onto a revolving stage to the sound of a trumpet fanfare. An American launch was no accident. The carefully orchestrated unveiling was in deference to what Aston Martin hoped would become the Volante's most profitable market.

'In January 1996 we were launching the DB7 coupe and Volante in the States,' remembered David Price. 'We had been away from America for a considerable time so the launch of the DB7 there was very significant; it was certainly the most significant thing during my time at Astons.

'When I got to Aston Martin we strengthened the US sales structure. I thought [we needed] a more robust and elegant sales strategy. That was essential before the launch and I think was relatively successful in the near term. We nevertheless struggled for a time there simply because it was a name that wasn't known to a lot of people by that time; we had been absent for so long. We even had one dealer who insisted on referring to us as "Austin Martin"!'

The convertible version of the DB7 wasn't designed side-by-side with the coupe, though a Volante had been envisioned from the start. Designer Ian Callum commented that the DB7's styling may have been compromised if a convertible was designed along with the coupe. Development of the open car started as soon as the coupe was signed off. Volante production started with chassis number AA4SK 200001 shortly after its launch.

'We did the Volante after the coupe,' said Callum. 'We knew from the beginning that we would be doing one because that's what the market would demand. It seemed to happen very naturally; it wasn't a struggle. Jaguar had learnt a lot from the convertible XJS, so we knew the platform was strong enough.

'We did a clay model of the Volante and we took pictures. Because it was an elegant design it wasn't too difficult to do. I mean we had to get the lines right; it wasn't as easy as just taking the roof off. It had to be more deliberate than that. The rear seats, rear deck and rear wings took a lot of reworking. There was a point on the rear wings where everything above that had

Volante versions of the DB7 contained all of the elegance of the coupe original but handling was inferior

The carefully orchestrated unveiling was in deference to what Aston Martin hoped would become the Volante's most profitable market.

Right: A DB7 Volante featuring a 'Visual Dynamics' body kit by Works Service
Below: The hood added weight but detracted nothing from the car's looks

to be different and everything below that point had to be exactly the same. It was a good exercise. It really is my favourite car.'

Callum's design was extremely handsome. The complete rear-end section of the car was changed, wheel arch flares smoothed out and fuel filler repositioned. The chassis too came in for some subtle changes. To compensate for the lack of fixed roof, extra strengthening was incorporated by way of tubular reinforcement in the sills, under-floor and windscreen.

Other revisions included stiffer springs with softer damping to suit the car's less overtly sporting market, revised steering, new 12-spoke alloy wheels and improved brakes.

The Volante featured a Newport Pagnell-made fully lined, electronically operated mohair hood with glass rear screen. The interior included restyled seats, also incorporated at the same time into the coupe, some upgraded switch gear with slightly revised ergonomics and better safety equipment.

The use of steel sheet, in place of the front end's composite materials, and the powered hood mechanism, pushed the DB7 Volante's weight to 4133 lb; almost as much as the contemporary Vantage. Predictably, performance was blunted – top speed was quoted at 155 mph. Still, the DB7 Volante proved very popular with 879 sales, further cementing the DB7 as Aston Martin's most successful model up to that time.

Top: Thoughtful details added to the DB7 Volante's beauty **Above:** While the lights remained the same, much of the rear deck was redesigned to accommodate the folding hood

DB7 Volante
1996–1999

Chassis: Steel semi-monocoque body shell

Body: Composite and pressed steel 2+2 convertible styled by Ian Callum

Suspension: Front – Independent with double wishbones incorporating anti-dive geometry, coil springs, monotube dampers and anti-roll bar
Rear – Independent with double wishbones, longitudinal control arms, coil springs and monotube dampers

Brakes: Servo-assisted 284 mm ventilated discs with alloy four-piston callipers (front); 305 mm solid discs with sliding aluminium callipers (rear). Drum handbrake. ABS

Steering: Power-assisted rack and pinion

Wheels: Speedline18-inch alloy

Tyres: Bridgestone Expedia 245/40 ZR18

Transmission: GM four-speed automatic; final drive 3.058:1 Getrag five-speed manual; final drive 3.54:1. Limited-slip differential. Rear-wheel drive

Engine: 3228 cc alloy in-line six-cylinder with a chain-driven double overhead camshaft and four valves per cylinder. Compression ratio 8.3:1. Single M90 Eaton supercharger. EEC-V engine management system with sequential fuel injection. Fully catalysed exhaust system

Power: 335 bhp/250 kW @ 5750 rpm
361 lb/ft/489 Nm of torque @ 3000 rpm

Top speed: 155 mph/249 km/h

Dimensions:
Length	15 ft 2 in/4646 mmⁱ
Width	5 ft 9.5 in/1830 mm
Height	4 ft 2 in/1260 mm
Wheelbase	8 ft 5in/2591 mm
Weight	4133 lb/1875 kg

Price when new: £86,500

Number built: 879

i   The American edition was 3 inches (76 mm) longer owing to the more bulbous bumpers needed to meet safety legislation

Vantage Special Type I
On His Majesty's Secret Service Part I

The story of the Vantage Special Series cars has remained a closely guarded secret at Aston Martin. These cars, all made for the same customer, are the greatest legacy of the company's coachbuilt era. Splendid, distinctive cars, each one truly unique, they are enticing reminders of a time when Aston Martin really could offer bespoke motoring, and did it better than anyone else.

The story of these cars began when a representative of a Far East customer approached Aston Martin, requesting some four-door Lagonda Saloons and Shooting Brakes for his client. While work commenced on these Virage-based cars, a number of brand-new special-edition production cars with 6.3-litre engines, bigger wheels and brakes and bespoke interiors were commissioned.

'So we did all that work and one day he came back to us and asked for seven more of each,' remembered Kingsley Riding-Felce. 'At this stage David Eales and I nearly fell on the floor; Mike Loasby, Keith Riddington and a few others who were here all looked at each other and said, "Wow!"'

'The entire programme was done in total secrecy; most of the people in the company didn't even know it was happening.'

Kingsley Riding-Felce

Initially the customer requested a totally new bespoke four-door design for a collection of three cars. Sketches were commissioned and taken to one of the UK's most respected design houses and to Shapecraft. Working with them, in particular Clive Smart at Shapecraft, an apprentice and former employee of Aston Martin, the Special Projects Group, led by Riding-Felce, began building these very important cars.

The commission was clearly an opportunity to develop the business at Works Service. Based on the success the group had with the four-door Lagondas, Riding-Felce collected illustrations and more detailed feasibility sketches of a Vantage-based four-door saloon to show the client.

The first of the Special Series Vantages, the Type I was a stretched Vantage coupe, but with many special features

'This was the start of a very interesting period in my working life,' said Riding-Felce. 'To manage a project that encompasses the building of special motor cars from concept to delivery was a rare opportunity, both for the company and for me. There is nothing for nothing in this world and when the particular order came through we had to be available 24 hours a day, seven days a week. It involved many trips out to the Far East, with very short notice and we were rarely there for less than a fortnight at a time.

'It was an incredible time. To have the opportunity to meet the client, receive his expectations, come back with an illustration and a plan, receive the orders, come back [to Newport Pagnell] to work with a small group of dedicated clever people, build a unique and high-performance motor car to the customer's requirements, test it, refine it, put it on an aircraft at Stansted airport, fly out, take it off the Antonoff aircraft at the other end, prepare it, check it and hand it over to the customer, was a unique opportunity. As a group, that's what we did, many times.

'Through all of this David Townsend was a tremendous strength because he had the job of servicing all of the cars and finding out all the things that could happen in that climate. He and I used to go out working very closely together and for me it was great, because during the day I could put my overalls on and work on the cars so that I could see first-hand what was happening. Then I could come back, inform the team along with David on what we should do and in the evenings, I could put my suit on and wait for an audience with the client.

'Steve Bolton was doing a wonderful job here doing engineering for us and Mike Loasby was then working with us on some special projects. Keith Riddington and John Janes in the meantime were doing a tremendous job managing the pressures of the daily business. We used a number of top-quality outside suppliers and specialists and we really met the customer's expectations. We built some absolutely superb motor cars; we were head-to-head with Rolls-Royce and Bentley, Ferrari and Pininfarina, Mercedes and AMG.

'I can honestly say that in a lot of ways we really did better than they did on a number of occasions with some top quality products because we were a small, dedicated and focused team. We didn't have to go through some of the laborious processes that they were going through, as large organisations having clay bodies made with teams of people signing them off and teams of people making decisions.

Above: While following the basic lines of the production interior the Type I featured special chrome-plated bezels and switch gear
Opposite: Highly polished 18-inch OZ alloy wheels were featured on all three cars

'We were very lucky in the sense that we could design the cars, do the quarter scale, blow it up to full scale, make the egg crate and fit it onto a chassis, run panels over the chassis, get a design, put it into the wind tunnel, do some work, come back, make the changes, re-check it, make the bucks and then start beating out the panels.

'We made the decisions as we went along; we didn't have a big committee that I was accountable to. Our only committee was the customer. He knew what he wanted, we knew what we wanted and we could deliver for him. Of course, it was made so much easier by then because we then went on to building these cars based on the Vantage that was in production, as the company had gone away from the Virage.

'The Vantage team, run by Mike Booth along with Steve Bolton, went back to the original rear axle de Dion setup. We had a wonderful, powerful 550-horsepower twin-supercharged engine, a superb chassis, a torque tube from the gearbox at the rear axle assembly, big brakes and a well-and-truly sorted car. Then we started doing all our special work and development on the Vantage that was in production, so we moved away from our 6.3-litre conversions and based all our work on the Vantage and 600-horsepower conversions. That meant we could produce special-bodied two-door and four-door versions of the Vantage.'

Arthur Wilson and Bolton developed a 600 bhp engine package, fitted with specially developed four-speed-plus-overdrive Chrysler

Torqueflite automatic transmissions, to give the heavier Type Is a projected 200-plus mph top speed.

'This entire programme was done in total secrecy; most people in the company didn't even know it was happening. The wonderful thing about it was that everybody respected the security that was needed and although a lot of people tried to find out and a lot of people from the press were quite keen to know, we managed to keep a lid on it. During that time there was a lot of interest because they were wondering what was going on, but we were absolutely signed-up to say that we could not let anybody know what was happening.'

'[With] the first one that we did, the Type I four-door version of the Vantage, I worked with our younger son on the drawing board to get the length and shape of the body right; we did the proportions, "taping-up" the black lines,' said Mike Loasby.

'I then took that sketch to Woodmasters, the pattern maker, in High Wycombe. We made a quarter-scale wooden model under my direction from that sketch and we produced a full-size buck and got the body work off that. Following that I spent quite a lot of time at Shapecraft and then I would be at Aston Martin every day building the cars.'

Styling-wise, the Type Is were similar to the production Vantages with the addition of rear doors and a longer wheelbase. The increased length didn't detract from the car's

Top to bottom: Mike Loasby inspecting the scale model; The four-door Vantage chassis and superstructure ready for panelling; The body taking shape; Shaun Rush inspecting the rear window mechanism

164

elegant lines and the familiar styling features remained. From the front or back the four-door saloons looked almost identical to the Vantage coupe. Non-standard fittings included highly polished six-spoke OZ alloy wheels and chrome door handles.

Each of the three Type Is was mechanically and bodily identical, but were painted in bespoke colours chosen by the client: chassis number 70051 (Cannock Black with black interior and reflective glass), 70053 (Titanium Silver with grey interior and reflective glass) and 70088 (Special Red with red and black interior and clear glass).

The interiors were different from the production cars, containing some bespoke switchgear and fittings including Asprey clocks and pens and writing slopes. A specially developed Nippondenso air-conditioning unit was also included to cope with the destined hot climate.

'The interior I did from pictures supplied by the artist,' said Loasby. 'We built all that up in the car at Newport Pagnell using a glass fibre basic shape [armatures] and top-quality leather trim.

'All of the cars had a similar interior; they were different in detail but in principle were all broadly similar. We did everything for that, we designed new air vents, including all the operating mechanism, all of the heavily chromed surrounds, new instrument bezels, the door handle surrounds, everything.

'We provided umbrellas, silver pens and high-quality stereo systems. All the rest was really high-quality chrome, the type you never see normally. It was done by a little father and son outfit out in a barn somewhere, who still knew how to do it properly. There are not many people who can or have the opportunity or requirement to do it properly.

'We did everything to the highest possible quality on those cars. The door cappings were done in various woods and had cross banding around the edges, the veneer was put at right angles to create the effect and a thin contrasting strip of boxwood stringing separated the two areas.

'I didn't design the interior – I took a picture and turned that into three-dimensional reality, but I would never call myself the designer. It was my responsibility because I took it from the picture but we did do some design work, in the sense that the trim had to be designed. That was done in conjunction with the trim shop. With regards to the seats we had the pictures and we wanted them to be comfortable so we altered the shape of the cushions. The trimmers did it to my specification ultimately after a great amount of discussion.

'The rear seats had electric adjustment [requiring each vehicle to have a double battery installation package]. The design had to be sorted out for that and all around the rear quarter areas for the companion mirrors. The mirrors were Kingsley's idea as the sketches didn't extend that far, they only went as far as door handles and things like that. All of the pull handles on the door

Walter Hayes

Walter Hayes started his working life in newspapers before joining Ford UK in 1961 as Public Relations Manager. He established World Championship-winning race and rally programmes for the Ford Escort, Cortina and Sierra and was instrumental in getting Ford involved in Formula One with Cosworth's DFV engines. He was also involved in the creation of the Le Mans-winning GT40 programme as Director of Ford's Advanced Vehicle Operations. He became President of Ford Europe in 1977 and was instrumental in persuading Henry Ford II to purchase Aston Martin.

Hayes joined the Aston Martin Board of Directors in 1990 and acted as Executive Chairman upon the resignation of Victor Gauntlett from 1991 to February 1994, when John Oldfield took control. Under his direction the company introduced the Virage Volante, Vantage, 6.3-litre Virage, Virage Shooting Brake, Lagonda Vignale concept car, Lagonda Saloon and Shooting Brake and, most importantly, the DB7. He also instigated the far-sighted 'Car for Life' policy.

After guiding Aston Martin into the safest position in its history, Hayes (pictured below with Bruce Blyth, left) retired in January 1994 after a very distinguished career in the motor industry. He continued to be very busy during his retirement, remaining Honorary Life President of Aston Martin and was the Founding Chairman of the Aston Martin Heritage Trust until his death on 26 December 2000.

were broadly shown but we had to interpret them to produce the real thing. The dash and the console: we did all that. We had very much of a free hand. Once the customer had seen the first one or two cars they just said to get on with it, so we did.

'Kingsley would go and see the client with a selection of drawings he had specified and commissioned. They would say what they wanted and how many they wanted of them. Kingsley would give me the drawings and I would make them a reality. He would drop in on a regular basis and help, in any way if necessary, and say whether he liked the styling or not and whether he wanted any changes made.

'Stylists are not always renowned for their reality or engineering practicality. So I would take the artist's drawings

Top to bottom: The body nearing completion; Constructing the interior; Final preparations inspected by Kingsley Riding-Felce (left); Mike Loasby acting as chauffer on the Type I's first outing at Newport Pagnell

Above: The Cannock Black car featured reflective glass **Opposite:** All Special Series cars were equipped with 600 bhp Vantage engines and four-speed-plus-overdrive transmissions

that they had done and make proper engineering drawings of the chassis and all the hard points. I would try to make the two go together, which usually involves quite a lot of subtle change, moving around bits and pieces.

'Having arrived at that, I would take seven to eight templates of the vehicle, set them up on my quarter-scale table, put the wheels in the right places and then build the car around that and shape the clay to suit, literally carve it out, put this on, take this off until I got the shape. Then if it didn't transfer terribly well from the picture to the model, I would make the model look right. I am reasonably good at three-dimensional work, but I can't draw.'

'We always said [the Type I] should have gone into production at Newport Pagnell,' said Riding-Felce. 'But again, the style, like all the styles, was done exclusively for the client.'

'The first Type Is had a standard Vantage front and rear that was from the 600 package,' recalled engineer Steve Bolton. 'It had the carry-over Vantage brakes that had grown out of the 6.3 Virage brakes, but the car was bigger and heavier and faster.

'So we went to the next generation of brakes, which went from four-piston to six-piston callipers and, again, we made some

Vantage Special Type I
1996

Chassis: Steel box-section chassis, steel superstructure

Body: Aluminium four-seat saloon styled by Special Projects Group

Suspension: Front – Independent with double wishbones, Eibach coil springs, coaxial spring dampers and anti-roll bar Rear – de Dion axle, radius arms, Watt's linkage, Eibach coil springs, telescopic dampers and anti-roll bar

Brakes: Servo-assisted 365 mm grooved and ventilated discs with AP Racing six-piston callipers (front); 310 mm ventilated discs with four-piston callipers (rear). ABS

Steering: Power-assisted rack and pinion

Wheels: 18-inch OZ alloy

Tyres: Goodyear Eagle GS-D 285/45 ZR18

Transmission: Torqueflite four-speed-plus-overdrive automatic. Final drive 3.31:1. Limited-slip differential. Rear-wheel drive

Engine: 5340 cc alloy V8 with twin chain-driven overhead camshafts per bank and four valves per cylinder. Compression ratio 8.2:1. EEC IV engine management system. Two Roots type M90 Eaton superchargers with additional intercooler radiator and water pump. Fully catalysed exhaust system

Power: 600 bhp/447 kW @ 6500 rpm
600 lb/ft/813 Nm of torque @ 4000 rpm

Top speed: 205 mph/330 km/h (approx)

Dimensions:
Length	16 ft 7 in/5050 mm
Width	6 ft 4 in/1918 mm (excluding wing mirrors)
Height	4 ft 4.5 in/1330 mm
Wheelbase	9 ft 6.2 in/2900 mm
Weight	4399 lb/1995 kg (approx)

Price when new: N/A

Number built: 3

suspension revisions. We started to make changes to the geometry at the front of the car to improve its ride on the road.'

The 'overseas client' was impressed with the high degree of quality and performance that Aston Martin's Special Projects Group delivered. For such a small team, they did a remarkable job. The success of the Type I led to the order of three, more highly evolved Type II four-door saloons; all badged as Aston Martins, not Lagondas.

V8 Coupe

Don't mention the 'V' word

With the DB7 in production and proving a sales success, Aston Martin was keen to re-establish a standard V8-engined coupe into the line up. A new car was needed that was cheaper than the Vantage, would complement the six-cylinder DB7 and sell better than the Virage. It was decided that a non-supercharged coupe should be produced, but under a different name and with many design improvements.

'During 1996 we launched what we called the V8 Coupe,' said CEO David Price, 'which really was a replacement for the Virage. It utilised the Vantage chassis, which was a more elegant chassis than the Virage, but it had the non-supercharged engine. The Virage had a mixed image and certainly the industry had advanced and the suspension was not really state-of-the-art. It made a lot of sense to use the Vantage suspension on the V8 Coupe as we had the parts and had done the engineering and it improved the product.'

The Vantage suspension set-up was independent at the front with double wishbones, coaxial spring dampers and anti-roll bar. A de Dion axle was utilised at the rear, located by four longitudinal radius arms and a transverse Watt's linkage.

The V8 Coupe featured unique six-spoke alloy wheels and specially developed 255/50 ZR18 Pirelli P Zero tyres. The flared Vantage-style wheel arches were therefore not necessary. Ventilated steel 362 mm discs and AP Racing four-piston aluminium callipers were fitted at the front with 286 mm discs at the rear. A four-channel antilock braking system was also supplied to improve safety and driveability.

Launched at the Geneva Motor Show on 5 March 1996, and starting with chassis number AMSVR79001, the V8 Coupe borrowed styling cues from the Vantage such as the grille and front and rear lights. The updates transformed the car; it wasn't as overtly aggressive as the Vantage and it had softer, more elegant lines than the Virage.

'The V8 Coupe project was the opposite of what had traditionally happened at Astons,' said Chief Body Engineer Shaun Rush who started as an apprentice at Aston Martin back in 1976. 'In the past we'd had a standard car and then done Vantage and Volante versions of it. However with the Virage no longer being made we did not have a "standard" car, all we had was the Vantage.

The V8 Coupe was unusual in Aston Martin history as it was based on a higher-performance model, not the other way around

The updates transformed the car; it wasn't as overtly aggressive as the Vantage and it had softer, more elegant lines than the Virage.

Bob Dover

Born in Essex in 1945, Bob Dover gained a First Class Honours Degree in Mechanical Engineering from Manchester University. 'I have been in the car industry all my life,' he said, 'mainly in the luxury end. I started off as a Mechanical Engineer at Manchester University and then I spent a year at Cambridge doing a Production Engineering and Management course in 1968. Then I was based at Cowley at what became British Motor Holdings. I started as a Facilities Engineer, planning and implementing body conveyor systems.

'I progressed through to Facilities Director at Solihull, then as now, a Land Rover facility. They were turbulent times; the merger with Leyland, the Ryder Report and so on. Somewhat frustrated, I left and joined Massey Ferguson in Coventry, ending up running its French operations.

'I rejoined the Solihull team some ten years later, this time as Manufacturing Director and went on to kick off what became the Discovery programme. After a failed bid to do a management buyout the team broke up.

'I joined Jaguar as Manufacturing Director and I was in charge of Manufacturing and Quality in 1987/88. I went from Manufacturing Director to Chief Programme Engineer for sports cars. I did the XK8 and when that was finished, Jim Padilla, who was my boss, asked me if I would like to go to Aston Martin. I actually didn't want to go – I would rather have stayed at Jaguar. But Aston Martin soon captivated me.'

Dover was appointed Managing Director and Chief Executive Officer of Aston Martin in January 1997 and became Chairman in April of the same year. Under his stewardship AML launched the V8 Volante, DB7 Vantage, Project Vantage and V8 Vantage Le Mans. He also instigated the Vanquish programme and was instrumental in the purchase of the Gaydon factory.

'I remember sitting in my office at Bloxham when Ford announced that it was going to try to buy Land Rover from BMW and my visitor said, "You know about Land Rover because you used to work there." I thought that I might be on the list, but not at the top. But I was appointed as Chairman and CEO ahead of the completion of the sale in June 2000.

'Initially this car was known within the factory as the Virage S. We didn't have a big budget and had to do as much as we could in house. Chief Engineer Jess Line headed the programme.

'By this time the Vantage full-size mahogany master model was at Newport Pagnell. We worked out what the wheel arch projections were and using these, Cecil Atkinson and I restyled the front and rear wings. This involved removing some of the flare and softening the lines.

'I styled a new front spoiler using the original Virage part as a start, but incorporating two driving lights. [We also did] revised GRP sill covers, a rear spoiler, mesh front grille and the front wing side repeater lamps were changed to elliptical items.

'In production we took Vantage wing pressings and modified them to the V8 Coupe on jigs made at Newport Pagnell. It worked very well mainly because it was based on a very good foundation – the Vantage. It was probably the car that Virage should have been.'

'The V8 Coupe, which followed the supercharged Vantage, used the new cylinder head and cylinder block,' said Arthur Wilson. 'It produced 350 bhp @ 6200 rpm and 368 lb/ft of torque @ 4300 rpm. We were not allowed to do a manual transmission version, so had to soldier on with the aging Torqueflite [automatic]. Nevertheless, we could still achieve 5.8 seconds to 60 mph and 13.5 seconds to 100 mph. The press didn't match this, but that is what we got.' Maximum speed was quoted at 'over 150 mph'.

The V8 Coupe was positioned in the middle of the company's range, between the DB7 and powerful supercharged Vantage models. It featured all the usual Aston Martin refinements including Connolly leather, Wilton carpet, burr walnut, climate control system, CD player, cruise control and optional driver's-side airbag.

While Aston Martin only sold around 20 V8 Coupes per year over its five-year lifecycle, it did provide a third tier to the company's range and life to the non-supercharged V8 engine.

The V8 Coupe's styling was more elegant than the Virage but not as overtly aggressive as the Vantage

Dual taillights were carried over from the Vantage

Left: The sumptuous interior followed the lines of the Virage Volante before it **Right:** The use of Vantage cylinder heads brought a welcome increase in power over the Virage engine which by this time had been eclipsed by the six-cylinder DB7

QV8

Starting life as a standard V8 Coupe, the QV8 was the result of a commission from a private customer. The aftermarket work was undertaken by transport consultancy Q Design, which designed and created conversions and prototypes for the automobile, aircraft and marine industries.

Initially Q Design's brief was to create interior modifications including the installation of a premium stereo system and bespoke switchgear. But the QV8 eventually grew into a £1-million project that saw 70 percent of the bodywork replaced with new panels, new glass areas fitted and a new custom-made interior created.

The V8 Coupe's original 18-inch alloy wheels were replaced by 19-inch Vantage units, while the tail lights were sourced from the Ferrari 550 Maranello. The new interior included a Jaguar S-Type-sourced steering wheel, a touch screen mounted on the centre console, bespoke interior door handles and a secure storage system in place of the rear seats. The engine remained standard.

V8 Coupe
1996–2000

Chassis: Steel box-section chassis, steel superstructure

Body: Aluminium 2+2 coupe styled by John Heffernan

Suspension: Front – Independent with double wishbones, coaxial spring damper units and anti-roll bar
Rear – de Dion axle, longitudinal radius arms, transverse Watt's linkage and coaxial spring damper units

Brakes: Servo-assisted ventilated steel 362 mm discs with AP Racing four-piston callipers (front); 286 mm steel discs with aluminium sliding callipers (rear). ABS

Steering: Power-assisted rack and pinion

Wheels: 18-inch alloy

Tyres: Pirelli P-Zero 255/50 ZR18

Transmission: Torqueflite four-speed automatic with electronic Sport and Touring modes; final drive 4.09:1. Limited-slip differential. Rear-wheel drive

Engine: 5340 cc alloy V8 with twin chain-driven overhead camshafts per bank and four valves per cylinder. Compression ratio 9.75:1. Alpha Plus engine management system. Fully catalysed exhaust system

Power: 350 bhp/261 kW @ 6000 rpm
368 lb/ft/499 Nm of torque @ 4300 rpm

Top speed: 150-plus mph/241-plus km/h

Dimensions:

Length	15 ft 7 in/4745 mm
Width	6 ft 4 in/1918 mm (excluding wing mirrors)
Height	4 ft 4.5 in/1330 mm
Wheelbase	8 ft 6.75 in/2610 mm
Weight	4233 lb/1950 kg

Price when new: £139,500

Number built: 100

Vantage Special Type II
On His Majesty's Secret Service Part II

The second four-door Vantages, the Type IIs, were much more radical and more evolved in design than the Type I, moving away completely from production-based styling. Still based on a stretched Vantage platform and V600 running gear, the Type IIs were much more distinctive than the Type Is, especially from the front and rear.

Although very pleased with the Type Is the customer requested a bespoke four-door-based Vantage with a distinctively unique body. '[With] the next model I actually did something I had never done before,' said Mike Loasby. 'I used one of the rooms in the cottage out in the garden as a styling studio and made the "clay" quarter-scale model in that.

'The first four-door, I did the body shape, which was an extended version of the Vantage, and I did that with our younger son to get the details and the shape right. The second [Type II], I did the quarter-scale clay on which Shapecraft loosely based the car without following it precisely.'

'Mike, perhaps understandably, always had a thing about these cars not being exactly what he wanted,' said Principal Body Engineer Shaun Rush. 'However, I should stress that all we had was a quarter-scale model and the renderings. Not only did we have to make the cosmetic aluminium skin, but all the steelwork to support it, together with working out the doors, hinges, locking, sealing, window frames glass operation, and so on.

> 'I used one of the rooms in the cottage out in the garden as a styling studio and made the "clay" quarter-scale model in that.'
>
> *Mike Loasby*

'The styling was pretty much as per the model. I did some detail work, such as parts of the front bumper, badges in the rear quarters and the high-mounted stop light on the boot.

'The car used the large round Vantage stop and tail lamps but the rear indicators were unique smaller diameter items, the lenses of which Peter Killick had specially manufactured and the bulb holder was made in the pattern shop/vac form facility at Newport,' recalled Rush.

The more bulbous Type IIs departed completely from Vantage-based styling

Top: Standard headlight and taillight units were incorporated into the Type II design **Above:** The scale model from which the car's design merits were evaluated **Right:** Works Coachbuilt badges graced all Special Series cars

The Type IIs had a more bulbous body theme. From the front they had chromed grilles and standard headlights. The bonnet was more rounded at the front and incorporated different openings at the rear. The high-powered cars were also very high-waisted and featured the famous dual Aston Martin air intakes as used on the 6.3-litre Virage. Other special features included Works Coachbuilt badges aft of the front wheels and discreet Aston Martin wings badging on the C-pillars.

While retaining four round taillights, the rear was extensively redesigned. Gone was the built-in spoiler, replaced with a curvaceous boot (inside of which was a Swaine, Adeney and Brigg umbrella) with built-in brake light, and bumper with hot air outlets and fog lights. The highly polished OZ alloy wheels and bright fittings used on the Type Is were carried over on the Type II, as were the bespoke interiors.

Once again, bodily and mechanically, the three Type IIs were identical save for the paint schemes, which followed exactly the Type Is: chassis number 70092 (Special Black with reflective glass), 70105 (Special Red with clear glass) and 70145 (Titanium with reflective glass).

A proposed Type II Shooting Brake was never constructed.

Top: More adventurous styling came at the request of the customer who was seeking a more individual bespoke design **Above left:** Special, luxurious rear seats were designed especially for the project **Above right:** Type II interiors remained the same as the Type I and featured special air conditioning units to cope with the hot climate of their intended destination

The three completed Type IIs shortly before dispatch to their new owner in the Far East

Vantage Special Type II
1996

Chassis: Steel box-section chassis, steel superstructure

Body: Aluminium four-door saloon styled by Special Projects Department

Suspension: Front – Independent with double wishbones, coil springs, coaxial spring dampers and anti-roll bar
Rear – de Dion axle, radius arms, Watt's linkage, coil springs, telescopic dampers and anti-roll bar

Brakes: Servo-assisted 365 mm grooved and ventilated discs with AP Racing six-piston callipers (front); 310 mm ventilated discs with AP Racing four-piston callipers (rear). ABS

Steering: Power-assisted rack and pinion

Wheels: 18-inch OZ alloy

Tyres: Goodyear Eagle GS-D 285/45 ZR18

Transmission: Torqueflite four-speed-plus-overdrive automatic; final drive 3.31:1. Limited-slip differential. Rear-wheel drive

Engine: 5340 cc alloy V8 with twin chain-driven overhead camshafts per bank and four valves per cylinder. Compression ratio 8.2:1. EEC IV engine management system. Two Roots type M90 Eaton superchargers with additional intercooler radiator and water pump. Fully catalysed exhaust system

Power: 600 bhp/447 kW @ 6500 rpm
600 lb/ft/813 Nm of torque @ 4000 rpm

Top speed: 205 mph/330 km/h (approx)

Dimensions:

Length	16 ft 7 in/5050 mm
Width	6 ft 4 in/1918 mm (excluding wing mirrors)
Height	4 ft 4.5in/1330 mm
Wheelbase	9 ft 6.2 in/2900 mm
Weight	4399 lb/1995 kg (approx)

Price when new: N/A

Number built: 3

Virage Lightweight
Works Service bespoke

After ordering a number of 6.3-litre Virages in 1992, a well-known client requested something more potent from Aston Martin. Works Service responded with three special Lightweight 6.3-litre Virages; chassis numbers 50421 (Titanium Grey), 50422 (Black) and 50423 (Cobalt Blue). Fitted with specially developed engines and transmissions, modified bodywork and interiors, they were another impressive example of Works Service's bespoke abilities.

The customer requested a higher-performance version of the standard 6.3-litre package in a lighter body. In order to accommodate the request two main briefs were undertaken: improve the power and torque output of the 6.3-litre engine and trim down the weight of the production car's considerable body.

The commission was received in 1994 and renderings for the body style were approved towards the end of 1995. A mock-up was produced in early 1996 but with the Type I and II under construction, and the Special Series coupes yet to be produced, the project was put on hold. 'Kingsley wanted to get them moving again,' said Shaun Rush, 'so I arranged for them to be paneled by the production panel shop and I supervised the build process.

'The chassis was modified to Vantage at the front, the Virage steel inner doors and door glass frames were removed and replaced with the later Vantage items. The cars were put down the production line for the second time in their short lives and were paneled using a combination of Shapecraft and standard Vantage tooling.

'Using the renderings. I styled sill covers and a front spoiler, front grille infill panel, cover for the rear number plate landing and a one-piece rear bumper/spoiler, which I was particularly pleased with. These along with the backs of the standard wing mirrors were finished in lacquered carbon fibre. The front grille on the original renderings and the mock up featured driving lights, however we did not include them on the actual cars.' Vantage-type boot lids with high-mounted stop lamps were fitted as were BMW headlamps.

The specially constructed bespoke bodywork involved modifying almost every panel of the donor Virage. Changes included a reprofiled bonnet featuring dual air vents, side flanks incorporating scalloping to aid brake cooling and twin cooling ducts, inspired by the 1960s Project Cars.

ASTON MARTIN: POWER, BEAUTY AND SOUL

Three Lightweight Virages were constructed, but their build was convoluted

A red starter button was fitted, as were carbon fibre
fascia panels, well ahead of their production
debut in the V8 Vantage Le Mans.

'A target was set and a lot of weight was taken out of the interior,' said Kingsley Riding-Felce. 'The cars only had two seats and a lot of carbon fibre was used on the dashboards, the doors and some of the exterior panels too.'

Inside the trim was pared down and the rear seats removed, while modifications were made to the dashboard to give the vehicles a racing car feel. Red starter buttons were fitted, as were carbon fibre fascia panels, well ahead of their production debut in the V8 Vantage Le Mans.

'David Morgan produced some very special engines for these cars,' said Riding-Felce, 'each with eight butterflies and eight individual throttle bodies. They were fabulous engines.' The 6.3-litre engines were coupled with Torqueflite four-speed-plus-overdrive automatic transmissions.

'Those three cars had further up-rated engines fitted with individual throttles and carbon fibre trumpets and air boxes, yet with higher-lift and profile camshafts fitted,' said David Morgan. 'The power ended up just short of 500 bhp. Unfortunately the automatic transmission masked the superb throttle response. Cars like these deserved a manual gearbox.'

The Lightweight Virages were delivered during September 1997 to the Far East.

Top to bottom: As featured on the rendering, a special grille with dual driving lights was fashioned in aluminium but it did not make the final build; Carbon-fibre dashboard trim and a starter button were part of the race-inspired interior; Underneath the skin, the 6.3-litre V8-powered coupe's chassis was modified to incorporate Vantage improvements

Virage Lightweight
1997

Chassis: Steel box-section chassis, steel superstructure

Body: Aluminium two-seat coupe styled by John Heffernan. Modified by Works Service

Suspension: Front – Independent with unequal length wishbones, coil springs, coaxial spring damper units and anti-roll bar
Rear – de Dion axle, radius arms, Watt's linkage, coil springs, telescopic dampers and anti-roll bar

Brakes: Servo-assisted 355 mm ventilated discs with AP Racing six-piston callipers (front); 280 mm ventilated discs with AP Racing four-piston callipers (rear). ABS

Steering: Power-assisted rack and pinion

Wheels: 18-inch OZ alloy

Tyres: Goodyear Eagle GS-D 285/45 ZR18

Transmission: Torqueflite four-speed-plus-overdrive automatic; final drive 4.09:1. Limited-slip differential. Rear-wheel drive

Engine: 6347 cc alloy V8 with twin chain-driven overhead camshafts per bank and four valves per cylinder. Compression ratio 9.5:1. Weber-Alpha sequential fuel injection

Power: 495 bhp/369 kW @ 5750 rpm
480 lb/ft/651 Nm of torque @ 4400 rpm

Top speed: 186 mph/299 km/h (approx)

Dimensions:
Length	15 ft 7 in/4737 mm
Width	6 ft 3 in/1944 mm
Height	4 ft 3.5 in/1321 mm
Wheelbase	8 ft 6.75 in/2610 mm
Weight	4000 lb/1814 kg (approx)

Price of conversion: N/A

Number converted: 3

V 8 V o l a n t e
Flying high

'The thing that we did to attract
more business was to stretch the
V8 Volante to provide more leg
room, giving Aston Martin a
true four-seater convertible.'
David Price

The V8 Coupe proved a popular choice for buyers who wanted a genuine handcrafted Aston Martin, but were not in the market for the ultra-expensive Vantage. To capitalise on this, and to introduce a further model into the stable, Aston Martin released a Volante version of the V8 Coupe.

Like the coupe before it, the V8 Volante replaced the Virage Volante and incorporated many of the styling changes and mechanical updates of the V8 Coupe. It was launched at the London Motor Show in October 1997 and production started in the same year with chassis number 89001.

'When the Vantage was up and into production, as a team we naturally thought that our next project would be Vantage Volante,' said Shaun Rush. 'It had been a popular car in the two-valve series and we already had the hood and other parts from the Virage Volante. I did a rough rendering in 1994, however there did not appear to be any intention or desire to do what most people thought would be an exceptional car.

'When the long-wheelbase project was first raised we were told that after the LWB there would be a normal wheelbase [SWB] version. I asked Jess Line [Chief Engineer of V cars] if we could do the normal wheelbase car first as we had most of the parts and it would give us more time to sort out the LWB which needed a new hood, revised interior trim, modified chassis, revised drivetrain and engine. However, Jess was told that [remaining stocks of] Virage Volantes [had to be cleared first]. So we had to do the LWB.

'At the time we had a Bentley provided for us to benchmark against, but they were really two different cars. The bodywork was basically V8 Coupe with the extra 200 mm in the rear wing between the door and rear wheel. I was asked to put some kind of feature in this area to try and break up what was a rather large bland panel. I did this although I was never really happy with it.

'We never did get to do a proper production run of the normal wheelbase Volante although a chassis was partly built; this was later used for trim and seat belt development on the Vantage Volante Special Edition project. Although we did eventually do the eight [short wheelbase] Special Edition cars, I believe, and those eight cars show, that we missed a tremendous opportunity to do a large run of these cars.'

Seating for four adults was a more realistic option than ever before with the LWB V8 Volante

Premier Automotive Group

The brainchild of Ford Chief Jac Nasser, the Premier Automotive Group (PAG) was established in October 1999. Ford's premium brands – Aston Martin, Jaguar, Volvo, Land Rover and Lincoln – were banded together under the leadership of former BMW boss, Wolfgang Reitzle, (pictured) who led PAG until 2002, when Mark Fields took over. Lewis Booth became head of PAG in 2005.

'Henry Ford II's acquisition of Aston Martin was the seed that planted the Premier Automotive Group,' said Jac Nasser. 'We had a collective brand of what was the best in the business. Because the brands are so different there is very little overlap and you're not forced into any unnatural acts between the brands to make them viable to a customer base.

'PAG was a Ford-brand project that was fully developed in terms of the breadth of products that it had. Ford is anything from GTs, Thunderbirds and Mustangs all the way to pick-up trucks and cars; it isn't dependent only on the mass market. We wanted to expand and offer our customers any vehicle that they may want in their garage. [We wanted PAG] not only in terms of our market representation and customer focus, but also as a good way of balancing our risks and using our economies and balance of scale to the advantage of the customer.

'I coined the phrase PAG. It was about the time I was recruiting Wolfgang Reitzle. We discussed it and we had three or four alternatives. We were in between Premium, Premier or Luxury and after a few telephone calls it was decided Premier would be the right and natural grouping of the three words for the name.'

'We were very fortunate with Aston Martin, we had icons of the automotive industry and enthusiasts. Without Walter Hayes we wouldn't really have got the momentum started and John Oldfield, who was one of the finest automotive engineers on the planet; he kept that tradition going and, of course, Bob Dover. He was a great leader of the product.

'I don't think (Ford) has ever thought of Aston Martin as the pinnacle of the company. Ford is what I consider the most important brand; [it] is the origin of the company and our major body. Each brand is different. When I was running the company I was very proud that Aston Martin and Jaguar were in connection with that product.'

The V8 Volante had different dimensions from both the Virage Volante and the V8 Coupe. In order to make a more practical four-seat car, approximately 7 inches were added to the wheelbase. Rear seat accommodation was more generous than previous models and, for the first time in an open car, provided comfortable seating for four adults and reasonable luggage space.

'The thing that we did to attract more business, which worked quite well, but was launched just after my time, was to stretch the V8 Volante to provide more leg room, giving Aston Martin a true four-seater convertible,' said David Price.

The Volante was mechanically the same as the V8 Coupe, with power still quoted at 350 bhp @ 6000 rpm and 368 lb/ft of torque @ 4300 rpm. It was a very heavy car, weighing 4500 lb, but it was still able to cruise at more than 150 mph and the 0–60 mph sprint was achieved in only 6.5 seconds. The Volante's four-speed automatic transmission was equipped with electronic sports and touring modes, but touring in the grand manner was this car's forte.

The new breed V8 Volante featured all the usual Aston Martin refinements including a fully electrically operated mohair hood with heated glass window and Connolly leather, Wilton carpet and walnut interior.

The V8 Volante and V8 Coupe were the last of the non-supercharged V8-engined cars produced at Newport Pagnell. (A supercharged convertible was later built, but this unique model is known as the LWB Vantage Volante Special Edition). Both V8 Volante, of which only 64 examples were built, and V8 Coupe models were sold up until 2000 when Aston Martin's coachbuilt era came to an end.

Traditional craftsmanship abounded in the Volante's sumptuous interior

V8 Volantes shared the V8 Coupe's 350 bhp engine

Above: The V8 Volante was among the last of the 'standard' traditionally coachbuilt cars produced by Aston Martin at Newport Pagnell **Right:** The wheelbase's extra length was most noticeable between the doors and rear wheel arches; the styling feature was added by Shaun Rush to break up the plain panel

Jac Nasser

Jac Nasser was born in Amyoun, Lebanon in 1947 and immigrated with his family to Melbourne, Australia in 1951. After gaining a business degree at Royal Melbourne Institute of Technology, he started his career with Ford Australia in 1968 as a Financial Analyst. He worked for Ford North America's truck operations from 1974 and in various roles in Asia Pacific and South America before becoming President and CEO of Ford Australia (1990–93), Chairman Ford Europe (1993–99), Vice President Ford Motor Company (1993–96), Executive Vice President Ford Motor Company (1996–99) and finally, President and Chief Executive Officer Ford Motor Company (1999–2001).

A genuine devotee, Nasser has owned several Aston Martins including a DBS V8 and DB4. 'I was fortunate that throughout the period of my career from 1983 to 2001, I was able to touch any product that the company was involved in,' said Nasser. 'I had a special affection for Jaguar and Aston Martin. I felt they represented not only a way of stretching our market penetration but also as a wonderful way of testing new technology, whether it was in product design, or electronics, or the manufacturing process. The flow-through would reach other Ford products.'

Nasser left the automotive industry altogether after leaving Ford in 2001 to pursue other business interests.

V8 Volante
1997–2000

Chassis: Steel box-section chassis, steel superstructure

Body: Aluminium 2+2 convertible styled by John Heffernan

Suspension: Front – Independent with transverse unequal length wishbones, coil springs, coaxial spring dampers and anti-roll bar
Rear – de Dion axle, radius arms, transverse Watt's linkage, coil springs and coaxial spring dampers

Brakes: Servo-assisted 330 mm ventilated discs with AP Racing four-piston callipers (front); 286 mm ventilated discs with aluminium sliding callipers (rear). ABS

Steering: Power-assisted rack and pinion

Wheels: 17-inch alloy

Tyres: Avon Turbospeed 255/55 ZR17

Transmission: Torqueflite four-speed automatic with electronic Sports and Touring modes; final drive 4.09:1. Limited-slip differential. Rear-wheel drive

Engine: 5340 cc alloy V8 with twin chain-driven overhead camshafts per bank and four valves per cylinder. Compression ration 9.75:1. EEC IV engine management system. Fully catalysed exhaust system

Power: 350 bhp/261 kW @ 6000 rpm
368 lb/ft/499 Nm of torque @ 4300 rpm

Top speed: 150 mph/241 km/h

Dimensions:

Length	16 ft/4945 mm
Width	6 ft 2.5 in/1918 mm (excluding wing mirrors)
Height	4 ft 6.5 in/1380 mm
Wheelbase	9 ft 2 in/2810 mm
Weight	4500 lb/2050 kg

Price when new: £169,500

Number built: 64

Alfred Dunhill DB7

Two paragons of English style unite

Twenty years before Lionel Martin and Robert Bamford began their modest motor business in London's Kensington, Alfred Dunhill inherited and subsequently reinvented his parent's business in Euston Road, London, selling exquisite accoutrements to the discerning English gentleman. Since 1893, Alfred Dunhill's name has been a byword for quality, elegance and the ultimate in style. Dunhill's maxim is, 'It must be useful, it must work dependably, it must be beautiful, it must last, and it must be the best of its kind.' Aston Martin has subscribed to those same qualities since the early days of the Lionel Martin cars.

A partnership between these two paragons of English style seemed to be inevitable, for Dunhill had sold 'everything but the motor' since moving into motoring accessories in 1897. Bob Dover, newly appointed Chairman and Chief Executive of AML and Callum Barton, Chief Executive of Alfred Dunhill, met early in 1997 with the idea of showcasing selected products from the Alfred Dunhill collection in a unique DB7.

For those who enjoyed a fine cigar, the smoker's edition contained an ebony Macassar humidor to keep cigars in pristine condition.

'It was immediately apparent that there was a natural synergy of thought and purpose between our two companies,' said Dover.

Callum Barton added, 'Alfred Dunhill and Aston Martin are strikingly similar in their design heritage and commitment to quality craftsmanship. Our clients are international, creative, modern, successful individuals who always seek the best. We have combined our strengths to develop the ultimate in "toys for boys". Thus this special edition Alfred Dunhill DB7 was born.'

While the mechanicals remained standard, many exterior and interior changes set the Alfred Dunhill DB7 apart

The prototype Alfred Dunhill DB7 was built in 1997 and for six months was previewed to potential customers in Europe, North America and the Asia Pacific region, including the Salon International de la Haute Horlogerie, the world's most prestigious watch fair and the Alfred Dunhill Queen's Cup Polo tournament. The model was met with such enthusiasm it was decided to pursue production. The car was finally officially unveiled at the North American Auto Show on 5 January 1998, with production and delivery taking place in that same year.

There were two different versions of the Alfred Dunhill DB7, which could be ordered in coupe or Volante form: the smoker's and non-smoker's edition. For those who enjoyed a fine cigar, the smoker's edition contained an ebony Macassar humidor to keep cigars in 'pristine condition', a silver-plated cigar and cigar lighter and a matching set of Alfred Dunhill AD 2000 fountain and ball point pens housed in the top of the central armrest.

For non-smokers, in place of the cigar humidor and smoking accessories was a special Alfred Dunhill grooming kit, containing Dunhill cologne and a set of Millennium cufflinks and a tie bar. Both editions included a tailored three-piece set of black and grey Alfred Dunhill CityScape leather luggage and an Alfred Dunhill AD 2000 key fob.

Outwardly, the car was distinguished by its exclusive Dunhill Millennium watch-coloured metallic platinum paint scheme.

Other DB7 specials

DB7 GTS (i6) – Offered by Aston Martin of Mayfair and produced by Car Care Works, the GTS was launched in June 1996. It featured a yellow nose cone, black Le Mans mesh grille, bonnet bulges and air louvres, split-rim Speedline alloy wheels, wood-rim steering wheel, white instrument dials, sports exhaust and tuned engine. 54 built.

DB7 GTS II (i6) – An updated GTS II (pictured below right) was produced by Care Car Works and sold through Aston Martin of Mayfair from August 1998. It featured the original GTS fittings plus Vantage-style round rear taillights. 16 built.

Neiman Marcus (i6) – Offered through the Neiman Marcus department store's 1998 Christmas catalogue *The Answer Book* and sold exclusively through Neiman Marcus stores. All were six-cylinder Volantes, available with manual or automatic transmissions. They were painted in the same unique shade of black with a black mohair hood and light grey interior with carbon fibre panels, chrome wheels and wire mesh grille. Costing US$150,000, Swaine, Adeney and Brigg fitted luggage and a monogrammed car cover came as standard. 10 built.

DB7 Beverly Hills (i6) – Available through the Aston Martin dealers in Beverly Hills, California, only two coupes and four Volantes were produced. The Beverly Hills model featured Midnight Blue paintwork, satin-finished alloy wheels, sheepskin over rugs, stainless steel mesh grille and a set of fitted luggage. Six built.

DB7 Stratstone Limited Edition (i6) – Completely built by Aston Martin and offered through Stratstone of Mayfair in 1999, the Limited Edition featured an all-black paint scheme with grey interior, polished alloy wheels, stainless steel wire mesh grille with chrome surround, carbon fibre interior trim, individually numbered sill plates and Stratstone of Mayfair-embossed seats. 19 built (10 convertibles and 9 coupes).

DB7 Vantage Jubilee Edition (V12) – Offered from January 2002 and built to celebrate Queen Elizabeth II's 50th anniversary as monarch, the Jubilee Edition, offered in coupe and Volante versions, was finished in a unique shade of Jubilee Blue with an ivory interior. Costing £120,950 it featured a stainless steel mesh grille, Jubilee-embossed seats, white-faced instruments, 19-inch alloy wheels, chrome door mirrors and Touchtronic transmission. 24 built.

DB7 LWB (V12) – Announced in early 2003 by RSD Automotive, the long wheelbase DB7 (pictured top) had 6 inches added to the wheelbase to create a more realistic four-seat carriage. The conversion was available on DB7 coupes or Volantes. Conversions cost around £75,000. One or two built.

Keswick (V12) – Finished in metallic black with 19-inch wheels, the Keswick model featured a black interior with metallic finishes and cappings, satellite navigation, white-faced instruments and DB7-embossed seats and carpets. 10 built.

DB7 Anniversary Edition (V12) – Launched in 2003 to mark the 10th anniversary of the DB7. The Anniversary Edition featured Touchtronic transmission, fluted leather seats, power-fold mirrors and premium sound and satellite navigation systems. It was finished in either Slate Blue with two-tone Caspian or Arctic Blue interior. Each was individually numbered and badged. 100 slated for production but only 33 built.

The gunmetal grille and 12-spoke alloy wheels, featuring centre hubs aping the watch design, complemented the body colour.

Inside, the modern millennium feel continued with the brushed aluminium dashboard, centre console, door cappings and gear knob and the chrome-rimmed white dials with black numerals. A stylised version of the Millennium watch design replaced the standard clock in the centre of the fascia panel. The car also featured Alfred Dunhill-embossed charcoal Connolly leather upholstery with contrasting silver-grey piping and charcoal Wilton carpet edged in silver grey and similarly embossed with the Alfred Dunhill name.

It was planned that 150 Alfred Dunhill DB7s were to be produced, but only 78 were ordered and built. The car was only superficially different from its standard production counterpart; the model designation was justified by the differences in paint, trim and special additions. The dimensions, engine, suspension and transmission specifications and performance figures were exactly the same as the standard DB7 coupe.

Alfred Dunhill DB7
1997–1999

Chassis: Steel semi-monocoque body shell

Body: Composite and pressed steel 2+2 coupe and convertible styled by Ian Callum

Suspension: Front – Independent with double wishbones incorporating anti-dive geometry, coil springs, monotube dampers and anti-roll bar
Rear – Independent with double wishbones, longitudinal control arms, coil springs, monotube dampers and anti-roll bar

Brakes: Servo-assisted 284 mm ventilated discs with alloy four-piston callipers (front); 295 mm ventilated discs with sliding aluminium callipers (rear). Drum handbrake. ABS

Steering: Power-assisted rack and pinion

Wheels: 18-inch Speedline alloy

Tyres: Bridgestone Expedia 245/40 ZR18

Transmission: GM four-speed automatic; final drive 3.058:1
Getrag five-speed manual; final drive 3.54:1. Limited-slip differential. Rear-wheel drive

Engine: 3239 cc alloy in-line six-cylinder with a chain-driven double overhead camshaft and four valves per cylinder. Compression ratio 8.3:1. Single M90 Eaton supercharger. EEC-V engine management system. Fully catalysed exhaust system

Power: 335 bhp/250 kW @ 5750 rpm
361 lb/ft/489 Nm of torque @ 3000 rpm

Top speed: 165 mph/266 km/h

Dimensions:

Length	15 ft 1.5 in/4646 mm[i]
Width	5 ft 9.5 in/1830 mm
Height	4 ft 1.5 in/1238 mm
Wheelbase	8 ft 5in/2591 mm
Weight	3913 lb/1725 kg (manual)
	4023 lb/1825 kg (automatic)

Price when new: £89,950 (coupe); £97,500 (Volante)

Number built: 78

Left: Alfred Dunhill DB7s featured brushed aluminium and special additions including cigar humidors and grooming kits **Bottom left:** Of the intended 150, only 78 Alfred Dunhill specials were built

i The American edition was 3 inches (76 mm) longer owing to the more bulbous bumpers needed to meet safety legislation

A M 3
On His Majesty's Secret Service Part III

During the construction of the Special Series Vantages, the same client had also ordered specially built cars from Rolls-Royce, Bentley, Mercedes-Benz/AMG and Ferrari; many of which had bespoke bodies, upgraded engines, and other unique features including four-wheel drive systems. The famous design house, Pininfarina in Turin had designed some of the bodies for this particular client, most notably for Ferrari.

On request from the customer, Pininfarina contacted Kingsley Riding-Felce at Aston Martin with the proposal that the two companies collaborate on a series of cars; Aston Martin would provide the rolling chassis and Pininfarina the unique bodywork styling and interiors.

'[The Special Series Vantages] were so well received and so well recognised within the industry and by our colleagues that Pininfarina came to Aston Martin and asked if it could do a joint project with us,' recalled Riding-Felce.

'In fact we did a special project with Pininfarina. We supplied a chassis with the upgraded 600-horsepower engine with bigger brakes and suspension. We surprised Pininfarina with a 600-horsepower packaged chassis for them to re-body the car. We worked very closely with them.

On request from the client, Pininfarina contacted Aston Martin with the proposal that the two companies collaborate on a series of cars.

'It was a fantastic opportunity to work with Pininfarina and it gave us an insight into its business. Despite the 20 weekends away overseas [in the Far East] and doing everything else, the time spent going to Italy and dealing with these things was superb. These cars went to the same customer in the Far East; we were all working for the same customer at the time.

'We built the Pininfarina cars as a delete-build chassis in production; they had a rolling chassis, effectively,' recalled Riding-Felce. 'We then brought it into Works Service and upgraded the performance. We then shipped the cars to Pininfarina for it to body and the car was sold to the customer.'

AM3 and AM4 were Pininfarina's first designs on Aston Martin cars

The delete-build chassis were constructed over the period of May 1996 to July 1997. Meanwhile, five separate styling exercises were produced by Pininfarina, codenamed AM1 through AM5. After presentation to the customer, designs one, two and five were rejected. Projects AM3 and AM4 were chosen, hence the names of these unique vehicles.

Pininfarina was supplied with five Vantage rolling chassis: numbers 70500–70504 (both types in red with clear glass and black with reflective glass), plus one standard car, which the Italian carrozzeria used as a development mule and was later turned into a completed rebodied AM3 or AM4 car.

Each chassis came complete with upgraded 600 bhp engines, specially developed Chrysler Torqueflite four-speed-plus-overdrive automatic transmissions with a 3.31:1 final drive and a fully developed performance package with the best brakes and suspension system available for this type of vehicle. In common with all the specially commissioned Vantages, AM3 and AM4 were produced in right-hand drive configuration.

The prototype, 70500, was built up by Turin-based prototype specialists Coggiola and tested at Goodyear's Miraval Test Track in southern France with the assistance of Aston Martin engineers. Coggiola finished bodying the six cars in 1997, and

Pininfarina sold the vehicles and directly freighted them to the customer in the Far East.

AM3 was by far the most radical design of all the Special Series Vantages; the Italian design house stretched the Aston Martin design language almost beyond recognition. The familiar grille was totally replaced with a separate removable composite nose section that incorporated both light clusters. A similar material was used at the rear. The taillights were encompassed in a shape aping Aston Martin's traditional grille and flared up into a Kamm tail, below which were dual exhaust pipes.

One concession to Aston Martin's recognised design language was the side strakes behind the front wheels. AM3 utilised specially designed six-spoke wheels with Goodyear 285/45 ZR18 tyres. Being a joint project, both Pininfarina and Aston Martin badges appeared on the car.

The dual coloured interiors were completely different from standard Vantage cabins. Most of the switchgear was unlike that used by Aston Martin and AM3's dashboard featured the car's instruments organised into a single row in front of the driver. One of the few immediately recognisable items was the Ford-sourced steering wheel.

One of the few recognisable Aston Martin design cues was the air vent aft of the front wheels

Clockwise from top left: The removable composite front was AM3's most controversial feature; The Kamm tail was fashioned into the Aston Martin grille shape; Aston Martin provided a chassis for Pininfarina's designers to mock up the interior; Rear accommodation was tight, but luxurious

AM3
1997

Chassis: Steel box-section chassis, steel superstructure

Body: Aluminium 2+2 coupe styled by Pininfarina

Suspension: Front – Independent with wishbones, Eibach coil springs, coaxial spring dampers and anti-roll bar
Rear – de Dion axle, radius arms, Watt's linkage, Eibach coil springs, telescopic dampers and anti-roll bar

Brakes: Servo-assisted 365 mm grooved and ventilated discs with AP Racing six-piston callipers (front); 310 mm ventilated discs with AP Racing four-piston callipers (rear). ABS

Steering: Power-assisted rack and pinion

Wheels: 18-inch alloy

Tyres: Goodyear Eagle 285/45 ZR18

Transmission: Torqueflite four-speed-plus-overdrive automatic; final drive 3.31:1. Limited-slip differential. Rear-wheel drive

Engine: 5340 cc alloy V8 with twin chain-driven overhead camshafts per bank and four valves per cylinder. Compression ratio 8.2:1. EEC IV engine management system. Two Roots type M90 Eaton superchargers with additional intercooler radiators and water pump. Fully catalysed exhaust system

Power: 600 bhp/447 kW @ 6500 rpm
600 lb/ft/813 Nm of torque @ 4000 rpm

Top speed: 205 mph/330 km/h (approx)

Dimensions:
Length	15 ft 7 in/4745 mm
Width	6 ft 4 in/1918 mm (excluding wing mirrors)
Height	4 ft 4.5 in/1320 mm
Wheelbase	8 ft 6.75 in/2610 mm
Weight	4300 lb/1950 kg (approx)

Price when new: N/A

Number built: 3

Vantage Special Series I
On His Majesty's Secret Service Part IV

While the four-door Type II models were being constructed, the Special Projects Group received a commission for a further series of three cars. This time, the customer sought further individuality and greater sportiness. Moving from four-door saloons, the client requested a vehicle more in the vein of a sports car and the two-door Series I and II supercars were the result.

'The client had expressed an interest for more of a sports car,' recalled Steve Bolton. 'A model had been done for what was called the Series I two-door, which was designed by Mike Loasby. It was on seeing this model that they said, "That's the car we want!"'

'The idea was that we would have a [common] two-door platform that could be skinned. So we developed what became the V600 platform, which had the ability to give us the full 600 horsepower in all temperatures.'

'We took the first two-door Series I car to the wind tunnel in semi-complete form and found that at 200 mph it had 70–80 horsepower to spare. It was quite a fast car.'

Mike Loasby

'I started on the Series I two-door and did a full quarter-scale [model],' said Loasby. 'It was modified by Shaun Rush to increase the size of the car so it was the same size as the production Vantage. I had made it a lot smaller in height particularly because that was what the artist's impression intended it to be. Then it was brought to completion using the same structure as the donor car. So that's why we reverted to that point; they used my general body shape, but [mine] was a bit smaller. If they'd used mine, it would have been somewhat faster because speed is proportional to frontal area, dependant to a degree on height.'

'The Series I programme started in earnest when Mike completed his quarter-scale black model,' recalled Shaun Rush. 'It was a lovely looking thing and everyone was keen to get on with it.

ASTON MARTIN: POWER, BEAUTY AND SOUL

A Special Series I coupe's aluminium body nearing completion; only three were built

The Series I rendering was quite different from the completed car

DB7 doors were used on the V600 Vantage-based coupes

'I had arranged the production of some delete build chassis, which were basically a running platform. After being built using the normal build procedures to a similar delete specification, these were driven across the road to be stripped by Works Service and the chassis, with no roof structure, were sent [to be panelled].

'The black model was used as an aid rather than the definitive model we thought it would be. I had to restyle the car, although we did use some of the styling cues from the original renderings and the model. At home in the evenings I did a revised layout drawing but lifted the roof, pulled the nose of the car forwards and up, changed the rake of the front screen so we could keep the windscreen wiper's lower screen rail and all the other packaging issues related to the front bulkhead as standard Vantage. To balance the car I had to pull the rear back, although the final car still had its rear bumper beam 4 inches further forwards than a standard Vantage.

'The other major thing I wanted to do was to incorporate the DB7 door package. This included the inner door [which would have a unique skin], a hinge, locks, dropping glass and seals. All [these] items had been proven and were readily available. The seals in particular had a lot of money spent on them; this would also give us a frameless door glass. So the side profile of the glass house was changed to incorporate the DB7 glass; it obviously ran into the small rear quarter glass, which retained the distinctive shape of the renderings and model and again we hoped to use the seal from the DB7 to hold it in.

'The door aperture was one area that I always felt we could improve on and I wanted to be able to open the door and be as impressed with the panels inside the door opening as the actual outer panels. We also incorporated special plinths to hold the unique coach building badges.

'I had my revised sections enlarged to full-size and Cecil Atkinson, the Production Pattern Maker, and I made half an egg box jig mounted on a Vantage slave chassis. We also took a pair of GRP reversals from the door apertures of a DB7 in the engineering workshop. These, together with the buck, were delivered just before Christmas 1997.

'The Series One was probably the most straightforward from a panel point of view. The major work was to sort out the structure underneath it. The architecture of mounting the DB7 doors and unique seat belt mountings together with the philosophy of how the panels were to be attached, were going to be the foundations for nine cars of three different body styles. As the bodies got progressively more detailed on Series II and III, these foundations, apart from some details, would remain the same, leaving us to concentrate on the cosmetic aluminium skin.

'[We] mocked up three-quarters of a car on our buck in January 1997, which we then pushed and pulled about until we were happy with the proportions. It was reviewed and then a complete body was mocked up. Steve Bolton had arranged some wind tunnel time for us in March. We made a few adjustments as a result of this work and then went ahead and made jigs and panelled three cars. The front-end from this wind tunnel mock up was subsequently grafted onto the engineering mule and used for testing at Miraval.

'The rear bumper was enclosed behind our fully enveloping rear-end as per Type II. The front bumper was also hidden behind the large DB4 Zagato-style front grille, but was clad in carbon fibre to give it an engineered appearance,' said Rush.

As further examples of the Special Series cars were produced, development continued unabated. 'Steve Bolton did all the suspension and the anti-roll bars,' said Loasby. 'The customers were always changing the damping and so forth and the anti-roll bars. I am not sure why.

'We took the first two-door Series I car to the wind tunnel in semi-complete form and found that at 200 mph it had 70–80 horsepower to spare. It was quite a fast car. I don't think they ever worked out the theoretical top speed on paper but working from those figures it would have been 205 to 206 mph.'

While unlike any other production car in appearance, the Series Is remained identifiable as Aston Martins and were the most handsome of the Special Series cars. Here the ever-

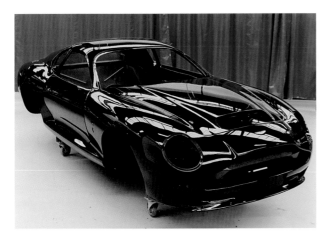

present spirit of Zagato can be seen in some of the design elements, including the abbreviated three-quarter rear window, powerful rear haunches and frontal treatment.

The aluminium grille and cowled headlights gave the car a technical look, while the pulled-out rear haunches, housing lightweight Dymag magnesium alloy wheels with Goodyear Eagle tyres, hinted at the car's immense abilities. The sides incorporated deeply dished sills and shapely doors with new wing mirrors and stylised air intakes.

The Special Series I cars spanned chassis numbers 70505–70507 (Black, Titanium Grey and Special Red respectively). Chassis 70507 has subsequently been resprayed black.

High-speed performance testing was undertaken at Goodyear's Miraval Test Track in southern France, where the warmer temperatures more closely replicated the Far East's demanding climate. All of the car's systems were thoroughly proven; the V600 performance package was developed, suspension was finely tuned and the tyres and brakes were exhaustively tested to ensure all aspects of the car worked as they should and complemented each other.

Security around all the Special Series Vantages was very tight. 'The principle was that I could go out in the cars if I wanted to,' said Loasby, 'but in the main, of course, we didn't take them out on public roads because we didn't want people to see them.'

The Vantage Special Cars were very important to Aston Martin in what was a difficult trading period, providing much-needed capital. CEO David Price recalled: 'All the time I was at Astons we were very strapped for cash, hence the cancellation of the (DB7 GT) race programme. I was very committed to the bespoke builds that Kingsley was doing for a well-known royal family. Without these, the company would have struggled even more.'

Top to bottom: The quarter-scale clay model at Mike Loasby's house; Loasby's completed model under evaluation; A painted body shell awaiting trim and mechanical components; Aerodynamic testing at MIRA

The Series I was the best looking of the Special Series cars

197

Members of the Special Projects Group: 1 Kingsley Riding-Felce 2 Arnold Heaton 3 Alan Walton 4 Gerald Woolhead 5 David Townsend 6 Mike Loasby 7 Alan Pooley 8 Steve Goodship 9 Ian Hartley 10 Ray Brown 11 Steve Bolton 12 Bernard Wise 13 Bob Pearce 14 Paul Smith 15 Neil Morris 16 Pat O'Connor 17 Paul Huewen 18 Peter Killick 19 Shaun Rush. The Series I mule with bespoke front and production rear body work is pictured at the rear

Vantage Special Series I
1998

Chassis: Steel box-section chassis, steel superstructure

Body: Aluminium 2+2 coupe styled by Special Projects Group

Suspension: Front – Independent with wishbones, Eibach coil springs, coaxial spring dampers and anti-roll bar
Rear – de Dion axle, triangulated radius arms, Watt's linkage, Eibach coil springs and telescopic dampers

Brakes: Servo-assisted 365 mm grooved and ventilated discs with AP Racing six-piston callipers (front); 310 mm ventilated discs with AP Racing four-piston callipers (rear)

Steering: Power-assisted rack and pinion

Wheels: 18-inch Dymag magnesium

Tyres: Goodyear Eagle GS-D 285/45 ZR18

Transmission: Torqueflite four-speed-plus-overdrive automatic; final drive 3.31:1. Limited-slip differential. Rear-wheel drive

Engine: 5340 cc alloy V8 with twin chain-driven overhead camshafts per bank and four valves per cylinder. Compression ratio 8.2:1. EEC IV engine management system. Two M90 Eaton superchargers with additional intercooler radiator and water pump. Fully catalysed exhaust system

Power: 600 bhp/447 kW @ 6500 rpm
600 lb/ft/813 Nm of torque @ 4000 rpm

Top speed: 205 mph/330 km/h (approx)

Dimensions:
Length	15 ft 7 in/4745 mm
Width	6 ft 4 in/1918 mm (excluding wing mirrors)
Height	4 ft 4.5 in/1320 mm
Wheelbase	8 ft 6.75 in/2610 mm
Weight	4232 lb/1919 kg (approx)

Price when new: N/A

Number built: 3

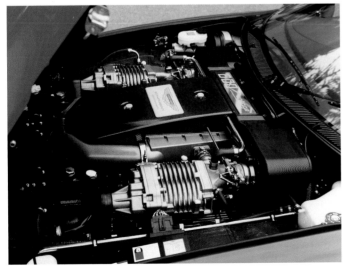

Top: Steve Bolton (right) and Steve Joyce of AP Racing at Miraval Test Track in France **Top right:** The Series I mule receiving attention after high-speed testing **Middle:** Nickel-plated instrument bezels and air-conditioning duct surrounds were a significant feature in all Special Series cars **Above:** The 600 bhp engine was sufficient to power the Series I to 205 mph

Project Vantage

Technological showcase

Project Vantage, with its new technology and brave styling, was a tremendously influential model in Aston Martin's new era, plunging the company firmly into the future. Its origins can be traced back to a meeting between the President of Ford Automotive Operations, Jac Nasser, Jaguar executives and Bob Dover in early 1997.

'Jac Nasser was a great supporter of Aston Martin,' remembered Dover, 'but he was also a great businessman. On one visit to Jaguar, where there was a big group of senior executives from North America, Jac asked the Jaguar people if they wanted a concept car. Their reply was that they did not; he turned to me and asked me if I wanted one and I responded that I did.

'He had some ideas and questions. We had sketched some cars out, with Kingsley's people actually, and he said that he would give us a million dollars for a concept car. I said that I couldn't afford it, that my business wouldn't stand it; his response was that he'd get Ford to pay for it. So that led into Project Vantage. Jac wanted to call it Project Vantage because it was synonymous with the higher-powered version of the Astons.

'I said to Jac that it would give Project Vantage a lot more credibility when he launched it if he could say that he had driven it. I suggested that we go to Millbrook where he drove the car and loved it.'

Bob Dover

'Jac wanted us to try and get it finished for Detroit [Motor Show] as a concept car the following January [1998], which meant we had to get it finished by about mid-December, and we had to freeze everything by about October.'

Dover quickly put plans and processes into place to have the concept car produced in the limited allocated time frame. One of the first things on the agenda was engaging a stylist.

Project Vantage took Aston Martin into a new high-tech era

'Bob Dover had a plan to grow the family and put [Project Vantage] out into the market,' said Ian Callum. 'Bob wanted to do a show car [for] Ford executives to see if they could get the confidence to put it into production. So they put out some tenders for a design to various British design houses and then somebody at Aston said to contact me.

'I, by the way, was not so presumptuous to think that because I had done the DB7 that I would automatically be considered for the job. I didn't think for a minute that I would automatically pick up the mantle at Aston Martin. I had earned some stripes but I wasn't that arrogant. So I went to meet Bob.

'I had done a couple of show cars in the past and in the end they said, "We want you to do a design". I remember doing a very simple design sketch, a simple line drawing but in that you could see Project Vantage. They put a lot of faith in me and we modelled that car in about 12 weeks. I said to Bob, "It's all in my head; I know we can do this".'

Project Vantage was gradually taking shape but as the deadline drew closer it appeared time may have run out for the design and engineering team. 'I didn't think at that moment that he would make it,' said Dover, 'but I asked Jac if he could get across to see the clay [model], which was at Leafield, TWR's headquarters. To my surprise he said he was flying over from the States on the Friday night, and had a couple of hours free on Saturday morning.'

Nasser was immediately enthusiastic about the design. 'When Jac Nasser saw the back of the car he said, "That's the car that I want",' recalled Callum.

'Jac saw the car and loved it,' said Dover. 'When we had it running we wanted to take some video footage to show at the launch at Detroit, so I said to Jac that it would give it a lot more credibility when he launched it if he could say that he had driven it. I suggested that we go to Millbrook, the proving circuit, where he drove the car and again loved it. Remember that this was a million-dollar car, which wasn't very highly tuned, it had the paddle shift and everything; it was a prototype.'

There is only one Project Vantage. It is and remains a concept car but its story does not end there. Launched at the North American International Auto Show in January 1998, one year before the V12 DB7 Vantage, Project Vantage was designed to whet the appetite of DB7 owners and would-be owners as to what may be in the pipeline at Aston Martin.

'We believe Project Vantage reflects all the essential elements of power, performance and driver involvement in a manner which is true to the traditions of Aston Martin,' said Dover upon the launch of Project Vantage.

'The concept of Project Vantage will enable everyone involved in the programme to investigate and explore techniques, concepts and materials which could all be employed at some time in the future, together with seeking options on the exterior and interior designs. We are looking forward to receiving feedback on all of the features incorporated into the concept.'

Ford had decreed that Aston Martin was to be its pilot for high-technology developments. Project Vantage was a design concept for a totally new, advanced-technology car that certainly fitted that description.

'Aston Martin is a tremendous real-world arena for some of Ford's most advanced technologies,' said Nasser. 'Project Vantage helps us refine some very important design and

Top to bottom: Ford's Indigo Concept Car, first shown at the Detroit Motor Show in 1996, featured the V12 engine that later powered Project Vantage; Ian Callum's 1:1 clay styling model; Ford's V12 engine, in modified form, powered many Aston Martin models

construction technologies that initially can be employed in low-volume manufacturing and eventually become employed in more mass market vehicles.'

Engineers and designers from Aston Martin, Ford Advanced Vehicle Technology, Magnetti Marelli, AP Racing, Cosworth Engineering, ITT and TWR were all involved in the development of the car. Project Vantage employed advanced technologies in the design and building of the body and chassis. The tub was constructed from aluminium honeycomb and the extruded aluminium chassis sections and roof pillars were reinforced with carbon fibre. It was claimed these materials and construction methods saved more than 50 percent in weight and increased torsional rigidity by more than 100 percent.

When news of Project Vantage broke it was the words 'V12 power' that drew most attention. A research and development programme to evaluate future Aston Martin engine requirements had begun between Ford Research and Vehicle Technology and Cosworth Engineering in July 1997. The early fruit of this research was the prototype 5.9-litre, 48-valve V12 engine used in Project Vantage.

A V12 was touted as the possible production engine for the Lagonda Vignale Concept Car back in 1993 and was first seen in mock-up guise at the Turin Motor Show in April 1994. It was then used in Ford's GT90 concept car, which debuted at the

Ian Callum

Ian Callum's styling work for both Jaguar and Aston Martin has produced some of the most elegant and exciting cars in recent history, including the Aston Martin DB7 line, Project Vantage and Vanquish and Jaguar XK8, F-Type concept, XK coupe and convertible and C-XF Concept.

Callum was born in Dumfries, Scotland and studied Industrial Design at the Glasgow School of Art, gaining a Masters Degree in Automobile Design at the Royal College of Art. 'I [then] went to Ford at Dunton Design and Research building in Essex for 11 years,' said Callum. 'During that period I worked in Australia, in Italy, with my brother Moray and then I worked in Japan.' Between 1979 and 1988 Callum worked on the Ford Fiesta, Mondeo, Escort RS Cosworth, mid-engined RS200 and Probe models.

Between 1988 and 1990, Callum was Design Manager at Ghia Design Studio where he worked on the Via, Zig and Zag concept cars. 'After 11 years I left Ford and went back to England and joined TWR Industrial Design Studios with Tom Walkinshaw in 1990. He had various concepts and ideas that we were trying to do and he used to do a lot of work for JaguarSport.'

At TWR Callum became Chief Designer and General Manager and it was here that he produced his most famous design: the DB7. After leaving Aston Martin in late August 1999, Callum took up the appointment of Head of Design at Jaguar, succeeding Geoff Lawson.

Detroit Motor Show in 1995 and finally in Ford's Reynard-engineered, hot-rod-inspired Indigo Show Car that was first seen at the Detroit Motor Show in 1996.

The engine was developed in cooperation with Aston Martin, Jim Clarke and his team at Ford Advanced Vehicle Technology and Cosworth Engineering. One of several engines considered for production, it was developed to give 200 mph performance while meeting or exceeding the world's strictest emissions standards.

Paddle-shift gears designed by Magnetti-Marelli and Ford enabled gear changes to be effected in only 250 milliseconds. The six-speed transmission, mated to a limited-slip differential, could also be operated in fully automatic mode.

AP Racing provided the braking package, which consisted of 352-mm front and rear ventilated steel discs with alloy six-piston callipers. Twelve-spoke, 19-inch lightweight magnesium alloy wheels were used with 255/40 ZR19 front, and 285/40 ZR19 rear Bridgestone tyres. The front and rear suspension set-ups employed independent double aluminium wishbones, coil springs, monotube dampers and anti-roll bars.

Like all previous Aston Martins, Project Vantage continued the classic sports car front-engine, rear-wheel drive configuration. It was also a strict two-seater; the first since the Virage Volante prototype of 1990.

Extended rear wheel arches gave the car a powerful stance

'In March [1997] we gave the [development] job to TWR,' said Dover. 'My brief to Ian [Callum] was that I wanted something a bit more aggressive than DB7, somewhere between the V8 and the six-cylinder DB7, which turned into Project Vantage.' While wholly elegant like its six-cylinder cousin, the Vanquish was more overtly aggressive, with hints of both the DB4 GT Zagato and the Vantage Special Series I.

'The DB7 was deliberately built to be a beautiful car with a more restrained shape than the big [V8] Astons in production,' said Callum. 'Having done that, I had to get more aggressive again with the Project [Vantage], to stress out the car's extra potential without losing its Aston purity. We pulled its front wheels forward, gave the car a very high belt line, an important Aston characteristic, and moved the wheels as far out in the arches as we could. I really wanted to give the feeling

that it belonged to the ground, that despite its performance it was anchored there no matter what.'

Although thoroughly modern on the outside, traditionalists could follow a common lineage in the design. But the interior alienated some potential customers. The controversial, far-sighted, two-seat cabin featured saddle brown Connolly leather, carbon fibre and aluminium trim, endowing the car with a contemporary ambience. The seats were trimmed in leather and quilted suede and contained four-point safety harnesses in deference to the car's sporting intentions.

Traditional walnut made way for a thoroughly contemporary look that matched Ford's idea of Aston Martin as flag bearer of its cutting-edge technology. A more traditional touch was the inclusion of fitted luggage in the boot and the addition of interior lockers for oddments. Because the development period precluded it, air conditioning was omitted, although the dashboard incorporated the controls and air vents.

Neil Simpson's interior design didn't make production, but his influence is seen in the later V8 Vantage Le Mans and Vanquish. 'I did the Project Vantage show car interior that became the Vanquish,' said Simpson. 'The interior [of the pre-production Vanquish] was changed by the engineering team. There were always people who were nervous about doing something so modern. The Project Vantage interior was done in a time frame expected of a show car, but I always felt it could have been developed into a very good interior. It was well-received by designers. I think some of the cues were used elsewhere and there are still cars coming out that make reference to that style. The [Vanquish] production car interior was saved at the 11th hour by Aston Martin; I didn't care for the early [pre-production] work. It may be an appropriate design, which is the main thing, but it's not a landmark piece of work.'

The unique metallic green Project Vantage, AMV03, is owned by Aston Martin and is on occasional display at its Headquarters in Gaydon, Warwickshire.

Opposite: Vanquish (left) and Project Vantage models, together at Aston Martin's Works Service in Newport Pagnell, look almost identical but there were many differences **Above:** Neil Simpson's far-sighted interior never made it into the production Vanquish

Project Vantage
1998

Chassis: Extruded and bonded aluminium and carbon fibre platform and superstructure

Body: Aluminium and composite two-seat coupe styled by Ian Callum

Suspension: Front – Independent with unequal length double aluminium wishbones, coil springs with pushrod-operated monotube damper units and anti-roll bar
Rear – Independent with electro-hydraulic active roll control, double aluminium wishbones incorporating anti-squat geometry, coil springs, monotube damper units and anti-roll bar

Brakes: Servo-assisted ventilated steel discs 352 mm with AP Racing alloy six-piston callipers (front and rear). ABS

Steering: Power-assisted rack and pinion

Wheels: 19-inch magnesium alloy

Tyres: Bridgestone SO2 255/40 ZR19 (front). 285/40 ZR19 (rear)

Transmission: Borg Warner six-speed manual with auto shift selection; final drive 3.69:1. Limited-slip differential. Rear-wheel drive

Engine: 5935 cc alloy V12 with twin chain-driven overhead camshafts per bank and four valves per cylinder. Visteon twin PTEC engine management and fuel injection system. Fully catalysed exhaust system

Power: 442 bhp/330 kW @ 5000 rpm
320 lb/ft/434 Nm of torque @ 3000 rpm

Top speed: 200 mph/322 km/h (claimed)

Dimensions:

Length	15 ft 3.5 in/4667 mm
Width	6 ft 2.5 in/1898 mm
Height	4 ft 3 in/1298 mm
Wheelbase	8 ft 10 in/2692 mm
Weight	3417 lb/1550 kg (quoted)

Price when new: Not available for sale

Number built: 1

A M 4

On His Majesty's Secret Service Part V

Outwardly, Pininfarina's AM4 design was elegant and more traditionally Aston Martin-like than AM3, with its side air vents and recognisable grille, yet it also contained typical Pininfarina signature styling cues.

The front of the car was dominated by an elongated black five-slat grille, DB7-style headlights and sweeping creases and round air outlets on the bonnet. The design's most radical feature could be witnessed from the rear where the all-encompassing light cluster featured an inverted Aston Martin grille shape, below which were dual rectangular exhaust pipes. AM4 shared the same Goodyear-shod Pininfarina-designed six-spoke alloy wheels as AM3.

Pininfarina also designed the organically flowing interior, which differed from AM3. Aston Martin supplied Pininfarina's designers with an unnumbered chassis for use as a trim buck, but from there, any resemblance to an Aston Martin cabin was difficult to trace.

> Aston Martin supplied Pininfarina's designers with an unnumbered chassis for use as a trim buck, but from there any resemblance to an Aston Martin interior was hard to trace.

The dashboard, switchgear, seats and door trims were thoroughly redesigned by Pininfarina's stylists using an Aston Martin-supplied chassis for interior mock-up purposes. The Vantage steering wheel, with airbag, remained and, like AM3, the dials were arranged in a straight line running across the right half of the dashboard. But in contrast, AM4 featured glossy colour-coded trim on the steering wheel, transmission lever, centre console and doors.

Like AM3, AM4's body was built by Coggiola in Turin. AM4 was completed in early 1998 and shipped from Italy directly to the customer in the Far East.

AM4 featured both Aston Martin and Pininfarina badges; the bodies were actually built by Turin-based specialists Coggiola

Pininfarina

Battista 'Pinin' Farina was born on 2 November 1893. At age 11 he began working at his brother's 'Stabilimenti Farina' body shop in Turin and during WWI he was involved in the construction of trainer aircraft.

Farina left his brother's workshop and founded Carrozzeria Pinin Farina on 22 May 1930. Beginning as a specialist body building company, Pininfarina grew to become one of the world's foremost design houses. The company's bodies have graced many of the world's most evocative cars including Cisitalia, Alfa Romeo Duetto, Fiat 124 Spyder and Peugeot 404.

But it is for its Ferrari designs, the first of which was penned in 1952, that the company will forever be known. Most notably, Pininfarina designed the Dino, Testarossa, GTO, F355, 360 Modena (pictured below) and 550 Maranello.

In 1961 Farina left the running of the carrozzeria in the hands of his son Sergio and brother-in-law Renzo Carli. He died on 3 April 1966. The AM3 and AM4 designs were the first collaboration between Pininfarina and Aston Martin.

Top to bottom: The steering wheel is Vantage-sourced but the dashboard bears no resemblance to any Aston Martin model; Heavily bolstered front seats featured in the cabin; AM4's styling was much more in the Aston Martin mould than AM3

AM4
1998

Chassis: Steel box-section chassis, steel superstructure

Body: Aluminium 2+2 coupe styled by Pininfarina

Suspension: Front – Independent with wishbones, Eibach coil springs, coaxial spring dampers and anti-roll bar
Rear – de Dion axle, radius arms, Watt's linkage, Eibach coil springs, telescopic dampers and anti-roll bar

Brakes: Servo-assisted 365 mm grooved and ventilated discs with AP Racing six-piston callipers (front); 310 mm ventilated discs with AP Racing four-piston callipers (rear). ABS

Steering: Power-assisted rack and pinion

Wheels: 18-inch alloy

Tyres: Goodyear Eagle 285/45 ZR18

Transmission: Torqueflite four-speed-plus-overdrive automatic; final drive 3.31:1. Limited-slip differential. Rear-wheel drive

Engine: 5340 cc alloy V8 with twin chain-driven overhead camshafts per bank and four valves per cylinder. Compression ratio 8.2:1. EEC IV engine management system. Two Roots type M90 Eaton superchargers with additional intercooler radiators and water pump. Fully catalysed exhaust system

Power: 600 bhp/447 kW @ 6500 rpm
600 lb/ft/813 Nm of torque @ 4000 rpm

Top speed: 205 mph/330 km/h (approx)

Dimensions:
Length	15 ft 7 in/4745 mm
Width	6 ft 4 in/1918 mm (excluding wing mirrors)
Height	4 ft 4.5 in/1320 mm
Wheelbase	8 ft 6.75 in/2610 mm
Weight	4300 lb/1950 kg (approx)

Price when new: N/A

Number built: 3

Top to bottom: Rolling chassis were prepared at Newport Pagnell and shipped to Italy for Coggiola to body; AM4s featured 600 bhp Vantage engines and four-speed-plus-overdrive automatic transmissions; An inverted grille shape was incorporated into the rear light cluster

Vantage Special Series II

On His Majesty's Secret Service Part VI

The Series II two-door sports cars proved to be the last of the line for the Special Projects Group. The subsequent Series III two-door coupes were destroyed part-way through their build and the other special cars, AM3 and AM4, were styled by Pininfarina and bodied by Coggiola in Italy.

Three cars were built: chassis numbers 70508 (black), 70509 (Titanium Silver) and 70510 (Special Red). The Series II, like the Type II, was a more radically evolved version of the first cars.

Once again, Kingsley Riding-Felce showed various design drawings to the client and a body style was agreed upon. Work began on the cars in July 1997 with the bodies based on the hard points and basic chassis devised for the Series I.

While resembling the Series I, the Series II had more complicated lines and shapes in the design. The grille was more traditional in profile and may have proved the inspiration for the restyled mouth of the Vanquish S. The front spoiler, however, was more overt, while the dual headlights sat behind unusually shaped perspex covers.

The bonnet scoop was reminiscent of the early DB4 and on either side of it were restyled air outlets. The side windows were steeply raked inwards, meeting the roof in a sharp crease. The shapely sills, first seen on the Series I, were emphasised with contrasting silver accents. The wheels were, once again, Dymag magnesium eight-spoke items fitted with Goodyear Eagle tyres.

'We did everything to the highest possible standard,' said Mike Loasby. 'We put the 600-horsepower engines in those vehicles. They were quite potent cars and would do something approaching 190 mph on the test-track.' In ideal situations the car could exceed 200 mph.

While the Series II coupes were still being manufactured, work on the Series III coupes had already began. Styling sketches were drawn, the body shape was agreed upon, bucks were made and the bodies created in aluminium. The chassis numbers 705011, 705012 and 70091 (a complete 600 bhp Vantage that had been used for testing which was to become a Series III) were allocated and the running gear was at the ready. The cars could successfully have been constructed.

The three Series II cars were the last Special Series Vantages produced by Aston Martin's Special Projects Group

'It was heartbreaking to see those three bodies, which were all in various stages of completion, have their aluminium skins taken off and destroyed.'

Shaun Rush

But a directive was received from the Far East that the project was to be stopped before the cars could be completed. As the Special Projects Group was bound to an exclusivity agreement all the bodies and the bucks upon which they were built were destroyed. They cannot and will not ever be produced.

'It was heartbreaking to see those three bodies, all in various stages of completion, have their aluminium skins taken off and destroyed,' said Shaun Rush. 'The Series III were the most radically styled of the two-door cars. [We] just used [the] renderings and our basic chassis layout with the DB7 door package to mock up a body and then we just "went for it". These cars, while not in my opinion as good an overall package as the Series I, were going to be stunning – with their large chromed brass grille and other body finishes, they were quite "over the top".'

The conclusion of the Special Series programme was not the finish of the Special Vehicle Operations, but the department did eventually close down. 'It was disappointing when Special Vehicle Operations was disbanded [at the end of 2000],' said Steve Bolton. 'The Series I and Series II had been particularly well received.'

'When you get a team and they work so well together, as we did, it's great,' said Kingsley Riding-Felce. 'There were so many in the team; they know who they are. They know how good they were and the contribution that they made. We really had a tremendous enthusiasm to make this work. The days were long and there was a huge amount of corporate pressure on us to deliver.

'Once a car was delivered, of course we could raise the invoices, which at that time were very important, because we needed to

Top left: The three Series III coupe bodies were built and chassis allocated but a directive from the Far East cancelled the order; they will never be constructed Top right: Rear accommodation was suitable only for children Above: Dymag 18-inch magnesium wheels were fitted to all three cars Opposite: Unique styling features included deep contrasting sills and sharp crease lines running from the head and taillights

show the company that we were delivering. It was also important that we absolutely met the quality requirements, because the customer was not going to accept anything other than the absolute best. So we worked together as a team – we worked very hard and delivered a number of very, very special cars. This work continued until the customer decided that he had enough in his collection and we decided to downsize the team.'

The days of truly bespoke motor cars are gone now at Aston Martin. On the winding down of the Special Projects Team, Aston Martin's priorities changed. Riding-Felce made Aston Martin's new directions clear, stating in Works Service's *Works Torque* magazine: 'Our commitment to present and future owners means we have taken the difficult decision to decline some offers to use our coachbuilding skills on one-off models, preferring instead to use all of our expertise to satisfy the growing demands of a company producing more new cars than at any time in history.'

'If it's chassis coachwork, to be honest I don't think we would do it because the laws and regulations have changed and product liability has changed,' said Riding-Felce, later. 'A lot of this is planning; there is a huge amount of time in the planning. You really do soak up your resources when you do some of these bigger projects. We certainly do engine, brakes and suspension upgrades, full re-trims, re-paints, servicing and accident repairs.

'Having got that group of people together, what do you then do with all that talent? We started to work on after-market ideas for the DB7; things like brake and performance upgrades. The team worked on a lot of the new ideas we offered within Works Service. Then as a result of our engineering, these were taken and put on line, which meant that we really had to disband the team, which was very sad.'

Cars like the Special Series Vantage are from a bygone era that will never be replaced.

Vantage Special Series II
1998

Chassis: Steel box-section chassis, steel superstructure

Body: Aluminium 2+2 coupe styled by Special Projects Team

Suspension: Front – Independent with wishbones, Eibach coil springs, coaxial spring dampers and anti-roll bar
Rear – de Dion axle, radius arms, Watt's linkage, Eibach coil springs, telescopic dampers and anti-roll bar

Brakes: Servo-assisted 365 mm grooved and ventilated discs with AP Racing six-piston callipers (front); 310 mm ventilated discs with AP Racing four-piston callipers (rear). ABS

Steering: Power-assisted rack and pinion

Wheels: 18-inch Dymag magnesium

Tyres: Goodyear Eagle GS-D 285/45 ZR18

Transmission: Torqueflite four-speed-plus-overdrive automatic; final drive 3.31:1. Limited-slip differential. Rear-wheel drive

Engine: 5340 cc alloy V8 with twin chain-driven overhead camshafts per bank and four valves per cylinder. Compression ratio 8.2:1. EEC IV engine management system. Two Roots type M90 Eaton superchargers with additional intercooler radiator and water pump. Fully catalysed exhaust system

Power: 600 bhp/447 kW @ 6500 rpm
600 lb/ft/813 Nm of torque @ 4000 rpm

Top speed: 205 mph/330 km/h (approx)

Dimensions:
Length	15 ft 7 in/4745 mm
Width	6 ft 4 in/1918 mm (excluding wing mirrors)
Height	4 ft 4.5 in/1320 mm
Wheelbase	8 ft 6.75 in/2610 mm
Weight	4399 lb/1995 kg (approx)

Price when new: N/A

Number built: 3

Vantage V600

Six hundred of the best

The Special Series Vantages had bespoke bodies, the highest quality build and components and one of the most potent drivetrains in production but they did suffer from one problem: a loss of power due to the hot Far East climate.

As a result, the Special Vehicle Operations team at Newport Pagnell, under the leadership of Arthur Wilson, developed ever more potent versions of the V8 engines in an effort to restore lost power. 'I started working for Kingsley Riding-Felce on a series of very special project cars for an overseas client in conjunction with Arthur Wilson, who was developing the base increase in power for the V600 engine concept,' said Steve Bolton. 'The name 600 came about because the previous project number was 590, so this became 600. It was just the next series of numbers. It was coincidental that that was also the power output.

'I had done some work previously with the Vantage and had established that one of the concerns with the car in extreme climates was that the intercooling system wasn't as efficient as it could have been. We needed to liberate more power, as well as revise the superchargers and the exhaust system to improve the intercooling system and thus, the performance was a necessity.

> 'Service did their bit on the engine and they brought it back up to 600 horsepower. This effectively meant taking the restrictive exhaust off and increasing the intercooling.'
>
> *Arthur Wilson*

'We found that by improving the cooling we could take advantage of the increased charge being developed by the new superchargers and get a robust 600 horsepower. Development of the projects for our special client gave us the spin-off for the V600 for other markets as well. [But] the first V600 was made solely for the special client.'

Having already done the engineering and development for these engines for the Special Series Vantages, it was decided to offer them to the public. Once again, it was not a production model, but rather an after-market package for road-registered 550 bhp Vantages; the Vantage V600 was not Type Approved.

Performance figures confirmed that the V600 Vantage was among the fastest cars in the world, but time was running out for the aging design

Works Service

'There has always been a Works Service, or a Service Department,' said Kingsley Riding-Felce. 'Even when Martin and Bamford founded the company in 1914, customers were always in a position to take their cars back to have them repaired and serviced.'

That tradition continued when the company moved to Feltham in Middlesex, where a Service Department and a Service Operations unit were created. Aston Martin and Lagonda were brought together at Newport Pagnell in the mid-1950s but it wasn't until around 1960 that a new dedicated service operation was created. When Riding-Felce joined the company in 1976 it was more of a Service Department looking after routine maintenance for Aston Martin and Lagonda cars.

'We recognised the need to develop it as a separate entity because calling it a Service Department wasn't giving it the credit it deserved,' explained Riding-Felce. 'We were undertaking a lot of coachwork and one of the things that inspired us was that other cars, such as the Vignale by Ghia, had their own beautiful coachbuilding badges. We needed something similar to show our own level of identity – Works Coachbuilt or Works Prepared – so we created our own distinct design and badges.'

Works Service has played an immensely important part in the company's history and many of the specialised and development cars in recent times have come out of its doors, including the original DB7 GT, Special Series Vantages, 6.3-litre two-valve V8 engine enhancement, Virage 6.3 conversion, Virage Shooting Brake, Lagonda Saloon and Shooting Brake, DB7 V8, V600 Vantage and Vantage Volante Special Edition.

There have been others, too. Works Service restored the first production DB4, chassis number DB4/101/R; a replica DB5 James Bond car, DB5/1456/R, complete with revolving number plates and water jets; the original DB4 GT, DP 199; and the famous DB4 GT Bertone Jet, DB4 GT/0201/L.

'We also offer a bespoke service that allows customers to add that personal touch to their cars. Over the years, we have installed specialist telephone systems and cocktail cabinets; we've fitted television sets in the back of headrests and put modern CD players behind old radio fascias with speakers hidden in the car,' said Riding-Felce.

Works Service still retains all the skills to service and repair the many early models customers bring to them at Newport Pagnell. 'Our restoration work is in strong demand and our objectives are now streamlined to meet the responsibilities of the new era of the DB9, V8 Vantage and beyond. Works Service has an important role to play in the company's future as well as its past.'

Many customers brought in their used Vantages for conversion, but not all. Some V600s were registered while still at Newport Pagnell's Works Service in order to have the revisions made while still brand new.

Tadek Marek's V8 engine was first bench tested at 275 bhp in July 1965 and 33 years later, Aston Martin was producing road-going versions, not speculative racing specials, at more than twice that power. The percentage differential between the Vantage V600 and the 350-horsepower V8 Coupe was 71.4 percent, while the differential between the original 4.8-litre V8 engine and the twin supercharged 600 bhp unit was 118.2 percent.

'We did a 600 horsepower up-rate for [Works] Service for the 1997 model Vantage, which had to be strangled by the exhaust system to get it past the 74Dba drive-by noise test,' remembered Arthur Wilson. 'The restrictive exhaust made it lose some power and to get it back we went slightly beyond the original service conversion. Then Service did their bit on it when it got to them and they brought it back up to 600 horsepower. This effectively meant taking the restrictive exhaust off and increasing the intercooling.'

Top: Approximately 81 cars shared the V600 package **Above:** Chrome grille surrounds and small badges were subtle indicators that the vehicle was a 600 bhp supercar

V600 engines were officially only available post-registration

Also available post-registration was a five-speed gearbox, in place of the standard six-speed unit

Model	Weight (lb)	0–60 mph (seconds)	Top speed (mph)	Power (bhp)
Vantage	4368	4.6	186	550
Vantage V600	4399	3.9	200-plus	600

Modifications to the engine included re-engineering of the charge air intake cooling system, an additional inter-cooler radiator, increased boost pressure for the superchargers and subtle changes to the throttle mechanism. The exhaust system was upgraded to a bigger bore tuned stainless steel, 'super sports' version that further enhanced engine performance.

Customers could also forego the production six-speed ZF manual gearbox and instead, opt for a close-ratio five-speed unit, post registration. As well, automatic cars could be fitted with an overdrive switch in the gear knob and have the differential ratio changed to maximise the automatic transmission's potential.

AP Racing brakes with six-piston brake callipers front and rear were added to help cope with the car's extra power. The existing rear brake calliper was retained as a park brake and traction control was also offered.

The front and rear suspension systems were completely reworked and incorporated stiffer Eibach springs, Koni adjustable sports dampers and stiffer anti-roll bar. Special hollow lightweight five-spoke Dymag alloy wheels with Goodyear Eagle GS-D 285/45 ZR18 tyres came with the standard package.

As the name suggests, the Vantage V600 engine was capable of 600 bhp @ 6500 rpm and 600 lb/ft of torque @ 4000 rpm; enough to propel the 4399-lb car to 60 mph in less than four seconds and on to a top speed in excess of 200 mph. Everything about the car was enormous, including the £233,682 price tag.

Visually, the V600 typically featured a revised chrome grille-surround, 'Works Prepared' badge and subtle body and engine 'Vantage V600' badging. First announced in 1998 at the British Motor Show, approximately 81 cars have been converted to the V600 package including the Special Series Vantages.

Vantage V600
1998–2000

Chassis: Steel box-section chassis, steel superstructure

Body: Aluminium 2+2 coupe styled by John Heffernan

Suspension: Front – Independent with double wishbones, Eibach coil springs, coaxial spring dampers and anti-roll bar Rear – de Dion axle, radius arms, Watt's linkage, Eibach coil springs, telescopic dampers and anti-roll bar

Brakes: Servo-assisted 365 mm ventilated and grooved discs with AP Racing six-piston callipers (front); 310 mm ventilated discs with AP Racing six-piston callipers (rear). ABS

Steering: Power-assisted rack and pinion

Wheels: 18-inch Dymag magnesium

Tyres: Goodyear Eagle GS-D 285/45 ZR18

Transmission: ZF five-speed manual; final drive 3.33:1 Torqueflite four-speed automatic; final drive 3.058:1 Limited-slip differential. Rear-wheel drive

Engine: 5340 cc alloy V8 with twin chain-driven overhead camshafts per bank and four valves per cylinder. Compression ratio 8.2:1. EEC IV engine management system. Two Roots type M90 Eaton superchargers with additional intercooler radiator and water pump. Fully catalysed exhaust system

Power: 600 bhp/447 kW @ 6500 rpm
600 lb/ft/813 Nm of torque @ 4000 rpm

Top speed: 200-plus mph/ 322-plus km/h

Dimensions:
Length	15 ft 7 in/4745 mm
Width	6 ft 4 in/1918 mm (excluding door mirrors)
Height	4 ft 4.5 in/1320 mm
Wheelbase	8 ft 6.75 in/2610 mm
Weight	4399 lb/1995 kg

Price when new: £233,682

Number built: 81 (approx) including 25 special projects and 56 customer conversions

DB7 V8

Eight into seven does go

There was a time when Aston Martin's bespoke capabilities meant almost any car could be constructed for a customer, within reason, provided they could pay for it. This unique DB7 V8, developed at Works Service in Newport Pagnell, is an important example of that bespoke era.

A customer requested the Special Projects Group build a very special DB7, then available only in six-cylinder guise, with a good deal more power than the production engine. The result was the fastest, most powerful road-going DB7 ever created.

'We were conscious at the Factory that the DB7 needed more power,' Kingsley Riding-Felce recalled. 'A V8 engine was tried, but allegedly didn't fit; this drove Aston Martin to ask Ford for a new powerplant and Jac Nasser made the V12 from the Indigo project available. We in Works Service always believed and knew that a Newport Pagnell V8 would fit into a DB7; this was when we did this bespoke V8 as a one-off development project for a customer.'

Various special DB7s had already been created but none as radical as this. 'We wanted to sell some DB7s to an overseas client,' said Steve Bolton. 'There were quite a large number with various trims and body colours and instruments, but they wanted something a bit more special. This was before the DB7 Vantage with the V12 engines, so we developed a version putting the Aston Martin V8 engine into the DB7.'

'Steve Bolton and I did this concept together,' said Riding-Felce. 'I liaised with the client and said that we could do it. Steve, as Project Engineer did the engineering, Ray Brown was the Leading Technician and I did the Project Management.

'We put a 452-horsepower, 6.3-litre engine in this DB7; we didn't put a 500-horsepower engine in it because of the automatic transmission. It had a new brake and suspension package and a special sump. It also required a new wiring loom for the engine management system. It was not much heavier than the six-cylinder car, therefore performance was tremendous.'

The DB7 V8 was the best of both worlds: it had the power of a V8 coupled with the agility of the lighter DB7. There wasn't much to suggest the car was equipped with a powerful V8 engine, save for the bulging bonnet and subtle DB7 V8 badging on the rear.

A rear wing and bespoke DB7 V8 badging were part of the one-off package

'We in Works Service always believed and knew that a Newport Pagnell V8 would fit into a DB7; this was when we did this bespoke V8 as a one-off development project for a customer.'

Kingsley Riding-Felce

It featured a full Driving Dynamics body kit, including side skirts, bolder front and rear bumpers and a rear, boot-mounted wing, OZ Racing 18-inch magnesium wheels and Bridgestone 245/40 ZR18 tyres.

Registered R40IFGP, the unique DB7 V8 was finished in Cheviot Red with oxblood and parchment leather trim, red carpet and parchment headlining. A bespoke brass mesh grille with a 'Works Prepared in Newport Pagnell' badge and matching brass-coloured side air intake completed the body modifications.

The car's most potent feature was the 6.3-litre, four-valves-per-cylinder V8 engine which was detuned slightly to produce 452 bhp @ 5500 rpm and 427 lb/ft of torque @ 5000 rpm. As requested by the customer, a specially modified four-speed-plus-overdrive Chrysler Torqueflite automatic transmission was fitted. Only 44 lb heavier, the potent V8 dwarfed the six-cylinder DB7's 335 bhp engine.

'We made [the V8 engine] fit by making some modifications here and there,' explained Bolton. 'It turned it into an absolutely phenomenal car. With all that horsepower in that lightweight body, coupled with the fact that it was an automatic, its ability to get off the line smoothly and quickly was unbelievable. We built a mule for that [project] and then built one proper car. The mule was subsequently destroyed.

'The DB7 V8 was surprisingly straightforward. It had the four-speed-plus-overdrive automatic transmission with a small switch on the steering wheel. Once the car was up and running the only gears you needed were third and fourth, so you could just use the flick switch to change between the two gears. The prop shaft was quite special; we used CV joints in order to get some driveline refinement.

Driving Dynamics body kit under development

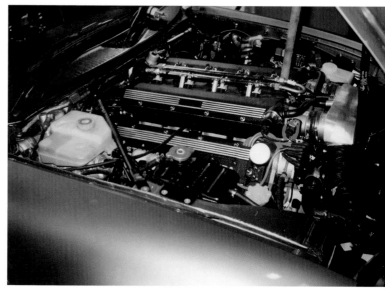

The DB7 V8 mule's engine bay undergoing evaluation

A DB7 V8 mule was used for testing and development purposes but was later destroyed

Works Service was able to fit a Newport Pagnell V8 into the DB7's engine bay, despite advice to the contrary

Left: Yellow brake callipers were chosen to harmonise with the brass accents on the grille, bonnet and air vents **Above:** A Driving Dynamics body kit and Dymag wheels were indicators that this car was not all that it seemed

'The chassis was totally reworked. That amount of power was doing a similar thing to when we supercharged the old Virage chassis and so that had trick springs and dampers to control it and minimise axle tramp. Again, for the brakes, we turned to our colleagues at AP Racing; they made a bespoke, race brake system for us. We also used magnesium wheels and our suggestion to the customer of gold-coloured mesh for the grille and side vents was accepted, which looked very good.'

Shaun Rush styled a one-off aluminium bonnet with twin bulges over the rocker covers to give the car a distinctive look. 'I oversaw the manufacture by the production panel shop of both an add-on section for the mule and a complete aluminium bonnet for the actual car,' said Rush. 'If my memory serves me correctly we also made aluminium front wings and boot lid for that car. We had the tooling from when the DB7 was first introduced and Newport Pagnell was asked to make aluminium parts as we were having problems with the composite panels.'

The DB7 V8 was road tested briefly by *Autocar* magazine in August 1998 just prior to delivery. Writer Steve Cropley reported that, 'the engine fired … at first crank of the starter. The beat was beautiful. The throttle blipped instantly with a potential that rocked the body on its firm suspension. I slipped the auto selector into D … we rolled out of Newport Pagnell below 2000 rpm, the engine showing off its relaxed nature, its immense low-down torque and with a whiff of four-valves-per-cylinder sizzle, its breeding, all at once. Floor the throttle and the car just erupts. The din is as delicious as anything from the great V8 days of Detroit, but it has the advantage of revving as well; the redline is 6500 rpm … if it won't whip two or three seconds off the normal DB7 six's 0–100 mph time of 14.4 seconds, I'll stand amazed … the steering was sharper than ever, the stability under braking and in corners was markedly enhanced and the brakes themselves were simply sensational. The whole package seemed so well integrated, so well developed.'[17]

Chassis number 100528, is the sole road-going DB7 V8 example; an exclusivity agreement between the customer and Aston Martin ensured no more were made.

DB7 V8
1998

Chassis: Steel semi-monocoque body shell

Body: Composite and pressed steel 2+2 coupe styled by Ian Callum with Driving Dynamics package

Suspension: Front – Independent with double wishbones, coil springs, monotube dampers and anti-roll bar
Rear – Independent with double wishbones, longitudinal control arms, coil springs, monotube dampers and anti-roll bar

Brakes: Servo-assisted ventilated steel discs 362 mm with AP Racing four-piston callipers (front); 286 mm with AP Racing two-piston callipers (rear). ABS

Steering: Power-assisted rack and pinion

Wheels: 18-inch OZ Racing magnesium

Tyres: Bridgestone Expedia 245/40 ZR18

Transmission: Torqueflite four-speed-plus-overdrive automatic; final drive 4.09:1. Limited-slip differential. Rear-wheel drive

Engine: 6347 cc alloy V8 with twin chain-driven overhead camshafts per bank and four valves per cylinder. Compression ratio 9.5:1. Weber-Alpha sequential fuel injection

Power: 452 bhp/337 kW @ 5500 rpm
427 lb/ft/579 Nm of torque @ 5000 rpm

Top speed: 190 mph/306 km/h (est)

Dimensions:

Length	15 ft 1.5 in/4646 mm
Width	5 ft 9.5 in/1830 mm
Height	4 ft 1.5 in/1238 mm
Wheelbase	8 ft 5 in/2591 mm
Weight	3846 lb/1745 kg (approx)

Price when new: £120,000 (approx)

Number built: 1

DB7 Vantage

V12 power once more

Although the DB7 was selling very well, it was obviously a little underpowered for some potential customers. In naturally aspirated form, the six-cylinder engine produced around 200 bhp. Equipped with an Eaton supercharger and with other modifications it put out 335 bhp in the DB7. As good as the engine was, it was not feasible to extend it too much further; a replacement was needed.

Various solutions had been considered, including using the Newport Pagnell V8. In 6.3-litre guise it powered one racing and one customer car, each with outstanding performance, but with ever-tightening emissions requirements, the days of the aging V8 were numbered. TWR had experimented with a 6.4-litre Jaguar V12 in the DB7, but that also came to naught. Finally, the answer lay with Ford.

'Aston Martin at the time was making V8s at, I guess, three a week at Newport Pagnell and was struggling to make DB7s,' recalled Bob Dover. 'The car, compared to the [Jaguar] XK8, wasn't different enough to justify the premium for it to be an Aston Martin. But at the same time it was beautiful. Ian [Callum] has said that it is the best work he has ever done. But the six-cylinder engine was just not special enough. We needed more power and more torque.

'So we got Ford to agree to the V12 engine, which was a crucial breakthrough and we got Ford Advanced Powertrain Group, Jim Clarke's team, to design and calibrate the new engine. That meant a comprehensive re-engineering of the car, not only design-wise, which I did with Ian Minards, David King and the team, but also chassis, suspension, gearboxes and also improving build quality.'

The Aston Martin V12 was launched in Project Vantage in 1998 at the Geneva Motor Show. While Project Vantage went on to become the Vanquish, the first fruit from the concept car was the DB7 Vantage, which utilised the car's V12 engine.

The DB7 Vantage was officially unveiled on 9 March 1999 at the Detroit Motor Show, with production starting around the same time with chassis number AA300001. 'We unveiled the DB7 V12, which was the first time anyone had seen it,' said Dover. 'A V12 engine was actually sitting in a lake in the corner of the stand covered in a silk cloth. The idea was that the silk seemed to disappear down a tube, which was actually sitting in

DB7 Vantage production soon overshadowed the six-cylinder DB7, which was phased out shortly after

While Project Vantage went on to become the Vanquish, the first fruit from the concept car was the DB7 Vantage, which utilised the car's V12 engine.

the lake and pulled through by guys with a winch out of sight. That was a spectacular day.'

With the more powerful car attracting only a modest premium over the DB7, the V12 Vantage proved so popular it quickly accounted for almost 90 percent of DB7 manufacture. As a result, it forced the six-cylinder model out of production in 1999, even though it stayed on the company's price list in 2000.

David King

David King began his automotive career in 1985 with Panther Cars, where he was involved in the development of the Panther Solo. He joined Jaguar in 1986 and was promoted to Programme Officer in 1991; he worked on the XJ40 before becoming Project Manager for saloon cars.

King joined Aston Martin in 1995 as Chief Programme Engineer. His early tasks included launching the DB7 Volante and introducing the DB7 to the North American market. He also led a team of 40 engineers in the development of the V12 DB7 Vantage and, later, the DB9, V8 Vantage, DBS and N24 racing car. In 2007 he was appointed Head of Product Communications and Motorsport.

Jaguar 6.4-litre V12 DB7

While the DB7 Vantage was in development, a silver prototype V12 DB7 was built for TWR boss Tom Walkinshaw. Fitted with a Jaguar 6.4-litre V12 engine producing 475 bhp @ 6000 rpm and 470 lb/ft of torque @ 4500 rpm, it endowed the car with a projected top speed of 182 mph.

'TWR was fishing to get the business for DB7 engines, to provide us with more powerful engines. The 6.4-litre Jaguar engine was one of its ideas,' said Kingsley Riding-Felce.

The car was designed as a running advertisement for TWR's expertise. It featured a host of enhancements including an Ian Callum-designed body kit, Borg Warner six-speed gearbox, upgraded suspension, AP Racing brakes with ABS, Cromodora wheels and Yokohama tyres. However, the 6.4-litre DB7 remained unique – the proposal was rejected and TWR later sold the car.

'TWR was trying to sell engines to us and the Jaguar engine was an obvious alternative because the V12 was such a huge mountain to climb financially,' said Bob Dover. 'But whether it is an Aston Martin or a Ferrari, it is important to have your badge on the engine.'

The V12 engine dramatically changed the DB7. With 20 percent more power and 17 percent more torque, a new close-ratio six-speed gearbox and with a modest weight increase of only 122 lb, the car was transformed from a 335-horsepower Grand Tourer into a 420-horsepower supercar.

Model	Weight (lb)	0-60 mph (seconds)	Top speed (mph)	Power (bhp)
DB7	3802	5.7	165	335
DB7 Vantage	3924	5.5	185	420

Erroneously labelled a 6.0-litre unit, the V12 was actually 5.9 litres, being 5935 cc. It was developed jointly between Aston Martin, Ford Research and Vehicle Technology Group and Cosworth Engineering and consisted of a 89 mm bore and 79.5 mm stroke, Cosworth aluminium alloy heads and cylinder block, four-valves-per-cylinder and a compression ratio of 10.3:1. In December 1999 Touchtronic transmissions became an option.

The DB7 Vantage's body was very obviously a development of the DB7. But in order to match the new car's stronger performance, a complementary, slightly more aggressive body was needed.

The sills were reshaped, the grille enlarged and new round fog/indicator lights were fitted. 'When it came to doing the DB7 Vantage I have to say I have some regrets,' said Ian Callum. 'It was obvious the car had more power so the car had to also look more powerful. But I was very reluctant to change anything about the car because I thought it was perfect the way it was. I realise now it was the wrong attitude to have, I have to admit. But that's how I felt at the time, with some justification I think.

'I love the front. The spotlights were directly from the DBR1 racing cars; it was something very Aston Martin that I could relate to, so that's the idea behind it. Because it had to have a bigger cooling area the front got lower and more dramatic but from the rear I had my reservations about some things. To my mind it should have been more aggressive but I think it worked quite well.'

Changes were not only made to the appearance of the car. The chassis came in for extensive alterations in structure, especially around the transmission tunnel and suspension geometry to give the car a sportier, stiffer ride. The steering was also revised to give a sharper feel. The body structure was strengthened and improved, too. David King, DB7's Engineering Manager said, 'The Vantage is more focused towards handling, whereas the six-cylinder car has an excellent balance between ride and handling.'[18]

Previously, Vantage models had consisted of revised and up-rated versions of production engines used in standard models.[i] The DB7 Vantage utilised a completely different engine, which contained six extra cylinders. It could have been called the DB8, but in any case it was a magnificent aberration in the annals of Vantage history.

i The 1972 AM Vantage used the DBS Vantage engine

Aston Martin's other V12s

During 1954 and 1955 the Lagonda brand was revived by David Brown with two V12-powered sports racing cars, DP115 and DP166. This was not the first time a Lagonda had used a V12 engine; WO Bentley had designed his masterpiece, the 4.5-litre V12, for Lagonda back in 1937. But it was the first time that an Aston Martin Lagonda had used such an engine.

Expectations were high for the Lagonda racing cars, but the projected 350 bhp was never achieved. Instead, a disappointing 321 bhp @ 6000 rpm was all the unreliable engine could muster. The Lagonda V12 failed in 1954, and although Aston Martin persevered with the engine in 1955, the car never reached David Brown's expectations. V12 power was finally abandoned at the end of the 1955 season, seemingly never again to be revived.

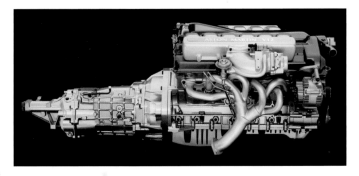

Top: Aston Martin's V12 engine became public knowledge at the launch of Project Vantage **Above:** Aston Martin took the opportunity to revamp the DB7's interior with the launch of the V12 car

Ian Callum had some regrets over the rear of the finished car

DB7 Vantage
1999–2004

Chassis: Steel semi-monocoque body shell

Body: Composite and pressed steel 2+2 coupe styled by Ian Callum

Suspension: Front – Independent with double wishbones incorporating anti-dive geometry, coil springs, monotube dampers and anti-roll bar
Rear – Independent with double wishbones incorporating longitudinal control arms, coil springs, monotube dampers and anti-roll bar

Brakes: Servo-assisted 355 mm ventilated and cross-drilled steel discs with alloy four-piston callipers (front). 355 mm ventilated steel discs with alloy four-piston callipers (rear). Drum handbrake. ABS

Steering: Power-assisted rack and pinion

Wheels: 18-inch alloy

Tyres: Bridgestone SO2 245/40 ZR18 (front). 265/35 ZR18 (rear)

Transmission: GM five-speed automatic; final drive 3.06:1
Getrag six-speed manual; final drive 3.77:1
Optional touchtronic operation available from December 1999. Limited-slip differential. Rear-wheel drive

Engine: 5935 cc alloy V12 with twin chain-driven overhead camshafts per bank and four valves per cylinder. Compression ratio 10.3:1. EEC V engine management system with sequential fuel injection. Fully catalysed exhaust system

Power: 420 bhp/328 kW @ 6000 rpm
400 lb/ft/542 Nm of torque @ 5000 rpm

Top speed: 185 mph/298 km/h

Dimensions:
Length	15 ft 1.5 in/4666 mm
Width	5 ft 9.5 in/1830 mm
Height	4 ft 2 in/1238 mm
Wheelbase	8 ft 5 in/2591 mm
Weight	3924 lb/1780 kg

Price when new: £92,500

Number built: 2110

DB7 Vantage Volante

Volante fortissimo

The Geneva Motor Show was once again the scene for the unveiling of an important new Aston Martin model: the DB7 Vantage Volante was revealed there on 9 March 1999, along with the V12 Vantage coupe. Production of the convertible started at chassis number AA40001 shortly afterwards.

The mechanical specification of the Volante was almost identical to the DB7 Vantage coupe. However, in line with customer demand, the Volante featured a stiffer suspension set-up than the six-cylinder DB7 convertible.

The Volante featured a stiffer suspension set-up than the six-cylinder convertible, in line with customer demand.

Automatic and manual transmissions were available, but shortly after the first production cars were delivered, a ZF Touchtronic transmission became an option. This transmission offered automatic ease with the option of manual shifting. Gear changes could be activated via buttons on the steering wheel, or operated in completely automatic mode.

Shamelessly aimed at the lucrative US market, the DB7 Vantage Volante proved to be another sales success for Aston Martin with 2046 cars produced during its four-year lifecycle. It seemed at this stage that Aston Martin could do no wrong.

DB7 Vantage Volante
1999–2004

Chassis: Steel semi-monocoque body shell

Body: Composite and pressed steel 2+2 convertible styled by Ian Callum

Suspension: Front – Independent with double wishbones incorporating anti-dive geometry, coil springs, monotube dampers and anti-roll bar
Rear – Independent with double wishbones incorporating longitudinal control arms, coil springs, monotube dampers and anti-roll bar

Brakes: Servo-assisted 355 mm ventilated and cross-drilled steel discs with alloy four-piston callipers (front); 330 mm ventilated steel discs with alloy four-piston callipers (rear). Drum handbrake. ABS

Steering: Power-assisted rack and pinion

Wheels: 18-inch alloy[i]

Tyres: Bridgestone SO2 245/40 ZR18 (front). 265/35 ZR18 (rear)

Transmission: GM five-speed automatic 3.06:1
Tremec six-speed manual 3.77:1
Optional ZF touchtronic operation available from December 1999. Limited-slip differential. Rear-wheel drive

Engine: 5935 cc alloy V12 with twin chain-driven overhead camshafts per bank and four valves per cylinder. Compression ratio 10.3:1. EEC V engine management system with sequential fuel injection. Fully catalysed exhaust system

Power: 420 bhp/328 kW @ 6000 rpm
400 lb/ft/542 Nm of torque @ 5000 rpm

Top speed: 165 mph/266 km/h (limited)

Dimensions:
Length	15 ft 1.5 in/4666 mm
Width	5 ft 9.5 in/1830 mm
Height	4 ft 1.5 in/1238 mm
Wheelbase	8 ft 5 in/2591 mm
Weight	4125 lb/1875 kg

Price when new: £99,950

Number built: 2046

Top to bottom: The open DB7 Vantage was powered by a 420 bhp engine but the suspension was 'softened' due to public demand; A lot of design work was needed at the rear to accommodate the Volante's folding fabric roof; The convertible's driving lights were inspired by the DBR1 sports cars of the 1950s

i 19-inch alloy wheels fitted with 245/35 (front) and 265/30 (rear) Yokohama tyres optional from 2002

V8 Vantage Le Mans

It was 40 years ago today

With the end of the V8 cars drawing near, Aston Martin devised a fitting tribute to Newport Pagnell's mainstay by producing the V8 Vantage Le Mans. Originally intended to be the celebrated swansong of the V8 engine and Vantage-based chassis, the V8 Vantage Le Mans was the most spectacular and expensive road car produced by Aston Martin to that time.

'We wanted to make a car to celebrate the anniversary of us winning Le Mans,' said Steve Bolton. 'I wanted to build a car, which in-house, we called the V200, because in testing we had managed to get 200 mph out of our mule vehicle. At that time there weren't a lot of cars that could do that, especially heavy cars like [the Vantage].'

'At the same time, Shaun Rush was styling a car celebrating our Le Mans win in 1959 and the two grew into each other. So the body style for the Vantage Le Mans, which Shaun had done, and the V200 package that allowed the car to go 200 mph, which I had done, came together and it was eventually called V8 Vantage Le Mans, which was a more fitting name than the code name.'

'I had the concept of a limited-edition car to commemorate the Le Mans victory, something I'd had in my mind since the 30th anniversary in 1989,' said Rush. 'Then with the 40th anniversary coming up in 1999 I approached Kingsley Riding-Felce with the idea of a car inspired by the DBR1, with aluminium racing fuel fillers, a different grille, starter button, large rev counter and Aston Racing Green paint scheme.'

Not all of Rush's initial ideas saw production. They included the 'lift-off' bonnet with quick-release pins, white roundels, 'bare bones' cockpit with deleted rear seats and racing-style front seats and exposed aluminium interior roof and fuel tank.

The car was available in either 550 bhp or in Works Prepared 600 bhp editions. To give it individual appeal though, and to set it apart from earlier Vantages, several body enhancements were included. The V8 Vantage Le Mans featured a unique blanked-off grille with elliptical openings each side, which were actually part of an original Vantage design proposal back in 1992, a large front spoiler and two contoured ducts on the bonnet.

Special machined aluminium Le Mans-type fuel filler caps were incorporated, as were five-spoke magnesium alloy wheels. Being produced to mark the 40th anniversary of Aston Martin's 1959 Le Mans victory, a fitting tribute was the DBR1-style air vents on the side flanks.

The V8 Vantage Le Mans grew from two different projects: one the work of Steve Bolton and the other from Shaun Rush

'This is all we know about making V8 cars, it is the final version of it, this is the best and fastest'
Bob Dover

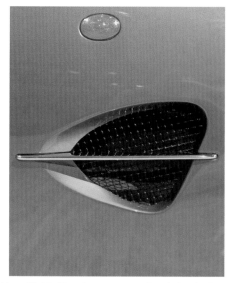

Left: Tony Brooks at the wheel of the successful DBR1/2; this model was the inspiration for the Vantage Le Mans **Right:** The air vents were directly inspired by the Le Mans-winning DBR1 **Below:** The car featured distinctive 'nostrils' in the grille

Dr Ulrich Bez

Dr Ulrich Bez was named CEO of Aston Martin in July 2000 upon the appointment of Bob Dover to a similar position at Land Rover. Born in 1943, Bez holds a Doctorate in Engineering and has had a long, distinguished career in the automotive industry.

He was formerly responsible for Product Design and Development at Porsche, BMW and Daewoo. Prior to joining Aston Martin, Bez was a business advisor to Ford Motor Company in the USA. He is a skilled test and development driver with experience in single-seat racing cars, sports cars and off-road vehicles.

His first decision at Aston Martin was to delay production of the Vanquish to sort out quality problems and the interior and exterior styling. He also scuttled the development of the mid-engined production sports car and the experimental mid-engined racing car.

He then instigated plans for the successful VH platform, which was the basis for the DB9 and V8 Vantage. Under his stewardship Aston Martin launched the Vanquish, DB7 Zagato, DB7 GT/GTA, DB AR1, DB9, DB9 Volante, Vanquish S, V8 Vantage, Aston Martin Rapide and DBS; the 20/20, Zagato Vanquish Roadster and Bertone Jet II concept cars were also shown at various motor shows. Dr Bez also oversaw Aston Martin's successful return to racing with the DBR9 and DBRS9.

As Aston Martin's longest-serving CEO since Victor Gauntlett, Dr Bez was revered as the man responsible for turning Aston Martin into a profitable business, modernising the company and making it a genuine competitor in the world sports car market.

During 2006 Dr Bez led the consortium that purchased Aston Martin. After the formal announcement on 13 March 2007, he continued as the company's CEO.

The modern interior featured modifications first incorporated into the Lightweight Virage. Aston Martin-embossed Wilton carpet and Connolly leather were standard, but titanium-finish metal replaced wood panels. Other touches included a machined alloy gear knob, drilled aluminium pedals and a red starter button fitted to the dashboard.

All 40 cars were painted in Aston Martin's evocative Racing Green and directions to the Le Mans circuit were included in the owner's handbook. A sterling silver key fob was included, as was a special plaque displaying the original owner's name.

The V8 Vantage Le Mans was launched at the Geneva Motor Show on 9 March 1999 where it joined the famous Le Mans-winning DBR1/2 on the Aston Martin stand. The 40 cars used chassis numbers AM70229, and AM70241–AM70279.

The V8 Vantage Le Mans looked menacing, and it was. The 600 bhp-engine version delivered 600 lb/ft of torque @ 4000 rpm and was capable of pushing the car to a top speed in excess of 200 mph. The 0–60 mph sprint was achieved in only 3.9 seconds while 0–100 mph took 9.1 seconds.

'The 600-horsepower Vantages were something we did as a run out before the DB9 was announced, as we did with the Zagato DB7s,' said Bob Dover. 'The V8 Vantage Le Mans was launched at Geneva. We had a nice line up that particular year, when we launched the V12, all painted in Aston Martin green. First of all we unveiled the DBR1, the Aston Martin that won the 1959 World Sports Car Championship. I said, "In 1959 this was everything we knew about how to make a quick car for racing," and we pulled the cover off the next one, which was the V8 600 and I said, "This is all we know about making V8 cars, this is the final version of it, this is the best and the fastest. If you want one, be quick." The V8 Vantage Le Mans should not be forgotten, it was a thunderous car.'

V8 Vantage Le Mans
1999–2000

Chassis: Steel box-section chassis, steel superstructure

Body: Aluminium 2+2 coupe styled by John Heffernan

Suspension: Front – Independent with wishbones, Eibach coil springs, coaxial spring dampers and anti-roll bar
Rear – de Dion axle, radius arms, Watt's linkage, Eibach coil springs and telescopic dampers

Brakes: Servo-assisted 365 mm ventilated discs with AP Racing six-piston callipers (front); 310 mm ventilated discs with AP Racing four-piston callipers (rear). ABS

Steering: Power-assisted rack and pinion

Wheels: 18-inch alloy

Tyres: Goodyear Eagle GS-D 285/45 ZR18

Transmission: ZF five- or six-speed manual; final drive 3.77:1 (3.31:1 optional)
Torqueflite four-speed automatic; final drive 3.058:1
Limited-slip differential. Rear-wheel drive

Engine: 5340 cc alloy V8 with twin chain-driven overhead camshafts per bank and four valves per cylinder. Compression ratio 8.2:1. EEC IV engine management system. Two Roots type M90 Eaton superchargers with additional intercooler radiator and water pump. Fully catalysed exhaust system

Power: 600 bhp/447 kW @ 6500 rpm
600 lb/ft/813 Nm of torque @ 4000 rpm

Top speed: 200-plus mph/322-plus km/h

Dimensions:

Length	15 ft 7 in/4745 mm
Width	6 ft 4 in/1918 mm (excluding wing mirrors)
Height	4 ft 4.5 in/1320 mm
Wheelbase	8 ft 6.75 in/2610 mm
Weight	4399 lb/1995 kg

Price when new: £190,130 plus £43,000 (approx) for V600 engine upgrade

Number built: 40

Vantage Shooting Brake
Life in the fast lane

Swiss Aston Martin specialist, Roos Engineering, created this Vantage Shooting Brake by converting a Vantage V600 Driving Dynamics coupe, chassis number AMSBL70165, into what could be the most powerful estate wagon in existence.

Roos Engineering began work on the Vantage Shooting Brake in 1997 when a German industrialist commissioned the project. By this time, Roos Engineering had already started the complicated Lagonda Shooting Brake conversion as well.

'We started off by doing detailed drawings in consultation with the customer,' said founder and proprietor, Beat Roos. 'This took a lot of time. You need to take time with this stage of the project because it is easier to change a bad design when it is on paper. It is too late to change the design once you have made the car; it is too expensive and time consuming. So we did the design and made an epoxy resin model; only when we, and the customer, were fully pleased with the design did we start making the tooling for the project. It took a long time, but it was worth it.' The conversion took around 10,000 hours and was extremely expensive.

'You need to take time with this stage of the project because it is easier to change a bad design when it is on paper.'

Beat Roos

Emphasising the car's uniqueness Roos added, 'Working exclusively by hand and using aluminium as the traditional coachbuilding material, the project was lovingly executed in every detail by Roos Engineering. In collaboration with local businesses in this sector, we presented the systematic implementation of a vision that is far beyond the concept of assembly-line manufacturing.'

One of the problems encountered on the Vantage conversion was that, with 600 lb/ft of torque, the rear section of the car needed to be as stiff as possible to cope with the immense turning force. As a result, much of the engineering and design work concentrated on engineering stiffness into the considerable bodywork to avoid body twist at the rear axle.

With an upward-lifting tailgate the Vantage Shooting Brake was a very practical high-speed carriage

Special coachbuilt touches included a replica double air vent on the rear three-quarter panels and the integration of twin fuel filler caps feeding the 100-litre fuel tank. Much of the original bodywork remained intact, the main feature being the recreated rear. The revised roofline, additional glass areas and rear tailgate were smoothly integrated; while lacking the elegance of the original coupe design, they were in harmony with the rest of the car.

The profile featured three electric side windows, the rear ending in an oval shape to complement the curved rear panel. The Vantage's round taillights were retained, above which was the specially designed, double-treated tailgate glass and single window wiper. The practical carpeted rear luggage area was capable of accommodating several suitcases, golf clubs or skis.

The Shooting Brake was finished in metallic green with black leather interior and grey carpets. A special sill plaque stating 'Aston Martin Lagonda Limited Coachwork by Roos Engineering Ltd Frauenkappelen/Bern Switzerland' was fitted. 'The interior was fairly standard,' said Roos, 'apart from the rear seats, which had to be altered. But we needed some more switches for the powered windows, tailgate and rear windscreen wiper.

Above: The pleasing proportions of Roos Engineering's Vantage Shooting Brake conversion **Opposite:** The dual air vents aft of the wheel arches were replicated on the rear panel, complete with Aston Martin and V600 badges

'It is nice to be known for making these special Shooting Brakes. I mean, when Bertone did the Jet II Shooting Brake, 200 people worked on it. We only have 14 employees and two panel beaters, so it is something to be proud of when a small company like ours can make such great cars,' said Roos.

Completed during 1999, the Vantage Shooting Brake was subsequently donated by its second owner, a Swiss banker, to the Traffic Museum in Switzerland, where it now resides.

Vantage Shooting Brake
1999

Chassis: Steel box-section chassis, steel superstructure

Body: Aluminium 2+2 Shooting Brake styled by John Heffernan, modified by Roos Engineering

Suspension: Front – Independent with double wishbones, coil springs, coaxial spring damper units and anti-roll bar
Rear – de Dion axle, longitudinal radius arms, transverse Watt's linkage and coaxial spring damper units

Brakes: Servo-assisted 362 mm ventilated steel discs with four-piston callipers (front); 286 mm ventilated steel discs with sliding aluminium callipers (rear). ABS

Steering: Power-assisted rack and pinion

Wheels: 18-inch alloy

Tyres: Goodyear Eagle GS-D 285/45 ZR18

Transmission: ZF six-speed manual; final drive 3.33:1. Limited-slip differential. Rear-wheel drive

Engine: 5340 cc alloy V8 with twin chain-driven overhead camshafts per bank and four valves per cylinder. Compression ratio 8.2:1. EEC IV engine management system. Two Roots type M90 Eaton superchargers. Fully catalysed exhaust system

Power: 612 bhp/456 kW @ 6500 rpm
600 lb/ft/813 Nm of torque @ 4000 rpm

Top speed: 200 mph/322 km/h (approx)

Dimensions:
Length	15 ft 7 in/4745 mm
Width	6 ft 4 in/1918 mm (excluding wing mirrors)
Height	4 ft 4.5 in/1332 mm
Wheelbase	8 ft 6.75 in/2610 mm
Weight	4450 lb/2018 kg (approx)

Price of conversion: N/A

Number built: 1

Lagonda Shooting Brake
Razor-sharp hatchback

Roos Engineering began working on this unique Lagonda Shooting Brake in 1996. The original 1987 left-hand drive Series 3 fuel-injected Lagonda, chassis number SCFDLO1S4HTL13511, was taken to Roos Engineering by a Hong Kong customer with the request that it be converted into a practical Shooting Brake. It was the first Shooting Brake project conducted by the Swiss company, but the complicated work involved meant that it was completed after the Vantage Shooting Brake.

'A customer had approached Aston Martin Works Service and asked if a Shooting Brake body could be made for his Lagonda. They said no and so he came to us,' said Beat Roos. 'We had made some designs for a Lagonda Shooting Brake, just for fun, in the 1980s, so when he asked us, the factory gave the okay, so we agreed.'

It was to be a very long project. 'We always work very closely with the customer, but with the Lagonda, it was a very difficult design to work on. It was not easy to make a different car on William Towns' design. I did the design drawings for the Lagonda Shooting Brake, and then we made a 1:1 model to show to the customer, who approved the design.'

Towns' original Lagonda design featured sharp angular lines, which resulted in the rakish Shooting Brake body. Its main features included the large, upward lifting tailgate and the practical rear luggage compartment. The tailgate, when upright, was supported by twin gas struts and was unusual in design in that it encroached well into the roof panel and featured a specially made angular rear glass panel. The rear side glass consisted of intricate separate sections, with strength-providing pillars required for stiffness.

Roos Engineering worked with local craftspeople and companies including Glas Trösch, manufacturer of the complicated glass sections; Walz Autosattlerei, which fitted out the car's new rear interior; and Brenca Fahrzeugelektrik, for the electrical systems. The car was engineered totally in-house by Erich Stäheli and the coachwork was constructed by Rudolf Hess.

'To modify a vehicle like this,' said Roos, 'first, the basic structure and secondly, the design and construction requirements needed to be accurately identified. It is the customer's money and it is too expensive to make mistakes.

William Towns' angular lines were retained in the Roos Shooting Brake conversion

'We always work very closely with the customer, but with the Lagonda, it was a very difficult design to work on.'
Beat Roos

'It is easier to do the design drawings than it is to make the car in aluminium. In the end, when you finish the car, you can't start it again if it is a bad design. For example the glass on the Lagonda Shooting Brake cost 40,000 Swiss francs. So when we started, all of the details had to be exactly right.' The Lagonda Shooting Brake took around four years to complete and was ready at the beginning of 2000.

The Shooting Brake was finished in midnight blue paintwork and featured a grey leather interior. In addition to the rear conversion, special enhancements were incorporated to distinguish the car from other Lagondas. A unique mesh grille and spoiler were integrated at the front, a special 'Roos Engineering' sill plaque fitted and Lagonda badges were placed on each C-pillar. In between the front seats was a tailored console for the extra switchgear for the remote rear windows and the rear wash/wipe feature.

All major mechanical components and engineering were kept fairly original, including the wheels and tyres, but the three-speed Chrysler Torqueflite automatic transmission was upgraded to a more modern four-speed unit and the fuel system was updated.

Although made for a Hong Kong-based customer, the Lagonda Shooting Brake is kept in Switzerland and is maintained by Roos Engineering in Frauenkappelen.

Top: The substantial rear tailgate was held in place by twin gas struts **Above:** The complicated glass sections cost 40,000 Swiss francs to manufacture

Roos Engineering

Automobile Roos was founded by Beat Roos in 1975 as a one-man business. By 1977 Roos Engineering had become an Aston Martin dealer and by 1990 had grown to incorporate both a body and engine shop.

Roos Engineering is a world-renowned Aston Martin specialist that offers expertise in servicing and restoration. Based in Frauenkappelen, Switzerland, Roos employs 14 people, including two panel beaters.

The firm is best known for its Aston Martin Shooting Brakes. It has constructed three, including conversions based on Lagonda, V600 Vantage and V8 Volante.

Lagonda Shooting Brake
2000

Chassis: Steel box-section chassis, steel superstructure

Body: Aluminium four-seat Shooting Brake styled by William Towns and modified by Roos Engineering

Suspension: Front – Independent with unequal length double wishbones, coil springs and anti-roll bar
Rear – de Dion axle with coil springs and Watt's linkage

Brakes: Servo-assisted Girling 273 mm ventilated discs (front). 263 mm inboard-mounted discs (rear)

Steering: Power-assisted rack and pinion

Wheels: 16-inch Ronal alloy

Tyres: Goodyear Eagle 255/50 VR16

Transmission: Torqueflite four-speed automatic; final drive 3.06:1. Limited-slip differential. Rear-wheel drive

Engine: 5340 cc alloy V8 with twin chain-driven overhead camshafts per bank and two valves per cylinder. Compression ratio 9.5:1. Weber-Marelli fuel injection. Fully catalysed exhaust system

Power: 309 bhp/230 kW @ 5000 rpm
321 lb/ft/435 Nm @ 3000 rpm

Top speed: 140 mph/225 km/h (approx)

Dimensions:
Length	17 ft 4 in/5300 mm
Width	5 ft 11.5 in/1815 mm
Height	4 ft 3 in/1300 mm
Wheelbase	9 ft 6.5 in/2915 mm
Weight	4622 lb/2150 kg (approx)

Conversion cost: N/A

Number built: 1

Top to bottom: Thoughtful touches included the addition of a rear-window wiper; Vast amounts of planning and artisan work went into creating the rear accommodation area; The Series 3 interior was less confronting than the 1970s original

Vantage Volante
Special Edition

End of an era

By mid-2000 and after a lifecycle spanning 30 years, Aston Martin's V cars were nearing the end of production. Plans were in place for the Newport Pagnell factory to be gutted, reorganised and re-tooled at a cost of £5 million in preparation for the Vanquish. But the story of the V8 was not quite over yet.

The V8 Vantage Le Mans was originally slated as the last of the hand-built V8 models, but Aston Martin had been approached by a number of customers asking to produce a missing variant. The V8 was given a last reprieve and a Vantage version of the V8 Volante was built for nine selected customers from England, the Channel Islands and Germany.

The Vantage Volante Special Edition was designed and developed jointly between the Special Projects Group at Works Service and Newport Pagnell manufacturing. They were built in production at Newport Pagnell, but most cars were wheeled across Tickford Street to Works Service to have the 600-horsepower upgrade and special options fitted.

'You always have your share of romantics who look backwards and like the way things were. I understand the misty-eyed bit, but in reality it's not the way of the world.'

Nick Fry

The craftsmen working on the line on these cars must have done so with a great sense of nostalgia and trepidation, for the end of coachbuilding at Newport Pagnell also meant the end of their jobs in some cases. Redundancies had to be made as the engine and body builders, many of whom had worked at the Factory for years, were no longer needed.

'There was a lot of emotion attached to these cars,' recalled Kingsley Riding-Felce, 'because these cars really represented the end of the era to some people. Some of the employees had been building cars in that way for 30 or 40 years and these were the last to be made that way. The V8 Vantage Volante Special Editions were a testament to those craftsmen in terms of the quality of the cars and the way in which they were built.'

It was only by accident that the Vantage Volante Special Edition became the last coachbuilt Aston Martin to come out of Newport Pagnell; this is chassis 005

It was the end of another era at Aston Martin. The V8 Vantage Volante Special Editions were the last cars to use the highly developed V8 engine, much-evolved V8 platform and coachbuilt bodies. It was time for a new era of prosperity, high technology and higher volume. Difficult decisions had to be made but without them, Aston Martin would be out of business.

'You always have your share of romantics who look backwards and like the way things were,' said Nick Fry, 'but the reality of car production is that even if it is a very low-volume vehicle it still has to meet the known legal requirements and safety requirements. But in the high level of customer expectations if you only have 20 or 30 engineers and limited resources it's pretty much impossible to meet those requirements. I understand the misty-eyed bit, but in reality it's not the way of the world.'

Offered in 550 and 600 bhp forms, the most potent version shared the same powerful engine as the Vantage V600 coupe, meaning the convertible produced 600 bhp @ 6500 rpm and 600 lb/ft of torque @ 4000 rpm. The engines were not speed limited by the Factory and, although a definitive top speed was not recorded, that kind of power was enough to rank it up with the fastest production convertibles ever made.

The Special Edition Volante's chassis was a cross between the Vantage and Virage Volante but with the additional stiffeners, albeit shorter, of the longer wheelbase V8 Volante. The wheelbase was the same as the Vantage coupe, which was shorter than the standard V8 Volante, hence the term, short-wheelbase Volante. But like the terminology DBS-6, this is totally unnecessary. This is a stand-alone model in its own right. To confuse matters, in addition to the five right-hand-drive and three left-hand-drive cars made, an additional right-hand-drive car was constructed on the long-wheelbase V8 Volante chassis.

To set the Special Edition convertibles apart from the standard V8 Volante, owners could specify several unique features. Chassis number 001 had cooling ducts similar to the Lightweight Virages, 002 had V8 Vantage Le Mans-type bodywork and number 004 had the distinctive Le Mans bonnet.

Most were given twin bonnet-mounted air ducts, flared wheel arches with restyled sills and six-spoke aluminium alloy wheels and featured 'Works Coachbuilt' badging. Typically the cars' specification included heated glass rear windows and electrically operated and heated external mirrors plus bespoke interiors.

Each of the nine cars was unique; chassis 004 featured a V8 Vantage Le Mans-style bonnet

Clockwise from top left: Although closely resembling each other, all Special Edition Vantage Volantes were different in trim and body specification; One long wheelbase Special Edition Vantage Volante was constructed – it was initially intended for well-known Aston Martin devotee HRH Prince Charles, but the order was cancelled; Chassis 007 featured mainly standard body work; Chassis 002 had body accoutrements developed for the V8 Vantage Le Mans; Only three left-hand drive versions were specified, this is chassis 003

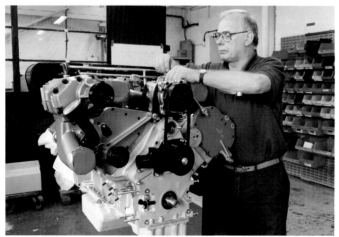

Top to bottom: Constructing the chassis of 006; The body of 001 nearing completion alongside a V8 Vantage Le Mans; Preparing the body of 008 for painting; Engines came in 550 bhp and 600 bhp specification

The nine cars all differed in specification and beautifully made owner's handbooks were specially written for each customer, taking into account the unique features of each car. The basic starting price was £229,950, but an extensive and expensive list of options could see the price rise dramatically.

The limited production ran through chassis numbers AM2R71001 (the first car built was AM2R71005) and finished with AM2R71008, the final coachbuilt, V8-engined car produced by Aston Martin, which was delivered on 20 October 2000.

'These cars were not supposed to be the last V8s,' said Shaun Rush, 'this is a myth that has been allowed to persist. When the first car, 71005, was completed by production there were still V8 Vantage Le Mans cars behind it on the production line. We had begun building some of the chassis and I think we may even have panelled the first cars when the then Managing Director, Ken Giles, had them removed from the production line and put into storage; he also issued instructions that no more of them were to be started.

'They sat in storage and by the time he let them back on site they had all been pushed back [originally the first car should have been completed by production in early November 1999 but it was not actually completed by production until the end of April 2000] and so it was entirely accidental that 71008 was the last V8 produced at Newport.'

The Islay Blue 550 bhp automatic long-wheelbase Volante, originally intended for HRH Prince Charles, used chassis number AM2R70514. This, unlike the other eight cars, was not a fully homologated vehicle and was registered using the Single Vehicle Type Approval Scheme. Chassis number 89035 was used as the development car for the long-wheelbase Volante. It contained a Vantage engine and Vantage front spoiler, otherwise it remained a standard Volante.

Autocar was given a brief taste of a unique Le Mans-bodied Vantage Volante Special Edition and, although a full road test was not possible, driving impressions were recorded by journalist Andrew Frankel. Well aware that he was driving the last of its kind he enthusiastically recorded, 'Find me a marque and motor combination more emotive than an Aston Martin V8. This engine not only has 600 bhp, it also has 600 lb/ft of torque, making it comfortably more than twice as grunty as a Ferrari 360 Modena. The result is the only car I have ever driven that, in the wet, will spin its wheels in four of its five gears.'

Frankel continued with the superlatives, 'I am piloting a nuclear-powered drawing room, waiting for the unique bellow of an Aston V8 at full chat. I hear it only briefly before reaching for another gear. But it is enough, as good a note on which to say goodbye as you'll hear. Some might be quicker still but none is more majestic than this. We will not see its likes again.'

Since beginning production in 1969, Aston Martin had hand-made 5016 V8-engined cars, which were dispatched to 31 countries.

Model	Weight (lb)	0–60 mph (seconds)	Top speed (mph)	Power (bhp)
DBS V8	3800	5.9	162	310–320
Vantage Volante Special Edition	4500	3.9[i]	200-plus	600

Vantage Volante Special Edition
2000

Chassis: Steel box-section chassis, steel superstructure

Body: Aluminium 2+2 convertible styled by John Heffernan

Suspension: Front – Independent with wishbones, coil springs, coaxial spring dampers and anti-roll bar
Rear – de Dion axle, radius arms, Watt's linkage, coil springs, telescopic dampers and anti-roll bar

Brakes: Servo-assisted 365 mm ventilated discs with AP Racing six-piston callipers (front); 310 mm ventilated discs with AP Racing four-piston callipers (rear). ABS

Steering: Power-assisted rack and pinion

Wheels: 18-inch alloy

Tyres: Goodyear Eagle GS-D 285/35 ZR18

Transmission: ZF five- or six-speed manual; final drive 3.33:1
Torqueflite four-speed automatic; final drive 3.058:1
Limited-slip differential. Rear-wheel drive

Engine: 5340 cc alloy V8 with twin chain-driven overhead camshafts per bank and four valves per cylinder. Compression ratio 8.2:1. Ford EEC IV engine management system. Two Roots type M90 Eaton superchargers. Fully catalysed exhaust system

Power: 600 bhp/447 kW @ 6500 rpm[ii]
600 lb/ft/813 Nm of torque @ 4000 rpm

Top speed: 200 mph/322 km/h (approx)

Dimensions:
Length	15 ft 7 in/4745 mm[iii]
Width	6 ft 4 in/1918 mm (excluding wing mirrors)
Height	4 ft 6 in/1357 mm
Wheelbase	8 ft 6.75 in/2610 mm
Weight	4500 lb/2041 kg[iv]

Price when new: £229,950 – £275,000 (approx. depending on exact specification)

Number built: 9[v]

Top to bottom: Installing the complicated electrical equipment on 007; The leather trim was all hand-made at Newport Pagnell; Each car had a unique interior, this is 008; Part of the Special Edition team with 008

i   3.9 seconds recorded for the 0–62 mph dash
ii 550 bhp engine also available
iii One car was constructed on the LWB chassis: length 16 ft; wheelbase 9 ft 2 in
iv LWB – 5280 lb/2395 kg
v   Eight cars were built on the standard chassis; one car on the long-wheelbase chassis

DB4 GT Zagato Sanction III

Three times a lady

The DB4 GT Zagato Sanction IIs proved a successful marketing strategy. They re-created the legend of the originals while making barely visible, sympathetic improvements to make them a better overall product to drive. They were controversial, but they also made a lot of money.

The DB4 GT Zagato story didn't end in 1991. Subsequently, several customers approached Richard Williams asking for more Sanction-type specials. In 1998 Williams approached Aston Martin for permission to produce two further Zagato replicas. Williams received permission from Walter Hayes, who insisted two DB4s be the basis for the copies, thereby saving them from extinction.

'The Sanction III cars are different to any other non-sanctioned Zagato cars because, firstly, they are allowed to wear the Zagato badge and secondly, a licence fee was paid to Zagato in conjunction with the build costs when they were bodied in Italy,' said Williams. 'Also, these cars were built with the knowledge and permission of the then-Life President of Aston Martin Lagonda Ltd, Walter Hayes. They were bodied at the Zagato Factory in Milan and wear the Zagato badge.

'Their specification is exactly the same as the Sanction II cars. The Sanction IIIs used chassis numbers DB4/344/R and DB4/424/R. They are painted, as were the Sanction II cars, in RS Williams Green. The true horsepower for these cars averages out at 350 bhp @ 6000 rpm with maximum torque at 330 lb/ft @ 4600 rpm. The Sanction car's weight, with ten gallons of fuel, was 2798 lb; heavier than the 1960s Zagatos, which weighed 2765 lb, as there is additional bracing welded into the chassis to improve their torsional rigidity.

'There was no official unveiling of the Sanction II cars,' Williams recounted. 'When Walter Hayes gave us permission to build these cars I contacted two clients who I believed would be interested, and they were. Work commenced in 1998 and they were both handed to their owners in 2000.'

It really does appear that the Sanction III cars were the last of the official Aston Martin DB4 GT Zagatos. 'Zagato will not be building any more special cars. It will, however, re-body a DB4 GT as a Zagato. This is exactly what happened in the 1960s. My company has rebuilt, and Zagato re-bodied, several DB4 GTs; one being the DB4 GT Special, DB4 GT/0148/R.'

One of two DB4 GT Zagato Sanction IIIs constructed on DB4 platforms

'When Walter Hayes gave us permission to build these cars I contacted two clients who I believed would be interested, and they were.'
Richard Williams

ASTON MARTIN LAGONDA LIMITED

Tickford Street, Newport Pagnell, Buckinghamshire MK16 9AN
Telephone: 0908 610620 Fax: 0908 613708 Telex: 82341 AML-G

From The Chairman's Office

29 January 1992

Richard Williams Esq.,
Protech House
Copse Road
COBHAM
Surrey KT11 2TW

Dear Richard

It was good of you to let me know about the two DB4GT
Zagatos. I have given the proposal some thought
since I find myself torn several ways.

I am sure that you care as much as we do about the
integrity of the marque and there is no doubt in my
mind that I have to be as firm a guardian as I can be
of every Aston that has ever been built. The
business today is so influenced by yesterday and by
yesterday's cars and I worry about anything that
dilutes their virginity.

Purists, I suppose, would insist that what you are
going to produce are essentially replicas, cannot -
in any event - be badged Zagato and that these are
tricky issues at the best of time.

I am, however, pragmatic about such things. And, in
view of your own sense of responsibility where Aston
is concerned, it would seem churlish to try to stop
you, even if I could.

If you do proceed, however, I think it fair for me to
ask that you will clearly identify the cars as
replicas so that nobody can come up with accusations
of dilution of the heritage which, after all, remains
our stock in trade.

Walter Hayes

Directors: Walter Hayes CBE (Executive Chairman) W. R. Bannard D. J. Graham M. R. Haysey J. R. W. Mansfield
Registered in England at the above address Number 1199255

ASTON MARTIN :: POWER, BEAUTY AND SOUL

Top to bottom: Built from shortened DB4 platforms, the Sanction III cars differed from the previous four Sanction Zagatos in that they retained their original chassis numbers; The Sanction IIIs were virtually indistinguishable from the originals; Zagato will no longer construct any Sanction cars

DB4 GT Zagato Sanction III
2000

Chassis: Steel box section chassis, steel superstructure

Body: Aluminium two-seat coupe styled by Ercole Spada of Carrozzeria Zagato

Suspension: Front – Independent with transverse unequal length wishbones, coaxial spring damper units and anti-roll bar
Rear – Live axle with coil springs, parallel trailing links, telescopic dampers and Watt's linkage

Brakes: Girling discs

Steering: Power-assisted rack and pinion

Wheels: 15-inch Borrani alloy

Tyres: Goodyear Eagle NCT 205/70 VR15

Transmission: David Brown four-speed manual; final drive 3.07:1. Limited-slip differential. Rear-wheel drive

Engine: 4212 cc alloy in-line six-cylinder with chain-driven twin overhead camshafts and two valves per cylinder. Compression ratio 9.82:1. Twin SU fuel pumps and three 50 DCO1/SP Weber carburettors

Power: 352 bhp/262 kW @ 6000 rpm
330 lb/ft/447 Nm of torque @ 4600 rpm

Top speed: 160 mph/257 km/h

Dimensions:
Length	13 ft 10.5 in/4229 mm
Width	5 ft 6 in/1676 mm
Height	4 ft 2 in/1271 mm
Wheelbase	7 ft 9 in/2362 mm
Weight	2798 lb/1269 kg

Price when new: N/A

Number built: 2

Vanquish
Project come to life

Although Bob Dover had said at its launch that there were no plans to put Project Vantage into production, when the concept car received such accolades, Aston Martin was forced to do just that.

'What nobody really knew outside Astons was that Project Vantage was actually the prototype for the Vanquish,' admitted Dover much later. 'We knew that if we got a lot of public support at the Detroit Show that we could build that car, which we obviously went on to do.

'After the show in Detroit, we put the business case together. We then took it to the Geneva show for the approval of the vehicle programme. By the end of the second press day, the top executives were racing around everywhere. Jac Nasser, Richard Parry-Jones, Ford's respected Chief Technical Officer, and I were actually in a hotel bar, and we finally got Jac to sign up. Jac is very much a people person. He is an eye-to-eye contact man and he looked at me and said, "You will do this and I will get my money back." That is how it was done. It was too small to go through the Ford Motor Company Product Approval process.

'I had always wanted to do it. There are a number of reasons for doing a concept car: to gauge opinion when you are not confident about the design, to see whether you can stretch the boundaries a bit. But we were confident of the design and that we could put Project Vantage into production, there was never any doubt about that in my mind. It was just giving Ford the confidence that it could do it with the V12 engine as well.'

Project Vantage remained a one-off concept car, but its spirit inspired the Vanquish and plans were soon implemented to put the car into production. 'With this car we go back to our roots, as we did with the DB4 in making it a totally driver-focused car,' said Dover before the car was officially launched. 'It has a six-speed gearbox and a paddle transmission, also an electronic throttle, a second generation V12 engine and all-aluminium and composite construction, which is a world first.'[19]

Ian Callum's Vanquish body design had hints of DB4 GT Zagato and Vantage Special Series I in its genes

'Jac (Nasser) looked at me and said, "You will do this and I will get my money back".'

Bob Dover

Gaydon

During 2001 Aston Martin acquired new headquarters when it took over the 900-acre site of the existing Land Rover test facility in Gaydon, Warwickshire. Only 11 miles from the Bloxham factory, Ford purchased the site from BMW as part of the Rover sale.

Aston Martin's engineers, until then located at Newport Pagnell, Bloxham and temporarily in Coventry, were then able to assemble under one roof. 'We could see we were going to run out of space and we started looking for another factory,' remembered Bob Dover. 'At that time we were just about to move and buy a new factory, because we had run out of space at Newport Pagnell; we had really squeezed Vanquish in there and it had been designed to do what we had been doing, which was building four or five [cars] a week. When I left I think we were building about 14 a week, so it was really caught in a tight layout.'

Aston Martin's engineering workforce subsequently increased from around 20 in 2001, to 200 only three years later. Engineering work that was largely contracted out could then be done in-house.

Gaydon is Aston Martin's ninth home in 90 years and its first purpose-built facility. It houses a reception and customer service area, cafeteria, offices, manufacturing and painting facilities. The new site also enabled Aston Martin to access Land Rover's aerodynamic and environmental wind tunnels, research laboratories, test rig facilities and test roads.

The modern lines and environmentally sound nature of Gaydon's architecture perfectly announced Aston Martin's new technology-driven, modern approach to car manufacture. Each car was made in a series of work areas inside, one step at a time, moving on to subsequent stations for each new process. A good deal of hands-on work was still applied to the construction of each new car. Newport Pagnell remains the home of Aston Martin Works Service.

Development of the Vanquish started in earnest after the Geneva Motor Show in March 1998. Launch Manager for the Jaguar XK8, Ian Minards, followed Dover from Jaguar to work on the Vanquish programme as Chief Programme Manager, and saw the programme through to production. According to Minards, the Vanquish development was originally known as 'Project Bolton' before being designated AMV03.

Bob Dover left Aston Martin to join Land Rover in mid-2000 and was replaced by Ulrich Bez in July that year. 'I left after we showed the Vanquish to the dealers in Monte Carlo – that's when I signed off and I went from there to full time at Land

Top: The Vanquish's unveiling was withheld while the newly arrived Dr Ulrich Bez ordered detail changes to the interior and other parts of the car **Above:** In 'Vanquish trim', the V12 engine produced 460 bhp

Rover,' said Dover. 'I went from drinking champagne in Monaco to a muddy field in Yorkshire, which was very interesting. Vanquish was just about done when I left.'

Seventy-three Vanquish prototypes were built, by far the most of any preceding model and one million miles of exhaustive hot and cold weather testing were covered at Ford proving grounds in Europe, Australia, USA and Canada.

The Vanquish was initially intended for release at the Birmingham Motor Show in 2000, but Dr Bez withheld the car in order to sort out interior and exterior styling and other mechanical quality issues. The production delay also allowed some invaluable time to further develop the car. Meanwhile pictures were released to the press in October, but interior photos were conspicuously absent. Vanquish was finally launched at the Geneva Motor Show in March 2001. Production started soon afterwards with chassis number SCFAC133341B500001.

The name Vanquish was chosen for the production car to continue Aston Martin's tradition of V names. It means to 'overcome in battle, to conquer, to reduce to submission by superior force.' The name came in for considerable criticism, but did grow on people.

Vanquish was a brave, more boldly conceived car produced in an era of confidence and financial security. The DB7 before it was made at a make-or-break time for the company; if it failed, Ford might have rethought its investment. It succeeded and became Aston Martin's biggest seller at the time. Its success allowed Aston Martin to create the Vanquish, a car that stretched the company's boundaries unlike any car before. It was a far cry from the necessarily cautious DB7.

The Vanquish was constructed unlike any other Aston Martin. It was hand-assembled at Newport Pagnell using some of the traditional craftsmanship used on the V8 models. But it was much more technically sophisticated than the V8 it replaced and therefore needed new production techniques. At the core of the Vanquish was its new carbon fibre central supporting structure that doubled as the transmission tunnel. The new tub employed aerospace construction techniques and created a cockpit of exceptional strength and torsional rigidity on par with contemporary Formula One cars.

The extruded aluminium chassis platform, bonded to the tub, benefited from the expertise of a range of people at Aston Martin, Ford and Lotus Engineering, including ex-Lotus Formula One drivers John Miles and Mike Cross. Dan Parry-Williams, a TWR structures expert, developed the renowned structure. A steel, aluminium and carbon fibre subframe supported the engine while carbon fibre windscreen pillars supported the roof. The underbody was completely flat, allowing air to travel into a venturi at the rear, enhancing downforce. The extremely strong structure exceeded all known and projected safety legislation.

Vanquish Launch Manager Ian Minards followed Bob Dover to Aston Martin from Jaguar and oversaw 'Project Bolton'

The Vanquish's handsome shell was built by Hydro Automotive systems in Worchester. After arriving at Newport Pagnell, craftsmen fitted the superformed aluminium panels individually to each car, which still required a degree of craftsmanship. Each car then received eight coats of paint and varnish.

'The key thing about Vanquish was the fact that the innovation in terms of the structure would really put us back where we were, which was always pretty advanced in terms of technology,' said Dover. 'I always wanted it to be a technology demonstrator for Ford. The carbon fibre crash structure up front was a first, no matter what Ferrari says, the carbon fibre crash structure at the rear was a first, the A-post, woven Kevlar on a solid foam master, was a first. So the car was extremely stiff in bending and in torsion.

'The technology was extremely important. The paddle shift, for instance: we could have used a manual shift very easily but the paddle shift was something I wanted to do. The V8 was getting very out of date technologically, the six-cylinder DB7 didn't break any new ground and we needed to get back at the top in terms of technology.'

The front and rear suspension consisted of independent double aluminium wishbones, coil springs, mono-tube dampers and anti-roll bars. Brakes were Brembo 355 mm front and 330 mm rear ventilated and cross-drilled steel discs with four-piston

callipers. A Teves anti-lock vacuum-assisted braking and traction control system was also supplied. The Vanquish used 19-inch alloy wheels shod in Yokohama 255/40 ZR 19 tyres (front) and 285/40 ZR 19 (rear).

Ian Callum's styling remained very similar to Project Vantage. At a casual glance the two were almost identical, but closer inspection revealed many detail changes. In fact, none of the surfaces on the Vanquish, except the roof, remained from the concept car.

The track was widened, the controversial crease on the rear haunches was softened and the side windows were teased out a little to create more cabin room. The side air intakes were mildly reshaped and the exhaust exit area was changed. Details such as door mirrors, fuel filler cap, side indicator lights, front fog lights and rear light clusters were all subtly changed.

The forward-looking interior of Neil Simpson's Project Vantage was highly modified and toned down on the Vanquish. The production interior featured leather and brushed aluminium. It was modern, but not as far reaching as Project Vantage.

A limitless colour palette and various leather and carpet combinations were available. A choice of two or two-plus-two seating could also be specified; the two-seat option contained a deck in place of the rear seats for additional luggage accommodation.

The 5935 cc V12 engine was not new; it had appeared in largely the same form in the DB7 Vantage of 1999 in Stage One tune. For the Vanquish, however, the Stage Two engine received a new air induction system, up-rated camshafts, manifolds and a revised crankshaft and valve gear, which increased power to 460 bhp @ 6500 rpm and 400 lb/ft of torque @ 5000 rpm. The Vanquish also utilised a fully catalysed stainless steel exhaust system fitted with a bypass valve, helping provide the car its unique and highly praised sound.

The Vanquish featured an electronic drive-by-wire throttle system and Tremec gearbox, similar to the six-speed unit used in the DB7 Vantage. Gear changes were actuated by an electro-hydraulic clutch via Magnetti-Marelli and Ford-developed Formula One-style paddles at the back of the steering wheel.

Top: The rear taillights were among the detail changes from the Project Vantage show car

Above: A Vanquish prototype undergoing hot weather testing in Australia in 2000

Sports Dynamic Pack

Announced in late 2003 and becoming available from May 2004, the Sports Dynamic Pack available for the Vanquish featured changes to the front suspension with revised damping and shorter springs and steering arms. The front brakes were changed to 378 mm ventilated and grooved discs with six-piston callipers and while the rear brakes remained 330 mm, they were widened by 2 mm. The new nine-spoke alloy wheels were 30 percent lighter than the previous set. Many of the developments from the Sports Dynamic Pack were incorporated into the later Vanquish S.

More Vanquish prototypes were built than for any other Aston Martin model before it; unlike in earlier times, they were all destroyed

A Winter Mode prevented the application of too much torque on slippery surfaces, while Sport Mode cut gear changing times to only 300 milliseconds. 'This will be the most dynamic, technically advanced and sophisticated model ever to be introduced by Aston Martin,' said Dr Bez.

Performance figures of 0–60 mph in 4.5 seconds and a top speed of 190 mph were quoted by Aston Martin prior to the car's launch. These targets could not be matched by road testers who mustered 4.9 seconds for 0–60 mph and a top speed of 186 mph.

The Vanquish received unanimous praise from numerous motoring magazines upon its launch. Most claimed it to be the best Aston Martin ever made; others said it was the best GT available. Certainly, when all the hysteria subsided, what remained was the best press received by Aston Martin to that time and the reputation of the company received a significant boost.

Model	Weight (lb)	0-60 mph (seconds)	Top speed (mph)	Power (bhp)
Project Vantage	3417	4.0	200	442
Vanquish	3969	4.9	186	460

Vanquish
2001–2004

Chassis: Extruded and bonded aluminium and carbon fibre platform and superstructure

Body: Aluminium and composite two-seat or 2+2 coupe styled by Ian Callum

Suspension: Front – Independent with double aluminium wishbones, coil springs, monotube dampers and anti-roll bar
Rear – Independent with double aluminium wishbones, coil springs, monotube dampers and anti-roll bar

Brakes: Servo-assisted 355 mm ventilated and cross-drilled discs with four-piston callipers (front); 330 mm ventilated discs with four-piston callipers (rear). ABS

Steering: Power-assisted rack and pinion

Wheels: 19-inch magnesium alloy

Tyres: Yokohama 255/40 ZR19 (front). 285/40 ZR19 (rear)

Transmission: Tremec six-speed manual with auto shift/manual select shift; final drive 3.69:1. Limited-slip differential. Rear-wheel drive

Engine: 5935 cc alloy V12 with twin chain-driven overhead camshafts per bank and four valves per cylinder. Compression ratio 10.5:1. Visteon twin PTEC engine management and fuel injection system. Fully catalysed stainless steel exhaust system with active bypass valves

Power: 460 bhp/343 kW @ 6800 rpm
400 lb/ft/542 Nm of torque @ 5500 rpm

Top speed: 186 mph/299 km/h

Dimensions:
Length	15 ft 4 in/4665 mm
Width	6 ft/1923 mm
Height	4 ft 4 in/1318 mm
Wheelbase	8 ft 6.75 in/2690 mm
Weight	3969 lb/1835 kg

Price when new: £158,000

Number built: More than 1300

255

2 0 / 2 0   C o n c e p t   C a r
Perfect vision

Aston Martin concept cars are rare. Over the years only a handful have been constructed and exhibited, so when one was unveiled to the public, especially one linked with the famous Giorgetto Giugiaro, it was big news indeed.

Giugiaro designed the one-off DB4 GT Bertone Jet, which was exhibited at the Geneva and Turin Motor Shows, when he was a young designer working at Bertone in 1961. Being a design study only, the Bertone Jet did not enter production. But it gave the world yet another glimpse of how Aston Martins could look in the hands of master designers.

Forty-one years later, at the Geneva Motor Show in 2001, another Giugiaro-designed Aston Martin was unveiled. Exhibited on Giugiaro's Italdesign stand, the 20/20 Concept Car, a vehicle designed to reflect Aston Martin's design direction, attracted considerable attention.

Dr Ulrich Bez had collaborated with Giugiaro previously when he was head of Research and Development at Daewoo. Bez was seeking new design ideas so asked Giugiaro to create a concept car for the Geneva Motor Show in 2001 with the understanding that the car be a Giugiaro project, not an official Aston Martin.

Bez made available a DB7 Vantage Volante chassis, running gear and windscreen to the father-and-son team of Giorgetto and Fabrizio Giugiaro who were jointly responsible for the final design. Bez was shown the concept car in October 2000, but at this point it lacked anything other than Giugiaro styling cues and could have belonged to any number of manufacturers.

An air intake was later positioned behind the front wheels, the rear wheel arches were built up and the familiar Aston Martin grille was incorporated. From the front, the car could have passed as an Aston Martin and the interior featured possible future themes, but from any other angle the car was pure Italian fantasy.

The 20/20 followed the lines of Giugiaro's Capsula of 1982 and Structura of 1998, which utilised a visible aluminium frame doubling as a styling feature. 'An evocative surface treatment,' said Giugiaro, 'often solves whims and trends but may present the product as frivolous, like a big toy. With 20/20, the car can return to its roots as a complete, meticulous piece of engineering.'

Based on a DB7 Vantage Volante platform, Giugiaro's 20/20 Concept Car did not reach production

From the front, the car could have passed as an Aston Martin and the interior featured possible future themes, but from any other angle the car was pure Italian fantasy.

Italdesign

The company now known as Italdesign was founded in February 1968 under the name Studi Italiani Realizzazione Prototipi SpA by the Giugiaro and Mantovani families. Now employing more than 1000 people, the Italdesign group of companies has produced more than 120 car designs.

In the post-Bertone Jet years, Giorgetto Giugiaro (pictured below right) went on to design cars as diverse as the Iso Grifo, Gordon-Keeble, Maserati Ghibli, VW Golf, Alfasud, De Lorean DMC 12, Maserati Bora, Lotus Esprit, BMW M1, Bugatti EB 112 and the Maserati 3200 GT. He was also given the great honour of being named 'Designer of the Century'.

The Aston Martin 20/20 Concept Car was designed by Giorgetto in collaboration with his son, Fabrizio (pictured below left).

The finished result was a two-plus-two-seat, Targa top, convertible sports car. The body was based on an exposed aluminium spaceframe with bonded non-load-bearing carbon fibre and plastic composite body panels. A reworking of Aston Martin's famous air vents incorporated a thick bar aping the distinctive door hinges and the bonnet incorporated twin louvres, allowing a glimpse of the V12 engine.

The rear bulkhead could be removed to make room for two occasional rear seats to accommodate children. The soft collapsible roof folded down into a special housing behind the Targa-style rollover bar. A very generous-sized boot was capable of taking several suitcases.

The interior was reminiscent of the futuristic Project Vantage. The seats, doors, dashboard and steering wheel, which incorporated a grille-shaped airbag cover, were all trimmed in terracotta-coloured leather. The large analogue dials were housed on the steering column instead of being set into the dashboard. Brushed aluminium accents in the cockpit gave the car a contemporary ambience.

The 20/20 shared the same mechanicals as the DB7 Vantage, but it was claimed the engine produced 500 bhp as opposed to the 420 bhp of the production model. Although it was a fully functioning car, performance figures were never released. Weight also was not disclosed. Like the DB4 GT Bertone Jet before it, the 20/20 Concept Car remained unique.

Exposed door hinges were incorporated into the air vent design

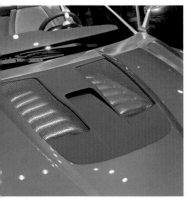

Clockwise from top: The cabin was only suitable for two passengers, with very small occasional rear seats hidden under the rear bulkhead; Unusual elongated taillights were incorporated into the rear design; Instruments were grouped around the steering column, easily facilitating left- or right-hand drive configurations; The car's V12 engine could be seen through twin wire mesh grilles on the bonnet

The 20/20 was a working prototype with a claimed engine output of 500 bhp

20/20 Concept Car
2001

Chassis: Steel box-section chassis, steel superstructure.

Body: Aluminium 2+2 convertible styled by Fabrizio and Giorgetto Giugiaro of Italdesign

Suspension: Front – Independent with double wishbones incorporating anti-dive geometry, coil springs, monotube dampers and anti-roll bar
Rear – Independent with double wishbones incorporating longitudinal control arms, coil springs, monotube dampers and anti-roll bar

Brakes: Servo-assisted 355 mm ventilated and cross-drilled steel discs with alloy four-piston callipers (front); 330 mm ventilated steel discs with alloy four-piston callipers (rear). Drum handbrake. ABS

Steering: Power-assisted rack and pinion

Wheels: 18-inch alloy

Tyres: Bridgestone SO2 245/40 ZR18 front. 265/35 ZR18 (rear)

Transmission: ZF six-speed manual; final drive 3.33:1. Limited-slip differential. Rear-wheel drive

Engine: 5935 cc alloy V12 with twin chain-driven overhead camshafts per bank and four valves per cylinder. Compression ratio 10.3:1. EEC V engine management system with sequential fuel injection. Fully catalysed exhaust system

Power: 500 bhp/373 kW @ 6000 rpm (claimed)
420 lb/ft/569 Nm of torque @ 5000 rpm

Top speed: 200 mph/322 km/h (claimed)

Dimensions:

Length	15 ft 4 in/4455 mm
Width	6 ft/1900 mm
Height	4 ft 4 in/1300 mm
Wheelbase	8 ft 6.75 in/2591 mm
Weight	N/A

Price when new: Not available for sale

Number built: 1

DB7 Zagato

Bespoke suit

By 2002 the nearly-ten-year-old DB7 was showing its age. It had already received a V12 engine transplant and body and interior modifications, but it was coming to the end of its lifecycle. To retain interest in the model until its successor arrived, Dr Ulrich Bez announced at that year's Geneva Motor Show that Aston Martin would be producing two new DB7s, both with Zagato-designed bodies.

The project had its origins at the 2001 Pebble Beach Concours d'Elegance when Bez found himself seated next to Dr Andrea Zagato at the judges' table. Much like when Victor Gauntlett, Peter Livanos and the Zagato brothers met at the Geneva Motor Show in 1984, conversation soon centred on the Aston Martin–Zagato connection. Over dinner on Sunday 19 August Bez broached the subject of renewing the celebrated collaboration with Zagato.

'Creating a new Aston Martin Zagato was my passion,' said Bez. 'I wanted a car that had all of the beauty of the DB4 GT Zagato with its style and excitement, but with a contemporary execution; the car would be based on DB7 technology with enhanced driving dynamics and greater agility.'

Initial sketches by Zagato's Chief Designer Norihiko Harada were presented to Bez and Aston Martin's new Design Director Henrik Fisker shortly after. During the Frankfurt Motor Show the brief was agreed and in December, further more detailed designs were shown to Aston Martin personnel. Final approval to proceed was given in early 2002.

The prototype, christened 'Georgia' by the project team, was crafted in hand-beaten aluminium at Zagato's studios in Milan under the direction of Zagato Project Manager, Luca Zanetti, Chief Engineer, Walter Messini and President, Dr Andrea Zagato.

Back at Bloxham, under the supervision of Mark Johnson (Chief Programme Engineer), Paul Barritt (Programme Manager) and Simon Butler (Programme Engineer), 'Georgia' and three additional engineering cars were thoroughly road tested and developed. The new exterior styling was only the beginning of a large number of changes the DB7 went through to bring it to market.

The Zagato was powered by the DB7 Vantage-derived V12 engine and some other mechanical components were carried

The gaping grille was the most striking feature of the Zagato DB7 design

Of particular note was the rear glass, which continued the 'double bubble' effect of the roof.

Above: The distinctive upswept rear quarter window became a Zagato trademark **Far left:** Zagato President and great grandson of the company's founder, Dr Andrea Zagato **Left:** Early styling sketches by Nori Harada were shown to Aston Martin's directors for approval; many detail changes were made for production

over as well. Unique features included an up-rated 435 bhp engine specification, improved brakes and suspension and a higher differential ratio of 4.09:1 was used for quicker acceleration. Manual transmission only was offered.

The front and rear suspension utilised double aluminium wishbones and coil springs with unique dampers developed to create a more driver-centred car. Up-rated anti-lock ventilated disc brakes were added as were unique Zagato-designed alloy wheels.

Where the new car differed dramatically from standard was in the body styling. Nori Harada, once a student of celebrated DB4 GT Zagato designer, Ercole Spada, worked with Zagato's CAD modellist, Alessandro Serra, under the guidance of Fisker.

Bodily, Harada's Zagato design owed little to the Ian Callum original. Save for the front windscreen, every panel was different. Lightweight aluminium was used for the bonnet, doors and boot, with pressed steel used for the front wings and roof, while the front and rear bumpers were constructed from impact-absorbing composite material.

Harada's design married both Aston Martin and Zagato styling features in a dramatically different-looking car. Based on a shortened DB7 Vantage Volante chassis, the front and rear overhangs were abbreviated by 0.5 inches and 6 inches respectively, creating a car 2.5 inches shorter in the wheelbase and 8 inches shorter overall, while being 1 inch wider and marginally taller. The famous air vents remained and Aston Martin's trademark grille was apparent, but it was enlarged in the Italian style like numerous past Maserati and Ferrari sports cars.

Zagato's styling cues were also in abundance with the famous double-bubble roof, up-swept rear quarter glass, short front and rear overhangs, muscular rear haunches and taut body panels. The grille-shaped rear featured a small luggage slot, reminiscent of the DB2, and new round rear taillights. Of particular note was the rear glass, which continued the 'double bubble' effect of the roof.

'We don't see it as really retro,' said Fisker, 'We see it as more of a Zagato in the tradition of Zagato and Aston Martin. The idea of this car was, like the original DB4 and DB4 GT Zagato, for the

DB7 and the DB7 Zagato to have a relationship in design. So you couldn't go off in some futuristic direction.'

Only three standard colours were offered – Aqua Verde, Zagato Nero and Mercury Grey – however, many customers ordered bespoke colour schemes. Eventually, 28 different body colours and 19 interior combinations were chosen.

Unlike previous Aston Martin-Zagatos, whose rolling chassis were constructed in England then transported to Zagato in Milan where the aluminium bodies were fitted, the DB7 version had pressed panels constructed by Italian company OPAC. The body shells were then phosphated and electroplated by Padanaforesi and primed by Rattalino in Italy before returning to Gaydon where they were painted. The cars were constructed at Bloxham, each taking around 250 hours to complete.

The interior retained the DB7 Vantage steering wheel and most switch gear, but featured quilted, Zagato-embossed aniline leather seats. The dashboard and doors, reconfigured to compensate for the car's higher waistline, were trimmed in matching leather. A parcel shelf, complete with leather straps, replaced the rear seats, providing additional luggage space.

To highlight the Zagato's bespoke nature, a Mercury Grey model with chocolate brown interior, chassis number AB3400008, was officially unveiled to a gathering of 120 potential customers at the

famous London tailors Gieves and Hawkes, at Number 1 Savile Row in July 2002.

'Steve Bray and the Garage team worked all night to get the car into Gieves and Hawkes,' remarked Kingsley Riding-Felce. 'We had to put it in through the front [window] on its side.' The Zagato DB7 was also previewed at the 2002 Pebble Beach Concours d'Elegance on 18 August and made its motor show debut at the Paris Salon on 28 September 2002.

Production was slated at anywhere from 75 to 99 cars depending on customer demand. Interest was strong and Aston Martin announced in October 2002 that 200 confirmed orders had been taken. Production however was capped at 99: chassis numbers 700001–700099. One additional car was retained by the factory.

Top: A small rear tailgate, like the DB2 before it, was incorporated in lieu of a hatchback **Above:** Quilted aniline leather seats were a unique feature of the two-seat interior

DB7 Zagato
2002–2004

Chassis: Steel semi-monocoque body shell

Body: Aluminium and steel two-seat coupe styled by Nori Harada of Carrozzeria Zagato

Suspension: Front – Independent with double aluminium wishbones incorporating anti-dive geometry, coil springs, monotube dampers and anti-roll bar
Rear – Independent with double aluminium wishbones with longitudinal control arms, coil springs and monotube dampers

Brakes: Servo-assisted 355 mm ventilated and grooved discs with four-piston callipers (front); 330 mm ventilated and grooved discs with four-piston callipers (rear). ABS

Steering: Power-assisted rack and pinion

Wheels: 18-inch (front); 19-inch (rear) alloy

Tyres: Pirelli P Zero 245/40 ZR18 (front). 275/35 ZR19 (rear)

Transmission: Tremec six-speed manual; final drive 4.09:1. Limited-slip differential. Rear-wheel drive

Engine: 5935 cc alloy V12 with twin chain-driven overhead camshafts per bank and four valves per cylinder. Compression ratio 10.3:1. EEC V engine management system with sequential fuel injection. Fully catalysed exhaust system

Power: 435 bhp/324 kW @ 6000 rpm
410 lb/ft/556 Nm of torque @ 5000 rpm

Top speed: 184 mph/296 km/h

Dimensions:
Length	14 ft 7 in/4488 mm
Width	6 ft 1 in/1861 mm
Height	4 ft 2 in/1248 mm
Wheelbase	8 ft 3 in/2531 mm
Weight	4079 lb/1850 kg

Price when new: £166,000 (approx)

Number built: 100

DB7 GT/GTA

Take two

A GT version of the DB7 had already been attempted back in 1995, but with only two examples built it, can hardly be considered a production model. The time seemed right, therefore, in 2002 for the release of a new GT version to continue interest in the DB7 while work was conducted behind the scenes on its replacement. The result was a significant improvement over the DB7 Vantage.

The DB7 GT became a finely honed performance car and, along with the Zagato, the most powerful DB7 road car ever. It was launched at the Birmingham Motor Show on 22 October 2002 and the short build run of only 302 cars was completed within 12 months.

It was created in less than a year and developed due to customer demand for a sportier, more driver-focused DB7. In keeping with the driver's car theme, the GT was only produced in coupe form.

There was a lot of input into the development of the DB7 GT, much of it learnt over the years by Works Service. Starting with the engine, 15 extra horsepower was liberated from the Vantage V12, raising power to 435 bhp, with torque up to 410 lb/ft from 400 lb/ft. This, combined with a revised final drive ratio of 4.09:1, ZF six-speed manual gearbox with quick-shift gear lever, twin-plate racing clutch and new sports exhaust system with bypass valve, turned the DB7 GT into a very quick motor car.

It was created in less than a year and developed due to customer demand for a sportier, more driver-focused DB7.

The GTA five-speed automatic version, apart from the transmission and detuned 420 bhp engine, was identical in specification and price but, predictably, top speed was reduced to 'only' 165 mph. It was outwardly identified by GTA badging.

Subtle changes to the body included a new undertray, wheel arch liner extensions, upswept boot lid, twin bonnet vents, mesh radiator grille with a lower air intake and five-spoke 18-inch alloy wheels with Bridgestone 245/35 ZR18 (front) and 265/30 ZR18 (rear) tyres.

The DB7 GT's rear spoiler and other aerodynamic aids were said to reduce lift by 50 percent

The interior featured cossetting leather sports seats, aluminium fascia inserts, white-faced intruments, aluminium gear knob and racing-style pedals. The revisions combined to endow the new DB7 GT with a distinctive modern ambience.

Large racing-style Brembo brakes with grooved discs and up-rated pads were incorporated, as was a Vanquish-style brake booster. The suspension was also up-rated to include new damper settings, stiffer bushes and improved location of the front lower wishbone and front sub-frame, while a brace was added to the lower rear suspension to improve stability. The revisions to the aerodynamic package were said to cut lift by 50 percent and increase high-speed stability. The DB7 GT was the best-handling DB7 of all.

Production was confined to 190 GTs and 112 GTAs. The future now lay with the 'VH' cars being developed at Gaydon.

Clockwise from far left: The interior featured an alloy gear knob and racing-style pedals; Special sill plaques were part of the DB7 GT specification; GT badges denoted a manual car, while automatic versions boasted GTA badges; Horsepower was raised to 435 bhp for the DB7 GT; The DB7 GT was one of several limited edition specials made towards the end of the DB7's lifecycle

DB7 GT/GTA
2002–2003

Chassis: Steel semi-monocoque body shell

Body: Aluminium 2+2 coupe designed by Ian Callum

Suspension: Front – Independent with double wishbones, coil springs and anti-roll bar
Rear – Independent with double wishbones, coil springs and anti-roll bar

Brakes: Servo-assisted 355 mm ventilated and grooved Brembo discs with four piston callipers (front); 330 mm grooved Brembo discs with four piston callipers (rear). ABS

Steering: Power-assisted rack and pinion

Wheels: 18-inch alloy

Tyres: Bridgestone 245/35 ZR18 (front) 265/30 ZR18 (rear)

Transmission: GT: Tremec six-speed manual; final drive 4.09:1
GTA: Five-speed automatic; final drive 3.77:1. Limited-slip differential. Rear-wheel drive

Engine: 5935 cc alloy V12 with twin chain-driven overhead camshafts per bank and four valves per cylinder. Compression ratio 10.3:1. Visteon twin PTEC engine management and fuel injection systems. Fully catalysed exhaust system

Power: GT: 435 bhp/324 kW @ 6000 rpm
410 lb/ft/556 Nm of torque @ 5000 rpm

GTA: 420 bhp/313 kW @ 6000 rpm
400 lb/ft/542 Nm of torque @ 5000 rpm

Top speed: GT: 184 mph/296 km/h
GTA: 165 mph/266 km/h

Dimensions:
Length	15 ft 1.5 in/4646 mm
Width	5 ft 9.5 in/1830 mm (excluding wing mirrors)
Height	4 ft 1.5 in/1238 mm
Wheelbase	8 ft 5 in/2591 mm
Weight	3913 lb/1775 kg (manual)
	4023 lb/1825 kg (automatic)

Price when new: £104,500

Number built: GT: 190; GTA: 112

D B 7   G T / G T A   –   T a k e   t w o

A M V 8   V a n t a g e

V8 power lives on

In January 2002, Aston Martin began testing a two-seat sports car then known as AM305. It was to become the AMV8 Vantage, which was previewed on 6 January 2003 at the Detroit Motor Show, more than two years ahead of production.

In what proved to be a smokescreen for the DB9, it came as a genuine surprise when Aston Martin revealed its new concept car so early. Under the cover of the AMV8 Vantage's considerable publicity, Aston Martin's designers and engineers were able to undergo development of the DB7 replacement in relative secrecy.

The AMV8 concept car was said to premier Aston Martin's new VH architecture, but in reality was DB7-based. It marked the debut of Henrik Fisker's design work for the British company.

The AMV8 was the first two-seat Aston Martin for many years and combined with short overhangs, wide track and long bonnet, the proportions were near perfect. It shared a strong family resemblance to the Vanquish and the later DB9 but this was no bad thing; the dimensions of the AMV8 Vantage were quite different, being a dedicated two-seater with a hatchback, the first since the DB2/4 of 1953.

The cabin, the work of interior designer Sarah Maynard, was also thoroughly modern. An important aspect of her work was that the trim and switchgear were bespoke items, not shared with any other brand. The finishings and switchgear hinted at premium watches and audio equipment. Although leather was prominent, yet again wood was replaced in favour of anodised aluminium.

It was a very advanced car, said to employ an aluminium platform with front mid-mounted V8 engine mated via a cast aluminium torque tube to the transaxle gearbox. The future VH architecture offered tremendous structural integrity and torsional rigidity while allowing various models to be produced from the same basic platform. Featuring composite body panels the AMV8 Vantage concept car was built by DC Design PVT Ltd. The company, led by Dilip Chabria, a one-time designer at Ford, specialised in constructing prototype and concept cars. The show car featured gun metal paintwork (later changed to dark metallic blue), orange trim and fitted luggage.

The AMV8 Vantage appeared at the Detroit Motor Show two years before planned production

In what proved to be a smokescreen for the DB9 it came as a genuine surprise when Aston Martin revealed its new concept car so early.

Henrik Fisker

Danish-born Henrik Fisker was appointed Director of Design at Aston Martin in September 2001 upon the departure of Ian Callum. Fisker came from BMW's US-based Designworks, where his credits included the BMW Z8 sports car. Combining Fisker's responsibilities at Aston Martin, he worked at Ford's London design house Ingeni.

He took over the design of the AMV8 Vantage and DB9 after Callum had begun both cars but influenced their finished production forms. He also contributed to the DB7 Zagato, DB AR1 and DB9 Volante. Fisker resigned from Aston Martin in December 2004 to begin his own design consultation business Fisker Coachbuild in the USA in 2005; among his first models was the Tramonto (pictured below).

Top to bottom: The AMV8 concept car was the first two-seat Aston Martin since the Virage Volante prototype debuted in 1990; The bold interior was toned down for the production cars; The upward-lifting tailgate allowed easy access to a surprising amount of luggage

VH architecture

Aston Martin's vertical/horizontal (VH) architecture represented the vertical integration of the platform's models throughout the Aston Martin range. The production V8 Vantage had the shortest wheelbase, followed by the DB9, with the long-wheelbase four-door Rapide Concept sitting on the longest platform. H stood for the horizontal incorporation of Ford's resources and expertise across the parent company's range, enabling Aston Martin to tap into PAG partner Volvo's expertise in safety systems and Ford Research and Vehicle Technology for engine development.

Mid-engine project

With the DB7 nearing the end of its lifecycle, Aston Martin and Ford executives created plans for a new volume-selling vehicle. Breaking with tradition, it was decided to engineer a mid-engined sports car. The plan for the £80,000 car gained momentum; a mid-engined racing car was also designed. But the projects were cancelled by Ford executives due to concerns the proposed car would damage Aston Martin's reputation; research had shown customers wanted a front-engined car. Upon Dr Bez's arrival at Aston Martin plans were developed for a new line of cars using a shared platform and the mid-engined concept was abandoned.

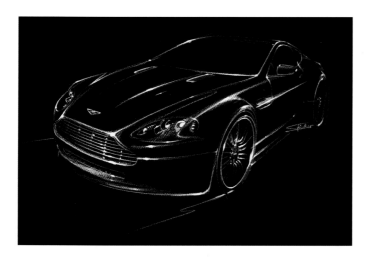

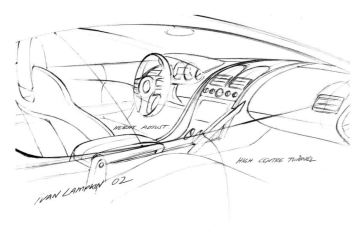

Top to bottom: The short wheelbase two-seater had superb proportions – the show car was based on a DB7 platform; Subtle details such as the mirrors changed but production versions proved to be quite faithful to the concept car; A Henrik Fisker-signed sketch of the AMV8 Vantage concept car demonstrates its purity of line; An early sketch of the car's interior

AMV8 Vantage
2003

Chassis: Extruded aluminium bonded monocoque (claimed)[i]

Body: Aluminium, steel, composite material and magnesium alloy two-seat hatchback coupe styled by Henrik Fisker[ii]

Suspension: Front – Independent with double wishbones, coil-over aluminium monotube dampers and anti-roll bar Rear – Independent with double wishbones, coil-over aluminium monotube dampers and anti-roll bar

Brakes: Servo-assisted 355 mm ventilated and grooved discs with Brembo four-piston calipers (front); 330 mm ventilated steel discs with four-piston callipers (rear). ABS

Steering: Power-assisted rack and pinion

Wheels: 18-inch Speedline alloy

Tyres: Bridgestone SO2 245/40 ZR18

Transmission: Six-speed manual; final drive 4.09:1. Limited-slip differential. Rear-wheel drive

Engine: Front mid-mounted 4281 cc alloy V8 with twin chain-driven overhead camshafts per bank and four valves per cylinder. Fully catalysed stainless steel exhaust system

Power: 500 bhp/373 kW @ 6000 rpm (claimed) 420 lb/ft/569 Nm of torque @ 5000 rpm (claimed)

Top speed: 200 mph/322 km/h (claimed)

Dimensions:

Length	14 ft 3.5 in/4347 mm
Width	6 ft 1.5 in/1874 mm
Height	4 ft 1.5 in/1298 mm
Wheelbase	8 ft 5.5 in/2600 mm
Weight	3307 lb/1500 kg (approx)

Price when new: Not available for sale

Number built: 1

---

i   The AMV8 Vantage concept car was DB7-based
ii Project started by Ian Callum

271

DB AR1

Yankee doodle

With scores of disappointed customers missing out on the DB7 Zagato, Aston Martin launched a Zagato-designed roadster specifically for the American market that had not officially received the DB7 Zagato. Unveiled on 2 January 2003 at the Los Angeles Motor Show, the DB American Roadster 1 (DB AR1) was, like the DB7 Zagato, also specified as a limited edition of only 99 vehicles.

It was based on a standard DB7 Vantage Volante platform; however, Zagato designed the bodywork purely as a two-seater, the rear seat area being used for additional storage. The DB AR1 was not a convertible version of the DB7 Zagato; it had a longer wheel base and was a genuine roadster, made without a roof and equipped only with rudimentary wet weather equipment.

It was a different design from the coupe, but shared some characteristics including the gaping grille and distinctive rear haunches. The roadster body was constructed from steel with front wings, sills, boot lid (with integral boot spoiler) and front and rear bumpers panelled in aluminium for weight saving.

Dr Ulrich Bez explained before the car's launch that a DB AR1 concept car was to be exhibited to US customers to judge reaction. If sufficient interest was shown, Aston Martin would consider putting it into production in 2003. 'If the reaction is as positive as that for the DB7 Zagato,' he said, 'we will produce a limited number of DB AR1 models solely for the United States market.'

The reaction was very positive. All 99 examples, chassis numbers 800001–800099, sold within a three-week period after a tour of the United States following the Los Angeles Motor Show. Chassis number 800100 was retained by the factory. All DB AR1s were constructed and delivered to customers during 2003 and 2004. A small number were also sold in Europe to some special customers. One right-hand drive car, chassis number 800016, was constructed.

The DB AR1 had much the same specification as the DB7 Zagato including Brembo disc brakes with four-piston callipers front and rear and Vanquish-sourced brake servo, twin AP Racing clutch, quick-shift gear lever and 435 bhp V12 engine (420 bhp for the automatic version) and active sports exhaust system with rear muffler bypass valves. To produce a wider track, specially designed Yokohama-shod 19-inch alloy wheels with offset were used.

The gaping grille of the DB7 Zagato remained, but the rest of the DB AR1 was quite different from the earlier coupe

The DB AR1 was not a convertible version of the
DB7 Zagato; it was a genuine roadster.

Clockwise from top: The DB AR1 was designed for the American market, but a small number were registered in Europe; DB AR1s were true roadsters with only rudimentary wet-weather gear; The production car remained faithful to the early styling sketches; Like the coupe design, the roadster featured a double contoured rear section; Despite the longer wheelbase compared to the DB7 Zagato, the DB AR1 could still only accommodate two passengers

Always intended as a runout model for the DB7 range, the final DB AR1 was begun on 19 January and left the Bloxham factory on 23 February 2004, bringing to an end both Aston Martin's most successful car in sales terms up until that time *and* construction at Bloxham. All new car manufacture would take place in Gaydon.

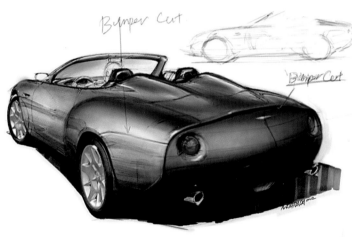

DB AR1
2003–2004

Chassis: Steel underframe, steel superstructure

Body: Aluminium and steel two-seat roadster styled by Nori Harada of Carrozzeria Zagato

Suspension: Front – Independent with double wishbones incorporating anti-dive geometry, coil springs, monotube dampers and anti-roll bar
Rear – Independent with double wishbones incorporating longitudinal control arms, coil springs, monotube dampers and anti-roll bar

Brakes: Servo-assisted 355 mm ventilated and grooved steel Brembo discs with four-piston callipers (front); 330 mm ventilated and grooved steel Brembo discs with four-piston callipers (rear). Drum handbrake. ABS

Steering: Power-assisted rack and pinion

Wheels: 18-inch alloy

Tyres: Pirelli P Zero 225/40 ZR18 (front). 275/35 ZR19 (rear)

Transmission: Six-speed manual; final drive 4.09:1
Five-speed automatic; final drive 3.06:1. Limited-slip differential. Rear-wheel drive

Engine: 5935 cc alloy V12 with twin chain-driven overhead camshafts per bank and four valves per cylinder. Compression ratio 10.3:1. Visteon EEC V engine management and fuel injection systems. Fully catalysed stainless steel exhaust system with active bypass valves

Power: 435 bhp/324 kW @ 6000 rpm (manual)
410 lb/ft/556 Nm of torque @ 5000 rpm
420 bhp/313 kW @ 6000 rpm (automatic)
400 lb/ft/542 Nm of torque @ 5000 rpm

Top speed: 185 mph/298 km/h (manual)
165 mph/266 km/h limited (automatic)

Dimensions:

Length	15 ft 1 in/4657 mm
Width	5 ft 10 in/1861 mm
Height	4 ft 2 in/1220 mm
Wheelbase	8 ft 5 in/2591 mm
Weight	4096 lb/1858 kg (manual)
	4211 lb/1910 kg (automatic)

Price when new: US$235,000

Number built: 100

DB AR1 – Yankee doodle

275

D B 9

Leaping into the future

The launch of the DB9 at the Frankfurt Motor Show on 9 September 2003 was both a figurative and literal leap into the future for Aston Martin. It replaced the DB7, but it was not its direct successor and, to highlight the many advances made and to avoid any misconceptions about eight-cylinder engines, Aston Martin bypassed the DB8 title altogether.

It was the most important car in the company's new high-tech era. In contrast with past practices, Aston Martin employed around 120 product designers using CAD (Computer Aided Design) and CAE (Computer Aided Engineering) technology to help design the major facets of the DB9. As a result it featured a host of technological advances and was built unlike any Aston Martin before.

The DB9 was the first car produced at the company's new purpose-built factory in Gaydon and also the first model based on Aston Martin's VH (vertical/horizontal) platform.[i] The tub was constructed from stamped aluminium sheets, cast aluminium joints and aluminium extrusions bonded together with advanced adhesives and self-piercing rivets.

Aston Martin's VH aluminium structure endowed the DB9 with a light, yet immensely strong, platform. The aluminium roof, bonnet and rear wings and composite front wings and boot were bonded to the frame, producing a body shell 25 percent lighter but twice as rigid than the DB7's.

The Gaydon factory featured a first for Aston Martin: a robot. The robot applied adhesive to body panels in the body shop in preparation for bonding. DB9 construction still involved a degree of hand craftsmanship: each car took around 200 hours to build and even the painting was done by hand.

Fine-tuned by ex-Lotus Formula One racer and chassis designer, John Miles, the suspension was by forged aluminium wishbones, front and rear aluminium dampers and anti-roll bars. The brake package consisted of ventilated and grooved discs with electronic braking distribution, traction control, electronic brake assist and dynamic stability control. Lightweight alloy wheels and specially developed Bridgestone Potenza tyres were standard equipment.

The DB9's safety systems were developed with the assistance of PAG partner, Volvo, which provided its crash test expertise and

Opposite: Performance was a DB9 strong point: 0–60 mph took only 4.7 seconds and the GT could reach a top speed of 186 mph

i   The V8 Vantage also shared the V/H platform and, although in concept guise it debuted before the DB9, it didn't go into production until 2005

Cologne engine facility

In one of Aston Martin's more controversial recent decisions, it was announced in mid-2003 that Cosworth Technology would no longer make Aston Martin's new engines in England. Production would move offshore to Germany at the Ford engine plant in Cologne.

Dr Ulrich Bez said that the move was no reflection on Cosworth but with Aston Martin's impending growth, the move was necessary. 'From 2005 our annual production will increase three-fold and the switch to Cologne for our V12 engine will enable this to happen. The production base will also be totally flexible, allowing us to assemble modular engine concepts and variants. All the engines built within this facility will be unique to Aston Martin and a perfect fit in terms of technology requirements, quality control and lean production techniques,' he said.

Officially opened on 28 October 2004, the Aston Martin Engine Plant (AMEP) was located within Ford's Niehl engine plant and produced engines solely for Aston Martin. The 12,500-square-metre facility was divided into four main areas: one to machine cylinder blocks, one to machine heads, one to assemble the engine and an inwards/outwards goods area. All engine testing was completed during assembly. V8 and V12 engines were built concurrently and, as in the days of the Newport Pagnell V8, each engine was built by one technician.

airbag and seatbelt sensor development. Crash testing was conducted at Volvo's Safety Centre in Sweden. 'Volvo is renowned as the automotive safety leader,' said DB9 Chief Programme Engineer, David King. 'It was the perfect partner to assist in delivering the DB9's outstanding safety performance.'[20]

During the design of AM803 Ian Callum left Aston Martin to take up the post of Chief Designer at Jaguar. Henrik Fisker saw the model through to production. The DB9's styling drew on evolutionary DNA from both DB7 and Vanquish models. It was more modern than the DB7 and sleeker than the Vanquish and was praised for being one of the best-looking GTs in the world. A unique design feature was the 'swan wing' doors, which swung up and out at a 12-degree angle, making entry and exit easier.

An undertray reduced both lift and drag helping achieve an aerodynamically efficient body. 'A low Cd figure was not an absolute priority,' said Henrik Fisker of the DB9's 0.35 drag coefficient. 'The goal was superb styling with high-speed stability and great front-to-rear balance.' Volvo also assisted with the aerodynamics, providing Computational Fluid Dynamic equipment in its studios in Sweden.

The DB9 was stretched by 2 inches in length and 4.5 inches in the wheelbase from the DB7 though the rear seats remained small. The cabin featured aluminium on the door grab handles, dashboard and dials and Bridge of Weir leather upholstery available in 20 different colours. The racing seats were manufactured by Recaro and re-upholstered by Aston Martin. Wood, including walnut, mahogany and bamboo, was only used on the top of the centre console and, optionally, on the tops of the doors.

'We spent a lot of time considering how best to use wood,' said interior designer, Sarah Maynard. 'Wood is typically used as an appliqué with strips of highly polished veneer simply adding decoration to the car. We wanted the wood in the DB9 to look more structural. We also wanted to use large strips of wood, rather than little strips.'

The message centre, or 'organic electroluminescent display', on the dashboard was said to be easier to read than more traditional LCD screens. The dials replicated finely honed Swiss watches and featured an anti-clockwise-swinging tachometer, a feature not seen on an Aston Martin for many years. The entertainment system featured a Linn-designed stereo, especially developed for the DB9.

The engine was the third-generation V12 first seen in Project Vantage, but due to Aston Martin's constant development the new unit was quite different from the engine used in the DB7 Vantage. Aston Martin's Chief Powertrain Engineer Dr Brian Fitzsimons explained that the majority of the engine's significant parts were new, having a revised intake and exhaust system, manifolds, new crankshaft, new cams and upgraded engine management system.

The cast aluminium torque tube and carbon fibre propshaft connected the rear-mounted transmission and front-mid mounted engine, endowing the DB9 with a 50:50 weight distribution. The transmission was a ZF drive-by-wire six-speed automatic with Formula One-style paddles.

The DB9 was subjected to the most rigorous testing and development programme of any Aston Martin in the company's history. Ninety-three prototypes were proven in the deserts of the USA, frigid conditions of Sweden, crash test centres at Volvo, and racetracks at Nardo in Italy and Lommel in Belgium. The DB9 had exceptional performance with a top speed of 186 mph and a 0–60 mph time of only 4.7 seconds.

Some styling cues from the AMV8 Vantage concept car made their way onto the DB9 but the later production car was a true GT with 2+2 seating and a boot

To highlight the many advances made and to avoid
any misconceptions about eight-cylinder engines,
Aston Martin bypassed the DB8 title altogether.

Clockwise from above: Continuing the Gran Turismo concept established by the DB2, the DB9 featured luxury 2+2 accommodation in a stylish, high-performance coupe body; The DB9's sleek interior, the work of Sarah Maynard, was among the best ever; The DB9 was the first production car to feature Aston Martin's new VH architecture

DB9 Sports Pack

Aston Martin announced the optional Sports Pack for the DB9 (pictured below) from July 2006. The package featured new lighter five-spoke wheels and revised suspension. Suspension changes included revised spring rates, front anti-roll bar and dampers and the ride height was reduced by 6 mm (¼ inch). The composite undertray was also replaced by a load-bearing aluminium panel, further adding structural stiffness. The DB9 Sports Pack was available for new cars and could also be retro-fitted.

DB9
2003–

Chassis: Extruded aluminium bonded monocoque

Body: Aluminium and composite panelled 2+2 coupe styled by Henrik Fisker[ii]

Suspension: Front – Independent with aluminium double wishbones incorporating anti-dive geometry, monotube dampers and anti-roll bar
Rear – Independent with aluminium double wishbones, monotube dampers and anti-roll bar

Brakes: Servo-assisted 355 mm ventilated and grooved steel discs with four-piston callipers (front); 330 mm ventilated and grooved steel discs with four-piston callipers (rear). ABS, electronic braking distribution, traction control, electronic brake assist and dynamic stability control

Steering: Power-assisted rack and pinion

Wheels: 19-inch alloy

Tyres: Bridgestone Potenza REO50 235/40 ZR19 (front). 275/35 ZR19 (rear)

Transmission: Graziano six-speed manual transaxle; final drive 3.54:1
Touchtronic 2 shift-by-wire ZF six-speed automatic transaxle; final drive 3.15:1
Limited-slip differential. Rear-wheel drive

Engine: Mid-front mounted 5935 cc alloy V12 with twin chain-driven overhead camshafts per bank and four valves per cylinder. Compression ratio 10.3:1. Visteon twin PTEC engine management and fuel injection. Fully catalysed stainless steel exhaust system with active bypass valves

Power: 450 bhp/336 kW @ 6000 rpm
420 lb/ft/569 Nm of torque @ 5000 rpm

Top speed: 186 mph/299 km/h (manual)

Dimensions:
Length	15 ft 5 in/4710 mm
Width	6 ft 2 in/1875 mm
Height	4 ft 2.5 in/1270 mm
Wheelbase	9 ft/2740 mm
Weight	3770 lb/1710 kg (manual); 3968 lb/1800 kg (automatic)

Price when new: £103,000 (manual)[iii]

---

ii Design started by Ian Callum
iii £106,000 (automatic)

DB9 Volante

High-tech drop top

Aston Martin's newest convertible, the DB9 Volante, was unveiled at the Detroit Motor Show in January 2004, shortly after the DB9 coupe was launched. Once again, as with the AMV8 Vantage concept car, the DB9 Volante was shown well ahead of schedule. Production cars were not delivered to customers until the first half of 2005.

The DB9 Volante was conceived from the beginning as a convertible and was engineered with structual rigidity in mind. This, however, was one of the car's greatest criticisms. It retained the rear seats and boot space of the DB9, small though they were, making it a relatively practical convertible.

Safety-wise, the car boasted tilt sensors that detected potential rollover accidents, deploying twin hoops from the seat headrests to protect occupants. The A-pillars were said to be capable of withstanding more than twice the weight of the vehicle. This, coupled with the DB9's proven safety record, meant the DB9 Volante was an extremely safe open car.

Emphasising the Volante's thorough engineering, Dr Ulrich Bez stated upon its launch, 'We made no compromises when we designed the DB9 Volante. It features the same light, yet strong bonded aluminium body frame as the coupe, which gives the best possible levels of rigidity. This in turn ensures the same high levels of handling as enjoyed by the coupe.' The technical specification remained the same as the DB9 coupe.

> It was unveiled in January 2004, well ahead of schedule. Production cars were not delivered until the first half of 2005.

Featuring taut aluminium and composite panels, the DB9 Volante was designed by Henrik Fisker. The lack of a soft tonneau cover departed from Volante tradition. Instead, the folded roof fitted neatly into the body under a hard flush-fitting panel, giving the car a very elegant profile. It was one of Aston Martin's best-looking convertibles ever.

The DB9 Volante was a very handsome car but there were criticisms of its lack of rigidity

Below: Unlike most earlier Aston Martin convertibles, the DB9 Volante's hood stored neatly and out of sight under a hard cover

DB9 Volante
2004–

Chassis: Extruded aluminium bonded monocoque

Body: Aluminium and composite panelled 2+2 convertible styled by Henrik Fisker

Suspension: Front – Independent with aluminium double wishbones incorporating anti-dive geometry, monotube dampers and anti-roll bar
Rear – Independent with aluminium double wishbones, monotube dampers and anti-roll bar

Brakes: Servo-assisted 355 mm ventilated and grooved discs with four-piston callipers (front); 330 mm ventilated and grooved discs with four-piston callipers (rear). ABS, electronic braking distribution, traction control, electronic brake assist and dynamic stability control

Steering: Power-assisted rack and pinion

Wheels: 19-inch alloy

Tyres: Bridgestone Potenza REO50 235/40 ZR19 (front). 275/35 ZR19 (rear)

Transmission: Graziano six-speed manual transaxle; final drive 3.54:1
Touchtronic 2 ZF six-speed automatic transaxle; final drive 3.07:1
Limited-slip differential. Rear-wheel drive

Engine: Mid-front mounted 5935 cc alloy V12 with twin chain-driven overhead camshafts per bank and four valves per cylinder. Compression ratio 10.3:1. Visteon twin PTEC engine management and fuel injection systems. Fully catalysed stainless steel exhaust system with active bypass valves

Power: 450 bhp/336 kW @ 6000 rpm
420 lb/ft/569 Nm of torque @ 5000 rpm

Top speed: 186 mph/299 km/h (manual)

Dimensions:

Length	15 ft 5 in/4710 mm
Width	6 ft 2 in/1875 mm
Height	4 ft 5 in/1318 mm
Wheelbase	9 ft/2740 mm
Weight	3770 lb/1710 kg (manual)
	3968 lb/1800 kg (automatic)

Price when new: £112,000 (manual)[i]

Top to bottom: Scandinavian furniture design and high-quality audio equipment inspired the car's interior designer, Sarah Maynard; The V12's 450 bhp ensured 186-mph performance; The fully catalysed exhaust system came with an active bypass valve; At 6 ft 2 in wide, the DB9 Volante was wider than the original V8 models

i   £115,000 for Touchtronic 2 transmission

DB9 Volante – High technology drop top

Zagato Vanquish Roadster

Topless Italian

With the backing of Aston Martin, Zagato produced a roadster version of the Vanquish in September 2003 to 'provoke interest' in an Italian-styled Vanquish. It was designed in cooperation between Zagato's Automotive Chief Designer, Nori Harada and Aston Martin's Design Manager, Peter Huchinson.

The Vanquish Roadster made its debut on the Zagato stand at the Geneva Motor Show in March 2004. It certainly provoked interest; around 100 requests for the roadster were received at the show even though it wasn't promoted as a production car. Despite customer demand, no further examples were made.

The roadster, while being largely based on the production coupe, included some notable new design features. The Zagato model introduced a clever three-way modular roof system; a hard top for winter that virtually converted the roadster into a coupe, thermal glass (the show car used Plexiglas) for warm weather and a soft cover, which when not in use, could be stowed away.

Due to the use of glass at the rear, there was no room for the optional rear seats offered with the Vanquish. In their place was a luggage compartment. Because of the Vanquish's rigid platform, no additional strength-related structural engineering was said to be needed, so weight remained the same as the coupe.

For the first time Zagato did not design an entirely new look for the donor Aston Martin, but produced a variation offering some Italian flair. The metallic blue body remained much the same as the coupe, except at the rear, where a new round light cluster was employed in the higher and wider tapered tail and rear bumper. The inside of the car remained very much the same although the Zagato model featured a striking red interior with anodised metal surfaces.

The Zagato Roadster differed from the Italian carrozzeria's earlier Aston Martin designs; it wasn't a completely reclothed chassis – much of the bodywork remained standard

Around 100 requests for the roadster were received even though it wasn't promoted as a production car.

Top to bottom: A styling sketch demonstrating the replaceable hard-top roof; There was no folding convertible roof on the Zagato Roadster: the car came complete with a removable hard top, a clear glass roof and a detachable soft-top; Zagato's Vanquish Roadster was the rarest working Aston Martin model produced by the famed Italian company

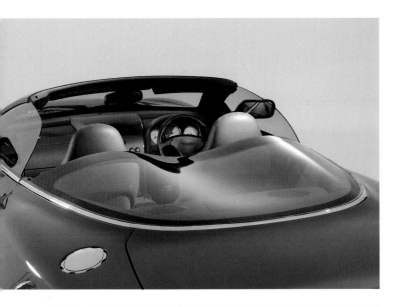

Top: The 'double bubble' rear was made from Plexiglas; customer versions were slated to be fashioned from thermal glass but the roadster did not enter production **Above:** Zagato introduced a completely new rear treatment on its roadster

NCE Convertible

Following in the footsteps of Radford and FLM Panelcraft, Newport Convertible Engineering (NCE) converted a Vanquish coupe into a stylish convertible for a customer in 2004 before Zagato's Roadster debuted. It was different from Zagato's design in that it utilised a traditional tonneau cover and all existing light fittings.

Aston Martin–Zagato Cars

Model	Year	Production
DB4 GT	1961–1963	19[i]
V8 Vantage	1986–1988	52
V8 Volante	1987–1989	37
Lagonda Rapide[ii]	1988	1
DB4 GT Sanction II	1991	4
DB4 GT Sanction III	2000	2
DB7	2002	100
DB AR1	2003	100
Vanquish Roadster	2004	1
Total		**314**

Zagato Vanquish Roadster
2004

Chassis: Extruded and bonded aluminium and carbon fibre platform and superstructure

Body: Aluminium and composite two-seat roadster styled by Ian Callum. Modified by Nori Harada of Carrozzeria Zagato

Suspension: Front – Independent with double aluminium wishbones, coil springs, monotube dampers and anti-roll bar Rear – Independent with double aluminium wishbones, coil springs, monotube dampers and anti-roll bar

Brakes: Servo-assisted 355 mm ventilated and cross-drilled discs with four-piston callipers (front); 330 mm ventilated discs with four-piston callipers (rear). ABS

Steering: Power-assisted rack and pinion

Wheels: 19-inch magnesium alloy

Tyres: Yokohama 255/40 ZR19 (front). 285/40 ZR19 (rear)

Transmission: Tremec six-speed manual with auto/select shift; final drive 3.69:1. Limited-slip differential. Rear-wheel drive

Engine: 5935 cc alloy V12 with twin chain-driven overhead camshafts per bank and four valves per cylinder. Compression ratio 10.5:1. Visteon twin PTEC engine management and fuel injection system. Fully catalysed exhaust system with active bypass valves

Power: 460 bhp/343 kW @ 6800 rpm 400 lb/ft/542 Nm of torque @ 5500 rpm

Top speed: 186 mph/299 km/h

Dimensions:
Length	15 ft 5.5 in/4685 mm
Width	6 ft /1923 mm
Height	3 ft 11.5 in/1265 mm
Wheelbase	8 ft 6.75 in/2690 mm
Weight	3969 lb/1835 kg

Price when new: Not available for sale

Number built: 1

---

i   One chassis number used twice

ii Styling exercise

Bertone Jet II

Bertone flies once more

In an unexpected renewal of Aston Martin's long-dormant association with the famous design house, the Bertone Jet II was unveiled at the Geneva Motor Show in March 2004. Back in 1960 the carrozzeria produced the DB4 GT Bertone Jet. Forty-four years later it designed a Shooting Brake based on a Vanquish platform. It too would remain unique.

'A custom-built vehicle in a made-to-measure suit by a great tailor,' was how Bertone described the Bertone Jet II. '… in modern terms [it is] linked to the traditional history of Italian coachbuilders which dressed the most enchanting engines of the time in "haute couture".'

While the Bertone Jet II was exhibited on the Bertone stand only, the project had the backing of Aston Martin. 'We always have to explore the limits of the brand and this Bertone Jet II is a very interesting concept,' said Dr Ulrich Bez. 'There are a number of ideas we could perhaps consider in the future. That's why Aston Martin supported this.'

'The choice of the Aston Martin brand really responds to two motivations,' said Lilli Bertone, Chairman of the Bertone Group. 'The first is linked to history; since 1953 Aston Martins have always stimulated and inspired Bertone's creativity, resulting in one-off vehicles of particular design merit and expressive strength. The second motivation derives from an emotive factor: an exercise in design and engineering is much more stimulating and demanding if a sports "pedigree" such as the Aston Martin Vanquish is in the leading role.'

Bertone's design retained the Vanquish windscreen, door rings and basic structure, but the car was lengthened by 8 inches to create a distinctive four-seat Shooting Brake body. Every body panel was altered.

According to Bertone, 'The point of difference for the styling definition was the search of a Bertone identity with respect to the classic Aston Martin features. The car body, originating from sinuous lines and tight geometrical features, is a synthesis of the two brand identities.'

The car's exterior styling was the responsibility of Design Director, Giuliano Biasio, overseen by Managing Director, Roberto Piatti. The concept was initiated in June 2003 and in July of that year a 1:1 scale model was shown to Aston Martin executives and the project was given approval to proceed.

Bertone's Jet II Shooting Brake body reinvented the Vanquish's styling themes to dramatic effect

Ideas from the concept appeared in the Aston Martin Rapide, including the panoramic roof, wooden-backed, folding seats and aluminium-ribbed wooden load area.

Bertone

Giovanni Bertone founded Carrozzeria Bertone in Turin in 1912. Initially making caravans, Bertone moved on to constructing motor car bodies after WWI and later became one of Italy's most evocative and respected design houses. Bertone has produced memorable body designs for many of the world's great car companies, most notably for Lamborghini, Iso, Lancia, Ferrari and Alfa Romeo.

Bertone Jet

During production of the DB4 GTs, chassis number DB4GT/0201/L was provided with unique bodywork designed by Giorgetto Giugiaro when he was working for Carrozzeria Bertone in Milan. The steel-panelled car was shown at the Geneva and Turin Motor Shows in 1961. The association between Giorgetto Giugiaro and Aston Martin was renewed 40 years later when the 20/20 Concept Car was unveiled at the 2001 Geneva Motor Show.

Other Bertone Aston Martins

Inspired by a visit to the Turin Motor Show in 1952, where he saw two Bertone-bodied MGs, Chicago-based British car importer Stanley Harold 'Wacky' Arnolt ordered Bertone-bodied designs on a run of eight Aston Martin DB2/4 Mk II chassis. Each unique and exquisite in their own way, the Bertone Aston Martins were the intended subject of a large batch of special cars for Arnolt's business. After eight chassis, however, Aston Martin stopped supply and the Bertone-Aston Martin collaboration was abandoned.

The Bertone Jet II was painted a light silver sage green and featured a subtle reworking of the frontal aspect including the air intakes and grille. It also had a stylised bonnet and side air intakes and unique Bertone headlamps.

'In the front part the classic Aston Martin grille remains,' said Bertone, 'with additional air ducts to cool the disc brakes. The flush cover headlights propose an evolved graphic with respect to the original model.'

The windscreen glazing was extended with Plexiglas to cover almost the entire roof, which incorporated T-bar bracing for strength. 'The idea of movement is resumed by a large transparent roof,' said Bertone, 'which emphasises the dynamism and the impetus of the vehicle.'

Perhaps the most striking view of the car was from the rear, where Biasio integrated the Aston Martin grille outline into the rear window and light clusters. Also at the rear, new exhausts and outlets were incorporated into the rear bumper. The finished design was customised by the addition of Bertone badging and sill plates.

Bertone Jet II was a working prototype driven by several journalists, but was never fully road tested with measured performance figures. All the running gear was tried and tested but not everything in the concept car was fully functioning including the tailgate, which could not be opened.

The cabin was the work of Interior Design Manager David Wilkie, the man responsible for the Lagonda Vignale's Art Deco interior. The cabin incorporated different trim and materials from the Vanquish and apart from basic items such as the Vanquish-sourced steering wheel, was thoroughly reworked.

A Vanquish dashboard, with a specially made instrument cluster was used, but the centre console was sourced from the DB9, as were the sage green and magenta leather seats. Most of the switchgear was unique to this car, as was the aircraft-type cabin lighting in the T-bar roof.

The cabin made extensive use of opaque, satin-finished pear-wood and satinised aluminium trim, clearly inspired by Italian motorboats of the 1950s and 1960s. It had a wooden rear floor and rear seat backs, which could fold down flush with the floor, turning the rear of the vehicle into a vast load-bearing area.

The Bertone Jet II gave valuable positive exposure to both companies, but although Aston Martin publicly praised the vehicle, there was obviously no thought of producing a limited run of these cars. Like the earlier Bertone Jet, the US$1.8-million concept car remained unique. Ideas from the concept, however, did appear in the Aston Martin Rapide, including the panoramic roof, wooden-backed, folding seats and aluminium-ribbed wooden load area.

Top: Bertone completely reinterpreted the Vanquish interior and added nautical themes such as wooden floors, a feature that would be seen later in the Aston Martin Rapide **Top right:** Much of the Bertone Jet II's roof was glazed, another theme used by Aston Martin at a later date **Middle:** Satinised wood and aluminium recalled the famous Riva boats of the 1950s **Above:** The rear window and taillights created an Aston Martin grille shape; the concept car's tailgate was not operational

Bertone Jet II
2004

Chassis: Extruded and bonded aluminium and carbon fibre platform and superstructure

Body: Aluminium and composite 2+2 Shooting Brake styled by Giuliano Biasio of Stile Bertone

Suspension: Front – Independent with double aluminium wishbones, coil springs, monotube dampers and anti-roll bar Rear – Independent with double aluminium wishbones, coil springs, monotube dampers and anti-roll bar

Brakes: Servo-assisted 355 mm ventilated and cross-drilled discs with four-piston callipers (front); 330 mm ventilated discs with four-piston callipers (rear). ABS

Steering: Power-assisted rack and pinion

Wheels: 19-inch magnesium alloy

Tyres: Yokohama 255/40 ZR19 (front). 285/40 ZR19 (rear)

Transmission: Tremec six-speed manual with auto/select shift; final drive 3.69:1. Limited-slip differential. Rear-wheel drive

Engine: 5935 cc alloy V12 with twin chain-driven overhead camshafts per bank and four valves per cylinder. Compression ratio 10.5:1. Visteon twin PTEC engine management and fuel injection system. Fully catalysed stainless steel exhaust system with active bypass valves

Power: 460 bhp/343 kW @ 6800 rpm
400 lb/ft/542 Nm of torque @ 5500 rpm

Top speed: 186 mph/299 km/h

Dimensions:

Length	15 ft 4 in/4675 mm
Width	6 ft/1930 mm
Height	4 ft 4 in/1330 mm
Wheelbase	8 ft 6.75 in/2900 mm
Weight	4000 lb/1835 kg

Price when new: Not available for sale

Number built: 1

Vanquish S
Back at the top

With the DB9 universally acclaimed upon its launch, Aston Martin found itself with a small problem. At over 50 percent more expensive and with only a 10 bhp and slight speed advantage, the Vanquish, on paper at least, looked overpriced. A Vanquish Vantage was needed to address the balance.

Development for an upgraded model began shortly after the first Vanquish customer cars were delivered in mid-2001. A one-off 500-plus horsepower Vanquish was developed in 2002 for an Aston Martin executive and was in regular use, providing valuable feedback to its engineers.

The Sports Dynamic Pack transformed the accomplished GT into a more potent car by improving handling and braking, but it stopped short of offering the ultimate in performance. It was, however, a developmental step along the way to the production Vanquish Vantage.

While, in name at least, a Vantage model never arrived, Aston Martin released the Vanquish S instead; Vanquish Vantage considered too much of a mouthful.

The Vanquish S was first shown in September 2004 at the Paris Motor Show. The first production model was sold soon afterwards. 'This derivative makes the car more special,' said Dr Ulrich Bez at the car's launch. 'It is the fastest and best handling car we have produced, the ultimate high-performance Aston Martin.'

Flagged as the 'Ultimate Aston Martin', the Vanquish S, with a 520 bhp engine and top speed in excess of 200 mph, put Aston Martin once again near the top of the supercar league. The Vanquish S was a substantially redeveloped new car incorporating suspension, mechanical and aesthetic enhancements that completely transformed the vehicle.

The engine had new cylinder head castings with fully machined inlet ports and combustion chambers to improve airflow, while new fuel injectors and revised engine mapping increased power to 520 bhp @ 7000 rpm and torque to 425 lb/ft @ 5800 rpm. A specially developed transmission and new differential ratio of 4.3:1 improved acceleration with the 0–60 mph sprint achieved in 4.8 seconds. The Vanquish S was tested at 205 mph at the Nardo test track in Italy.

Opposite: Subtle details such as the front splitter distinguished the Vanquish S from its earlier iteration, but it was a much better performer

Aston Martin ironically created a small problem for itself. At over 50 percent more expensive and with only a 10 bhp and slight speed advantage, the Vanquish, on paper at least, looked overpriced.

The performance of the Vanquish S was impressive: top speed was more than 200 mph

Other changes included Sports Dynamic suspension, new quick-ratio steering rack, larger front disc brakes with six-piston callipers and race-derived brake pads, plus brake pedal improvements to reduce travel.

Subtle styling changes were also made to distinguish the 'S' model from the standard Vanquish and to improve overall performance including new lightweight 11-spoke alloy wheels, re-worked grille (which grew out of development work on Middle East-bound Vanquishes) and a new aerodynamic front splitter designed to improve high-speed grip. At the rear a new aero profile boot lid was added to reduce lift. This helped to produce a handsome variant with an impressive Cd of 0.32 with improved high-speed balance and stability. Inside, a DB9-sourced glass starter button and leather-covered console were incorporated.

Although officially still available, the standard Vanquish was virtually superseded by the similarly priced Vanquish S and went out of production shortly after the higher-performance model was released.

Vanquish S Ultimate Edition

With the Vanquish S no longer able to be sold in the US market, production of Aston Martin's flagship model was no longer viable. In February 2007 Aston Martin announced the last of the Vanquish variants with a special limited run of 50 Vanquish S Ultimate Edition models.

Each car was painted in Ultimate Black, a new colour unique to this model. The interior, which was only available in 2+2 seating configuration, was finished in semi-aniline leather with special coarse stitching and featured a leather headlining and black chrome-finish interior highlights. Further, each car was fitted with personalised sill plaques bearing the owner's name and the limited edition number of the car. The enhancements came at no extra charge to the Vanquish S' £182,095 (2007) price.

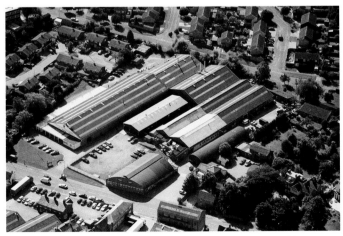

The demise of the Vanquish S brought production to an end at Newport Pagnell; until the acquisition in 2001 of the Gaydon manufacturing facility, Aston Martin's home since 1955

Vanquish S
2004–2007

Chassis: Extruded and bonded aluminium and carbon fibre platform and superstructure

Body: Aluminium and composite two or 2+2 seat coupe styled by Ian Callum

Suspension: Front – Independent with double aluminium wishbones, coil springs, monotube dampers and anti-roll bar Rear – Independent with double aluminium wishbones, coil springs, monotube dampers and anti-roll bar

Brakes: Servo-assisted 378 mm grooved and ventilated discs with six-piston callipers (front); 330 mm grooved and ventilated discs with four-piston callipers (rear). ABS

Steering: Power-assisted rack and pinion

Wheels: 19-inch forged alloy

Tyres: Yokohama 255/40 ZR19 (front). 285/40 ZR19 (rear)

Transmission: Six-speed manual with auto/select shift; final drive 4.30:1. Limited-slip differential. Rear-wheel drive

Engine: 5935 cc alloy V12 with twin chain-driven overhead camshafts per bank and four valves per cylinder. Compression ratio 10.8:1. Visteon twin PTEC engine management and fuel injection system. Fully catalysed stainless steel exhaust system with active bypass valves

Power: 520 bhp/388 kW @ 7000 rpm
425 lb/ft/576 Nm of torque @ 5800 rpm

Top speed: 200-plus mph/322-plus km/h

Dimensions:
Length	15 ft 4 in/4665 mm
Width	6 ft/1923 mm
Height	4 ft 4 in/1318 mm
Wheelbase	8 ft 6.75 in/2690 mm
Weight	3969 lb/1835 kg

Price when new: £174,500

Number built: 1289

DBR9

Returning to the track

Rumours of Aston Martin's return to racing as a Works team began in February 2002 when Jeremy Main was appointed Director of Product Development and Motor Sport. On arriving at the company he conducted a motorsport feasibility study and upon analysis it was agreed to establish a separate motorsport division in partnership with Prodrive.

Aston Martin Racing was later formed as a separate wholly-owned division responsible for overseeing the development, design and construction of the DB9-based racing cars and the organisation of Aston Martin's sports car racing.

Prodrive Head, David Richards said before the launch, 'Aston Martin and Prodrive have created a new venture: Aston Martin Racing. At Aston Martin Racing we'll take care of all racing activity for Aston Martin in the next five years. The first venture in this is to build the DB9 race car. It's a joint thing we have been talking to Aston Martin about for many years.

'Prodrive's position historically has always been to be at the top level of World Championship activities in Formula One and the World Rally Championship. In sports cars, which I believe should be the third leg of World Championship motor racing, we will have Aston Martin Racing.'

Worldwide interest in sports car racing was rising by this time and new regulations from the Automobile Club de l'Ouest were drafted allowing for production-based cars to compete on equal terms.

By July 2004 a photo-etched image of the proposed DB9 race car and initial information became available. In a sentimental, but not unpredictable move, the new car was named DBR9.

The title was a nod in the direction of the famed DBR sports and Formula One cars of the 1950s and early 1960s, which spanned DBR1 to DBR5. There was no DBR6, 7 or 8, but much like the skip from DB7 to DB9, the DBR9 was a leap into the future and the perfect name for Aston Martin's new generation of racing cars.

The DBR9 was built within GT1 (formerly GTS) regulations as specified by the FIA. It used a DB9-based bonded aluminium platform, bespoke double wishbone suspension with Koni dampers and Eibach springs, OZ Racing forged magnesium alloy wheels with slick Michelin tyres and lightweight 330 mm carbon disc brakes front and rear with Brembo six-piston callipers.

Styled using Computational Fluid Dynamics to optimise aerodynamic efficiency, the body followed the profile of the DB9 from the wheel hubs upwards, but was both shorter and wider. Unlike the road car, its panels were carbon fibre composite, while the roof, one of the few parts actually borrowed from the DB9, was aluminium. The body was fitted with a full high-strength roll cage, large carbon fibre rear wing and flat underbody.

The cockpit, as stipulated by the rules, retained the dimensions of the road car and featured a carbon composite dashboard and lightweight racing seat. The car weighed only 2425 lb, providing a power-to-weight ratio of 550 bhp per ton.

The DBR9's V12 engine was based on the DB9 aluminium block and cylinder heads but was modified to produce 600-plus bhp, rev limited to 8000 rpm. It had a dry sump, double overhead camshafts, four valves per cylinder and two 31.2 mm air restrictors. Like the DB9, the competition X-trac six-speed gearbox was mounted at the rear axle.

Following the example of the DB3S, it was planned to build 12 Works cars (chassis numbers 01–12) and 20 customer cars (chassis numbers 101–120) for private racers and collectors. Customer cars were said to cost £475,000, while a Works franchise was reputed to have cost £2,750,000 over three years.

The DBR9 was officially unveiled to the press on 4 November 2004 at Gaydon. Finished in Aston Racing Green with a yellow nose cone, it sported the number 59 in recognition of Aston Martin's 1959 Le Mans victory. At the unveiling Dr Bez stated that motorsport would create heightened awareness for Aston Martin around the world. 'The DBR9 is the first step in our return to motorsport,' he said. 'I know that our customers and enthusiasts alike are looking forward to seeing Aston Martin racing again at an international level.'

David Richards added, 'I personally believe that sports car racing is the purest form of motor racing. Not the prototype racing we have seen in recent years but based upon production sports cars, the dream cars like Aston Martin. We have already seen new entrants like Maserati and Lamborghini coming in and we could well see even more coming to a possible World Series.'

The day after the launch, Darren Turner tested the DBR9 at Snetterton. Fellow test drivers Tomas Enge and David Brabham were also engaged during the end-of-year testing programme at both Snetterton and Donington circuits in order to develop the cars in preparation for their debut in March 2005.

Two Aston Martin Works teams were established to compete in the GT1 category in the 2005 international sports car racing season, including the American Le Mans series and FIA GT championship. Both teams, with three drivers apiece, were run independently with the full support of the Works.

Aston Martin's return to Le Mans in 2005 was warmly greeted but a class victory eluded the team

299

Both DBR9s taking on fuel at Sebring during practice

On 31 January, the two three-member driving teams met during testing at Sebring in preparation for the year's first event; the Sebring 12 Hours. The driver line up was announced in February 2005 and included the international team of David Brabham, Tomas Enge, Pedro Lamy, Stephane Ortelli, Peter Kox and Darren Turner. French Rally Champion, Stephane Sarrazin, joined the team soon after for the first race.

The opening of the American Le Mans Series (ALMS), the Sebring 12 Hour race on 19 March, saw the debut of the DBR9. Wet weather hampered a full practice schedule, but DBR9/02 (58), driven by Kox, Lamy and Sarrazin qualified fourth in class. DBR9/01 (57), piloted by Brabham, Turner and Ortelli came in fifth, only 0.2 seconds adrift.

In its first competitive event Aston Martin Racing claimed GT1 class victory when Brabham took the chequered flag in 57. It was a superb and unexpected result and the team was clearly elated with the win against such established competition.

Aston Martin Racing's next race was at the RAC Tourist Trophy on 15 April at Silverstone, the scene of Aston Martin victories in 1958 and 1959. Aston Martin Racing dominated from the start with Kox and Lamy in DBR9/02 (29) on pole and Brabham and Turner driving DBR9/01 (28) close behind. The two cars finished in that order with a Corvette C6-R in third place; Aston Martin once again winning the Tourist Trophy.

Great anticipation greeted the Aston Martin team on its return to Le Mans in June and expectations were high when DBR9/01 (59) with Brabham, Turner and Sarrazin qualified first in class with Enge, Kox and Lamy in DBR9/02 (58) claiming second place ahead of the Corvette Racing C6-Rs. The two cars were extremely competitive, leading the GT1 class at certain stages, swapping the lead periodically with the Corvettes.

But with one-and-a-half hours remaining, 59 entered the pits with radiator problems, and 58 stopped on the track: out of fuel. To enable a finishing result, Frenchman Stephane Sarrazin was sent back out in 59 with ten minutes remaining to claim a third-in-class result behind the two Corvette C6-Rs.

Spa, the scene of an Aston Martin triumph in 1957, was contested in wet conditions on 31 July 2005. DBR9/02 (29), piloted by Kox, Lamy and local driver Marc Goosens, who was brought in to replace Tomas Enge, qualified in third place.

Sister car DBR9/01 (28), driven by Brabham, Sarrazin and Turner, was seventh on the grid. The race was not a good one for the two teams with 29 finishing in fifth place and 28 one place behind. But both cars proved their reliability by finishing the gruelling 24-hour endurance event.

During practice for Petit Le Mans in Georgia at the end of September, new driver, Northern Irishman Jonny Kane, crashed DBR9/01 (57), damaging the car. The team worked furiously to repair it in time for the race; Kane, Brabham and Turner qualified in third position. The DBR9/02 (58) of Lamy, Enge and Kox qualified one place behind.

During the race car 58 lost time due to a lengthy pitstop for a drive-shaft replacement, and lost 19 laps. Later, the same car suffered minor damage after a collision with the Audi of JJ Lehto, finishing in 11th place overall and fifth in class. Car 57 fared better finishing in fourth place and second in class slotting in between a Corvette C6-R and one place ahead of ACEMO Motorsport's Saleen S7-R.

At Laguna Seca two weeks later, the DBR9/02 (58) of Kox and Lamy qualified fourth in class. DBR9/01 (57), with Turner and Brabham at the wheel, this time was fifth on the grid. At one stage Lamy, in 58, was leading but after a stop-and-go penalty and a puncture, finished ninth overall and third in GT1 class. Turner and Brabham in car 57 experienced handling problems, finishing one place behind their team mates in tenth place and fourth in class with the two Corvette Racing C6-Rs once again taking the first two places in GT1.

The season started better than it finished but for a development year, 2005 was a remarkable success.

Aston Martin Racing concentrated on the American Le Mans Series in 2006, allowing private teams Aston Martin Racing BMS, Cirtek, Labre Competition, Team Modena, Phoenix Racing and RaceAlliance, running DBR9s, to compete in the FIA GT and Le Mans Series Championship. The private DBRS9s of Autosport Designs Racing, Barwell Motorsport and BMS Scuderia Italia S.p.A. competed in the GT3 championship and SCCA Speed World GT events.

Aston Martin Racing's first race of 2006 was on 18 March at Sebring, the scene of its memorable class victory the year before. Pedro Lamy put DBR9/02 (009) on pole with DBR9/03

Jeremy Main

Jeremy Main was appointed Director of Product Development and Motorsport at Aston Martin in February 2002. Recruited from Ford UK, where he had worked since joining as an apprentice in 1971, he was given responsibility for future product development and engineering as well as the technical direction of the company.

During his tenure with Ford, Main managed Special Vehicle Engineering and was Chief Process Engineer in the USA. Later he became Chief Engineer on the Ford Fiesta and B Car programmes in the UK.

At Aston Martin he was commissioned to do a feasibility study into returning to Factory racing and was responsible for overseeing the formation of Aston Martin Racing in 2003. Main left Aston Martin in May 2006 to pursue private interests.

The Sebring 12-hour race was the site for Aston Martin's return to World Sports Car racing in March 2005; the team won first time out

DBR9 57, piloted by Brabham, Turner and Ortelli, raced faultlessly during the night to clinch victory from the highly fancied Corvette Racing team at the 2005 Sebring 12-Hour race

(007) one place behind in GT1 class, so victory was once again in the equation. But AMR could not repeat its triumph in the American classic.

In hot conditions and with new Pirelli tyres, Jason Bright, Pedro Lamy and Stephane Sarrazin achieved a second in class placing for 009, 1 minute 28 seconds behind the winning Corvette C6-R. Darren Turner, Tomas Enge and Nicolas Kiesa came home in third position; Enge completing a double stint at the end of the race to edge out the second Corvette.

AMR scored a further podium finish at the Lone Star Grand Prix on 12 May in Houston. Enge and Turner, after running as high as second in class, brought DBR9/03 (007) home in fourth place overall and third in class in the 2- hour, 45-minute event. Sarrazin and Lamy had a difficult race in DBR9/02 (009) when Sarrazin spun and, after the safety car was deployed, found himself one lap down. Low on fuel, 009 was forced to pit, but the crew was not allowed to refuel the car until the pits were declared open. Sarrazin and Lamy finished fifth overall and fourth in class.

The following week, on 21 May at American Le Mans in Mid Ohio Tomas Enge, driving DBR9/03 (007), claimed pole position with third-placed Pedro Lamy in DBR9/02 (009) splitting the second- and fourth-placed Corvette Racing C6-Rs. However, a puncture and a number of untimely safety car periods meant the best AMR could secure was a third place for Enge and Turner in 007. Sarrazin and Lamy in 009 finished close behind the sister car in fourth position.

Hoping to avenge its disappointing outing at Le Mans in 2005, Aston Martin Racing once again fielded a two-car team for the French classic. It begun well with Tomas Enge in DBR9/03 (007) claiming class pole position but on lap four the BMS Scuderia Italia DBR9, in the hands of Fabio Babini, spun on some oil and crashed badly. The safety car was deployed and Turner was called into the pits where his car suffered a cracked oil pipe. The pit crew worked for six laps to cure the problem but 007 never fully recovered. But Turner, Enge and Andrea Piccini battled back from 48th place to secure a second placing in GT1 class and sixth overall.

The DBR9's cockpit shared the basic dimensions of the road car but little else

Qualifying in second position, DBR9/02 (009), driven by Lamy, Sarrazin and Ortelli ran a strong race. Leading for a good deal of the enduro, a class victory looked promising. But like the previous year AMR was robbed of triumph within sight of the finish line. With three hours remaining, Ortelli was experiencing gear selection problems and, losing time to the second-placed Corvette, entered the pits for a 45-minute clutch replacement. After the lengthy pitstop the car ran faultlessly to cross the finish line fifth in class and tenth overall. Corvette Racing repeated its 2005 victory with car 64 finishing first with 355 laps.

On 1 July AMR achieved its first victory since the Tourist Trophy at Silverstone in April 2005 at the New England Grand Prix. Despite five changes of leadership in GT1 class, Pedro Lamy in DBR9/02 (009) claimed victory by the narrow margin of 0.033 seconds, defeating the Corvette Racing C6-R in the 2-hour-45-minute race. After qualifying in first place, and twice leading the race, Turner and Enge in DBR9/03 (007) finished in third position.

Aston Martin Racing claimed its second class victory in a fortnight in the ALMS at Salt Lake City on 15 July. In very hot temperatures, Turner and Enge, driving DBR9/03 (007), were victorious despite an alternator problem, cured during the car's final pit stop. Andrea Piccini and Pedro Lamy in DBR9/02 (009) finished in second position after a close battle with the Corvette Racing C6-R (4).

The title was a nod in the direction of the famed DBR cars, which spanned DBR1 to DBR5.

The DBR9 name was a direct nod to Aston Martin's sporting past; DBR was last used on the DBR4 (pictured) and DBR5 Grand Prix cars

Car 59 claimed third place in the GT1 class at Le Mans 2005

Top: A 'customer' version of the DBR9 was unveiled at Le Mans in 2005 (this is chassis DBR9/101)

Above: DBR9 007 passes under the famous Dunlop bridge late in the 2006 Le Mans 24 Hours; after a troubled race, the car driven by Darren Turner, Tomas Enge and Andrea Piccini finished second in GT1 class and sixth overall

With Enge nursing a broken hand following a bicycle accident, Andrea Piccini was on standby to replace the Czech if required at Portland International Raceway on 22 July. He was not needed, as Enge and Turner drove a very strong race, bringing DBR9/03 (007) home in second position. The DBR9/02 (009) of Sarrazin and Lamy suffered a puncture and was given a one-minute stop-and-go penalty for a pit stop infringement, relegating it to fourth position.

At Road America on 20 August, AMR was once again denied victory when Turner/Enge and Sarrazin/Lamy achieved a further third and fourth in class after another promising start. Sarrazin, driving DBR9/02 (009), collided with the number 2 Audi and spun into the gravel trap, requiring a tow. After pit stops Turner, in DBR9/03 (007), was in first position with Sarrazin and Lamy three laps behind. Both cars later suffered punctures, putting them out of contention for a class victory.

On 3 September AMR returned for the eighth round of the ALMS at the Grand Prix of Mosport at Mosport International Raceway in Canada. In wet conditions during qualifying AMR was positioned on the front row of the GT1 grid after the final 20-minute qualifying session was cancelled and grid positions calculated on the combined times of the previous two practice sessions. Stephane Sarrazin recorded the fastest time, putting DBR9/02 (009) on pole with Tomas Enge close behind in second position.

Pedro Lamy in 009 led away from the start but Peter Kox in 007 had a spin when hit by one of the Corvette C6-Rs, leaving him well down the field. While Lamy maintained his lead, Kox worked his way through the field to be in second position. After a pit stop and driver change Sarrazin found himself behind the leading Corvette but with 20 minutes remaining the Frenchman reclaimed the lead after a bold overtaking manoeuvre. He remained in front until the finish of the race with Enge bringing home 007 in third position, one lap behind 009.

The penultimate round of the ALMS championship, Petit Le Mans at Road Atlanta, was held on 30 September. Pedro Lamy qualified DBR9/02 (009) in third position in GT1 class with a lap of 1:18.547; Darren Turner driving DBR9/03 (007) was close behind in fourth place.

Aston Martin Racing achieved first and second placing in the 1000-mile race, which was interrupted by seven safety car periods. Lamy and Stephane Sarrazin led for much of the race but a late puncture and pit stop meant 009 was caught behind the safety car, which was deployed after an incident with a LMP1 car. Number 007, shared by Turner and Tomas Enge, inherited the class lead, which they held until the end, beating the second-placed sister DBR9 by one lap.

The final round of the ALMS, the Monterey Sports Car Championships, was held at Mazda Raceway, Laguna Seca in California on 21 October. Stephane Sarrazin put DBR9/02 (009) on pole in GT1 Class with a time of 1:21.012 seconds, while Tomas Enge qualified DBR9/03 (007) in fourth position after electrical problems precluded a full qualifying session.

Pedro Lamy led the race from the beginning in 009 while Darren Turner raced up to second position by the end of the first lap. Lamy and Turner later handed over the cars to Sarrazin and Enge but at the three-hour mark of the four-hour race, 007 suffered yet another puncture while leading the race. After pitting, Enge rejoined the contest in fourth position, which is where he finished the race.

Sarrazin in 007 inherited the lead but was overtaken 30 minutes before the finish by the 4 Corvette C6-R driven by Olivier Beretta. But he regained the lead shortly afterwards finishing victorious. Aston Martin Racing finished the 2006 season in second position in both the Teams' and Manufacturers' Championships behind Corvette Racing.

For 2007, Aston Martin Racing concentrated solely on a Le Mans GT1 class victory, entering two DBR9s in the 24-Hour race that year. In a rain-interrupted event DBR9/10 (009) finally gave Aston Martin Racing their GT1 class win, with David Brabham steering home 009 under the safety car in treacherous conditions. Car 007 finished fourth. All four Works-supported customer team-entered DBR9s were also classified finishers.

Prodrive

Based in Banbury Oxfordshire, Prodrive was formed by David Richards (pictured) and Ian Parry in 1984 and has grown to become a world leader in motorsport and automotive technology employing around 900 staff in Europe, North America, Asia and Australia. It held a unique position, having been involved in three major world wide racing series simultaneously: Formula One, World Rally Championship and Sports Car racing.

Prodrive had tremendous success in GT racing with its Ferrari 550 GTS Maranello throughout 2001 and 2002 and in 2003 achieved overall first and second positions in the FIA GT Championships. It also won three driver's and three manufacturer's titles in the World Rally Championships with Subaru and five British Touring Car Championships with BMW, Ford and Alfa Romeo. Prodrive was also involved in running the BAR Honda Formula One team before joining F1 in its own right in 2008.

While Prodrive was not involved, David Richards independently became a major shareholder in Aston Martin when a consortium purchased the company in 2007. Richards then became a non-Executive Chairman of Aston Martin.

David Brabham driving DBR9/10 to a GT1 Class victory late in the 2007 24 Hours of Le Mans

DBR9
2004–2006

Chassis: Extruded aluminium bonded monocoque (modified DB9)

Body: Carbon fibre composite and aluminium coupe incorporating steel roll cage styled by Aston Martin Racing

Suspension: Front – Independent with aluminium double wishbones, adjustable Koni dampers and Eibach springs
Rear – Independent with aluminium double wishbones, adjustable Koni dampers and Eibach springs

Brakes: Servo-assisted 330 mm carbon discs with Brembo six-piston callipers (front and rear)

Steering: Power-assisted rack and pinion

Wheels: 19-inch OZ Racing forged magnesium

Tyres: Michelin 235/40 ZR19 (front). 275/35 ZR19 (rear)

Transmission: X-trac six-speed sequential transaxle. Limited-slip differential. Rear-wheel drive

Engine: Mid-front mounted 5935 cc alloy V12 with twin chain-driven overhead camshafts per bank and four valves per cylinder. Two 31.2 mm air restrictors. Visteon twin PTEC engine management and fuel injection systems. Pi Data system. Pectel engine ECU

Power: 600 bhp/447 kW @ 7000 rpm
516 lb/ft/700 Nm of torque @ 5000 rpm

Top speed: 200-plus mph/322-plus km/h (approx)

Dimensions:

Length	15 ft 7 in/4767 mm (including rear wing)
Width	6 ft 5.5 in/1978 mm
Height	4 ft 4.5 in/1318 mm
Wheelbase	9 ft/2740 mm
Weight	2425 lb/1100 kg

Price when new: N/A (customer cars approx £475,000)

Number built: 19 (10 Factory cars/9 Customer cars)

V8 Vantage

Return of the two-seater sports car

The production version of the AMV8 Vantage concept car was publicly unveiled on 1 March 2005 at the Geneva Motor Show. It was the culmination of Aston Martin's five-year plan and completed the company's new three-tier line up, which included the Vanquish S, DB9 and DB9 Volante. Like the DB9 range, the V8 Vantage was produced at Aston Martin's new factory in Gaydon, while the 4.3-litre V8 engine was assembled at the new engine facility in Cologne, Germany.

The V8 Vantage took Aston Martin into unchartered territory and up against new rivals, most notably the famed Porsche 911. With a younger customer in mind, it was the most affordable model in the line up and took Aston Martin into unprecedented production numbers. Around 3000 cars were slated for production per year; by far the most of any Aston Martin in its long history.

While the 4.3-litre V8 engine was unique to this car, it had its origins with the Jaguar 4.2-litre V8 used in the XKR. Most of its internal parts, however, were unique to Aston Martin, including the bore and stroke. 'We share expertise within the PAG organisation but this design is totally new and not a shared engine,' declared Jeremy Main. 'Every significant part of it is unique, from the specification of the cylinder block, to the cylinder heads, crankshaft, connecting rods, pistons, camshafts, inlet and exhaust manifolds, lubrication system and engine management. The V8 engine is unique to Aston Martin.'

The engine was located behind the front axle and as low under the bonnet as possible. Coupled with a rear-mounted manual (a Sportshift 'paddle' system was announced in late 2006) transaxle gearbox, this provided a near perfect 49:51 weight distribution for ultimate balance and handling. The new car was endowed with high performance, too, if not in the same league as the heady figures quoted for the concept car. Aston Martin claimed a top speed of 175 mph and 0–60 mph in 4.9 seconds.

The production car was Aston Martin's second built on the VH architecture of aluminium extrusions, castings and pressings. The body was made of composite, aluminium and steel panels glued to the supporting frame, much the same as the DB9. The use of high-technology materials and processes meant the car weighed just 3461 lb; the lightest Aston Martin production car for some time, but still heavier than the Porsche 911.

While lacking some of the DB9's elegance, the V8 Vantage was fiercely styled

V8 Vantage by Prodrive

In late 2006 Prodrive announced a range of performance options available for the V8 Vantage, including engine, suspension and aerodynamic improvements.

Prodrive engineers tuned the 4.3-litre V8 engine to increase power from 380 bhp to 425 bhp and torque from 302 lb/ft to 325 lb/ft. This increased the car's top speed from 175 mph to 182 mph and reduced the V8 Vantage's 0–62 mph time from 5.0 seconds to 4.7 seconds. Also included in the engine package was a modified exhaust system which allowed drivers to manually override the exhaust valve.

Prodrive, in collaboration with Bilstein and Eibach, also developed an adjustable suspension package. A switch allowed the driver to dial-up normal or sports mode, which firmed the suspension for more responsive handling. A new set of unique forged wheels, based on the DBR9's design, was also available.

A discreet aero package, consisting of carbon composite front lip and boot spoilers, was also offered, and was said to reduce lift by 45 percent, improving the coupe's grip and high speed stability.

Prodrive's V8 Vantage options became available in early 2007 and were available only for road-registered vehicles.

Clockwise from top: Dashboard dials were modelled on high-quality stereo equipment; A standard six-speed manual gearbox was originally the only transmission option, but a 'Sportshift' paddle system was introduced at the Paris Motor Show in September 2006; Both 18- and 19-inch lightweight alloy wheels were optionally available; Aston Martin's latest two-seat sports car was more than worthy of the badge;

With a 380 bhp V8 engine, the lightest Aston Martin for many years could sprint to 60 mph in only 4.9 seconds

The V8 Vantage took Aston Martin into unchartered territory and up against new rivals, most notably the famed Porsche 911.

Clockwise from top left: The understated two-seat cabin carried over interior themes premiered in the DB9; The 4.3-litre V8 engine had Jaguar roots, but its many unique parts, including the cylinder heads and crankshaft, meant Aston Martin claimed it as their own; The V8 Vantage remained faithful to the AMV8 Vantage concept car previewed two years earlier; While they shared the same name, the two V8 Vantage generations were completely different cars

Suspension was by independent double aluminium wishbones, coil over aluminium monotube dampers and anti-roll bars front and rear. Two wheel options were available: 18-inch and 19-inch spoke aluminium alloy, shod in Z-rated Bridgestone Potenza tyres.

It differed in minor details, but remained faithful to the AMV8 Vantage concept car unveiled in January 2003. It was said that 94 percent of the concept car remained but the production version had different front and rear lights and door handles and a reworked interior. Its origins were the work of Ian Callum, but the production version had input from Henrik Fisker.

The interior carried on in the vein of the DB9 with bespoke switchgear and instrumentation. 'We wanted to continue to evolve the interior design we started with the DB9,' said interior designer, Sarah Maynard. 'The V8 Vantage has all of those attributes and like the DB9 everything you can touch and see within the cabin area is special to Aston Martin.'

Aston Martin's unusual step of announcing its intentions to build the V8 Vantage more than two years ahead of release gave engineers and designers ample testing and development time on the production version. Seventy-eight prototypes were built and tested over 1.5 million miles in Dubai and Sweden, while high-speed testing was conducted at the Nürburgring circuit in Germany and the Nardo test track in Italy.

The name, already used in the 1970s, remained controversial and confusing. 'We decided to call it the V8 Vantage,' said Dr Ulrich Bez, 'so as not to lose an important Aston Martin name. In the past, Vantage has denoted a higher performance derivative, but this was no longer going to be possible ... We wanted to keep the name, and we felt it fitted perfectly with the character of the new V8.'[21]

V8 Vantage
2005–

Chassis: Extruded aluminium bonded monocoque

Body: Aluminium, steel, composite and magnesium alloy two-seat hatchback coupe styled by Henrik Fisker

Suspension: Front – Independent with double aluminium wishbones, coil-over aluminium monotube dampers and anti-roll bar
Rear – Independent with double aluminium wishbones, coil-over aluminium monotube dampers and anti-roll bar

Brakes: Servo-assisted 355 mm ventilated and grooved steel discs with Brembo four-piston callipers (front); 330 mm ventilated steel discs with four-piston callipers (rear). Separate handbrake calliper. ABS, EBD, TC, EBA, PTC and DSC

Steering: Power-assisted rack and pinion

Wheels: 18-inch or 19-inch alloy

Tyres: Bridgestone Potenza 235/45 ZR18 (front). 275/40 ZR18 (rear)[i]

Transmission: Six-speed Graziano manual or Sportshift transaxle; final drive 3.909:1. Limited-slip differential. Rear-wheel drive

Engine: Front mid-mounted 4281 cc alloy V8 with twin chain-driven overhead camshafts per bank and four valves per cylinder. Fully catalysed stainless steel exhaust system

Power: 380 bhp/283 kW @ 7300 rpm
302 lb/ft/409 Nm of torque @ 5000 rpm

Top speed: 175 mph/282 km/h

Dimensions:
Length	14 ft 3.5 in/4382 mm
Width	6 ft 1.5 in/1866 mm (excluding mirrors)
Height	4 ft 1.5 in/1255 mm
Wheelbase	8 ft 5.5 in/2600 mm
Weight	3461 lb/1570 kg

Price when new: £79,995

i Optional 19-inch alloy wheels were fitted with 235/40 ZR19 (front), 275/35 ZR19 (rear) Bridgestone Potenza tyres

D B R S 9
Customer satisfaction

Aston Martin Racing released details of the DBRS9 in mid-2005 and unveiled the model at that year's Le Mans 24-Hour Race in June. The racing arm had already committed itself to constructing customer versions of the successful DBR9 back at the car's launch in late 2004, but it was felt a 'bridging' car for developing drivers and teams would also be successful.

Built purely for track use, the DBRS9 followed the styling of the DBR9. However, the body was less overtly aggressive, following more closely the smoother lines of the road car. It was based on the DB9's aluminium platform and contained a DBR9 roll cage. It also featured removable carbon composite body panels and polycarbonate side and rear windows, Brembo ceramic brakes, X-trac six-speed manual gearbox (with the option of a sequential unit) and competition-tuned suspension with two-way adjustable Koni dampers and stiffer springs. The interior featured an adjustable steering wheel and competition racing seat. The option of a second passenger seat was also available.

Developed for GT and club racing to GT3 American Le Mans Series (ALMS) and FIA international regulations, the DBRS9 featured many of the developments employed in the customer DBR9s except it had a detuned V12 engine developing 550 bhp @ 7000 rpm and 457 lb/ft of torque @ 5000 rpm. It was 375 lb heavier too, with a power-to-weight ratio of 430 bhp per ton meaning that performance was not in the same league; but neither was the price. Claimed performance was a top speed approaching 200 mph, 0–60 mph in less than 4.0 seconds and 0–100 mph in less than 9.0 seconds.

Deliveries began in December 1995 and the DBRS9's first competitive tests were conducted at Paul Richard circuit in France on 3 December. Works driver Darren Turner completed much of the development test driving. The DBRS9's competition debut was at the Speed GT World Challenge at Sebring on 18 March 2006.

The DBRS9 was used by privateers across the globe; this example competed in the Australian GT Championship

Developed to GT3 international regulations,
the DBRS9 featured many of the developments
used in the customer DBR9s.

Clockwise from top left: Special lightweight magnesium OZ Racing wheels were specified; Carbon fibre was used on items such as the door and interior trims; For a race car the DBRS9 was nicely, if sparsely, trimmed; Many of the features of the more expensive DBR9s were incorporated into the DBRS9, which was intended for GT3 FIA racing; Powerful brakes came as standard, but this example had AP Racing callipers instead of Brembo units; The DBRS9 was first unveiled at the 2005 Le Mans 24-Hour race but it never raced there

DBRS9
2005–

Chassis: Extruded aluminium bonded monocoque (modified DBR9)

Body: Carbon fibre composite and aluminium coupe incorporating steel roll cage styled by Aston Martin Racing

Suspension: Front – Independent with aluminium double wishbones, adjustable Koni dampers and Eibach springs
Rear – Independent with aluminium double wishbones, adjustable Koni dampers and Eibach springs

Brakes: Servo-assisted 330 mm carbon discs with Brembo six-piston callipers (front and rear)

Steering: Power-assisted rack and pinion

Wheels: 19-inch OZ Racing forged magnesium

Tyres: Michelin 235/40 ZR19 (front). 275/35 ZR19 (rear)

Transmission: X-trac six-speed manual transaxle. Optional sequential gearbox also offered. Limited-slip differential. Rear-wheel drive

Engine: Mid-front mounted 5935 cc alloy V12 with twin chain-driven overhead camshafts per bank and four valves per cylinder. Two 31.2 mm air restrictors. Visteon twin PTEC engine management and fuel injection systems. Pi Data system. Pectel engine ECU

Power: 550 bhp/410 kW @ 7000 rpm
457 lb/ft/620 Nm of torque @ 5000 rpm

Top speed: 195 mph/314 km/h (est)

Dimensions:
Length	15 ft 4 in/4687 mm (including rear wing)
Width	6 ft 5.5 in/1979 mm
Height	4 ft 4.5 in/1318 mm
Wheelbase	9 ft/2740 mm
Weight	2822 lb/1280 kg

Price when new: £190,000 (approx)

Number built: 26

Aston Martin Rapide Concept

Four-door sports car

Aston Martin has always been a sports car company. Two-door cars have been its forte but over the years several attempts have been made to incorporate four-door saloons into the range. Post-war, they have mainly been badged as Lagondas. For a time during the 1970s and 1980s the Lagonda sold well but customer demand had never been strong enough to sustain a continuous line of four-door saloons in the Aston Martin range.

Aston Martin eliminated Lagonda from its trading name in 2001 and it looked for a time that a four-door car would not be seen again. So it came as a genuine surprise when the Aston Martin Rapide Concept was launched in early 2006.

The Rapide Concept grew out of the thought that the DB9 didn't offer realistic seating for four adults and a long-wheelbase version would give Aston Martin greater market penetration. A long-wheelbase two-door DB9 was investigated, but once the extension had been made and room created it was decided to include rear doors to provide the necessary access. 'If there's a space,' explained Dr Ulrich Bez, 'then you should also offer accessibility, otherwise you're not being honest.'

As with all Aston Martin's Gaydon-produced vehicles, the Rapide Concept was built upon the extruded aluminium VH architecture. Using a tested and proven platform meant Aston Martin could quickly develop a different range of cars, in different sizes, that all met safety requirements. Proving the versatility of this platform, the long-wheelbase four-door 'coupe' gave Aston Martin a greater range of cars spanning two, 2+2 and a more realistic four seater.

In line with post-war tradition, consideration was given to calling the four-door car a Lagonda. But that strategy had never worked particularly well before and this time it was thought better to call the car what it really was: a four-door Aston Martin, the first since the Special Series Vantages of the mid-1990s. The Rapide name came straight from the Lagonda history book. Discounting the Zagato Lagonda Rapide styling exercise, it was last used for a four-door DB4-based saloon produced between 1961 and 1964. Only 55 were made.

The remarkable aspect of the Rapide Concept's design was how well proportioned it was. In order to retain the scale of the DB9, all dimensions of the Rapide were altered. It was 11.5 inches longer in wheelbase, 1.5 inches taller, 1.5 inches wider

The Rapide Concept took Aston Martin back into four-door territory for the first time since the Special Series Vantage Type II

Aston Martin dropped Lagonda from its trading name in 2001 and it looked for a time that a four-door car would not be seen again.

The Rapide's passenger accommodation and luggage space were the best in the Aston Martin line-up

Marek Reichman

Born in Sheffield, England, Marek Reichman studied Industrial Design at Teesdale University and Vehicle Design at the Royal College of Art in London. After graduating in 1991 he began working at Land Rover. When BMW took control of that company he moved to BMW's Designworks studio in the USA.

In 1998 he established a design studio in London. He then worked as part of the Rolls-Royce team designing the Phantom before moving on to Ford Motor Company in 1999 as Chief Designer of Lincoln and other Ford brands, later becoming Director of Design for Product, Interior Design Strategy and Process.

At the request of Dr Ulrich Bez, Reichman became Design Director at Aston Martin in May 2005, succeeding Henrik Fisker. The Rapide Concept was his first design work for Aston Martin.

and 15 inches longer overall. It still retained sports car looks however, being much lower than many of its competitors.

It was built in four months by a team of 26 people led by General Manager of Prototype operations Ian Calnan and Marek Reichman. Bez gave Reichman the brief in May 2005 when awarded the post at Aston Martin. Before arriving at the company he studied Aston Martin's DNA and had already made preliminary sketches for the four-door concept. Reichman completed the design within seven weeks in August 2005 working with a team of clay modellers.

The car was obviously built upon the DB9's make up: the roofline remained low and sleek and all four 'swan wing' doors opened up and out at a 12-degree angle to assist access. The carbon fibre-panelled rear was much altered however, with different seats, floor and fuel tank arrangements. From the back, the Rapide was reminiscent of the V8 Vantage, containing a vast hatchback and generous load area. The roof featured a panoramic transparent polycarbonate section with dial-up transition from clear to opaque, like the Bertone Jet II.

Passenger comfort was improved, providing greater head and legroom over the DB9. Rear passengers were supplied with DVD screens and separate controls for the sound and climate systems. Similar in basic architecture to the DB9, the Rapide Concept's interior contained a number of unique touches including a mobile phone recharger, bespoke switch gear, Jaeger-LeCoultre clock and a champagne chiller below the rear compartment floor.

Apart from the DB9 fascia, most of the Rapide Concept's trim was unique. The show car's cabin was trimmed in light-toned leather, with contrasting exotic sharkskin. There was no carpet, leather being used to trim the floor. Satinised wood and aluminium were used as highlights and also in the load area at the rear.

The running gear was DB9-sourced, including the 5.9-litre V12 engine, but to compensate for the Rapide's extra 309 lb, power was increased by 30 bhp to 480 bhp and the ZF Touchtronic transmission adjusted to suit the more refined role of the four-seater. Performance was claimed to be in the realms of the DB9 meaning a 180-plus mph speed and a 0–60 mph sprint time of around 5.0 seconds.

A first for Aston Martin was the introduction of carbon ceramic disc brakes on all four wheels. New lighting supplied by LED systems, new-design wing mirrors, an altered grille, aluminium fuel filler cap and new 20-inch polished alloy wheels were also featured on the show car. Suspension was DB9-based but adjusted to take into consideration the car's new dimensions and weight.

The Rapide was built to offer an alternative to sporting, luxurious four-door carriages like the Maserati Quattroporte and Porsche Panamera. It was a new niche for Aston Martin, ensuring its presence in this growing market segment.

The fully functioning prototype was completed by the deadline of 22 December and unveiled at the Detroit Motor Show on 9 January 2006. At the time of the launch Aston Martin claimed the car was only a concept to gauge possible customer interest and that no firm production timetable had been developed.

Clockwise from top left: With four doors and an upward-lifting tailgate, the Rapide Concept was a very practical high-performance motor car; While recognisably DB9-based, the Rapide's interior featured bespoke switchgear; The Rapide Concept featured trimmings such as a chessboard and champagne set; Satellite navigation and rear DVD screens were part of the technologically advanced concept car's specification

Aston Martin Rapide Concept
2006

Chassis: Extruded aluminium bonded monocoque

Body: Aluminium and composite four-door coupe with polycarbonate roof styled by Marek Reichman

Suspension: Front – Independent with aluminium double wishbones incorporating anti-dive geometry, monotube dampers and anti-roll bar
Rear – Independent with aluminium double wishbones, monotube dampers and anti-roll bar

Brakes: Servo-assisted 355 mm ceramic discs (front); 330 mm ceramic discs (rear). ABS, electronic braking distribution, traction control, electronic brake assist and dynamic stability control

Steering: Power-assisted rack and pinion

Wheels: 20-inch alloy

Tyres: Bridgestone Potenza REO50 235/40 ZR20 (front). 275/35 ZR20 (rear)

Transmission: ZF Touchtronic shift-by-wire six-speed automatic transaxle; final drive 3.15:1. Limited-slip differential. Rear-wheel drive

Engine: Mid-front mounted 5935 cc alloy V12 with twin chain-driven overhead camshafts per bank and four valves per cylinder. Compression ratio 10.3:1. Visteon twin PTEC engine management and fuel injection. Fully catalysed stainless steel exhaust system with active bypass valves

Power: 480 bhp/358 kW @ 6000 rpm
420 lb/ft/569 Nm of torque @ 5000 rpm

Top speed: 186 mph/299 km/h (approx)

Dimensions:
Length	16 ft 8 in/4997 mm
Width	6 ft 4.5 in/1915 mm
Height	4 ft 6 in/1358 mm
Wheelbase	9 ft 11.5 in/2990 mm
Weight	4079 lb/1850 kg

Price when new: N/A

Number built: 1

V8 Volante Shooting Brake

Shooting star

Having a world-wide reputation for building Shooting Brakes, Roos Engineering was approached by a Russian businessman in 2002 with a request to convert a V8 Volante, chassis number SCFDAM2CCWBL89034, into the most radical Shooting Brake yet.

Once the commission was accepted, Beat Roos approached Englishman Andrew McGeachy to sketch various design proposals that were then shown to the client. When the owner agreed to the design, McGeachy made further detailed sketches and technical engineering drawings were created.

'We started working on this project in 2002,' said Beat Roos. 'The car took [four years to complete] because it was our first project where we changed almost everything you can change on a car. It had a completely new interior and the bodywork included [new] front, rear and even side panels on the car. Everyone who knows the base of this Shooting Brake, the LWB V8 Volante, will see all the changed details and the time we spent on this vehicle.'

After the conversion, little of the original car remained: virtually every panel had been altered, the wheels were changed to 20-inch alloy Mille Miglia multi-spoke items and the interior was almost entirely new. Mechanically the car remained largely unchanged from the donor V8 Volante.

The V8 engine was left unmodified but the standard Chrysler Torqueflite four-speed automatic transmission was replaced by a specially prepared five-speed ZF gearbox. The car also featured a Works Prepared Driving Dynamics option including uprated suspension and bigger front brakes.

The V8 Volante Shooting Brake was painted Rolls-Royce Royal Blue and the new interior trimmed in terracotta alcantara with Bordeaux piping. The interior was completely changed from the original with only the front seats remaining, but retrimmed in all-new leather.

Starting life as a V8 Volante, almost every panel was altered by Roos Engineering in Switzerland to create its third Shooting Brake

'The car took four years to complete because it was our first project where we changed almost everything you can change on a car.'

Beat Roos

Clockwise from top: Mille Miglia 20-inch alloy wheels were yet another change in the car's specification; V8 Volante, Lagonda, Vantage, Virage, DBS, DB6 and DB5 Shooting Brakes reunited; Roos Engineering used traditional aluminium coachbuilding techniques to create the Shooting Brake body; Andrew McGeachy's design sketches were shown to the customer for approval before the car was constructed in aluminium; Vantage-style taillights were stacked vertically either side of the tailgate

It featured a complex, redesigned dashboard, interior panels, rear seats and luggage compartment. The rear seats were moved backwards to offer extra leg room and space for passengers and allowed the owner to transport skis inside the car.

The interior proved a considerable challenge for the Swiss specialists. 'The design of the interior was planned from day to day because of the difficulties that appeared after every step,' Roos said.

The Shooting Brake body was finished during 2005 but a redesign of the interior at the customer's request delayed completion of the car until mid-2006. The project took four years and 10,000 hours of labour to complete.

V8 Volante Shooting Brake
2006

Chassis: Steel box-section chassis, steel superstructure

Body: Aluminium 2+2 convertible styled by John Heffernan, restyled Shooting Brake designed by Andrew McGeachy and converted by Roos Engineering

Suspension: Front – Independent with transverse unequal length wishbones, coil springs, coaxial spring dampers and anti-roll bar
Rear – de Dion axle, radius arms, transverse Watt's linkage, coil springs and coaxial spring dampers

Brakes: Servo-assisted 362 mm ventilated discs with AP Racing four-piston callipers (front); 286 mm ventilated discs with aluminium sliding callipers (rear). ABS

Steering: Power-assisted rack and pinion

Wheels: 20-inch Mille Miglia alloy

Tyres: Pirelli P-Zero Rosso 275/40 R20

Transmission: ZF five-speed automatic; final drive 3.06:1. Limited-slip differential. Rear-wheel drive

Engine: 5340 cc alloy V8 with twin chain-driven overhead camshafts per bank and four valves per cylinder. Compression ratio 9.75:1. EEC IV engine management system. Fully catalysed exhaust system

Power: 350 bhp/261 kW @ 6000 rpm
368 lb/ft/499 Nm of torque @ 4300 rpm

Top speed: 150 mph/241 km/h

Dimensions:
Length	16 ft/4945 mm
Width	6 ft 2.5 in/1918 mm (excluding wing mirrors)
Height	4 ft 6.5 in/1380 mm
Wheelbase	9 ft 2 in/2610 mm
Weight	4500 lb/2050 kg

Price when new: N/A

Number built: 1

D B S
Movie star

News of a new Aston Martin model, initially thought to be made especially for the movie *Casino Royale*, was announced in late 2005, accompanied by a provocative white on black styling sketch by Aston Martin's Design Director Marek Reichman. In reality it predated the movie deal. The first photographs of the car were released on 4 May 2006, preempting spy shots.

The DBS, a title first used by Aston Martin in 1966 for the two-seat motor show prototypes by Touring of Milan, was designed by Reichman and produced in secrecy at Aston Martin's headquarters in Gaydon by a small team under his direction.

The DBS shared the same VH architecture as the DB9; its aluminium roof, bonnet and rear wings, along with its composite front wings and boot, were all bonded to the extruded aluminium monocoque frame. While clearly based on the DB9, the DBS contained elements of the purpose-built DBR9 racing derivative including twin bonnet air vents, a gaping air intake below the grille, bootlid spoiler, carbon fibre splitter and powerful-looking sculpted sills.

The engine was reputed to develop in the region of 500 bhp and featured a Graziano six-speed manual gearbox. Like the Rapide, the DBS specification included new ceramic disc brakes and 20-inch chrome 10-spoke alloy wheels. The DBS also contained stiffer springs and possessed a lower ride height than the DB9.

The interior was DB9-based but contained many unique touches including alcantara quilted seats, alcantara-lined instrument binnacle, carbon fibre steering wheel and unique switch gear on the centre panel. Where the DBS differed completely from the DB9 was that it contained only two seats, the rear being used for additional storage.

'This car encapsulates the link between our elegant DB9 road car and the powerful DBR9 race car. It signals an evolutionary development of Aston Martin's world-renowned style and elegance,' commented Reichman upon the DBS's launch. 'While hinting at our future direction, the DBS also has very clear links with our heritage.'

The DBS made its screen debut in *Casino Royale* on 14 November 2006 and while Aston Martin initially made no announcements as to possible manufacture, it did enter production with the first deliveries taking place in 2007.

The DBS' DB9-based body was styled by newly arrived Design Director Marek Reichman

While clearly based on the DB9, the DBS contained elements
of the purpose-built DBR9 racing derivative.

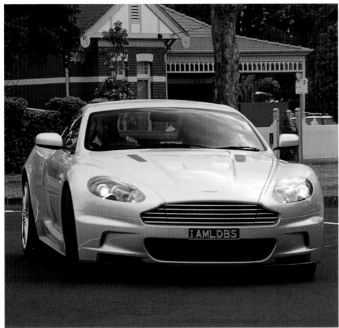

Clockwise from far left: The rear spoiler helped rear-end grip; A more aggressive body was not an improvement over DB9's clean lines; The interior could only accommodate two occupants; 5.9-litre V12 boasted 500 bhp; Top speed was quoted as 186 mph

DBS
2006–

Chassis: Extruded aluminium bonded monocoque

Body: Aluminium and composite panelled two-seat coupe styled by Marek Reichman

Suspension: Front – Independent with aluminium double wishbones incorporating anti-dive geometry, monotube dampers and anti-roll bar
Rear – Independent with aluminium double wishbones, monotube dampers and anti-roll bar

Brakes: Servo-assisted 355 mm ceramic discs (front); 330 mm ceramic discs (rear). ABS, electronic braking distribution, traction control, electronic brake assist and dynamic stability control

Steering: Power-assisted rack and pinion

Wheels: 20-inch alloy

Tyres: Bridgestone Potenza REO50 235/40 ZR20 (front). 275/35 ZR20 (rear)

Transmission: Graziano six-speed manual transaxle; final drive 3.54:1. Limited-slip differential. Rear-wheel drive

Engine: Mid-front mounted 5935 cc alloy V12 with twin chain-driven overhead camshafts per bank and four valves per cylinder. Compression ratio 10.3:1. Visteon twin PTEC engine management and fuel injection. Fully catalysed stainless steel exhaust system with active bypass valves

Power: 500 bhp/373 kW @ 6000 rpm
420 lb/ft/569 Nm of torque @ 5000 rpm (approx)

Top speed: 186 mph/299 km/h (manual)

Dimensions:
Length	15 ft 4.5 in/4697 mm
Width	6 ft 2 in/1875 mm
Height	4 ft 2.5 in/1270 mm
Wheelbase	9 ft/2740 mm
Weight	3770 lb/1710 kg (approx)

Price when new: N/A

V8 Vantage N24
Road racer

During the same 17–18 June weekend as the 2006 Le Mans 24-Hour race, Aston Martin entered a V8 Vantage in the ADAC Nürburgring 24-Hours in Germany. Driven by Aston Martin's Chairman and CEO Dr Ulrich Bez, Vehicle Engineering Manager Chris Porritt, editor-in-chief of *Sport Auto* magazine Horst von Saurma and development driver Wolfgang Schuhbauer, the Aston Martin team achieved 24th place (fourth in class) from a field of 220, of which only 141 finished. At the completion of the race Porritt drove the road-legal car back to Aston Martin's headquarters in Gaydon.

Aston Martin announced later at the British International Motor Show on 18 July 2006 that it would produce a small number of Nürburgring V8 Vantage replicas, aimed at amateur racing drivers. In deference to its race debut, the new car was called V8 Vantage N24.

At the completion of the race Chris Porritt drove the road-legal car back to Aston Martin's headquarters in Gaydon.

The N24 in action at the 2006 ADAC Nürburgring 24-Hours where it finished fourth in class

Built at Aston Martin's Gaydon factory, the V8 Vantage N24 was largely production standard. Modifications from the stock V8 Vantage included the fitting of an FIA roll-cage, larger 105-litre bag-fuel tank with interior fuel pump reset and battery master switch, Recaro racing seats, built-in air jack, lightweight 18-inch magnesium Speedline wheels with 250/650 18 (front) and 280/650 18 (rear) Yokohama slick racing tyres and an altered differential ratio of 3.54:1.

Sound-deadening material and door trims were removed as were all air conditioning, electric window, airbag and central locking systems. In the interests of weight saving, all windows, except the front windscreen, were made from polycarbonate, the standard battery was replaced by a smaller item and the leather trim was replaced by lighter alcantara that reduced the car's dry weight to 2932 lb.

The front grille featured only four horizontal slats to aid cooling and while the suspension, with front and rear independent double aluminium wishbones, coil-over aluminium monotube dampers and anti-roll bars, was largely standard, stiffer springs and anti-roll bars were incorporated to improve handling.

The first N24's V8 engine and gearbox were said to be completely stock but 'production' versions featured a lighter, balanced crankshaft, conrods and pistons, reprofiled cylinder head and recalibrated engine management system with free-flow exhaust system. The result was a 30 bhp increase for the V8 engine to 410 bhp @ 7500 rpm. Available only with a six-speed manual gearbox, the N24 also featured a Valeo twin-plate ceramic clutch and lightweight flywheel. The N24's top speed was limited to 175 mph, the same as the standard road car, while the 0–60 mph sprint was trimmed to a claimed 4.3 seconds.

Production of the V8 Vantage N24 began in December 2006 in time for the 2007 race season at a price starting at £82,800, depending on the exact specification.

Top right: Production began in late 2006 with the first customer cars available in early 2007 Above: Aston Martin's CEO, Dr Ulrich Bez, was one of the drivers at the car's debut in Germany

V8 Vantage N24
2006–2008

Chassis: Extruded aluminium bonded monocoque

Body: Aluminium, steel, composite and magnesium alloy two-seat hatchback coupe with roll-cage styled by Henrik Fisker

Suspension: Front – Independent with double aluminium wishbones, coil-over aluminium monotube dampers and anti-roll bar
Rear – Independent with double aluminium wishbones, coil-over aluminium monotube dampers and anti-roll bar

Brakes: Servo-assisted 355 mm ventilated and grooved steel discs with Brembo four-piston callipers (front); 330 mm ventilated steel discs with four-piston callipers (rear). Separate handbrake calliper. ABS, EBD, TC, EBA, PTC and DSC

Steering: Power-assisted rack and pinion

Wheels: 18-inch Speedline magnesium

Tyres: Yokohama A048 250/650 18 (front), 280/650 18 (rear) racing slick

Transmission: Six-speed Graziano manual; final drive 3.54:1. Limited-slip differential. Rear-wheel drive

Engine: Front mid-mounted 4281 cc alloy V8 with twin chain-driven overhead camshafts per bank and four valves per cylinder. Fully catalysed stainless steel exhaust system

Power: 410 bhp/306 kW @ 7500 rpm
302 lb/ft/409 Nm of torque @ 5000 rpm

Top speed: 175 mph/282 km/h

Dimensions:

Length	14 ft 3.5 in/4382 mm
Width	6 ft 1.5 in/1866 mm (excluding mirrors)
Height	4 ft 1.5 in/1255 mm
Wheelbase	8 ft 5.5 in/2600 mm
Weight	2932 lb/1330 kg (dry)

Price when new: From £82,800

Number built: 53

Aston Martin Rally GT

Street machine

Aston Martin had enjoyed a deserved reputation as a successful challenger in sports car racing over several decades. Less celebrated were the company's minor achievements in Formula One and rally competition.

Works Aston Martin teams had participated in rally contests in the mid-1950s with drivers such as Reg Parnell, Peter Collins and Maurice Gatsonides piloting DB2/4s entered in the famous Monte Carlo Rally, RAC British Rally and Mille Miglia events. Private teams had also competed in numerous rallies before and since.

But for 50 years Aston Martin had officially been absent from the world of rallying, until 2006 with the announcement of a new V8-engined rally competitor developed by Prodrive. The British company responsible for the running of Aston Martin Racing's successful DBR9 sports cars had extensive experience in the World Rally Championship, winning six World Rally titles with the Subaru team.

Aston Martin Racing DBR9 driver Stephane Sarrazin performed some of the test driving duties and competed in several French Rally Championship events in the new car.

In late September 2006, Aston Martin Racing announced what it called 'the world's most exclusive rally car' – the new Aston Martin Rally GT. Based on the V8 Vantage, but extensively re-engineered, it boasted a tuned 4.3-litre V8 engine; fitted with a competition exhaust it was said to produce 420 bhp and 302 lb/ft of torque. A six-speed V8 Vantage-sourced transaxle with an AP Racing centre-plate clutch and limited-slip differential was fitted as standard but a specially developed close-ratio six-speed dog box could be optionally installed.

The Rally GT used a standard V8 Vantage platform but was fitted with an integral Prodrive-developed roll cage and featured modified suspension including Eibach springs and three-way adjustable EXE-TC dampers, 355 mm (front) and 330 mm (rear) disc brakes and 18-inch (front) and 19-inch (rear) alloy wheels.

Aston Martin Racing driver Stephane Sarrazin testing the Rally GT in France

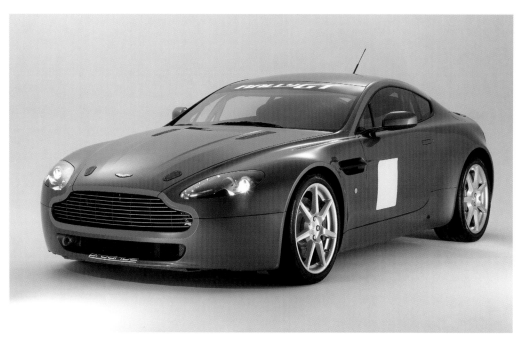

Clockwise from top: The Rally GT was fitted with a tuned 420 bhp V8 engine and competition exhaust; Prodrive's extensive experience in the World Rally Championship was used to develop the Rally GT; A roll cage and modified suspension more suited to the demands of rally competition were standard equipment

Aston Martin Racing DBR9 driver Stephane Sarrazin performed some of the test driving duties and competed in several French Rally Championship events in the new car, coming second on debut in the Lyon to Charbonniers Rally with co-driver Stephane Prevot in April 2006.

Constructed at Prodrive's Banbury factory, the Aston Martin Rally GT was made available to private teams from later that same year at approximately £145,000–150,000 depending on specification.

Aston Martin Rally GT
2006

Chassis: Extruded aluminium bonded monocoque

Body: Aluminium, steel, composite and magnesium alloy two-seat hatchback coupe with roll-cage styled by Henrik Fisker

Suspension: Front – Independent with double aluminium wishbones, three-way adjustable EXE-TC dampers, Eibach springs and anti-roll bar
Rear – Independent with double aluminium wishbones, three-way adjustable EXE-TC dampers, Eibach springs and anti-roll bar

Brakes: Servo-assisted 355 mm ventilated and grooved steel discs with Brembo four-piston callipers (front); 330 mm ventilated steel discs with four-piston callipers (rear). Hydraulic handbrake.

Steering: Power-assisted rack and pinion

Wheels: 18-inch (front); 19-inch (rear) alloy

Tyres: Bridgestone Potenza 235/45 ZR18 (front). 275/40 ZR19 (rear)

Transmission: Six-speed Graziano manual or Sportshift transaxle; final drive 3.909:1. Limited-slip differential. Rear-wheel drive

Engine: Front mid-mounted 4281 cc alloy V8 with twin chain-driven overhead camshafts per bank and four valves per cylinder. Competition stainless steel exhaust system

Power: 420 bhp/328 kW @ 7300 rpm
302 lb/ft/409 Nm of torque @ 5000 rpm

Top speed: 175 mph/282 km/h

Dimensions:
Length	14 ft 3.5 in/4382 mm
Width	6 ft 1.5 in/1866 mm (excluding mirrors)
Height	4 ft 1.5 in/1255 mm
Wheelbase	8 ft 5.5 in/2600 mm
Weight	2976 lb/1350 kg (approx)

Price when new: £145,000–150,000 (depending on specification)

Number built: 4

V8 Vantage Roadster

Road burner

Aston Martin's V8 Vantage Roadster was unveiled on 29 November 2006 at the Los Angeles Auto Show, with the first customer deliveries taking place in mid-2007. The new convertible V8 Vantage was a handsome motorcar endowed with high performance and a claimed top speed of 175 mph and 0–60 mph in 4.9 seconds despite a 239 lb weight increase over the coupe version.

Like the two-seat DB AR1, the open-top V8 Vantage was labelled a Roadster; Aston Martin retained the traditional Volante name for its four-seat convertible models. The fully lined hood (which can be raised or lowered in 18 seconds, while driving at speeds of up to 30 mph), with glass rear window followed the set-up of the DB9 Volante: a flush-fitting panel completely concealed the fabric hood, which allowed for a neat rear line with maximum rearward vision.

The cabin followed the modern lines of the V8 Vantage coupe, with optional timber inserts, Bridge-of-Weir leather seats and trim and full carpeting. The leather trim was extended at the rear of the cabin with twin pods, reminiscent of Zagato's DB AR1.

> Like the two-seat DB AR1 the new open-top V8 Vantage was labelled a Roadster; Aston Martin retained the traditional Volante name for its four-seat convertible models.

Built on Aston Martin's VH architecture, the Roadster was suspended by independent double aluminium wishbones, coil-over aluminium monotube dampers and anti-roll bars front and rear. Considerable engineering went into ensuring the open car had coupe-like stiffness after criticism of the DB9 Volante. It had 18-inch aluminium alloy wheels shod in Z-rated Bridgestone Potenza tyres, with 19-inch wheels available as an option.

The new Roadster shared the same running gear as the V8 Vantage coupe, including its 380 bhp 4.3-litre V8 engine and was equipped with either the six-speed Graziano manual gearbox or the newly available 'Sportshift' six-speed automated manual paddle-shift transmission.

The V8 Vantage Roadster debuted at the Los Angeles Auto Show in late 2006; production cars became available in mid-2007

Above: Despite increased weight, the V8 Vantage Roadster had a top speed of 175 mph

V8 Vantage Roadster
2006–2008

Chassis: Extruded aluminium bonded monocoque

Body: Aluminium, steel, composite and magnesium alloy two-seat roadster styled by Henrik Fisker

Suspension: Front – Independent with double aluminium wishbones, coil-over aluminium monotube dampers and anti-roll bar
Rear – Independent with double aluminium wishbones, coil-over aluminium monotube dampers and anti-roll bar

Brakes: Servo-assisted 355 mm ventilated and grooved steel discs with Brembo four-piston callipers (front); 330 mm ventilated steel discs with four-piston callipers (rear). Separate handbrake calliper. ABS, EBD, TC, EBA, PTC and DSC

Steering: Power-assisted rack and pinion

Wheels: 18-inch alloyⁱ

Tyres: Bridgestone Potenza 235/45 ZR18 (front). 275/40 ZR18 (rear)

Transmission: Six-speed Graziano manual or Sportshift transaxle; final drive 3.909:1. Limited-slip differential. Rear-wheel drive

Engine: Front mid-mounted 4281 cc alloy V8 with twin chain-driven overhead camshafts per bank and four valves per cylinder. Fully catalysed stainless steel exhaust system

Power: 380 bhp/283 kW @ 7300 rpm
302 lb/ft/409 Nm of torque @ 5000 rpm

Top speed: 175 mph/282 km/h

Dimensions:
Length	14 ft 3.5 in/4382 mm
Width	6 ft 1.5 in/1866 mm (excluding mirrors)
Height	4 ft 5.5 in/1265 mm
Wheelbase	8 ft 5.5 in/2600 mm
Weight	3770 lb/1710 kg

Price when new: £91,000

Top: The fully-lined hood can be raised or lowered in 18 seconds
Above: The V8 Vantage Roadster featured a sculpted rear like the Zagato-designed DB AR1 and Vanquish Roadster before it
Bottom: A six-speed 'Sportshift' transmission was an available option

i 19-inch alloy wheels optional

Epilogue
And so the story comes full circle

Under the ownership of Ford Motor Company since September 1987, Aston Martin had flourished. Numerous new products, a modern manufacturing facility in Gaydon, a return to international motor racing and – for one of the few times in the company's history – a profit, were among the milestones of the American company's stewardship. But on 31 August 2006, William Clay Ford, Executive Chairman of Ford Motor Company announced that Ford was to dispose of Aston Martin after almost 20 years of ownership.

It is true that severe economic circumstances and an underperforming Premier Automotive Group, which lost US$327 million in 2006, put pressure on Ford but, contrary to early reporting, it was Aston Martin that initiated the split.

Early in 2006, Dr Ulrich Bez had approached William Ford with a US$1-billion (£503-million) offer to purchase Aston Martin. Initially agreeing to the purchase, Ford later offered the company for sale by tender and appointed Swiss bank UBS to handle the negotiations.

The formal announcement of Aston Martin's sale was made on 13 March 2007 and ownership passed to a consortium headed by Prodrive boss David Richards for a reputed US$952 million (£479 million), well short of the estimated US$1.5 billion Ford Motor Company was initially seeking for the company.

The consortium consisted of David Richards; banker, John Sinders; and Kuwaiti companies Investment Dar (the largest listed investment company in the Gulf) and Adeem Investment Company. Under the new arrangement the consortium took an 85 percent share of Aston Martin, while Ford Motor Company retained a 15 percent stake in the company.

A condition of the agreement was that Dr Ulrich Bez remained as Chief Executive, while David Richards joined the Aston Martin board as non-Executive Chairman.

Once again, a new era was dawning …

Notes

1   D Burgess-Wise, *DB7 A Legend Reborn*, Automobile Quarterly, 1996.

2   C Nixon, *Aston Martin Virage*, Osprey, 1989.

3   RW Schlegelmilch & H Lehbrink, *Aston Martin*, Konemann, 2005.

4   Burgess-Wise, 1996.

5   Michael Bowler/Brian Joscelyne in *AM Magazine*, Spring 1986.

6   G Courtney, *The Power behind Aston Martin*, Oxford Illustrated Press, 1978.

7   Michael Bowler in *AM Magazine*, Summer 1987.

8   Brian Joscelyne in *AM Magazine*, Autumn 1991.

9   Nixon, 1989.

10 Paul Chudecki in *AM Magazine*, Summer 1994.

11 Schlegelmilch & Lehbrink, 2005.

12 Brian Joscelyne in *AM Magazine*, Spring 1994.

13 *Autocar and Motor*, 3 March 1993.

14 *AM Magazine*, Spring 1994.

15 Burgess-Wise,1996.

16 *The Daily Telegraph*, 4 November 1995.

17 *Autocar*, 1996.

18 Garry Taylor in *AM Magazine*, Summer 1999.

19 *Car* magazine (UK), 2000.

20 *Aston Martin Journal.*

21 *Aston Martin Journal.*

AMV8 *January 1986*

V8 Volante *January 1986*

V8 Vantage Zagato *March 1986*

V8 Vantage *October 1986*

Zagato Lagonda Rapide *March 1988*

Virage *October 1988*

AMR-1 *October 1988*

DB4 GT Zagato Sanction II *July 1991*

Lagonda Vignale Concept Car *March 1993*

DB7 *March 1993*

Lagonda Saloon *November 1993*

Lagonda Shooting Brake *November 1993*

Vantage Special Type I *March 1996*

V8 Coupe *March 1996*

Vantage Special Type II *March 1997*

Virage Lightweight *September 1997*

V8 Volante *October 1997*

DB7 Alfred Dunhill Edition *late-1997*

AM3 *1997*

Vantage Special Series I *January 1998*

Vantage Special Series II *June 1998*

Vantage V600 *1998*

DB7 V8 *August 1998*

DB7 Vantage *March 1999*

Vantage Shooting Brake *1999*

Lagonda Shooting Brake *January 2000*

Vantage Volante Special Edition *2000*

DB4 GT Zagato Sanction III *2000*

AMV8 Vantage *January 2003*

DB AR1 *January 2003*

DB9 *September 2003*

DB9 Volante *January 2004*

V8 Vantage *March 2005*

DBRS9 *June 2005*

Aston Martin Rapide Concept *January 2006*

V8 Volante Shooting Brake *June 2006*

V8 Vantage Volante *October 1986*

Lagonda *March 1987*

V8 Zagato Volante *March 1987*

V8 Vantage Volante PoW Specification *July 1987*

6.3-litre Virage *January 1992*

Virage Volante *March 1992*

Virage Shooting Brake *March 1992*

Vantage *October 1992*

Limited Edition Coupe *October 1994*

DB7 V8 Le Mans *April 1995*

DB7 GT *October 1995*

DB7 Volante *January 1996*

A p p e n d i x

Aston Martin race results

Production figures

Introduction dates

Specifications

Production figures 1987–2006

Photographs

Bibliography

Index

Acknowledgments

Project Vantage *January 1998*

AM4 *1998*

DB7 Vantage Volante *March 1999*

V8 Vantage Le Mans *March 1999*

Vanquish *March 2001*

20/20 Concept Car *March 2001*

DB7 Zagato *July 2002*

DB7 GT/GTA *October 2002*

Zagato Vanquish Roadster *March 2004*

Bertone Jet II *March 2004*

Vanquish S *September 2004*

DBR9 *November 2004*

DBS *June 2006*

V8 Vantage N24 *July 2006*

Aston Martin Rally GT *September 2006*

V8 Vantage Roadster *November 2006*

Aston Martin race results

AMR-1 race results 1989

Race/Distance	Date	Car	No.	Drivers	Result	Comments
Suzuka, Japan (480 km)	9/4/89	-	-	-	-	Did not enter. (Protech fined £250,000)
Dijon-Prenois, France (480 km)	21/5/89	AMR-1/01	18	David Leslie, Brian Redman	17th	Qualified 18th
Le Mans, France (24 hours)	10-11/6/89	AMR-1/01	18	Brian Redman, Costas Los, Michael Roe	11th	Qualified 35th. Finished 10th in Group C.
		AMR-1/03	19	David Leslie, Ray Mallock, David Sears	Retired	Qualified 43rd. Retired after 10 hours 23 minutes (engine failure; 20th position).
Jarama, Spain (480 km)	25/6/89	-	-	-	-	Did not enter. (Each team was allowed to miss one European race)
Brands Hatch Trophy, UK (480 km)	23/7/89	AMR-1/04	18	David Leslie, Brian Redman	4th	Qualified 14th. Highest finishing position.
ADAC Trophy-Nürburgring, Germany (480 km)	20/8/89	AMR-1/04	18	David Leslie, Brian Redman	8th	Qualified 21st
Wheatcroft Gold Cup-Donington Park, UK (480 km)	3/9/89	AMR-1/05	19	David Leslie, Michael Roe	6th	Qualified 10th
		AMR-1/04	18	David Sears, Brian Redman	7th	Qualified 20th
Spa-Francorchamps, Belgium (480 km)	17/9/89	AMR-1/04	18	Brian Redman, Stanley Dickens	7th	Qualified 32nd
		AMR-1/05	19	David Leslie, Michael Roe	Retired	Qualified 13th. Retired with a broken connecting-rod while in 8th position.
Trofeo Hermanos Rodriguez, Mexico (480 km)	29/10/89	AMR-1/05	19	Brian Redman, David Leslie	8th	Qualified 15th. Version II 6299 cc V8 engine used.

DBR9 race results 2005

Race	Date	Car	No.	Drivers	Result	Comments
Sebring 12 Hours, USA	19/3/05	DBR9/01	57	David Brabham, Darren Turner, Stephane Ortelli	4th (1st in GT1 class)	Qualified 5th in GT1 class. Class victory on debut.
American Le Mans Series (ALMS)		DBR9/02	58	Peter Kox, Pedro Lamy, Stephane Sarrazin	15th (8th in GT1 class)	Qualified 4th in GT1 class
RAC Tourist Trophy, Silverstone, UK	15/4/05	DBR9/02	29	Peter Kox, Pedro Lamy	1st	Qualified 1st
(FIA GT Round 3)		DBR9/01	28	David Brabham, Darren Turner	2nd	Qualified 2nd
Le Mans 24 Hours, France	18-19/6/05	DBR9/01	59	David Brabham, Darren Turner, Stephane Sarrazin	9th (3rd in GT1 class)	Qualified 1st in class. Cooling and heating problems late in race. Completed 333 lap
		DBR9/02	58	Tomas Enge, Peter Kox, Pedro Lamy	Did not finish	Qualified 2nd in class. Stopped on track with fuel related problems.
Proximus 24 Hours of Spa, Belgium	31/7/05	DBR9/02	29	Marc Goosens, Peter Kox, Pedro Lamy	5th	Qualified 3rd. Completed 557 laps.
(FIA GT Round 6)		DBR9/01	28	David Brabham, Stephane Sarrazin, Darren Turner	6th	Qualified 7th. Completed 555 laps.
Petit Le Mans, USA (ALMS)	1/10/05	DBR9/01	57	David Brabham, Darren Turner, Jonny Kane	4th (2nd in GT1 class)	Kane crashed during practice. Qualified 3rd in GT1 class.
(1000 miles or ten hours)		DBR9/02	58	Pedro Lamy, Tomas Enge, Peter Kox	11th (5th in GT1 class)	Qualified 4th in GT1 class
Laguna Seca, USA (ALMS)	15/10/05	DBR9/02	58	Peter Kox, Pedro Lamy	9th (3rd in GT1 class)	Qualified 4th in GT1 class
		DBR9/01	57	Darren Turner, David Brabham	10th (4th in GT1 class)	Qualified 5th in GT1 class

DBR9 race results 2006

Race	Date	Car	No.	Drivers	Result	Comments
Sebring 12 Hours, USA	18/3/06	DBR9/02	009	Jason Bright, Pedro Lamy, Stephane Sarrazin	4th (2nd in GT1 class)	Qualified 1st in GT1 class. Completed 337 laps.
American Le Mans Series (ALMS)		DBR9/03	007	Darren Turner, Tomas Enge, Nicolas Kiesa	6th (3rd in GT1 class)	Qualified 2nd in GT1 class. Completed 324 laps.
Lone Star Grand Prix, Houston, USA (ALMS)	12/5/06	DBR9/03	007	Darren Turner, Tomas Enge	4th (3rd in GT1 class)	Qualified 1st in GT1 class. Completed 137 laps.
		DBR9/02	009	Pedro Lamy, Stephane Sarrazin	5th (4th in GT1 class)	Qualified 2nd in GT1 class. Completed 137 laps.
American Le Mans , Mid-Ohio, USA (ALMS)	21/5/06	DBR9/03	007	Darren Turner, Tomas Enge	8th (3rd in GT1 class)	Qualified 1st in GT1 class. Completed 115 laps.
		DBR9/02	009	Pedro Lamy, Stephane Sarrazin	9th (4th in GT1 class)	Qualified 3rd in GT1 class. Completed 115 laps.
Le Mans 24 Hours, France	17-18/6/06	DBR9/03	007	Darren Turner, Tomas Enge, Andrea Piccini	6th (2nd in GT1 class)	Qualified 1st in class. Completed 350 laps.
		DBR9/02	009	Pedro Lamy, Stephane Sarrazin, Stephane Ortelli	10th (5th in GT1 class)	Qualified 2nd in class. Completed 342 laps.
New England Grand Prix	1/7/06	DBR9/02	009	Pedro Lamy, Stephane Sarrazin	4th (1st in GT1 class)	Qualified 4th in GT1 class. Completed 166 laps.
Lime Rock Park, USA (ALMS)		DBR9/03	007	Darren Turner, Tomas Enge	6th (3rd in GT1 class)	Qualified 1st in GT1 class. Completed 166 laps.
Utah Grand Prix	15/7/06	DBR9/03	007	Darren Turner, Tomas Enge	7th (1st in GT1 class)	Qualified 1st in GT1 class. Completed 62 laps.
Miller Motorsport Park, USA (ALMS)		DBR9/02	009	Andrea Piccini, Pedro Lamy	8th (2nd in GT1 class)	Qualified 2nd in GT1 class. Completed 61 laps.
Portland Grand Prix	22/7/06	DBR9/03	007	Darren Turner, Tomas Enge	9th (2nd in GT1 class)	Qualified 3rd in GT1 class. Completed 133 laps.
Portland International Raceway, USA (ALMS)		DBR9/02	009	Stephane Sarrazin, Pedro Lamy	11th (4th in GT1 class)	Qualified 4th in GT1 class. Completed 131 laps.
Generac 500 Road America, USA (ALMS)	20/8/06	DBR9/03	007	Darren Turner, Tomas Enge	11th (3rd in GT1 class)	Qualified 3rd in GT1 class
		DBR9/02	009	Stephane Sarrazin, Pedro Lamy	16th (4th in GT1 class)	Qualified 1st in GT1 class
Grand Prix of Mosport	3/9/06	DBR9/03	007	Peter Kox, Tomas Enge	9th (3rd in GT1 class)	Qualified 2nd in GT1 class
Mosport International Raceway, Canada (ALMS)		DBR9/02	009	Stephane Sarrazin, Pedro Lamy	7th (1st in GT1 class)	Qualified 1st in GT1 class
Petit Le Mans	30/9/06	DBR9/03	007	Darren Turner, Tomas Enge	1st (8th in GT1 class)	Qualified 4th in GT1 class. Completed 374 laps.
Road Atlanta, USA (ALMS)		DBR9/02	009	Stephane Sarrazin, Pedro Lamy	2nd (9th in GT1 class)	Qualified 3rd in GT1 class. Completed 373 laps.
Monterey Sports Car Championship	21/10/06	DBR9/02	009	Stephane Sarrazin, Pedro Lamy	8th (1st in GT1 class)	Qualified 1st in GT1 class
Mazda Raceway, Laguna Seca, USA (ALMS)		DBR9/03	007	Darren Turner, Tomas Enge	11th (4th in GT1 class)	Qualified 3rd in GT1 class

DBR9 race results 2007

Race	Date	Car	No.	Drivers	Result	Comments
Le Mans 24 Hours, France	16-17/6/07	DBR9/10	009	David Brabham, Rickard Rydell, Darren Turner	5th (1st in GT1 class)	Qualified 4th in GT1 class
		DBR9/07	007	Johnny Herbert, Peter Kox, Tomas Enge	9th (4th in GT1 class)	Qualified 10th in GT1 class

Production figures

Model	Production
AMV8 (Weber fuel injection)	61
V8 Volante (Weber fuel injection)	216
V8 Vantage Zagato	52
V8 Vantage (1986-1989)	137
V8 Vantage Volante	167 [i]
Lagonda (Series 4)	98
V8 Zagato Volante	37
V8 Vantage Volante PoW Specification	27 [ii]
Zagato Lagonda Rapide	1
Virage	411
AMR-1	4 [iii]
DB4 GT Zagato Sanction II	4
6.3-litre Virage	65 (approx)
Virage Volante	223
Virage Shooting Brake	8 [iv]
Vantage	511
Lagonda Vignale Concept Car	3
DB7	1605
Lagonda Saloon	9
Lagonda Shooting Brake	7
Limited Edition Coupe	9
DB7 V8 Le Mans	1
DB7 GT	2
DB7 Volante	879
Vantage Special Type I	3
V8 Coupe	100
Vantage Special Type II	3
Virage Lightweight	3
V8 Volante	64
DB7 Alfred Dunhill Edition	78
AM3	3
Vantage Special Series I	3
Project Vantage	1
AM4	3
Vantage Special Series II	3
Vantage V600	81
DB7 V8	1
DB7 Vantage	2110
DB7 Vantage Volante	2046
V8 Vantage Le Mans	40
Vantage Shooting Brake	1
Lagonda Shooting Brake	1
Vantage Volante Special Edition	9 [v]
DB4 GT Zagato Sanction III	2
Vanquish	1300
20/20 Concept Car	1
DB7 Zagato	99 [vi]
DB7 GT/GTA	302 [vii]
AMV8 Vantage	1
DB AR1	99 [viii]
DB9	N/A
DB9 Volante	N/A
Zagato Vanquish Roadster	1
Bertone Jet II	1
Vanquish S	1289
DBR9	19
V8 Vantage	N/A
DBRS9	26
Aston Martin Rapide Concept	1
V8 Volante Shooting Brake	1
DBS	N/A
V8 Vantage N24	53
Aston Martin Rally GT	4
V8 Vantage Roadster	N/A

i   Includes 58 USA Specification cars
ii   Includes five USA Specification cars
iii   Plus one car, AMR-2/01, which was completed and sold after the AMR team was disbanded
iv   Includes three V8 Coupe conversions
v   Includes one long-wheelbase car
vi   Plus one car retained by the Factory
vii   GT: 190 / GTA: 112
viii   Plus one car retained by the Factory

Introduction dates

Model	Introduction
AMV8 (Weber fuel injection)	January 1986
V8 Volante (Weber fuel injection)	January 1986
V8 Vantage Zagato	March 1986
V8 Vantage (1986-1989)	October 1986
V8 Vantage Volante	October 1986
Lagonda (Series 4)	March 1987
V8 Zagato Volante	March 1987
V8 Vantage Volante PoW Specification	July 1987
Zagato Lagonda Rapide	March 1988
Virage	October 1988
AMR-1	October 1988
DB4 GT Zagato Sanction II	July 1991
6.3-litre Virage	January 1992
Virage Volante	March 1992
Virage Shooting Brake	March 1992
Vantage	October 1992
Lagonda Vignale Concept Car	March 1993
DB7	March 1993
Lagonda Saloon	November 1993
Lagonda Shooting Brake	November 1993
Limited Edition Coupe	October 1994
DB7 V8 Le Mans	April 1995
DB7 GT	October 1995
DB7 Volante	January 1996
Vantage Special Type I	March 1996
V8 Coupe	March 1996
Vantage Special Type II	March 1997
Virage Lightweight	September 1997
V8 Volante	October 1997
DB7 Alfred Dunhill Edition	late-1997
AM3	1997
Vantage Special Series I	January 1998
Project Vantage	January 1998
AM4	1998
Vantage Special Series II	June 1998
Vantage V600	1998
DB7 V8	August 1998
DB7 Vantage	March 1999
DB7 Vantage Volante	March 1999
V8 Vantage Le Mans	March 1999
Vantage Shooting Brake	1999
Lagonda Shooting Brake	January 2000
Vantage Volante Special Edition	2000
DB4 GT Zagato Sanction III	2000
Vanquish	March 2001
20/20 Concept Car	March 2001
DB7 Zagato	July 2002
DB7 GT/GTA	October 2002
AMV8 Vantage	January 2003
DB AR1	January 2003
DB9	September 2003
DB9 Volante	January 2004
Zagato Vanquish Roadster	March 2004
Bertone Jet II	March 2004
Vanquish S	September 2004
DBR9	November 2004
V8 Vantage	March 2005
DBRS9	June 2005
Aston Martin Rapide Concept	January 2006
V8 Volante Shooting Brake	June 2006
DBS	June 2006
V8 Vantage N24	July 2006
Aston Martin Rally GT	September 2006
V8 Vantage Roadster	November 2006

Specifications

Model	Years	Engine	Power (bhp)	Top speed (mph)
AMV8 (Weber fuel injection)	1986-1989	5340 cc V8	305	150
V8 Volante (Weber fuel injection)	1986-1989	5340 cc V8	305	145
V8 Vantage Zagato	1986-1988	5340 cc V8	410/437 (opt)	186
V8 Vantage	1986-1989	5340 cc V8	410/437 (opt)	175
V8 Vantage Volante	1986-1989	5340 cc V8	410/437 (opt)	164
Lagonda (Series 4)	1987-1990	5340 cc V8	305	145
V8 Zagato Volante	1987-1988	5340 cc V8	305	155
V8 Vantage Volante PoW Specification	1987-1989	5340 cc V8	410/437 (opt)	168 (est)
Zagato Lagonda Rapide	1988	Not used	N/A	N/A
Virage	1988-1994	5340 cc V8	306	155
AMR-1	1988-1989	5998 cc V8/6299 cc V8	687/721	217
DB4 GT Zagato Sanction II	1991	4212 cc six-cylinder	352	160
6.3-litre Virage	1992-	6347 cc V8	465	174 mph (claimed)
Virage Volante	1992-1995	5340 cc V8	306	155
Virage Shooting Brake	1992-1999	5340 cc V8	306	152
Vantage	1992-1999	5340 cc twin-supercharged V8	550	186
Lagonda Vignale Concept Car	1993-1997	4605 cc V8	190	140 (claimed)
DB7	1993-1999	3228 cc supercharged six-cylinder	335	165
Lagonda Saloon	1993-1999	6347 cc V8	495	170 (claimed)
Lagonda Shooting Brake	1993-1999	6347 cc V8	495	170 (claimed)
Limited Edition Coupe	1994	5340 cc V8	335	155-plus
DB7 V8 Le Mans	1995	6299 cc V8	619	200 (est)
DB7 GT	1995	3228 cc supercharged six-cylinder	385	180 (approx)
DB7 Volante	1996-1999	3228 cc supercharged six-cylinder	335	155
Vantage Special Type I	1996	5340 cc twin-supercharged V8	600	205
V8 Coupe	1996-2000	5340 cc V8	350	150-plus
Vantage Special Type II	1997	5340 cc twin-supercharged V8	600	205
Virage Lightweight	1997	6347 cc V8	495	186 (approx)
V8 Volante	1997-2000	5340 cc V8	350	150
DB7 Alfred Dunhill Edition	1997-1999	3228 cc supercharged six-cylinder	335	165
AM3	1997	5340 cc twin-supercharged V8	600	205
Vantage Special Series I	1998	5340 cc twin-supercharged V8	600	205
Project Vantage	1998	5935 cc V12	442 (claimed)	200 (claimed)
AM4	1998	5340 cc twin-supercharged V8	600	205
Vantage Special Series II	1998	5340 cc twin-supercharged V8	600	205
Vantage V600	1998-2000	5340 cc twin-supercharged V8	600	200-plus
DB7 V8	1998	6347 cc V8	452	190 (est)
DB7 Vantage	1999-2004	5935 cc V12	420	185
DB7 Vantage Volante	1999-2004	5935 cc V12	420	165 (limited)
V8 Vantage Le Mans	1999-2000	5340 cc twin-supercharged V8	550/600 (opt)	200-plus
Vantage Shooting Brake	1999	5340 cc twin-supercharged V8	600	200 (est)
Lagonda Shooting Brake	2000	5340 cc V8	309	140 (est)
Vantage Volante Special Edition	2000	5340 cc twin-supercharged V8	550/600 (opt)	200-plus
DB4 GT Zagato Sanction III	2000	4212 cc six-cylinder	352	160
Vanquish	2001-2004	5935 cc V12	460	186
20/20 Concept Car	2001	5935 cc V12	500 (claimed)	200 (claimed)
DB7 Zagato	2002-2004	5935 cc V12	435	184
DB7 GT/GTA	2002-2003	5935cc V12	435 GT/420 GTA	184 GT/165 GTA

Model	Years	Engine	Power (bhp)	Top speed (mph)
AMV8 Vantage	2003	4281 cc V8	500 (claimed)	200 (claimed)
DB AR1	2003-2004	5935 cc V12	435 (manual)/420 (auto)	185 (manual)/165 (auto)
DB9	2003-	5935 cc V12	450	186
DB9 Volante	2004-	5935 cc V12	450	186
Zagato Vanquish Roadster	2004	5935 cc V12	460	186
Bertone Jet II	2004	5935 cc V12	460	186 (est)
Vanquish S	2004-2007	5935 cc V12	520	200-plus
DBR9	2004-	5935 cc V12	600	200-plus
V8 Vantage	2005-	4281 cc V8	380	175
DBRS9	2005-	5935 cc V12	550	195 (est)
Aston Martin Rapide Concept	2006	5935 cc V12	480	186 (est)
V8 Volante Shooting Brake	2006	5340 cc V8	350	150
DBS	2006-	5935 cc V12	500-plus (approx)	190 (est)
V8 Vantage N24	2006-2008	4281 cc V8	380	175
Aston Martin Rally GT	2006	4281 cc V8	420	175
V8 Vantage Roadster	2006-2008	4281 cc V8	380	175

Production figures 1987-2007

1987	219	1990	201	1994	159	1999	622
1988	208	1991	168	1995	723	2000	1029
1989	222	1992	46	1996	654	2001	1461
		1993	88	1997	654	2002	1465
				1998	625	2003	1511
						2004	2069
						2005	4450
						2006	6500
						2007	7400

Photographs

Aston Martin Ltd

Aston Martin Heritage Trust

Mark Bean

Paul Blank

Michael Bowler

Callaway Cars Inc

Carrozzeria Zagato SpA

Tim Cottingham

Ellen Dewar

David Dowsey

David Eales

eastonchang.com

Ford Motor Company

Holden Racing Team

Honda F1

Darren House

Harry Kielstra

Paul Kane

Mike Loasby

David Morgan

Michael Pinchard

Wayne Preusker

Kingsley Riding-Felce

Fabrice Rezaiguia

Roos Engineering

Shaun Rush

Stile Bertone SpA

Roger Stowers

Gareth Tarr

Richard Williams

Arthur Wilson

David Wright

Artwork by Mike Harbar: car-artist.com

Bibliography

Archer, Alan, Ted Cutting, Neil Murray and Richard Williams, *Aston Martin: The Compleat Car*, Palawan Press, 1994.

The Aston Martin Journal, Aston Martin, 2004.

Aston Martin Owners Club Register, Aston Martin Heritage Trust.

Bowler, Michael, *Aston Martin V8*, Cadogan Publications, 1985.

Burgess-Wise, David, *DB7 A Legend Reborn*, Automobile Quarterly Inc, 1996.

Chudecki, Paul, *Aston Martin and Lagonda, a Collector's Guide, Volume Two: V8 Models from 1970*, Motor Racing Publications, 1990.

Chudecki, Paul, *Aston Martin V8 Race Cars*, Osprey Publishing Ltd, 1990.

Clarke, RM, (ed), *Aston Martin Gold Portfolio, 1985–1995*, Brooklands Books, 1995.

Courtney, Geoff, *The Power behind Aston Martin*, Oxford Illustrated Press, 1978.

Edwards, Robert, *Aston Martin: Ever the Thoroughbred*, Hayes Publishing, 1999.

Gershon, Dudley, *Aston Martin 1963–1972*, Oxford Illustrated Press, 1975.

McComb, F Wilson, *Aston Martin V8s*, Osprey Publishing, 1981.

Nixon, Chris, *Aston Martin Virage*, Osprey, 1989.

Noakes, Andrew, *The Ultimate History of Aston Martin*, Marks and Spencer, 2003.

Pritchard, Anthony, *Aston Martin: The Post-War Competition Cars*, Aston Publications Ltd, 1991.

Schlegelmilch, Rainer W and Hartmut Lehbrink, *Aston Martin*, Konemann, 2005.

Styles, David, *Aston Martin and Lagonda: The V-Engined Cars*, Crowood Press Ltd, 1994.

Wyer, John, *The Certain Sound: Thirty Years of Motor Racing*, Edita SA, 1981.

Index

Acknowledgments

Though my name is on the cover, a book of this magnitude is not the work of one person. My respects and gratitude are extended to the following individuals and companies for granting interviews, sharing information and/or photographs to make this book a reality:

Aston Martin Ltd, Aston Martin Owners' Club, Aston Martin Heritage Trust, Dr Ulrich Bez, Steve Bolton, Michael Bowler, Max Boxstrom, Ray Brown, Reeves Callaway, Ian Callum, Moray Callum, Adriana Cerminara, Ted Cutting, Bob Dover, David Eales, David Flint, Nick Fry, Darren House, Harry Kielstra, Michel Hommell, Honda F1, Gavin van Langenberg, Peter Livanos, Mile Loasby, Ray Mallock, Ian Minnards, David Morgan, Jac Nasser, Simon Petrig, Michael Pinchard, David Price, David Richards, Kean Rogers, Beat Roos, Jose Rosinski, Shaun Rush, Adrian Ryan, Neil Simpson, Arthur Sinclair, Stile Bertone SpA, John Surtees, Roger Stowers, Gareth Tarr, Tim Watson, Richard Williams and Arthur Wilson.

Special mention must be made of respected author and historian Neil Murray of the Aston Martin Heritage Trust, who assisted with archival photographs and read my manuscript, offering gentle recommendations while pointing out some errors in my research. Neil was also the one-time producer of the excellent Aston Martin Owners' Club Register, which was consulted many times during my research for this book.

Thank you to my friend David Wright, one of the great motorsport enthusiasts and a very talented photographer. David provided some of his excellent photos for this book and we spent a memorable week together at Le Mans in 2006 collecting material. 2007 was less memorable.

To Wayne Preusker, who provided photographs for three chapters and who spent countless hours assisting me with the photographic material I owe my thanks and a couple of dozen pink doughnuts.

Australia's foremost Aston Martin expert and friend Paul Sabine has been a great supporter of mine for years. Not only did he offer valuable advice during my research and read my manuscript, he also made a very important telephone call that lead to the publication of this book. Thank you.

To Kingsley Riding-Felce of Aston Martin goes a great debt of gratitude. Kingsley was a great supporter of this project very early on. When we met at Newport Pagnell for the first time in 2003, for what proved to be the first of several interviews, Kingsley confounded me by describing a number of very special cars Aston Martin's Works Service had built in secrecy for a very special customer. Showing great faith in me, Kingsley detailed the story, which contained much sensitive information, for the first time and supplied me with dozens of photos, some of which have been reproduced in this book. I can only hope that this work is some form of repayment.

The artwork gracing this book's pages was created by the very talented Mike Harbar. I had met Mike at an Aston Martin Owners' Club dinner in Melbourne not long after Mike had arrived from the UK in 2000. I approached him with the idea of producing the artwork for this book early in the project and he agreed to supply the images. As the work grew in scope so did his work load, but Mike soldiered on, always with a smile, and created 65 separate drawings to introduce each chapter. Individual drawings and made-to-order montages are available from his website: car-artist.com

Finally to my friend Tim Cottingham, who was involved in the project from almost the beginning, a special thank you. Tim, who runs the excellent website www.astonmartins.com, is a well-known enthusiast and respected Aston Martin expert who now compiles the Aston Martin Owners' Club Register. He supplied much of the photography in this book and in addition, read my manuscript, answered countless questions and tracked down some hard-to-find archival photos as well.

David Dowsey